AF513115

RAJ TO SWARAJ

Attention Authors

'We Convert Fighters into Writers'. That's the motto of Manas Publications for more than four decades. Our message to the world is that India can win the battle not only by the bullet but also by the pen. There is no dearth of intellectuals in our country, but their knowledge is confined only to them. No sincere effort has, so far, been made by any other publisher to channelise their knowledge in the national interest. That is why the talent of a large number of intellectuals remains latent. An author transforms his knowledge into a manuscript, and it is our job to spread his / her knowledge by converting it into a beautiful book. For over four decades, Manas Publications has been motivating the intellectuals by publishing their manuscripts and would like to publish your manuscript too. If you or your colleagues have any manuscript ready for publication or are working on it, kindly contact us with detailed synopsis and list of contents. We will transform your work into a valuable publication. If you wish, we can also suggest you the suitable subjects for writing the books related to your area of expertise. Manas is known for its publishing quality and commitments. We take utmost care in production and give wide publicity to the book as well as its author through our national and international distribution network.

RAJ TO SWARAJ

Lt Gen (Retd) SK SINHA, PVSM

Former

Governor : J&K
Governor : Assam
Acting Governor : Arunachal Pradesh
Acting Governor : West Bengal
India's Ambassador : Nepal
Vice Chief : Indian Army
GOC-in-C : Western Command

Manas Publications

(We Convert Fighters into Writers)

New Delhi - 110 002 (INDIA)

MANAS PUBLICATIONS
(We Convert Fighters into Writers)
(Publishers, Library Suppliers, Importers & Exporters)
4402/5-A, Ansari Road (Opp. HDFC Bank)
Darya Ganj, New Delhi - 110 002 (India)
Phones: Off.: 011-23260783, 23265523, Res.: 011-23842660
E-mail: manaspublications@gmail.com
manaspublications@yahoo.com
Website: www.manaspublications.in

© **Lt Gen (Retd) SK Sinha**
2017

Cover designed by Shri Neeraj Nandkeolyar, a nephew of the author.

ISBN 978-81-7049-541-3
₹ 995

All rights reserved. This book is sold subject to the condition that it shall not, by way of trade or otherwise, be lent, resold, hired out, or otherwise circulated, without the publisher's prior written consent, in any form of binding, soft cover or e-version, etc, except by the authorised companies and without a similar condition including this condition being imposed on the subsequent purchaser and without limiting the rights under copyright reserved above, no part of this publication may be reproduced, stored in or introduced into a retrieval system, or transmitted in any form or by any means (electrical, mechanical, photocopying, recording or otherwise) without prior written permission of the publisher of the book.

The complete text/datas etc have been written and provided by the author only. The publisher is not responsible for the views of the author and authenticity of the data, in any manner whatsoever.

All disputes are subject to Delhi Jurisdiction only. No other court will have the Jurisdiction to entertain any case except the competent court of Delhi.

Designed at
Manas Publications

Printed in India at
R.K. Printers, Delhi
and published by Mrs Suman Lata for
Manas Publications, 4402/5-A,
Ansari Road (Opp HDFC Bank),
Darya Ganj, New Delhi - 110 002 (INDIA)

Dedicated to

The ever-lasting memory of my mother

RADHA NANDKEOLYAR SINHA

Who passed away when I was too young to

Remember her and

Who always guided me from her

Abode in Heaven

And to whom I owe so much

Queen Empress Victoria - 1897

Mahatma Gandhi - 1947

RAJ TO SWARAJ

Viceroy House, Kolkata - 1903

India Gate, New Delhi - 15 August 1947

Dependent to Independent

Lt Gen (Retd) SK Sinha, PVSM

Foreword

A Soldier's Stellar Service to the Nation,
In and Out of Uniform

India's Armed Forces are the pride of India. They safeguard the honour of our motherland, protect our sovereignty, defend our land and sea boundaries from external aggression, and when necessary, also render invaluable service to the Nation in times of calamity and conflict.

Our Army has produced many heroes. Just to name a few, Gen KM Cariappa, the hero of the first India-Pakistan War in 1947-48, became the first Commander-in-Chief of the Indian Army and was given the five star rank of Field Marshal in 1986. Gen Sam Manekshaw, the hero of the 1971 India-Pakistan war for the liberation of Bangladesh, was promoted to the five star rank of Field Marshal. This rank did not exist in the Indian Army. It was introduced for the first time in 1972. So far the Indian Army has two Air Marshals and its equivalent one Marshal of the Air Force, Arjan Singh.

We should also remember, with everlasting gratitude, martyrs such as Major Somnath Sharma, PVC and Brigadier Usman, MVC "Lion of Naushera" (first India-Pakistan War 1947-48); Major Shaitan Singh, PVC (Chinese War of aggression in 1962); Havildar Abdul Hamid, PVC (India-Pakistan War of 1965); Lieutenant Arun Khetarpal, PVC, Flying Officer Nirmal Jit Singh Shekhon, PVC and Mahendra Nath Mulla, MVC (India-Pakistan War in 1971); and Captain Vikram Batra, PVC and Captain Manoj Kumar Pandey, PVC (Kargil War in 1999). The roll of honour is long, but I have mentioned here only a few names from the three Services.

And how can we forget Lt Gen Jagjit Singh Aurora, Lt Gen Sagat Singh and Lt Gen JFR Jacob, whose brave and brilliant leadership in the 1971 war resulted in India's spectacular victory and forced the defeated and humiliated 92,000 Pakistani soldiers to surrender in Dhaka.

Yes, all these and many more names come to mind when one thinks of the valour and sacrifices of the Indian Army. One cannot overlook the enormous service rendered by the Indian Navy and Indian Air Force, too.

Yet, one name stands out in this constellation, shining uniquely with a presence that both compels recognition and commands respect. It is Lt Gen SK Sinha. He is the hero of several battles. "One of India's most outstanding Post-Independence Generals" is how Stephen Cohen, an eminent American expert on South Asia, has described him in his book *The Indian Army: Its Contribution to the Development of a Nation*.

§

In September 1947, Sinha was a General Staff Officer Operations in the rank of Major at the newly raised skeleton Command Headquarters in the West with Headquarters at Delhi. Lt Gen Sir Dudley Russell was the Army Commander. There were a dozen staff officers in the Headquarters of this Command. They were all British except for Sinha. At that time the British Officers were in the process of quitting the Indian Army and going back to Britain.

Pakistan, using a rag-tag army of tribal warriors equipped with modern weapons and Pakistan Army personnel in civilian clothes under the leadership of Maj Gen Akbar Khan invaded Jammu and Kashmir on October 22, 1947. Sinha's first-hand account of the first Indo-Pak War of 1947 in Kashmir is an interesting reading.

§

After a costly delay, Maharaja Hari Singh of Jammu and Kashmir acceded to India on October 26, 1947. Pakistan took advantage of this period of uncertainty and confusion by sending thousands of its armed tribals to invade the State. Pakistani invaders soon overcame the resistance put up by Maharaja's small Kashmir State Army and reached Baramulla by 25 October 1947. They were indulging in most brutal plunder and rapine of the town. The Maharaja fled Srinagar and went to Jammu. Srinagar lay defenceless.

Lt Gen Sir Dudley Russell, a veteran of First World War with a very distinguished war record in North Africa and Italy, was given the task of conducting operations in Jammu and Kashmir. At that time British officers were serving in both Indian and Pakistan Armies. The British Government for obvious reasons directed that no British officer of either Army will be allowed to go to Jammu and Kashmir theatre. Russell sent for Sinha late in the afternoon of 26 October 1947 and told him that Kashmir has acceded to India and that his Command had to conduct operations against Pakistani Forces that had invaded Kashmir. Troops had to be flown early morning next day from Safdarjung Airport at Delhi to the then grass airfield at Srinagar. A brigade group of 5,000 personnel with ammunition and stores to last the winter months had to be sent by air to Srinagar. The window of opportunity was only two to three weeks because after snowfall Srinagar airfield could not be used. The following morning only six Dakota aircrafts were available, but the next day all the Dakotas in India with private airlines, totalling 40, were made available. Sinha was made responsible for organising the airlift besides his duties as a General Staff Operations officer. Besides, Russell also gave him the task of acting as his eyes and ears to keep him updated about the progress of operations in the Valley.

800 Dakota sorties were successfully flown from Delhi to Srinagar in 15 days without any mishap and the task completed. Mountbatten wrote, "In my long experience of war, I have not come across another such massive airlift carried out at such short notice and so successfully."

§

Sinha's account of military operations on the first few days of 1947-48 war in the Valley is interesting. Lt Col Dewan Ranjit Rai, commanding 1 SIKH with half his unit comprising some 400 soldiers was flown to Srinagar on the first day. Sinha went with the second lot of sorties on that day and stayed the night at Srinagar. The situation was very critical. There were only 400 troops in Srinagar that day while the enemy was 5,000 to 8,000 strong at Baramulla. Ranjit Rai took a bold decision moving forward with the bulk of his force to contact the enemy at Baramulla and delay his advance with a fighting withdrawal. This brave officer got killed the first day but the enemy's advance was delayed. From the next day more troops started arriving and our troops fought a delaying operation to an intermediate position at Pattan while falling back to a well prepared defence sector at Shelatang on the outskirts of Srinagar. On

3 November we launched a counter offensive and won a decisive battle at Shelatang. The enemy was routed and fled leaving behind 369 dead bodies on the battlefield. Our troops pursued the enemy, liberated Baramulla and advanced some 60 miles to Uri. Russell wanted to continue the pursuit to Muzaffarabad, clear the Valley of raiders from Pakistan and seal the border. Government at the highest level overruled him and the Army was not allowed to go beyond Uri. The advance was halted. A golden opportunity was lost. May be the Government decision on this was taken on the advice of three senior military officers in Delhi at that time. Lord Mountbatten was the Governor General, Gen Sir Rob Lockhart was the Amy Chief and Lt Gen Sir Archibald Nye was the British High Commissioner. Possibly, they may have been influenced by Britain's strategic requirement on the sub-continent.

§

Sinha's description of his own activities in the days and months that followed, and of the heroism of our fledgling Army, is no doubt gripping. But there is something of immense value in his observation of how the people of Kashmir reacted to Pakistan's invasion. He writes:

> "To my very pleasant surprise I found no communal tension or violence in the city (Srinagar). It was all very peaceful. I heard the slogan raised by the people, *"Hamalewar khabardar, Hum Kashmiri Hindu-Sikh-Muslim Tayar."* This was at a time when the whole sub-continent, including the Jammu region of the State, was engulfed in unprecedented communal violence during the Partition Holocaust."

This is the authentic, original reality of *Kashmiriyat*. This is why, Sinha tells us, Mahatma Gandhi described Kashmir as "a ray of light" in the pervasive darkness. But he also tells us how Gandhiji supported the Indian Army's determined fight against Pakistani invasion. He writes:

> "I returned to Delhi to brief the Army Commander about what had happened at the battle of Shelatang. I found Maj Gen Cariappa, who was then the General Staff Officer of the Commander-in-Chief at Army Headquarters, was also present

> with Russell for my briefing. After having heard me, Cariappa said that he had to go to Mahatma Gandhi to apprise him of what had happened in the Valley. He asked me to accompany him. We went to the Harijan Colony in Delhi where the Mahatma was staying. This was the first and the last time I had an opportunity to see the Mahatma from close quarters. Cariappa briefed him of the details of the decisive victory we had achieved at Shelatang. It was a day of silence of the Mahatma. After listening to Cariappa, he wrote on a slate, "I am proud of the Indian Army. Non-violence is the weapon of the brave and not of the coward". We saluted the Mahatma and returned."

Another passage from this book is worth quoting. It refers to the martyrdom of Brigadier Usman.

> "The Pakistanis were targeting Brigadier Usman for being loyal to India. A Muslim being so was not acceptable to them. They had announced a reward of ₹50,000 to anyone who killed or captured Usman. One day we received a telephone call from Usman's younger brother Subhan who was a journalist in Delhi. He had heard rumours of Usman having been killed in Jhangar. We assured him that this could not be true because had it been so, we would have been immediately informed but in any case we will check and inform him soon. We sent a signal to Usman and he sent a reply, "I am still in the world of living." We duly informed Subhan of this. However, two days later the enemy shelled Jhangar heavily. There was only one casualty and that was Usman. While coming out of his bunker, he received a direct hit and was killed. After the Battle of Naushera, Usman had become a National Hero. His body was flown to Delhi and he was given a military funeral at Jamia Millia. President Rajendra Prasad, Prime Minister Nehru and other top dignitaries attended the funeral."

§

After tasting defeat in 1947-48, 1965 and 1971, Pakistan started a proxy war against India in the form of cross-border terrorism, fuelled by religious extremism. Indian government, India's security forces and Indian people are fighting this menace to this day. Sinha's book is a useful reminder that this war can be won by the combined efforts of the Armed Forces and the unbreakable unity of the people, transcending religious differences, especially in Jammu and Kashmir.

§

His career would have surely ended - and it deserved to end - with him serving as the Chief of the Army Staff (COAS), had the then Prime Minister Indira Gandhi not chosen his junior to supersede him in 1983.

As Sinha convincingly narrates in his memoirs, and as was well known to all well-informed people at the time, this was a politically inspired decision. Never before, and never after, has the principle of seniority been overlooked in the appointment of COAS. To Sinha, this was not just a matter of personal injustice. It amounted to an attempt at politicisation of the Indian Army. He reacted to this by doing what was expected of any self-respecting but disciplined soldier - he took premature retirement immediately, but gracefully, without challenging or questioning the authority of the political executive.

Naturally, the Government's unprecedented decision set off a national controversy. I remember that I had joined Atal Bihari Vajpayee and other members of the Opposition in raising this issue in the Parliament. The general feeling in the country was that an officer with a shining record in uniform was denied his rightful promotion to head the Indian Army.

But what makes Sinha's place in India's public life unique, is not just his distinguished soldierly career. Rather, it is this fact: no Army, Navy or Air Force officer, post-retirement, has served the Nation so long, in so many critical official assignments, and with such an emphatic stamp of positive transformation. Even if Sinha had never served in the Army, his work as the Governor of Assam and later as the Governor of Jammu and Kashmir -in times of extreme turbulence in both the strategically located States - and also his earlier stint as India's Ambassador to Nepal at a time when India-Nepal relations had unfortunately touched a nadir, would have been enough to earn him the Nation's admiration and accolades.

§

It is rightly said that people's admiration, affection and respect is the best reward a public servant can get in his or her life. In Sinha's case, this reward will certainly be enhanced when his memoirs *Raj to Swaraj* reaches readers' hands. I say so for two reasons. First, writing this book at a time when its author has already entered his Nineties is in itself an incredible achievement. God has been excessively kind to Sinha by enabling him to retain his photographic memory. One can also say that the highly disciplined life he has lived is the key to his enviable health. Yet, it is one thing to have a treasure-house of memories and quite another to write them down in a manner that grips the attention of the reader. This book testifies to the fact that Sinha is not only a riveting orator but also an engaging writer.

The second reason why our admiration for Sinha is bound to grow lies in the highly educative content of this book. It tells the story of the diverse challenges to national unity and security India faced right from the time of its independence and how Sinha, a man of soaring patriotism, confronted them both in and out of uniform. Of course, India continues to face some of these problems even today. Sinha's narration offers insights and lessons that can greatly help us in overcoming these challenges.

§

I have had the pleasure of knowing Sinha for many years. He too mentions in his book that he deeply cherishes his close association with "Atal Bihari Vajpayee (who is two weeks older than me) and LK Advani (who is two years younger than me)." After his retirement from the Army, we admired his activities as an independent and influential public figure who spiritedly espoused various national causes, especially the need for value-based politics.

My interaction with Sinha became more focused on achieving common objectives when I was made Home Minister in Vajpayee's government in 1998. In the previous year, he had been appointed as the Governor of Assam by the government of IK Gujral. Another example of how leaders across the political spectrum admired Sinha and trusted his ability to handle difficult challenges. Insurgency in Assam was at its peak then. And the problem was compounded by uncontrolled infiltration of illegal migrants from Bangladesh into the State. He served as the Governor of Assam until 2003, when our government decided that his services were needed in Jammu and Kashmir. Remarkably, the Congress-led UPA government continued with him as the Governor in Srinagar when Vajpayee left office until 2008.

During his six years in Guwahati, Sinha brought about a sea change in the situation in the State. Since he was himself an Army General, he ensured that there was a Unified Command in conducting military-police operations against the United Liberation Front of Assam (ULFA), a separatist organisation. Along with my officials in the Home Ministry, I monitored these operations closely from New Delhi. Our combined and well-coordinated efforts delivered a body blow to ULFA within a few years.

Sinha also initiated many development-oriented programmes, which were highly appreciated by the people. One of them was installation of one lakh shallow tube wells in Brahmaputra Valley, which turned Assam "from a rice-deficit State into a rice-surplus State." This also helped in weakening the appeal of insurgents.

The third prong of his gubernatorial policy was psychological - an innovative way to win over the hearts and minds of Assamese people. He did so by highlighting the inseparable bonds between their State and the rest of India, especially by eulogising (both within and outside Assam) three great sons of Assam - Mahapurush Shrimant Shankar Dev, a spiritual warrior; Lachit Borphukan, a military warrior; and Gopinath Bordoloi, a political warrior. How he did this is best told in Sinha's own words:

> "I organised an annual function at Guwahati on Victory Day of Lachit Borphukan in the Battle of Sarai Ghat in 1670 defeating Aurangzeb's nearly 1,00,000 invading force, at a time when Mughal Imperial and Military power was at its zenith. I also had a bronze statue of Lachit Borphukan put up at the National Defence Academy at Pune. I ceremonially unveiled that statue at the Academy and also delivered a lecture on his military leadership. The Lachit Borphukan Gold Medal was instituted at the Academy to be given to the best passing out Cadet in Officer-Like Qualities."
>
> "As for Gopinath Bordoloi, I had the Guwahati airport named after him and persuaded the Central Government to give the Nation's highest award, Bharat Ratna to him, 40 years after his death. His life-size bronze statue was installed in the Lok Sabha in New Delhi which was unveiled by Prime Minister Atal Bihari Vajpayee. All these measures undertaken by me had high emotional content and virtually swept the people of Assam off their feet making them feel proud of their past."

"The propaganda of the ULFA militants that Assam had never been part of India till the British incorporated it in their Empire in early 19th Century and Assamese were not Indians, was effectively contradicted. ULFA wanted to break away from India and make Assam a separate Nation. I countered this by various measures. I developed a large tree grove on the banks of a small river near Guwahati as a tourist spot. It is believed that Guru Vashishtha during the time of the *Ramayana* epic had his Ashram at this spot. I went on a pilgrimage to Dwarka, which was the capital of Lord Krishna. Before going to the main temple of the Lord, I chose to first go to the temple of his consort, Rukmini. The Press correspondents enquired why I had chosen to do so. I replied that Rukmini came from Sadiya district of Assam and as Governor of Assam, it was my duty to pray at this temple before doing so at the main temple of Lord Krishna. Many in Assam were not aware about Rukmini being from Assam."

"I tried to underscore the fact that from the days of the *Ramayana* and *Mahabharata,* Assam had been an integral part of India. Samudragupta's iron pillar at Allahabad mentions that Kamrup (modern Assam) was part of his empire in 5th Century. Throughout the ancient period, Assam was integrated with India. During the medieval period, Assam had defeated invasions of Muslim Armies while the rest of India had succumbed and became part of Muslim Empires for seven centuries. Two major invasions of Muslim Armies were defeated in Assam resulting in Assam being independent of Muslim rulers. The first invasion was that of Bakhtiyar Khilji in early 13th Century. He had conquered Bihar, burnt the famous Nalanda University, and then captured Bengal. He invaded Assam with 10,000 Turkish Horses. King Prithu of Pragjyotishpur (modern Guwahati) ambushed Khilji's Army while it was crossing the Brahmaputra. His forces were completely decimated and Bakhtiyar Khilji died in Assam. It is interesting that the account of this big ambush as written by Minhas, the chronicler of Bakhtiyar Khilji is corroborated by an inscription in stone written in Sanskrit at Konai Bulso Sil, South of Brahmaputra near Guwahati. I had this place with its stone inscription translated into Hindi, Assamese and English, put up at the site and developed a park at that location as a tourist spot."

> "The second major invasion was of Aurangzeb's Army of nearly one lakh which, as mentioned earlier, was decisively defeated in the battle of Saraighat in 1671. As a result of Assam defeating these invasions, unlike the rest of India, it never came under Muslim rule. Whereas from Kashmir to Kanya Kumari Muslim Rule was established for seven centuries in the rest of India and Persian became the official language, in Assam, Sanskrit remained the official language till the British conquered Assam in early 19th Century. In this respect Assam was more Indian than the rest of India. I also emphasised that Mahapurush Shrimant Shankar Dev in his writings often referred to Bharat Punya Bhumi. I highlighted these facts to bring out the fallacy of ULFA propaganda that Assamese were a separate Nation."

Readers of this book would surely applaud Sinha's successful efforts, which he sums up in these words:

> "The cumulative effect of my three-prong strategy of Unified Command, Economic Development and Psychological Initiative resulted in the people of Assam getting back to the National Mainstream. ULFA militants who at one time were hailed as heroes in Assam started being viewed as criminals losing popular support. My psychological initiatives that were directed towards winning hearts and minds of the people of Assam had been very successful but in the process, I myself had lost my heart and mind to the people of that State."

These passages from the book are enough to show that Sinha brought a profoundly intellectual approach to bear on his work in the various public offices he held. DN Bezboruah, former editor of *The Sentinel* and former President of Editors Guild of India as also one of the best journalists Assam has produced, praised him as "a Governor who far outshone all his predecessors in not being just a titular Head of State, but a Governor who served the State brilliantly with deep commitment to its people for six glorious and eventful years. He sought to rebuild the psychological alienation that crept in between Assam and the Indian heartland."

Not surprisingly, long after Sinha, a Bihari by birth, departed from Assam, he is still popularly referred to as "a true son of the soil of Assam."

I must also mention here Sinha's pivotal role in highlighting the problem of large-scale migration of Bangladeshis into Assam and the grave threat it posed to India's national unity and security. As Governor of Assam, his report on illegal migration into Assam backed by meticulous research, greatly strengthened our Government's stand on the need to scrap the IMDT or Illegal Migrants (Determination by Tribunal) Act. Far from stopping illegal migration, the loopholes in this Act had actually facilitated it, because these had been deliberately introduced by the Congress Government for electoral considerations. When the Supreme Court finally struck down this Act in 2005, calling it unconstitutional, its judgment quoted extensively from Sinha's report.

Sinha's contribution in Assam has drawn attention at National War College in the US. Dr Emma Simons in a Monograph on Counter Insurgency Operations for study at that College, has referred to it as one of the success stories of such operations in the 20th Century.

§

Sinha followed the same approach when he was appointed Governor of J&K in 2003. He was widely praised for his efforts, in his capacity as Chairman of Shri Amarnathji Shrine Board, to remove hurdles in the smooth organisation of the annual Amarnath Yatra on the one hand, and to revive Kashmir's syncretic Sufi culture on the other. Predictably, he also had to face many difficulties due to the political instability and rivalries in the State. Yet, it is a tribute to Sinha's non-partisan conduct as Governor that he won the trust, confidence and admiration of people across the political spectrum. He writes:

> "I developed very close relations with Ghulam Nabi Azad (the Congress leader who became the Chief Minister of J&K in 2005) and this helped me to continue my efforts to win the hearts and minds of the people of the State. AK Antony, the then Defence Minister, on a visit to Kashmir, told us that he had been the Chief Minister of his home State for a few years and he had not seen more cordial relations between a Governor and a Chief Minister as he found between Azad and me in Jammu and Kashmir."

§

I should also draw readers' attention to what Sinha writes about his days in Nepal as India's ambassador. A diplomat's foremost duty is to create, and consolidate, goodwill and support for his country among the people and in the ruling establishment of the country of his posting. This is especially important when the relations between the countries are strained. When Sinha went to Kathmandu in 1990, our bilateral ties had taken a big hit due to the Rajiv Gandhi government's ill-advised decision, in the previous year, not to renew the Trade and Transit Treaty between India and Nepal. This had resulted in India closing 13 of the 15 border check posts that regulated Nepal's trade with India and the rest of the world. Anti-India sentiments were on the rise in a country, with which India traditionally enjoyed very close socio-cultural relations.

Moreover, the pro-democracy movement in Nepal was fast gaining ground at the time, creating friction between the monarchy and political parties. The King had developed apprehensions that India was supporting them. How Sinha succeeded in calming the turbulence in Indo-Nepal ties is evident from the following excerpt.

> "The King (Birendra) and Queen of Nepal did us the rare honour of coming to the Embassy for a quiet dinner with us. Normally, a King or a Head of the State does not go on a private visit to an Ambassador's house. He broke this protocol in doing so to express his appreciation for what I had done in Nepal."
>
> "The Prime Minister of Nepal wrote to the Prime Minister of India saying, "General Sinha is a true friend of Nepal. He was as much India's Ambassador to Nepal as Nepal's Ambassador to India." For me it was a matter of great satisfaction that in a short tenure of one year we could restore the strained Indo-Nepal relations to a high level of cordiality. We ensured that instead of heading for chaos and anarchy, Nepal became a democracy and had a new Interim Constitution in such a short time. As India's Ambassador to Nepal, I had the satisfaction to be loyal to both my country of birth and the country of my profession. I am known in the Army as a Gorkha General."

§

Sinha's book is worth reading for many more reasons than the ones I have mentioned above. He has combined anecdotes with historical facts, and observations with comments, in a manner that readers will find both readable and profitable. Anyone who has devoted so many decades of his life – in Sinha's case, seven decades – to service of the Nation invites upon himself the responsibility to share his self-portrait, in the form of memoirs, with his countrymen. In a small way, such a book also becomes a portrait of the Nation itself. It chronicles the Nation's joys and sorrows, its achievements and failures, also its current problems and future potential for readers to reflect upon.

I congratulate Sinha for presenting his self-portrait within the larger portrait of India honestly and vividly. I also commend his family for prodding him to write this book.

Lastly, many thanks dear Sinhaji, for asking me to write the Foreword to your memoirs. India is proud of you!

October, 2016

LK Advani

Preface

I belong to a vanishing generation which heard first-hand accounts of events of the High Noon of the British Empire, from people who had lived in that era. The British Empire was the largest empire known to history, on which the sun never sets. Its decline started with the First World War. However, the sun continued to shine on it for another quarter of a century. Imperial splendour continued undiminished, almost till the end. Having gone past the meridian, the sun started descending to twilight. This descent became faster during the Second World War and ended shortly thereafter in sunset. I witnessed the latter days of the twilight years and the end of the Raj. I had a glimpse of the advent of India's Independence at Delhi. The much-cherished dawn arrived on 15 August 1947. India became Independent. Jawaharlal Nehru's memorable speech on the occasion, wonderfully articulated the momentous event. It was a piece of literature. Addressing the Parliament on that occasion, he stated,

> "Long years ago we made a tryst with destiny, and now the time comes when we shall redeem our pledge, not wholly or in full measure, but very substantially. At the stroke of the midnight hour, when the world sleeps, India will awake to life and freedom. A moment comes, which comes but rarely in history, when we step out from the old to the new, when an age ends, and when the soul of a nation, long suppressed, finds utterance."

I vividly recall those exhilarating days marred by unprecedented violence but holding much hope. The Prophets of gloom predicted that India being a behemoth, having tremendous diversity and numerous gigantic problems, would not be able to hold together. They were proved wrong. India has held together. Once described by Chester Bowles, the then US Ambassador to India, as a functioning anarchy, India has been a big success story of democracy in the developing world. No doubt, we have had our share of many failures but our successes have outweighed them. India is now on course to become a leading world power of the twenty-first century. Of late our political leadership had retarded national progress by putting things in the reverse gear, taking the country to the pits of corruption, misrule, dynastic succession, feudal culture, policy paralysis and economic bankruptcy. Being an optimist, I was convinced even in those dark days that a new dawn would come. The results of the parliamentary election of 2014 has ushered what one may call a New Dawn under a new leadership. This holds great promise for the future. The aberrations of the immediate past have started disappearing but much remains to be done to usher *Achhe Din*.

In the past, during the freedom struggle and the decade and a half that followed, India flourished despite the 1962 debacle. This was because of the extraordinarily high quality of its political leadership even though our people were then steeped in ignorance, poverty and backwardness. They were resigned to their fate. Mahatma Gandhi raised them out of dust to aspire and be enthused by a bright future in an India free from the shackles of colonialism. DF Karaka's biography of the Mahatma published in the early 30s is aptly titled, *Out of Dust*. I read this book when I was a college student, well before Independence. It greatly influenced and inspired me. The events that followed leading to our Independence and immediately thereafter confirmed what Karaka had written in early 30s.

No doubt our human resource material has improved exponentially in material terms but not morally. My generation witnessed various exciting events that shaped the course of history not only of our country but also the world. We saw the emergence of a new India and what has followed for seven decades thereafter.

I am now past ninety but thank God, my memory has so far not faded. My friends and relations, particularly my wife and our daughter Minnie, have been urging me to record some of the anecdotes and jokes that I have been narrating to them, from time to time. Minnie and our other two daughters, Meena and Manisha have done their PhD in History from universities in the US. Meena has been making her contribution in academics in Spain. She has been Principal of a leading English school and has now retired but is pursuing her interest in academics. Our son Yash, is a post-graduate in History with a good academic record. He is now a senior diplomat and until recently was India's High Commissioner to Sri Lanka. He now stands posted as India's High Commissioner to the UK, a prized appointment for a diplomat. Our two younger daughters Minnie and Manisha, born after him, are now senior professors in US universities who have earned high recognition in the field of their specialisation, Minnie in modern Indian history and feminist studies, while Manisha in the abolition of slavery in the US. They have both become Endowed Professors in their fields in leading universities in the US. This is the highest distinction for an academic. All of them feel that anecdotes can be of historical interest. There is a new trend in the study of history. Apart from the lives of monarchs, statesmen and military leaders who shaped the course of history, there is an urge to know what life was like for the common people in different eras. Personal anecdotes and an account of the styles of life of different classes in the past also need to be known for a better understanding of the past. Be that as it may, I stand persuaded and I undertook to write this book, while my memory serves. This is neither a book of history nor an autobiography. Yet it cannot be divorced from either. It provides a glimpse of the changing panorama of history seen from the prism of personal accounts of the past. The narrative in this book brings out the feudal life-style of the middle class in which I grew and how that class in different ways contributed towards India emerging from the shackles of colonialism to freedom and Independence. In the process, I have tried to convey the flavour of life in those bygone times and how it has now been changing. I have mentioned several family events pertaining to my ancestors and to myself. My ancestors on both my father's and mother's side were land-owning middle class emerging from a feudal to a modern era. On the paternal side my immediate ancestors had chosen government service and served the nation in that capacity. On my maternal side, my ancestors joined the freedom struggle led by the Mahatma. The way of life of the two families was vastly different. I had exposure to both in a fair measure. Much of the old values and ways of life have now changed, some for the better and some not so. The whole world seems to have changed so much over the years. Yet old memories linger, investing the past with nostalgia. No wonder, one tends to romanticise the good old days. Cicero said, "O Tempora, O Mores" (Oh What Times, What Customs).

I have tried to capture the style and ethos of the old days. I have narrated some anecdotes laced with humour that should amuse the reader. I have done this without any malice and with no intention of hurting anyone's feelings. Many of the jokes and incidents in this book pertain to the Army. Having joined the British Indian Army during the closing years of British rule and continued serving in the Indian Army post-independence, I have witnessed many changes that have taken place in the Army. I am often asked as to what life was like during British rule. Present day Army officers ask about my experience of serving with British colleagues and under British superiors in the Army. They also want to know about my relations in the Army with Muslim officers and soldiers who later opted for Pakistan Army. I have tried to provide answers to these queries by recounting a few anecdotes. I spent forty years of my active life in the Army. The anecdotes I have narrated of the period before I joined the Army pertain to civil life and are largely based on what I heard from earlier generations. The later anecdotes narrated in this book are mostly my personal recollections.

My wife and children have not only encouraged me to write this book but have been a source of great strength to me. Our middle daughter Minnie who had been pressing me for long to record old anecdotes had come to us from the US on a short holiday when I completed writing the manuscript of this book. She with her expertise in Indian History gave me some useful suggestions which I have incorporated. Our eldest daughter Meena, also on a visit to us, carefully edited the script of this book and also made useful suggestions. I had the support of all my family while writing this book. My Personal Assistant Sarvottam Kumar has been of great help in putting together the manuscript of this book, typing and retyping the script. I am grateful to him. I am also grateful to my nephew. Neeraj Nandkeolyar who has designed the cover of this book.

I cannot adequately express my gratitude to my respected close friend of over thirty years LK Advani, the BHISHMA PITAMAH of Indian politics for the valuable addition to this book by writing a generous Foreword.

New Delhi
1 October 2016

SK Sinha
Lt Gen (Retd)

Photo 1: Honourable Rai Bahadur Gajadhar Prasad (b 1850), paternal great-grandfather, Member Bengal Council.

Photo 2: Alakh Kumar Sinha (author's paternal grandfather), 1907.

Photo 3: Nomination letter for RK Lall Nandkeolyar (author's maternal grandfather) to the Middle Temple, 1912.

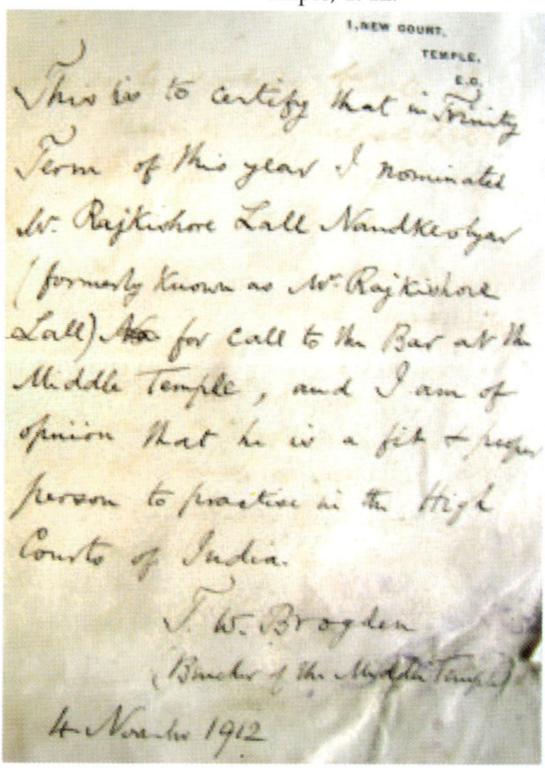

1, NEW COURT,
TEMPLE,
E.C.

This is to certify that in Trinity Term of this year I nominated Mr Rajkishore Lall Nandkeolyar (formerly known as Mr Rajkishore Lall) for call to the Bar at the Middle Temple, and I am of opinion that he is a fit & proper person to practise in the High Courts of India.

T. W. Brogden
(Bencher of the Middle Temple)

4 Novr 1912

Photo 4a: Barrister RK Lall Nandkeolyar in Western clothes before his political conversion.

Photo 4b: RK Lall Nandkeolyar after his conversion to Khadi.

Photo 5a: Nandvila, Residence of the Nandkeolyars (author's maternal grandparents).

Photo 5b: Party at Baraangan (courtyard) at the Nandkeolyars residence.

Photo 6: MK Sinha (author's father), IG Police, Bihar, in his office. A photograph of his father, AK Sinha, who was one of his predecessor's in the office, hangs on the back wall.

Photo 7: Members of the author's paternal side of the family who served the British government in India in different capacities. Bottom – author.

Photo 8: SK Sinha (author), 3rd from right second last row, at OTS, Belgaum, 1944.

Photo 9: Economic Development – Author visiting Shallow Tubewell Project in Assam.

Photo 10a: Psychological Initiative – Lachit Borphukan Dwar (Gate) Built at Raj Bhawan, Guwahati, Assam.

Photo 10b: Psychological Initiative, Gopinath Bordoloi Airport, Assam.

Photo 11a: Economiuc Development – Author visiting Microhydel-Power Project, Jammu and Kashmir.

Photo 11b: Author visiting Microhydel-Power Project in Jammu and Kashmir.

Photo 11c: Microhydel-Power machines for Jammu and Kashmir.

Photo 12a: Promoting Kashmiriyat – Author at Charar-e-Sharif, Jammu and Kashmir.

Photo 12b: Author at Pathar ka Gurdwara, Jammu and Kashmir.

Photo 12c: Author at the Amarnath Gufa (Cave), Jammu and Kashmir.

Photo 13: Plan for proposed Civilization Gate at Patna.

Photo 14: Author with Prime Minister Narendra Modi.

Note: General Sinha passed away on November 17, 2016 before being able to see the manuscript in print. He had, however, approved the copy-edited manuscript from the press. His family is very grateful to Manas Publications, Mr Sarvottam Rana, his Personal Assistant, and Mr Neeraj Nandkeolyar, his nephew, for preparing the manuscript for publication.

Contents

High Noon: The Raj at its Zenith

The British Empire reached its zenith under the rule of Queen Empress Victoria. That was the Golden Age of the Raj. My grandmother told me that one night in her village Dona, in Gaya district, she saw a broom-like constellation of stars in the sky. The entire village came out to see the strange phenomenon. The village priest stated that it was a very bad omen. It indicated that a calamity would befall the people. The village elders agreed to the suggestion of the priest to hold *havan* (special prayers) to ward off evil. The priest conducted prayers and earned a good amount. No calamity befell the village but a few days later, news came that the Great Empress had died. As loyal subjects, the people of the village went into mourning. In the old days there used to be professional mourners. They went to the house of bereaved families to beat their chests and cry loudly. They earned a living out of this. The landlords of the area hired some of these mourners and went with them to the house of the District Magistrate, the head of the administration in the district, to condole the death of the Queen Empress. In those days all heads of districts were British officers. The District Magistrate appreciated this display of loyalty and the landlord leading the delegation was given the title of Rai Saheb. No wonder, Mahatma Gandhi had used the term slave mentality for such ultra loyalty. In those days the Indian people kissed the chain that bound them. Nationalist feelings which had been stirred by the 1857 Uprising seemed to have evaporated in the rural areas of Bihar.

§

Calcutta (now Kolkata) was then the capital of India and Lord Curzon was the reigning Viceroy. My grandfather graduated from Calcutta University and was studying for a post-graduate degree in that university, when Queen Victoria died. My father was born a couple of years later. Nationalist feelings and the urge for independence had surfaced among the students and the intelligentsia in Calcutta. Swami

Vivekanand's soul stirring speech at the World Parliament of Religions at Chicago in September 1893 had aroused national pride among those who had taken to English education. Bengal was in the forefront in this regard. Sir Surendra Nath Banerjee was the silver tongue orator of India. His speeches had aroused national aspirations in Bengal. My grandfather told me that there was no outpouring of grief in the city on the news of the passing away of Queen Victoria. However, people were sad as she was a benevolent ruler, who had been considerate towards Indians. She had an Indian Munshi from Agra at Buckingham Palace in London to teach her Urdu. She was reported to be keen to visit India. Her desire remained unfulfilled. There was official mourning on her demise in Calcutta. Officials and uniformed personnel wore black bands on their left arm. Lord Curzon in his Convocation Address told the students that a suitable memorial overlooking the Calcutta Maidan will be constructed to commemorate the memory of the Great Queen. It took twenty years to complete the building. Victoria Memorial was inaugurated in 1921 and became the most prominent landmark of the city. However, it does not match the unique architectural beauty of the Taj Mahal.

§

Queen Victoria was the symbol of the High Noon of the British Empire. Curzon eloquently personified that High Noon in India, the jewel of the Empire. The Viceroy of India was considered the most powerful man of the world. It used to be said that the King of England reigns but not rules, the President of America rules but not reigns while the Viceroy of India both reigns and rules. Lord Curzon was perhaps the most imperialist and most capable incumbent of that high office. He gave ample display of both his reigning and ruling abilities.

Curzon decided to hold a magnificent Coronation Durbar, outdoing the Mughals in a dazzling display of pomp and pageantry, to proclaim the accession of the new sovereign as the Emperor of India. He preferred to hold this Durbar, billed to be the greatest show on earth, at Delhi and not Calcutta, the then capital of India. Delhi used to be the capital of the Mughals before their rule was extinguished by the British. It was considered a more congenial and more appropriate location to hold a Durbar in Mughal style. As Prince of Wales, the new King Emperor had visited India in 1876 and had spent eight months touring the country. He is reported to have said, "Because a man has a black face and is of a different religion from ours, there is no reason why he should be treated as a brute." This remark had gone down well with Indians and also liberal-minded British rulers. Curzon was hopeful that the King Emperor would come for the Coronation Durbar that he was organising at Delhi in Mughal style. It took nearly two years to complete preparations for the Durbar. Every detail, no matter how small, connected with the Durbar, was personally planned by him. The open plain North of Delhi of some 20 square miles was selected as the site for the Durbar. A tented city was established to house 2 lakh people. Roads, narrow gauge railway circuit, electric lights, post offices, hospitals, eating places, a central amphitheatre and so on, were put in place. The Viceroy's entourage consisted of a thousand people. Various Maharajas and Nawabs, Sheikhs from Aden and Shan Chiefs from Burma attended the Durbar. Special railway sidings had been constructed for numerous railway saloons in which these rulers came to Delhi. The Maharana of Udaipur hesitated to come to Delhi. His great ancestor Rana Pratap had sworn during Mughal rule not to visit Delhi, till India became free. Curzon persuaded the Maharana to come to Delhi. The latter felt that he should not displease the Viceroy and at the same time he could not betray his family's commitment to the oath taken by his great ancestor. As a compromise, he came in a special train to Delhi Railway Station but did not alight from his saloon. He returned to Udaipur without setting foot in Delhi.

§

As heir apparent, the new Sovereign had waited for half a century to ascend the throne. It was said that he was now having a gala time in London. The age of Victorian rectitude was over and the era of Edwardian gaiety had dawned. It was rumoured that the King had many mistresses and was loath to leave London for a tour to India which would mean being away from the glamorous life of London for a few months. Travel by sea to India then used to take the best part of a month each way. He deputed his younger brother, the Duke of Connaught to attend the Durbar. Journalists from all over the world came to cover the dazzling events of the Durbar.

On the first day, a procession of more than a hundred richly caparisoned elephants with liveried attendants moved through the streets of Delhi to the tented city. The elephants were lavishly decorated and had gold and silver *howdas* (throne-like structures) mounted on them. Attendants in colourful livery walked on either side of the elephants. My granduncle, whom I called Hira Phupha Dada, married to my grandfather's cousin a few years older to him, was the Manager of the railway restaurant at Delhi Railway Station. He had seen the procession of a hundred elephants going down Chandni Chowk to the tented city erected for the Durbar. He told me that the procession of elephants was a sight to see. Curzon rode on the leading elephant accompanied by Lady Curzon with her glittering jewels. The Duke of Connaught was on the second elephant followed by Maharajas and Nawabs with all their pomp and pageantry. Curzon took the salute at the military review with the Royal Duke, a Field Marshal of the British Army, on a horse beside him. There was much criticism of Curzon for taking precedence over a Royal Duke. Curzon justified this on the ground that he represented the Sovereign and had to take precedence over everyone except the King Emperor himself. His not doing so would have amounted to insulting the Emperor. No doubt the stand taken by Curzon was logical but it hurt the sentiments of the British people, bound by a deep sense of loyalty to the royal family. It was decided that thereafter when a Royal Duke visits India, the Viceroy and Governor-General would be relegated to being only Governor-General. The royal personage during his stay on Indian soil would be the Viceroy. This was a sensible decision to prevent any ceremonial hassle in the future.

The first major event at the Durbar was four hundred veterans of the 1857 'Mutiny', marching into the amphitheatre with the band playing 'See the Conquering Heroes Come'. The Viceroy read the proclamation of King Edward VII's accession as Emperor of India, to the thundering applause of the audience at the amphitheatre and the firing of 101 gun salute. Fireworks, folk dances and elaborate social functions like the Coronation Ball and Garden Parties were held on a grand scale. The later 1911 Durbar attended by King George V was equally elaborate. That was the first and only occasion when a ruling British sovereign visited India during two centuries of British rule. In 1911, King George V and Queen Mary in their royal horse carriage imported from London and escorted by a large contingent of cavalry in their ceremonial gear, rode down Chandni Chowk to the tented city North of Delhi. My granduncle told me that this procession was not as impressive as Curzon's procession of elephants. The following day the King rode on a small bay horse to the amphitheatre surrounded by a cavalry escort of tall horses. The King looked an insignificant figure. The band again played 'See the Conquering Hero Come'. This song may have been appropriate for the entry of the veterans of the 'Mutiny' into the amphitheatre in 1903 but it was hardly so, for entry of the King in the 1911 Durbar. The old generation of 1857 vintage had passed away. Lord Hardinge, the then Viceroy, tried to outdo Curzon's Durbar of 1903 but he could not do so, even though the King Emperor had himself attended the 1911 Durbar.

A special coronation medal was struck for the 1911 Durbar and awarded to dignitaries and selected uniformed personnel. My grandfather serving in the Police got this award. At this Coronation Durbar, it was announced that the capital of India will be shifted from Calcutta to Delhi and a new province of Bihar and Orissa, will be carved out from Bengal Presidency. Perhaps, the British felt that Calcutta was no longer a congenial place for a capital with increasing nationalist activities for freedom and outbreak of anarchist violence. Shifting the capital would be a bit of a setback for the Bengalis and they deserved this jolt. The announcement of the shifting of the capital from Calcutta to Delhi had been kept a carefully guarded secret. The reaction to this move was mute but the people of Bengal felt the pinch. Lord Curzon from London cynically observed that Delhi had been 'the graveyard of empires'. Curzon's foreboding turned out to be true. Thirty-six years later and only 16 years after the construction of New Delhi was completed in 1931, the mighty British Raj ceased to exist.

The Durbars of 1903 and 1911 were the high-water marks of British rule in India. War clouds had started gathering in Europe around 1903. Germany had emerged as a leading industrial power with a large Army. To counter the supremacy of the Royal Navy (British Navy), Germany had built a number of submarines. The British Far-East Fleet based at Hong Kong was withdrawn to home waters to counter the emerging naval threat from Germany. Some scholars have opined that this was the beginning of the retreat of the mighty British Empire from the East, ultimately leading to its demise some four decades later. Three years after 1911, the First World War started, and with it the descent of Britain from the position of a leading world power commenced. The USA increasingly started acquiring that position. After the Second World War this process culminated in the USA becoming a super power and Britain losing its eminent position.

§

There were some interesting titbits connected with the 1911 Durbar. A new bejewelled crown costing £ 60,000 was made for the coronation at Delhi, by Garrard the Crown Jewellers on Regent Street in London. The British Government was then on an economy drive. It declined to pay this huge amount for the crown. It was suggested that the money for the crown be raised from the Princes of India. The Viceroy felt that this would not be in keeping with the dignity of the Raj. The Government of India decided to foot the bill. The question now arose as to who should place the crown on the King's head. Considering that the coronation was being held in India, it was suggested that the crown be placed on the King's head by three Princes, a Hindu, a Muslim and a Sikh. The Archbishop of Canterbury threw a tantrum at this unchristian way of consecration. He argued that the King's consecration ceremony had already taken place at Westminster Abbey in London. Ultimately, it was decided that the King should arrive at the Durbar with the crown already on his head. The King and Queen sat on a specially erected throne. While a 101 gun salute was being fired for the occasion, all Princes in their regalia walked up to the King, took a deep bow, and paid obeisance offering *Nazar* (present) and then walked seven steps back in Mughal style. The Gaekwad of Baroda deviated from this protocol. Before entering the Durbar Hall, he took off all his jewels and his formal dress. Dressed like a Maratha *Sardar,* he walked to the throne, bowed slightly and to the 'horror of horrors', turned about without taking the seven mandatory backward steps. While doing so, he showed his back to the King. He walked away nonchalantly with a smile on his face and twirling a gold-top walking stick in his hand. There was a murmur of dismay among the audience. The Gaekwad got away with this flagrant violation of protocol. He pleaded that he got so nervous on seeing His Majesty that he forgot the laid down protocol. Surprisingly this explanation was accepted. Later the Gaekwad was given the high decoration of Grand Knight Commander of the Indian

Empire. After the Durbar, and when the King and dignitaries had left, the large crowd of common people watching the proceedings from an adjacent high ground broke the cordon and rushed towards the Durbar amphitheatre.

On the following day, the King Emperor laid the foundation stone for New Delhi, the proposed new capital around Raisina Hill. The main shopping centre of the new capital was to be named after the Duke of Connaught, in memory of the Duke's visit to India in 1903 when he had been slighted at the Durbar organised by Curzon. In the 90s, the inner and outer circles of Connaught Place were renamed Indira and Rajiv Chowks, after the new ruling family of India. Two decades after this renaming, the people still continue to refer to Connaught Place by its old name.

The construction of New Delhi was delayed due to the First World War. It was completed only in 1931, 16 years before the end of the Raj. Curzon's remark about Delhi being the graveyard of Empires came true. The two last empires enriched Delhi with magnificent buildings. Shahjahanabad (Delhi) of the Mughal era has the imposing structures of Red Fort, Jama Masjid and Humayun's tomb. The British Empire's legacy is Lutyen's Delhi with the imposing structures of Rashtrapati Bhavan, North and South Blocks and the Parliament House. Lutyen's New Delhi is the best laid out national capital in the world.

§

Going back in time, let me briefly narrate my family history and the vagaries of fortune that affected the family. My ancestors were well-to-do landlords living in Raipur Khajuri, a village about 20 miles from the city of Patna. During the great famine of 1770 which affected Bengal, Bihar and Orissa, some ten million people had perished. At that time, an ancestor of mine, Lakshmi Narayan, was one of the rich landlords of the area. He fed one meal of roasted gram and jaggery to 1,000 people every day. He and his family ate the same food. Warren Hastings decided in 1789 to have a huge granary for storing 1,40,000 tons of grain at Patna. He invited landlords to contribute for its construction and grains to be stored in it. Lakshmi Narayan was one of the contributors. This granary called Gol Ghar still exists in Patna and is the most important landmark of the city. Lakshmi

Narayan's name along with that of other contributors was inscribed on the outer wall of Gol Ghar. That inscription is now extinct.

As per the Sunset Law enacted at that time, land revenue had to be deposited in the District Treasury before Sunset on the designated date. In case of failure to do so the land would be auctioned to the highest bidder. Govind Sahay, the son of Lakshmi Narayan started from his village a day after the required date. He travelled in a palanquin with a large number of friends and attendants. Camping stores were carried on bullock carts. They spent three nights en route camping and relaxing. Dancing girls with generous supply of alcohol accompanied the convoy to entertain Govind Sahay and his friends during night halts. He arrived a few days later than the prescribed date for depositing the revenue in the District Treasury. He found that his land had been auctioned off. He now had very little property to sustain him and his family. His son Ram Lal lived in difficult circumstances. The latter's only son Gajadhar Prasad, my great-grandfather, was born in 1850 (Picture 1). He died at the age of 80 when I was four years old. I have no recollection of him. A year or so before he died, I had been sent to my mother's family as my mother was not well. I was told that Gajadhar Prasad had a vivid recollection of Indian soldiers who had rebelled against the British in 1857. They passed through our village to Ara going to join Veer Kuer Singh. The latter was an 80-year old landlord who had joined the fight against the British. He defeated a large contingent of British soldiers pursuing the mutinous Indian soldiers.

Gajadhar Prasad was keen to acquire English education. At the age of 16 he left the village against the wishes of his father and went to a distant relation in the city to study English. He would often read on the street under a lamp post. Starting with learning English alphabets at the age of 16, he passed Class 11, which was then known as Entrance Examination, in six years by earning a few double promotions. He was now eligible to join a university for higher education. In my time Entrance Examination was called the Matriculation Examination. There was no college in Patna at that time and Gajadhar Prasad could not afford to go to Calcutta for higher education. He took the law examination after doing his Entrance and qualified to practise in district and lower courts. He became a brilliant lawyer and within five years of his practice he began earning ₹1,000 a month. That amount in those days perhaps was like 1 lakh or more today. After a few years, his practice reached its zenith and his practice was now over ₹10,000 per month. This was a colossal amount then. He acquired several acres of land on the outskirts of the city fairly close to the District Courts. He built a big house with a compound of a few acres. It had a lawn and two gates in the front and a large water tank in the rear for boating and fishing. He gave several acres of land nearby to his relatives and others from his village. A virtual colony of our ancestral village now got established in the city.

The house built by Gajadhar Prasad was a single-storey building with tiled roof. Patna hardly had any cement roof or double-storey houses at that time except for the godowns built by European traders like the Dutch, the Portuguese and the British on the river bank. Patna was then a river port from which goods like indigo, rice, and saltpetre were exported to all over Europe. The latter was an essential ingredient for gunpowder. The best quality of saltpetre was found in Patna. It is said that the guns that fired shells at the battle of Waterloo from both sides were using shells with saltpetre ingredient, imported from Patna. As a child in 1933, I had seen the old house built by my great-grandfather before it was demolished. I remember that behind the front public rooms it had a large courtyard with a veranda all around with several rooms opening on to it. The large courtyard was connected to three small courtyards. Each of these had verandas around it and several small rooms. These three were meant for the families of his three sons.

§

My grandfather, Alakh Kumar Sinha, was born in 1884 and was brought up in the lap of luxury. His father had over one hundred servants. Each member of the family, male or female, had a personal male or female servant serving him or her. There were separate cooks for vegetarian and non-vegetarian food which used to be cooked in separate kitchens. There were several tradesmen also on the family's staff of servants, like barber, shoemaker, washerman, goldsmith, tailor, *syce* for horses, coach drivers and so on. My grandfather's eldest brother was very fond of shooting. He had about a dozen guns with a staff of about half a dozen gunmen who used to go out on *shikar* with him. The second brother was very fond of wrestling. He was known as the gentleman wrestler of Bihar. He had an *akhara* (wrestling pit) with a few wrestlers working for him. I have mentioned these details to give an idea of the style of living of the family during the heydays of my great-grandfather.

§

At the turn of the twentieth century the British introduced administrative reforms. Bengal Presidency comprised present Bihar, Jharkhand, Orissa, West Bengal, Bangladesh, the North-Eastern States and Burma. Bengal Council was set up to act as Advisers to the Governor. The Council had no legislative or executive authority. Its members were elected from a very restricted electorate. Only members of district boards and municipal committees of their region, including officials connected with them, could vote to elect a member of the Council. There was only one member in the Council from the present State of Bihar. Gajadhar Prasad was elected to this council. Members of the Bengal Council were given high protocol status almost like present day Ministers of States. They were given the designation of Honourable. Gajadhar Prasad had already earned the title of Rai Bahadur. He was now called Honourable Rai Bahadur Gajadhar Prasad and had attained much eminence.

In 1897 Gajadhar Prasad was elected President of All India Kayastha Sabha. It was a social organisation dealing with the problems of the caste. He presided over the annual session of the Sabha at Bareilly in 1898. He was taken in a decorated landau pulled by one member from each of the eleven sub-castes of Kayasthas instead of horses. Two important resolutions were passed at this session. The first pertained to inter-marriage between the eleven sub-castes. In those days marriages were arranged within sub-castes and inter-sub-caste marriages did not take place. Despite this resolution, it took some time to commence inter-sub-caste marriages. In his own family the first inter-sub-caste marriage took place in 1933, three years after he had died. Thereafter that virtually became the norm in the family. The second resolution pertained to the place of Kayasthas in the caste hierarchy. The Calcutta High Court had observed that they were in the *Shudra* (Scheduled Caste) category. It was proposed that the matter be taken up in Allahabad High Court to get a verdict to have Kayasthas included in *Kshatriya* caste. The High Court ruled that the Kayasthas are *Kshatriyas,* that is the ruler/martial class. I wish Kayasthas had remained in the depressed category because then they would have had much advantage in present day India. In the concluding session a poem was recited in honour of Gajadhar Prasad, eulogising his efforts to unite the eleven sub-castes, *"Har ek ko har ek se Bawista kar Dia, Sara Chaman Lapet kar guldasta kar dia."* (United one with one and made them into a bouquet of flowers.)

In view of the verdict of the High Court on the Kayasthas being *Kshatriyas,* my eldest granduncle and his brothers decided to adopt the *Kshatriya* surname of Singh to assert their new identity. Singh's anglicised spelling, as in vogue in Bengal, was Sinha. Thus Sinha was adopted as our family surname. The earlier generations had no surname as such. They were Narayan, Sahay, Lal and Prasad.

In 1908 Gajadhar Prasad fell seriously ill with typhoid which was considered a very serious disease in those days. A British doctor was brought from Calcutta to treat him. He recovered under his treatment. The doctor advised that he should give up practice and retire otherwise he may have a relapse which may prove fatal. He had to retire and give up his very lucrative legal practice that was the main source of income for the family besides the agricultural land he owned in the village. His sons ensured that he gave up his legal practice. They did not even allow him to meet clients at home to give legal advice in their cases in courts. He now led a completely retired life for over twenty years. The lavish living style of the family could not continue for long when the main source of income had vanished.

§

As a member of the Bengal Council, Gajadhar Prasad used to make useful contributions to its deliberations. The Governor was appreciative of this. He became quite friendly with him. He would write letters to him addressing him as Dear Friend. He sent word that while in Patna he would come to see him when he was recovering from his illness. This caused consternation in the family because there were then no chairs in the house. The Governor could not be expected to sit in the Indian style seating arrangement on a mattress over a large wooden platform. There was a large white sheet to cover the mattress. This had *Masnads* (large pillows) covered in white to recline on. My grandfather was dispatched to Calcutta to bring sofa-sets to set up an English-style sitting room in the house. He brought a couple of these from

Whiteways Laidlaw in Calcutta with tables, small peg-tables and carpets. A European style sitting room was set up for the Governor. The visit went off well. Some items of the furniture bought for the occasion are still part of our family heirloom.

§

Ganga Babu was a close friend of my grandfather. They had studied at school together. He would often come to stay with him and was treated like a family member. He came from a rich land-owning family. He was extraordinarily fair and could pass off for a European. He was full of life even in his old age and would crack jokes with children. He would tell us anecdotes which we as children would listen to with rapt attention. He told us that a Sheikh from Arabia visited London during the days of Queen Victoria. He was invited for dinner at Buckingham Palace. When finger bowls with water and rose petals were served, the Sheikh picked it up and drank the water. The Queen also did the same so that the Sheikh did not feel embarrassed. Everyone at the table followed suit. This showed how considerate she was and had no feeling of any racial superiority. Although she herself was kind and considerate towards Indians, her British officials in India were mostly racists and imperialists. They treated Indians with disdain. An Indian passing the house of a British official in the districts, or that of a British Indigo planter in North Bihar, had to dismount from his elephant, horse or palanquin at the gate and do a *salaam* in the Mughal style, before proceeding further. This practice was confined to *mofussil* districts and was not followed in cities like Calcutta or Patna. However, in cities, it was common for an Indian to bend and *salaam* a white man when he passed him on the road. One day, Gajadhar Prasad was out for his morning walk with his friend and colleague, Fakrudin Ali. They were both leading lawyers and the latter, later became a High Court Judge. Ganga Babu, then a young man, had accompanied them. A British Police Sergeant on a horse passed them from the opposite direction. On seeing him, Fakrudin bent low and did a *salaam*. My great-grandfather told him, "Fakrudin Bhai, you do not have to do that. He is only a Sergeant." The latter replied, "Bhai Gajadhar, he is an Englishman, he is a *Ferishta* (Angel). He is Sergeant today; he will be a *Lat* (Governor) tomorrow."

§

We learnt from Ganga Babu that Mahatma Gandhi had been thrown out of a first-class railway compartment by a British ticket examiner in South Africa even when he had a valid first-class ticket. Notwithstanding this, the ticket examiner felt that a coloured person should not travel in the same compartment as a white man. In India there used to be reserved compartments for 'Europeans Only' on railway trains. There were separate compartments for Indians. Ganga Babu, then a student, told his friends, including my grandfather, that he would show them how he could travel without a ticket from Patna to Calcutta in a first-class compartment reserved for Europeans. He dressed up in a smart three-piece suit and tie. Hardly any Indian wore English clothes in those days. He had gold-rimmed glasses and a gold chain attached to a pocket watch. He confidently entered a first-class coupe reserved for Europeans. There was no other passenger in the compartment. His friends including my grandfather were also boarding the same train in compartments for Indians. A dark Anglo-Indian ticket examiner demanded to see his ticket. He pretended to be deaf and shouted at the ticket examiner, "You black man, how dare you disturb me." Being of dark complexion, the ticket examiner had a complex. Soon people assembled at the scene. As arranged, a few of his assembled friends pretending to sympathise with the ticket examiner advised him not to get into trouble with a white man. The ticket examiner decided that discretion was the better part of valour and walked away from the scene. Ganga Babu travelled comfortably overnight to Calcutta and no one asked him for his ticket at Howrah Railway Station. I was very amused to learn that my grandfather's generation, when young, could play such pranks. In this connection, it would not be out of place to narrate what happened in Bihar, four generations later. A nephew of mine was studying at Jamshedpur and was coming by train to Patna. Several students were coming to Patna by the same train, to appear at an examination for a government job. They tore the reservation charts on a bogie and wrote on the compartment, 'Reserved for Ticketless Travellers'. The passengers who had their reservations had to either forego travelling on that train or manage to get into some other compartments. Whereas the former incident could be dismissed as an amusing prank, the latter was something which should not happen in a civilised society.

§

My great-grandfather had three sons, my grandfather being the youngest. All the three brothers were educated in Calcutta and graduated from Calcutta University. This was something rare in those days because normally rich families in Bihar did not bother about giving their children higher education. My eldest granduncle, Kali Kumar Sinha, had a law degree but he never practised. A rich man's son, he had expensive habits. He was very fond of hunting. He died young while on a tiger shoot. He was a gifted writer in English. His first book *Sanjogita,* was a historical novel published in the late nineteenth century. It got a favourable review in *The London Times.* During the First World War, he wrote a book, *Conflict of Nations,* very supportive of Britain. He was given the title of Rai Sahab by the Government for that book. His third book was also a novel titled *Star of Sikri.* These books are lost and we do not have them in our family. I recall that on a visit to London I found to my delight a copy of his book *Sanjogita* in the India Office Library. He also edited and published *Bihari,* an English daily from Patna.

My next granduncle Awadh Kumar Sinha, after graduating was appointed Deputy Magistrate, the highest rated government service next to the Indian Civil Service. Only about six Indians used to be appointed every year to the latter, on the basis of competitive examination held in London. As mentioned earlier, he was fond of wrestling and was the champion gentleman wrestler of the province. He was fond of stylish living. He was very fastidious about his clothes and his horse carriages. He had an imported two-wheeler horse carriage called *trap* and used to have a liveried attendant standing on a step in the rear of the *trap.* Being the son of a rich father he could afford to live in great style and some of his colleagues were envious of him. In 1905, he was posted as Deputy Magistrate at Ara, the headquarters of Shahabad district. He was in charge of the District Treasury and had to initial several entries in account books every day. He found it cumbersome to initial these with pen and ink supplied by the government which required every initial to be dried with a blotter. Stylo pens had come into the market in Calcutta. These did not require a blotting paper and as such were more convenient. He bought one for ₹2 from government funds for legitimate official work. A colleague who was envious of him carried tales to Sifton, the British District Magistrate. Sifton was a racist and a great stickler for rules.

He sent for my granduncle and accused him of misusing government funds. He politely explained to Sifton that the new ball-point pen helped him to initial entries faster than using the conventional, pen, ink and blotter. Sifton was not convinced and said that he was offering a lame excuse to cover his misdeed. He accused him of cheating the government. My granduncle had come prepared as he had learnt of the complaint made against him by his colleague. He took out half a dozen fountain pens from inside his coat pocket, one being of gold and another of silver. He placed them on Sifton's table saying that he had enough pens of his own and there was no need for him to buy a ₹2 Stylo pen from government funds for his personal use. This infuriated Sifton who called him a cheeky bloody Indian. He could not take that and caught Sifton by the neck. The latter shouted for help and soon his peon and clerks rushed into his office to separate them. This was something unimaginable in the heydays of British imperialism, when apart from being a white man, the District Magistrate was the supreme authority in the district and was looked up to as a demigod. Sifton ordered a case of assault registered against him and also wrote to Oldham, the Commissioner at Patna, recommending his dismissal from service. Oldham was well-known to my great-grandfather. The latter met him and briefed him about what had happened. Oldham told him that what had happened was something very serious and he would personally investigate the case and go to Ara the next day. He also assured him that he would do justice in the matter. Oldham visited Ara and met both Sifton and my granduncle. He reprimanded Sifton for the use of offensive language which had led to that most unfortunate incident. My granduncle was told that he should have sought redress in a proper manner and not got provoked to act in that reprehensible way. The Police case against him was withdrawn and he was immediately posted out to another district. Although my granduncle escaped any other action for that incident, that was virtually the end of his promising career. He never got any promotion nor did he get any good posting during the rest of his service. However, he became a bit of a hero amongst the Indian officials of Bihar. To make matters worse for him, Sifton later became the Chief Secretary of Bihar and thereafter Governor of the province. Despite this setback in his career, he was not bothered about this and continued to lead a stylish life. I recall as a child seeing him carefully select a tie to wear from an album of ties that he used to have. He would always be immaculately dressed in three-piece suit, with his gold-rimmed glasses, gold chain pocket watch and a gold-top walking stick. I was 9 years old when he died.

§

My grandfather studied in Calcutta for the first few years of the twentieth century. He did both his graduation and post-graduation from Calcutta University. Bihar was then part of Bengal. He often used to tell us stories of his student days in Calcutta. *Amrit Bazar Patrika* was a Bengali daily newspaper published from Calcutta in the nineteenth century. The Bengali Press had become very critical of the government. The British-owned English newspapers were of course pro-government. Lord Lytton, the then Viceroy, had passed the Vernacular Press Act imposing restrictions on the Vernacular Press. There was to be no restriction on the English Press. The *Amrit Bazar Patrika* overnight became an English daily. The following day it came out with a heading, "Good morning Lord Lytton. We appear in a new garb today." There was a scathing criticism of the government in that issue of the newspaper. No action could be taken against the English version of the newspaper because the Vernacular Press Act did not apply to its English edition. The British always tried to maintain the facade of legality and abided by the law.

§

Bengal had taken to English education much earlier than Bihar and was well ahead of Bihar. Biharis being more backward than Bengalis were looked down upon. The Bihari population in Calcutta at that time was mostly of the labour class. Peons, *Darwans* (guards), labourers and Police constables in Calcutta were almost all Biharis. They were called *sattukhors* (eaters of ground gram with water), the normal diet of the Bihari labourer. There were very few Bihari students in the University. Rajendra Prasad joined the University two years after my grandfather. He had passed his Entrance Examination from the Chapra Zila School in Bihar, standing first in Calcutta University which covered present day West Bengal, Bangladesh, Assam, Bihar, Jharkhand, Orissa and Myanmar. On his first day in college, he was ragged by the senior students. They called him *Sattukhor*. My grandfather advised him to discard the cap that he was wearing, which was a common practice in Bihar. Bengalis did not wear any cap. He also advised him to pick up Bengali. Rajendra Prasad followed his advice. He picked up Bengali in a remarkably short time. He and my grandfather became good friends. He always showed a lot of regard for him as his senior at college. Many years later when he was President of India, I found him showing the same regard for my grandfather. Unlike nowadays, even a two-year difference in age and seniority mattered a lot to that generation. As President of India, Dr Rajendra Prasad addressed a centenary function at Presidency College Calcutta of which he was an alumni. He spoke in flawless Bengali which greatly impressed the audience. I learnt from a Bengali friend who had attended the function that he spoke chaste Bengali which was in vogue in his time. Nowadays the spoken language had changed a lot.

§

I also recall my grandfather telling me about two big events that took place when he was a student in Calcutta. These were the Russo-Japanese War and the Partition of Bengal. The war between a leading European power and a rising Asian power had commenced in Korea and Manchuria. The Russians had suffered reverses both on land and on sea. The Czar decided to send his 'invincible' Black Sea Fleet to teach Japan a lesson. At that time the whole of Asia except Japan had been subjugated by European countries, with Britain and Russia as the leading imperial powers of the world. Britain had taken the sea route to establish its hegemony in Asia while Russia had done so following the land route. Japan was a very small power, compared to Czarist Russia. The Russo-Japanese War was seen as a clash between a David and a Goliath. Indians had sympathy for the Japanese in their fight against a European nation. The Czar dispatched his Black Sea Fleet comprising eight large battle ships and several other small warships. The six-weeks, 15,000-nautical miles, journey of the Fleet made headlines in Calcutta daily newspapers. The Fleet would stop at ports to collect coal and replenishments. It was apprehended that Russian naval superiority will spell the doom of Japan. And then one day came the surprising and stunning news that the Invincible Black Sea Fleet had been destroyed overnight by the Japanese in the battle of Tshushima off Japanese waters. All the eight Russian battleships were sunk and the mighty Black Sea Fleet ceased to exist. The Japanese lost only three torpedo ships in that decisive battle. There was much jubilation in Calcutta among the people, particularly the students. It was seen as a victory of Asia over Europe and of a coloured people over a white people. It gave hope and confidence to the Indian people that they could throw off British yoke. It provided a fillip to our national movement for freedom. Two generations later something similar happened when Japan joined the Second World War and had initial success against white colonial powers in Asia. Like my grandfather in the early twentieth century, I was a University student during the early years of the Second World War. We used to get thrilled to hear of Japanese victories over our Imperial masters. Initial Japanese victories in the Second World War broke the myth of the supremacy of the White Man. This hastened the independence of India and other Asian countries from the rule of European colonial powers.

§

Curzon partitioned Bengal in 1905. The reason given for this step was that Bengal Presidency was too unwieldy to administer. Hence for administrative reasons it was necessary to partition Bengal into two provinces. East Bengal with its capital at Dacca had the province of Assam merged with it. The rest of Bengal with its capital at Calcutta had present day West Bengal, Bihar, Jharkhand and Orissa. There was widespread opposition to this move as the people believed that there was a hidden communal agenda behind it. They viewed this as a part of the British Divide and Rule policy. In 1906 the All India Muslim League had been formed. At its first session in Dacca, it demanded the creation of an independent Muslim State named Bang-e-Assam, comprising East Bengal and Assam. The elite of Calcutta came largely from East Bengal, owning landed property there. Assam's population was one tenth of East Bengal. Apart from losing a province of their own, the Assamese people felt that they would get totally engulfed by a very large Bengali population. The population ratio between Bengalees and Assamese would be about ten to one. The agitation against the partition of Bengal gathered momentum and became a major national issue all over India. During his student days, my grandfather had also been associated with this agitation. Ultimately the British agreed to annul the partition of Bengal. This was seen as victory for the national movement for freedom.

§

There was a demand for Bihar being made a separate province and detached from Bengal Presidency. Apart from Bengal Presidency being too unwieldy for efficient administration, it was argued that Bihar being a Hindi-speaking region and culturally different from Bengal, should be made a separate province. Assam, with a much smaller population than that of Bihar, had been detached from Bengal Presidency and became a separate province in 1884. Dr Sachchidanand Sinha, Sir Ali Imam and the Lal brothers of Gaya (my maternal great-grandfather and great-granduncle) were in the vanguard of the movement for a separate Bihar from Bengal Presidency. My paternal grandfather, then a student at Calcutta, had opposed this movement. He felt that dismemberment of Bengal would break national solidarity. He wrote a well-argued booklet against separation of Bihar from Bengal. This was titled *Sir MacDonald's False Step*. MacDonald was the then Secretary of State for India. However, the dye was cast. Bihar and Orissa became a new province in 1911. Perhaps, the British got a vicarious pleasure in doing so and clipping the wings of the troublesome Bengalees! This happened much before my parents got married.

§

As mentioned earlier, my grandfather was the youngest of three brothers. Unlike his elder brothers, his living style was simple and even austere. He was the first in the family to have obtained a post-graduate degree. As a child, he had strayed into a segregated area on the platform during a plague epidemic. A Police Constable rudely held his hand and brought him out from that area. He got very upset at being treated in such a rough manner. He vowed to join the Police and teach Policemen to behave politely. His ambition to join the Police persisted with him when he grew older. Both his father and elder brothers tried to dissuade him as officer rank in the Police was not open to Indians. He would have to join the Police in a subordinate rank as Sub-Inspector, which would not be in keeping with the dignity of the family. Moreover, all the higher education that he had received would go waste. No graduate used to join as Sub-Inspector for which the required educational qualification was Entrance Examination. It was too idealistic to hope that he would be able to make any significant contribution in reforming the Police particularly from a subordinate rank. Destiny has its own ways. Soon after he got his MA degree from Calcutta University, the All India Police Reforms Commission announced that officer ranks in the Police will be thrown open to Indians. A new service called Superior Police Service will be started for Indians and would be at par with the Indian (Imperial) Police. The latter would continue to have only British officers. Probationers from both these services would train together at the Police Training College, Ranchi. My grandfather applied for the Superior Police Service and was selected for the same. He had a brilliant career in the Police and had the distinction of being the only Indian in the entire country to reach the highest rank in the Police during British rule (Picture 2). He rose to be the Chief of Police of Bihar. I may mention that BN Mullik, the legendary top ranking Policeman of Post-Independent India, wrote a book on *World's Great Policemen* in 1978, long after my grandfather had passed away. In his book, he wrote a brief life sketch of fourteen great policemen of the world from twelve different countries. My grandfather is the only Indian among these fourteen great policemen in this book. Two British Police Officers of the Indian (Imperial) Police, Sir William Henry Sleeman and Sir Charles Tegart are also in that list of fourteen. My father followed in the footsteps of my grandfather and competed into the Indian (Imperial) Police which by then had been opened for Indians. After Independence, he also rose to be the Chief of Bihar Police. He held this appointment for a record period of seven years followed by IG on special duty for four years. After the Second World War, I was selected for permanent commission in the Army and also for the Indian Police. I chose to stay on in the Army. My grandfather was not disappointed as he believed that one should have the freedom to choose one's career. After he passed away, my younger brother Jyoti competed into the Indian Police Service, maintaining the family tradition. He rose to be Special Secretary in Government of India.

§

My grandfather joined the Police Training College at Ranchi along with both Indian and British probationers. Among the probationers under training was MacDowell. He had served in the Army during the Boer War and had been seconded to the Police. All the probationers wore one star on their uniform but MacDowell having been a Lieutenant in the Army wore two stars. On the first day, he ticked off my grandfather for not saluting him as he was wearing two stars while my grandfather and other probationers wore only one star. My grandfather maintained that irrespective of what he wore on his shoulders, they were both probationers and he did not have to salute him. All probationers, both British and Indian, supported my grandfather's stand. The Principal of the college ruled that all probationers were equal and there was no need for anyone to salute the other. On passing out from the Police Training College, MacDowell got ante date of seniority for his service in the Army. Despite their initial spat, MacDowell became quite friendly with my grandfather while they were probationers at the Police Training College and did not hold any grudge against him. During the course of their service, MacDowell held higher ranks than my grandfather. He became DIG and then IG while my grandfather was SP and DIG. Of course, my grandfather had now to salute him. He succeeded MacDowell as IG before the Second World War. During the Second World War, MacDowell, after his retirement from the Police, was re-employed in the Army in the rank of Brigadier. He was appointed Commander of the Italian Prisoner of War Camp at Ramgarh in Bihar. More then quarter of a century later, I was posted as Brigade Commander in Ramgarh. When the Occupancy Register of the Flagstaff House was put up to me for my signature, I was amused to find MacDowell's signature in it as the first occupant of the house. I also recall that when as President of Ramgarh Cantonment Board I saw the names of past Presidents on a Board in my office, the first name was that of MacDowell. Had my grandfather been alive, he would have been amused to see the names of both MacDowell and his grandson on that Board. MacDowell was my grandfather's immediate predecessor as IG and also one of my father's much earlier predecessors.

§

In 1912 my grandfather was officiating as Superintendent of Police of Shahabad with about five year's service. He was one of the earliest Indians in the country to function as Head of the Police in a district. It was the same place where a few years earlier his elder brother had got into trouble with Sifton. A British Sergeant Major from the Army was on deputation with the Police and was serving under him. Being from the ruling race, he did not appear comfortable serving under an Indian. He put up a draft letter for my grandfather's approval. The draft was full of grammatical and spelling mistakes. My grandfather corrected the draft and sent it back to him. The Sergeant Major was unhappy about it and came to his office saying that English was his mother tongue, implying that he knew English better. My grandfather told him that English may have been his mother tongue, but he had apparently not been properly educated in that language. Having been an MA in English, he would try to help him make up that deficiency. He asked him to bring back the draft and he would explain the corrections to him, giving appropriate references from a book on grammar and also got him to check the spellings from the dictionary. After he saw all the references, the Sergeant Major realised his folly and thanked my grandfather for taking so much pain to teach him his own language.

§

With the start of the First World War, British officers on deputation from the Army to the Police were recalled for service in the war and a few other Police officers volunteered to serve with the Army in that war. This created several vacancies. This worked to my grandfather's advantage. Some did not get back after the war because they became casualties. My grandfather now got confirmed as Superintendent of Police and absorbed in the Indian (Imperial) Police which was opened to Indians after the First World War.

§

In 1917 there were widespread communal riots in Gaya and Shahabad, two bordering districts of Patna. Communal violence normally used to be an urban phenomenon, but the Bakrid riots that year had spread far and wide in rural areas. There were reports of rampaging crowds crossing the rivers on the boundaries of those districts and violence spreading to Patna. Being the capital of the province, Patna required special attention. My grandfather was then the Superintendent of Police of Patna. The Muslims were apprehensive of a Hindu in that appointment during communal riots. He took vigorous preventive action to ensure peace in the district. He formed peace committees of eminent Hindu and Muslim citizens in the city and organised heavy deployment of Police in sensitive areas of the city. He toured the rural areas extensively by car and on horse, contacting influential Hindu and Muslim landlords. They wielded considerable influence in their areas. He adopted a carrot and stick policy, threatening the landlords with police action against them, if there was an outbreak of violence in their area. He would initiate action against them if a communal riot broke out in their area, irrespective of whether or not they were in anyway personally responsible for it. At the same time, he promised them rewards like tax concessions, cash gifts and titles, if they prevented communal riots in their area. This approach worked and Patna was kept free of any communal violence. The widespread Bakrid riots in Bihar in which a few thousand casualties occurred found mention in the proceedings of the House of Commons in London. During the debate it came out that an Indian Superintendent of Police had maintained peace in his district, but British Superintendents of Police in neighbouring districts had not been able to do so. This underscored the case for Indian officers being given senior positions in the administration hitherto denied to them.

§

There was an interesting incident during the 1917 Bihar riots in Patna. A rich Muslim millionaire from Calcutta had come on a visit to Patna. His life was threatened. The Police took prompt action to provide him security. Before departing for Calcutta he visited my grandfather to express his gratitude. In the course of conversation, he enquired from my grandfather about his children. He told him that he had only one child, and he was studying at a local school. My father was then his only child. The businessman was surprised at my grandfather sending his son to a school with sons of common people. He told him that he too had only one son. He did not send him to any school. He got the school to come to his house. He used to get teachers from the school to come to teach him at his house. In any case, he said that education or passing examinations did not matter. He would leave enough money for his son, so that even if he spent ₹1,000 a day for the rest of his life he could live in comfort without having to earn any money himself. In those days ₹1,000 was like ₹1,00,000 or more today. My grandfather's monthly salary at that time was less than a thousand a month and he could live comfortably on his salary. Some twenty years later a young man in torn clothes came to see him. He introduced himself as the son of the millionaire from Calcutta who had met him in 1917. He had run through all the fortune that his father had left him. He used to hire a complete liner and go on tour by sea all over the world with his friends. He had led a very fast life. He came to him seeking financial assistance to buy a railway ticket to go back to Calcutta. My grandfather would tell us all this to impress upon us the importance of education in life.

§

My grandfather also served as Superintendent of Police in a district of North Bihar for a short time. There were many British Indigo planters there. They were a law unto themselves. They would force the peasant to give up tilling land for food crops which was more profitable for them and grow indigo instead. The farmers had to virtually starve to meet this demand. The planters had a prison of their own to lock up the poor farmers whom they punished. It was reported to him that a British planter had kicked a *Pankha*-puller as a result of which the latter had died. He asked the Sub-Inspector in charge of the Police Station to take action. The latter hesitated asking how could he register a case against an Englishman. He ordered him to do so immediately, to arrest the planter and take him to the Police Station. He personally interrogated the planter. After a beer session at the Club the planter had retired for his afternoon siesta. The *Pankha*-puller was pulling the *Pankha* sitting on the veranda outside. After a while he dosed off and the *Pankha* stopped. The planter woke up covered in sweat. He came out of the room and saw the *Pankha*-puller sleeping. In a fit of temper, he kicked the poor man hard and the latter collapsed. It was not a case of murder but one of culpable homicide not amounting to murder. After the planter's statement was recorded, he was released and law was now to take its course. There was uproar among the planters and even among European officials. Perhaps for the first time a planter had been arrested and taken to a Police Station. It was felt that such an outrageous act would adversely affect the prestige of the White Man. The English Press in Calcutta was highly critical of what they called an Indian officer's high-handedness. However, his superiors upheld the legally correct action taken by him. Later he was posted to Purnea where widespread dacoities were taking place. Purnea borders Nepal. Dacoits had been ravaging the district from sanctuaries in Nepal. He toured the border areas and established Police Stations in sensitive locations with armed police detachments suitably deployed for taking immediate action. An effective intelligence network was established and he personally supervised anti-dacoity operations. He was remarkably successful against dacoit gangs. Normalcy was restored in Purnea. He proved to be a competent Police officer in dealing with communal violence, in upholding the law without fear or favour and in combating dacoity. For his outstanding work in combating dacoity in Purnea, he was awarded the coveted title of Order of the British Empire which was very seldom given to a SP, whether Indian or British. Successful Police officers in higher ranks would normally be given this title. My grandfather got this award the year I was born and people would tell him that I had brought him good luck. He earned various other coveted awards in terms of medals and titles. He became one of the best decorated Police officers in the country.

§

My ancestors on my mother's side were from a village in Gaya district. In the late eighteenth century, my mother's ancestor was the only literate person in the village. He maintained the accounts of the local *Bania* (trader). The Dowager Maharani of Tekari used to make a lot of purchases through the *Bania*. The Tekaris, though not feudatory chiefs, had the title of Maharaja and were one of the richest landlords of Bihar. One day the Maharani wanted to check her accounts with the *Bania*. He produced the account book maintained by my maternal ancestor. She was impressed by his accurate and neat account keeping. She asked the *Bania* to bring his accountant before her. She offered him a job on her staff, which he readily accepted. He rose steadily in her service to become her Dewan (Prime Minister). This appointment was made hereditary. Three generations later, my great-grandfather Nand Kishore Lall having completed school education in Gaya went to Calcutta for higher education. There was no college in Bihar in those days. He joined Calcutta University and passed the MA examination from there in 1891. He was the first Bihari to get a post-graduate degree. He was offered the appointment of Deputy Magistrate, the highest service after ICS (Indian Civil Service). He declined the offer of appointment as Deputy Magistrate. He preferred to work under his father and later succeed him as Dewan. He felt that he would be better off financially as Dewan and have the advantage of staying at his home in Gaya without being posted to other places which government service would entail. However, as Deputy Magistrate, he would have enjoyed power and authority but that did not attract him. His sons chose Nandkeolyar as their surname just as my paternal grandfather and his generation had chosen Sinha as our family surname. There are conflicting versions of why Nandkeolyar surname was adopted. One is that it is derived from *Nand Kul* (Nand family) and adopted by the descendents of Nand Kishore Lall. The other version is that Nandkeolyar was the name of the family *Gotra* (clan). The concept of surname did not exist among Indians at that time. We adopted the British custom of surnames. Interestingly, the Nandkeolyars also adopted a crest as a coat of arms. This was a crossed sword and pen with a motto Knowledge is Strength and Nandkeolyar written below in the shield. This was in keeping with Kayasthas being declared ruling/martial class as per the verdict of Allahabad High Court.

§

My grandfather Raj Kishore Lall Nandkeolyar went for studies to London soon after the death of Queen Victoria. He wanted to become a Barrister. One could become a Barrister only after qualifying at a law examination in England and attending a certain number of dinners at the Inner Temple in London. Lawyers who got a law degree in India were known as advocates. Barristers had a higher status than Advocates. My grandfather met two other Indians going for higher education to England on the ship, during the journey from Bombay (now Mumbai) to London. One was from Madras (now Tamil Nadu) and the other a very fair Kashmiri. In those days, mostly fabulously rich Indian Princes used to go to England. Besides them, few Indian students from middle-class Indian families had started going there for higher education. The perception of the common man in England was that India was a land of rich Maharajas and poor uncivilised people, comprising snake charmers and rope tricksters. Soon after their arrival in London, my grandfather and his two friends were walking down the street. A lady with her small son was coming from the opposite direction. The boy on seeing them said, "Black, Blacker and Blackest." The Kashmiri replied, "You have got it wrong my boy. We are Fair, Fairer and Fairest." The lady apologised saying that they had never interacted with Indians and did not know that Indians could speak English. There were some other anecdotes of his stay in England which he narrated to me.

A Maharaja went to a show room of Rolls-Royce, the most expensive car in the market. He was being shown a car when some Englishman dropped in to see a Rolls. The salesman left the Maharaja and went to attend the Englishman. The Maharaja got annoyed at being so slighted. He was fuming but waited. The Englishman enquired about the price of the car. On being told the price, he said that it was too expensive for him and he left. The salesman came back to the Maharaja saying that the Englishman was not a serious buyer and he had wasted his time. The Maharaja replied that it served him right and enquired how many Rolls he had readily available. The salesman answered four. The Maharaja bought all the four and paid for them by cheque at the counter. He asked the cars to be shipped to his State in India and he would show him what he would do with those cars. He then left in a huff. He had those cars modified to carry garbage and handed them over to the Municipality. Pictures of those cars were published in the newspapers. The executives of Rolls Royce felt this was an insult to the world's most expensive car manufactured by them, giving adverse publicity. A senior executive of Rolls Royce came all the way to India to apologies to the Maharaja and request that those cars be not used as garbage vehicles. He offered to replace them with new cars for normal use and to take away those modified cars. The Maharaja was appeased and he agreed. There was also the story of another Maharaja who asked his Secretary to fix an appointment for him with a Harley Street specialist. The Maharaja went to see the Doctor and asked him to cure his baldness. The latter took out a guinea from his pocket and showed it to the Maharaja. The guinea had the face of King Edward VII on it. He told him that if there was a cure for baldness, we would have certainly cured the King.

§

My grandfather was much impressed by the London Bobby. He found them courteous but firm in dealing with people. He would say that the British Police was a people-friendly force unlike the Indian Police which was an oppressive colonial force. He recalled that he had invited an Indian friend to his apartment. The friend asked the Bobby on the road for directions to his apartment. The Bobby was very polite. He told him, "Go down this road, Sir, take the first turning Left and then second turning Right. You will smell it." He was obviously referring to the aroma of Indian cuisine being cooked in the kitchen. Use of such polite language by Police Constable towards an Indian, despite the then widely prevalent racist feelings and superiority complex over natives (term used for Indians) under British rule, was remarkable. There was also another incident which showed how the Bobby would do his duty without fear but in a polite manner. The King was driving down the road with his car flying the royal standard. The car was being driven fast, exceeding the prescribed speed limit. The Bobby stopped the King's car. The driver told the Bobby, "Can't you see that His Majesty the King is in the car?" The Bobby replied, "Drive carefully. His Majesty is in the car." The King was very pleased with the Bobby's reply. He was given a reward. This needs to be compared with what happens in our country nowadays. A Cabinet Minister in Srinagar, while travelling in his car with a police pilot ahead, was given a stop signal at a road junction by a traffic constable to allow moving vehicles from another direction to pass. The Minister's escort in his presence beat up the traffic constable mercilessly while the Minister watched this without saying a word. The constable had to be hospitalised. Of course, no action was taken against the Minister or his escort.

§

Orthodoxy was rampant in Bihar in those days. No one had gone from Gaya to England crossing the seven seas. On his return home, my maternal grandfather was made to do penance for the 'sin' he had committed by undertaking a forbidden journey. Failure to do so would have entailed his being declared an outcaste. He was required to go through self purification. The hair on his head, his eyebrows and the hair on the body was shaved off as an act of purification. He had to live in a thatched hut on the bank of the river and sleep on the ground for seven days. Every morning he had to bathe in the river and a prayer conducted for him with the Pandit sprinkling Ganga water on him. During this penance, he had to be on one vegetarian meal a day, sans onion and garlic. I asked him why he agreed to go through that silly ritual, which I am sure he could not have believed in. He agreed that he did not believe in that hocus-pocus, but went through that for the sake of my mother, who was then a baby. In those days of arranged marriages within the caste, it would have been difficult for him to find a groom for his daughter if he had been declared an outcaste. Arranging the marriage of a daughter was a sacred duty of a father. According to the prevalent belief in Bihar, a man's life was not complete without performing *kanyadan* (ritual of giving away one's daughter in marriage to a son-in-law). I asked him why his younger brothers who had also gone to England after him did not go through that silly self-purification ritual. He replied that they had gone abroad a few years after him and by then times had changed. Moreover, their daughters were born much later.

§

An anecdote of those days that I heard from my maternal grandfather was very amusing. Being the head of the joint family after his father had passed away, my grandfather had arranged the marriage of his sister with a groom from a family in Patna. Prior to the wedding, an uncle of the bridegroom came one morning to settle arrangements for the stay of the bridegroom's party comprising a hundred-odd people. As per custom, the bridegroom's party had to be put up by the bride's side. My grandfather and his two younger brothers, who had also been to London, were having their morning tea on the veranda wearing their dressing gowns. Tea was offered to the guest. He enjoyed the morning cup of tea. His first demand was for tea to be served every morning for the bridegroom's party during their stay for the wedding. Tea was not a common beverage in Bihar at that time. My grandfather readily agreed. The other arrangements including dowry details were settled. The guest was impressed by the fact that the brothers were all England-returned. Such people were looked up to in society then. On the wedding day, my grandfather had invited a number of local guests including a few English gentlemen in Gaya. He was greatly embarrassed to find the members of the bridegroom's family in the wedding procession wearing dressing gowns! They thought that dress was the latest fashion in England and they chose to wear that during the wedding procession.

§

Mahatma Gandhi returned from South Africa in 1915 where he had earned a great name for his non-violent resistance. Field Marshal Smuts, the ruler of that country had to modify the discriminatory law against Indians in South Africa. The Mahatma also had an exposure to war in Africa. During the Boer War, he organised volunteers to work as stretcher bearers for evacuating casualties from the battlefield. He personally took part in carrying out this humanitarian work. The British Government awarded him the Kaiser-i-Hind Gold Medal for his services. When the First World War started, he had gone to England and offered to raise an ambulance corps for service in France. As a loyal subject of the empire, he exhorted Indians to help in the war effort. He returned to India in 1915 with a big name and decided to join the Indian National Congress which was then a political party of educated Indian middle class, loyal to the British. They demanded self-rule for Indians within the British Empire. Hitherto the Congress would hold meetings in halls and petition the government for their demands. There were also some extremists who resorted to violence against the British and were known as Anarchists. They were eliminated ruthlessly.

The Mahatma decided to change the character of the Congress party. He desired that the Congress became a mass-based party and undertake a non-violent struggle for freedom instead of submitting petitions to the government asking for self-rule within the empire or indulging in senseless violence. Prior to starting such a movement, he undertook a familiarisation tour of the country to see ground realities for himself. He also went about talent spotting, to pick up local leaders for the party in various provinces.

§

Gandhiji came to Delhi in 1915. Along with his friend, CF Andrews, he stayed with Mr Rudra, the first Indian Principal of St Stephens College. Mr Rudra's son was proceeding shortly to England for higher studies. He was keen to join the Army, but he was being dissuaded by his father from doing so. He asked Gandhiji for his advice. He encouraged him to join the Army. The young Rudra went to England and studied for a couple of years as desired by his father. While in England, he joined the British Army as a Private. He served in the trenches in France. After the war, he was selected to go to Sandhurst for training as an officer. He got his commission in 1920 and was posted to the Indian Army. Soon after Independence, he was promoted Major-General and took part in Hyderabad operations advancing from Madras, while the main thrust was from Pune. After retirement, he had settled down at Dehradun where he was in touch with my Gorkha Regimental Centre. When I used to visit the Centre, I often met him during Dussehra functions. He lived up to the age of over ninety and would join us in Gorkha dance with the troops. He used to recall the encouragement he had received from the great saint of non-violence to join the profession of arms. He would tell us anecdotes about Gandhiji when he had stayed with his father, like his fondness for goat's milk and his punctiliousness about punctuality. He would say that those were the days when he was still just Mr MK Gandhi wearing normal clothes. He later became the Mahatma and started wearing loin cloth. When I was serving as Adjutant General at Delhi, a BBC team came from England to interview Army officers who had fought both in the First and Second World Wars. General Rudra was the only Indian officer who met that requirement. The BBC team interviewed him. A year or so later he passed away.

§

The Mahatma did an outstanding job of talent hunting in picking up leaders of great calibre to join him in the freedom struggle. Sardar Patel from Gujarat, the Nehru's, father and son duo, from UP besides Govind Ballabh Pant, Lala Lajpat Rai from Punjab, C Rajagopalachari from Madras, Rajendra Prasad from Bihar, Dr BC Roy from Bengal, Harekrishna Mahtab from Orissa and Gopinath Bordoloi from Assam. Normally nothing grows under the shadow of a Banyan tree but the Mahatma was a unique banyan tree under whose shadow many Banyan trees grew.

I heard an interesting anecdote about how Rajen Babu (Rajendra Prasad) became a disciple of the Mahatma. Rajen Babu had a brilliant academic career having always stood first in all University examnations, from Entrance to MA, and in his law examinations of BL and ML. He was a leading lawyer of Patna High Court and he had a flourishing legal practice. Gandhiji wanted to enlist him for his movement. He wrote to him seeking a meeting with him. Rajen Babu invited him to stay with him. There was some misunderstanding about dates. When Gandhiji arrived at his house, he found Rajen Babu was not in town. He decided to wait for his return. The servants showed him a vacant room in the servants' quarters. The following day Rajen Babu arrived and was horrified to learn that Gandhiji was staying in his servants' quarters. He apologised profusely and made immediate amends. He was greatly influenced by Gandhiji's magnetic personality and became his ardent disciple. Gandhiji developed implicit faith in his legal ability and his total loyalty to him. He would insist that all important resolutions of the Congress be drafted by Rajen Babu or approved by him. Gandhiji used to say that if he asked Rajen Babu to drink a cup of poison, he would unhesitatingly do so. A unique relationship developed between them.

Similarly it is interesting how he got Vallabhbhai Patel to join the Congress Party. Patel was a leading Barrister at Ahmedabad and an active member of Ahmedabad Club where he drank whisky and played bridge. It was only after a few attempts by Gandhiji that he agreed to meet him. Patel became a devotee of Gandhiji after their very first meeting. He agreed to join the Congress party and gave up his lucrative practice. He completely changed his life style. He became a very loyal follower of the Mahatma. He worked hard in the party and held a strong grip on the party organisation. He was the hero of the successful Bardoli agrarian movement. The Mahatma now gave him the title of Sardar. He became the Iron Man of the party. After independence, he became the Great Integrator of the Nation.

§

The poor peasants of Champaran in Bihar were suffering grave hardships. They were forced to grow indigo by British planters instead of crops which sustained them. The British planters committed much atrocity against them and they were not given sustenance wage. Gandhiji was invited to help in ameliorating their miserable conditions. He went to Champaran and launched a peaceful *Satyagrah* Movement. He was arrested. On pleading guilty in court, he was given a sentence of imprisonment. A widespread peaceful mass movement erupted. The government was forced to appoint an Inquiry Commission to look into the grievances of the peasants. The Mahatma was appointed a member of the Commission. My paternal grandfather was then posted as Superintendent of Police in the Special Branch of the CID. He dealt with political intelligence providing valuable inputs to the government for decision-making. He was the first Indian in the country to be given this sensitive appointment. He had closely monitored the progress of this widespread Agrarian Movement. On the basis of the Inquiry Commission report, the government passed the Champaran Agrarian Act. This provided much relief to the poor peasants. The Governor of

Bihar held an 'At Home' to which Mahatma Gandhi was invited. My grandfather attended the function and had the great honour of meeting Gandhiji. He was wearing his Gujarati dress of a red Turban, long Jacket and *Dhoti*. He was the cynosure of all eyes, both British and Indian. The success of the Champaran movement was hailed all over the country. With his record in South Africa and now in Champaran, Gandhiji became the most dominant personality on the political scene of India for the next three decades. It was at this stage that Rabindranath Tagore called him Mahatma which soon became his popular title. His successful non-violent movement led to his achieving a miracle in the history of mankind. The largest empire known to history was dismantled as a result of a unique non-violent movement. His non-violent movement became the role model for Martin Luther King, Jr to fight for equality for Blacks in the USA. As a result, the US had a Black President Mr Barak Obama for eight years. Similarly Nelson Mandela used the non-violent approach to give apartheid a burial in South Africa.

§

India's response to Britain in her hour of need during the First World War was widely acknowledged and appreciated. As mentioned earlier, Mahatma Gandhi volunteered to raise an ambulance unit of stretcher bearers to go to France as he had done previously during the Zulu and Boer Wars. He also exhorted Indians to join the Army. The outstanding performance of the Indian Army on the battlefields of Europe and the Middle-East was acclaimed worldwide. The gallant performance of Indian soldiers in that war filled Indians with a sense of national pride. It was hoped that the British Government would be generous in its recognition of India's contribution during the war. There were high expectations. The British Government did make some gestures, but they fell far short of expectations.

§

One of the earliest and persistent demands of the Congress party was to throw open the officer cadre for Indians in the Army. The first batch of Indians commissioned as officers was in 1919. A Royal Indian Military College was inaugurated by the Prince of Wales at Dehradun in 1920. This was a preparatory school to prepare young Indian boys in their teens to go for training to the Royal Military College at

Sandhurst before being commissioned as officers in the Army. This school continues to this date and is now called Rashtriya Indian Military College. Indians were now made eligible for the highest gallantry award of Victoria Cross. The Indian (Imperial) Police was also thrown open for Indians. My paternal grandfather who had joined the Superior Police Service was among the first few Indians taken into the Indian (Imperial) Police. Lord Sinha was the first Indian to be made a peer and the only Indian appointed a permanent (not officiating) Governor of a province during British rule. These gestures fell far short of what the Congress wanted.

§

The Congress demanded real devolution of political power and for India to be given Dominion Status. The Montagu-Chelmsford Reforms of 1919 provided only for Diarchy in the provinces. Education, Health, Local Bodies and Agriculture were placed under Indian Executive Councillors responsible to the State Legislatures whose strength was increased to 144 in Bihar with 49 nominated members. The strength of the Central Legislature was also increased. Elections were to be held on the basis of limited franchise. There was no provision for Executive Councillors at the Centre responsible to the Central Legislature. The British Government maintained that in view of ground realities, democracy could be introduced in India gradually and not overnight.

The Congress rejected the Montagu Chelmsford Act as not being good enough. Mahatma Gandhi decided to launch a mass movement to protest against it. To gather Muslim support he made common cause with the Khilafat Movement to restore the deposed Sultan of Turkey as the Khalifa. The government utilized the highly repressive Rowlatt Act which gave draconian powers to the State to quell agitation. Curbs were also introduced on the Press. A protest march was organised at Amritsar on 9 March 1919 led by a Hindu and a Muslim leader. These leaders were Dr Satya Pal who had served as an officer in the Army Medical Corps during the war and Saifuddin Kitchlew, a popular Muslim Barrister. They were taken into custody while leading a non-violent procession. The Police fired at the procession which resulted in a few deaths. There were disturbances in the city. *Hartal* was observed in the whole of Punjab. Three British employees of a bank were killed in Amritsar. Miss Sherwood, from a local missionary school, while going on a bicycle on a street in Amritsar was assaulted by a mob. Some Indian residents living on that street rescued her and gave her shelter. The Governor Sir Michael O'Dyer declared martial law in Punjab. Army assistance was summoned and Brigadier General Dyer arrived in Amritsar. On 13 April 1919, which was *Baisakhi* day, a large crowd gathered at Jallianwala Bagh, for a public meeting. Congress leaders were to address this meeting. On being informed about this meeting, Dyer rushed to the place in an armoured car with a mixed force of Indian soldiers. On arrival at the spot, he immediately deployed his troops and without any warning ordered firing on the non-violent crowd. Jallianwala Bagh was enclosed from all sides and there was only one entrance which was blocked by the troops firing at the crowd. As per official figures, 379 people were killed and 1,000 injured. As per a committee set up by the Congress, the casualty figures were more than 1,000 killed and 1,500 injured. Dyer also ordered that Indians using the street where the English lady had been assaulted would have to crawl on all fours. Such brutal savagery shocked the entire Nation. Widespread protests took place all over the country. Nobel Laureate Sir Rabindranath Tagore returned his knighthood along with a scathing letter to the Viceroy. Sir Shankaran Nair a member of the Viceroy's Executive Council resigned in protest.

The government appointed the Hunter Committee of Inquiry into the Jallianwala Bagh massacre. General Dyer gave evidence before this Committee. He said that he wanted to teach the whole country a lesson so that such agitation did not take place. He even said that his ammunition got exhausted. Had he more ammunition with him, he would have ordered more firing. He admitted that no medical aid was provided to the wounded. His macabre action, and subsequent defiant evidence before the Hunter Committee, shocked the conscience of all right-thinking people in the world. It was condemned in the House of Commons in London. Even a dyed-in-the-wool imperialist like Winston Churchill, who was then Secretary of State for War, severely condemned his outrageous and barbaric acts in the House of Commons. Asquith, the British Prime Minister, stated in the House of Commons that it had been the most monstrous act in the history of Britain. Dyer was made to quit the

Army. Yet there were many British people both in India and in Britain who hailed him as a hero and one who had saved the Empire. The House of Lords voted funds for Dyer and so did a newspaper chain in England. Many British citizens in India including Army officers also donated money for the purse that was presented to Dyer on his return home. Yet it appears that the memory of Jallianwala Bagh haunted Dyer till the last. He suffered from hallucinations and died a lonely man in 1927. His last words were Jallianwala Bagh. Sir Michael O'Dyer, who had been the Governor of Punjab during Jallianwala Bagh massacre and declared martial law, had fully supported General Dyer. Twenty-one years later, Udham Singh Azad in 1940 took revenge and shot Sir Michael O'Dyer at a public meeting in London. I was then an undergraduate at Patna University. We were happy that the massacre had been avenged. Jallianwala Bagh left a deep scar in Indo-British relations which could never be healed and the relations between the two nations would not be the same again. It is interesting that David Cameron, Prime Minister of Britain nearly a century later, while laying a wreath at the Jallianwala Bagh memorial, offered an apology for that most reprehensible act of brutality.

§

In 1919 my paternal grandfather had continued as Superintendent of Police in the Special Branch of Bihar CID. He felt highly perturbed with the reports about what had happened at Jallianwala Bagh. He felt like resigning but he had personal compulsions. His father had been stopped for health reasons to continue with his lucrative practice. The main source of income of the family had stopped but it had continued to live in the old lavish style incurring debts. My grandfather's eldest brother had died leaving his wife and children dependent on the joint family. My grandfather's second brother was serving in remote places from Patna. It fell upon my grandfather to manage the affairs of the joint family. He also had to look after his sister and her son who stayed with him. Given his family commitments, my grandfather could ill afford to resign.

While my grandfather found himself in a predicament, Lord Sinha was posted as Governor of Bihar. He had been President of the Indian National Congress a few years earlier and was respected for his nationalist views. The prospect of serving under an Indian

Governor attracted my grandfather and he made up his mind to continue in service to serve the nation loyally. He had earlier shown how as a Policeman he could discharge his duties without fear or favour when dealing with a British Indigo Planter. At that time, even in the Congress there had been divided opinion on whether or not to join the State Legislature. My maternal grandfather and his brother, despite being ardent Congressmen interacting closely with the Mahatma, had followed different parts. One joined the State Legislature and the other had boycotted it.

§

There was a feeling among many, both British and Indians, that the tragedy at Amritsar was a great aberration and the guilty had been punished. They felt that things would get sorted out. Slow but gradual movement towards self-rule would continue. The announcement of Lord Sinha being appointed Governor of Bihar raised high hopes. My father then a student at school was enamoured of the Police uniform and the colours of the Indian (Imperial) Police which he used to see his father wear. The IP tie and blazer were very colourful. He set his heart on competing into that service following in his father's footsteps, now that the Indian (Imperial) Police had been thrown open to Indians. He was friendly with Jayaprakash Narayan who was in college with him. The latter decided to respond to Gandhiji's call to boycott British educational institutions. In those days of early marriage, he was already married. His wife Prabhavati, daughter of a leading Congressman of Bihar, joined Gandhiji's Ashram. The Mahatma had no daughter. He and his wife Kasturba brought up Prabhavati for a few years while Jayaprakash Narayan had gone to the US for higher education. People used to go to England for higher studies. Hardly anyone went to the US those days. Facing much hardship, Jayaprakash Narayan even did menial work to support himself in the US and managed to complete his higher education there. He returned to India and joined active politics. I have mentioned these details because later Jayaprakash Narayan (JP) influenced my father's post-retirement career and my father's connection with him affected my army career. I shall dwell on these aspects later in this book.

§

Lord Sinha's appointment as Governor of Bihar in 1919 was unique and was widely welcomed all over the country, particularly in Bihar. It was a great morale booster for Indian officials in Bihar. They wanted to give of their best serving under an Indian Governor. Lord Sinha's meteoric career was a source of great pride for all Indians. Satyendra Prasanna Sinha came from a wealthy family of Raipur in Bengal. After graduating from Presidency College Calcutta, he went to England to study law in London. He qualified as a Barrister from Lincoln's Inn and returned to India in 1886 to practice law in Calcutta High Court. He also joined the Indian National Congress and remained a member of that party till 1919. He became a leader of the Calcutta Bar and was appointed to the coveted post of Advocate General of Bengal. After the Morley-Minto Reforms of 1909, he was inducted into the Viceroy's Executive Council and became the first Indian to be made a member of that Council. He was Law Member of the Council, equivalent of today's Law Minister in the Union Cabinet. He earned a Knighthood. In 1915 he became the President of the Indian National Congress, the year Mahatma Gandhi returned to India from South Africa. Lloyd George, the British Prime Minister, appointed Sir SP Sinha, a junior Minister in his Cabinet as Parliamentary Under Secretary of State in India Office. This was in recognition of the great contribution that India was making in the First World War. He now started attending meetings of the Supreme War Council at Paris along with Lloyd George and representatives of the Dominions in the Commonwealth and other allied countries. These meetings were presided over by Clemenceau, the French Prime Minister. After the war, he represented India at the Versailles Peace Conference. He was raised to Peerage as Lord Sinha of Raipur and appointed the Governor of Bihar and Orissa. Not only was he the one and only Indian to be appointed Governor during British rule but he was also the only Peer, British or Indian, who had been appointed Governor of a province. The three Presidency Governors of Bengal, Bombay and Madras used to be from public life in England and were often Peers of the Realm. I have mentioned these details to bring out that even the arrogant British ruling class in Bihar had a feeling of inferiority when interacting with Lord Sinha. The morale of Indians in the administration got a great boost in seeing one of their own in that exalted office. Next to the Viceroy, the Governor in his province was the most powerful person. Whatever my grandfather may have felt about disassociating himself from the British administration was dispelled both due to his family commitments and in no small measure by having the privilege of serving in a province over which an Indian was supreme.

Sinha was then not a common surname in Bihar as it is now. Lord Sinha was from Raipur in Bengal and our family is from a village called Raipur Khajuri in Bihar. There was no connection whatsoever between Lord Sinha's family and ours, yet many believed that my grandfather was connected to him. Reports and political assessments by Special Branch were then, as now, sent to the Governor for information. Lord Sinha was interested in these and would often send for my grandfather for discussion. At times, he agreed on file with his views, overruling contrary views of his British superiors. This gave my grandfather a privileged position which I am sure he must have enjoyed. He told me two interesting anecdotes of those days which I shall narrate.

Lady Sinha was fond of *Sandesh*. Bengali sweets were not available in Bihar in those days. A sweetmeat shop from Calcutta opened a branch in Patna. A special design of *Sandesh* made at this branch called Lady Sinha *Sandesh* was produced. A box of this sweet was sent to the Government House (now called Raj Bhavan) for Lady Sinha. The British ADC told the staff that native sweets could not be served on the table of His Excellency. He directed that these sweets be sent to the bedroom of Lady Sinha. When Lord Sinha heard of this, he sacked the ADC and got an immediate replacement for him. The second anecdote also pertains to Lady Sinha. As per the tradition among Indian wives, she wanted to occasionally cook Bengali dishes for her husband. The kitchen was some distance away from the main building. She could not go to the general cook house outside the main building because that would not have been proper for a Governor's wife. She mentioned her predicament to an Indian visitor telling him that she wished she could have a private kitchen of her own. The Indian Superintendent Engineer of Patna, Bishen Swaroop heard of this conversation. Within twenty-four hours, he had a private kitchen built on the same floor close to the Governor's apartment. The British Secretary to the Governor heard of this and inspected the kitchen to check if provisions had been made for fire precaution. This had been duly catered for. The Secretary was wise enough not to raise any objection after what had happened to the British ADC.

Due to his failing health, Lord Sinha resigned in 1921, much to the regret of my grandfather and all Indians in the administration. As former President of the Congress, he must have felt great strain in dealing with the Non-Cooperation Movement launched by the Congress, under the leadership of Mahatma Gandhi.

§

The Non-Cooperation Movement was gaining momentum by the day. Hindus and Muslims were fully united making things difficult for the British. Subsequent movements led by the Mahatma, the Civil Disobedience Movement of 1930 and the Quit India movement of 1942, did not have the same extent of communal unity. There was a general feeling that success was now within grasp. Some British colleagues of my grandfather told him that they were seriously thinking of packing their bags and going home to England as British rule may not now last. The British felt that they had no answer to deal with such a massive non-violent movement. At the height of this movement, the Chauri Chaura incident took place in 1922. Congressmen, in an act of retaliation, had attacked a police station and burnt it down. Some policemen inside the police station were burnt alive. The Mahatma immediately called off the movement when victory was within his grasp. His reason was that he did not want to gain independence through violence. The end could not justify the means. Both the end and the means had to be noble.

§

The maternal side of my family was caught in the political debates surrounding the Freedom Movement. A couple of years after my maternal grandfather, his younger brother also qualified as a Barrister from London and returned to Gaya. Both brothers joined the Congress and had the privilege of interacting with the Mahatma. My granduncle's wife Priyamvada also joined the Congress and was an active Congress worker. As a child, I saw some letters written by the Mahatma to the Nandkeolyar family, most of them are now not traceable. However, the family has been able to retrieve some of these letters of the Mahatma. I have included photocopies of a couple of these letters in this book (Appendix). They make an interesting reading and show how the Mahatma, inspite of his busy schedule, found time to go into small issues.

§

On return from England in 1913, fully qualified as a Barrister, my maternal grandfather had joined the Gaya District Bar (Picture 3). I am told he worked hard as a Barrister and made a mark for himself in his profession. He became President of the Gaya Bar Council. He had been in touch with Dr Annie Besant and her Home Rule Movement. Dr Besant was a theosophist and her society started a boarding school for girls in Benares (now Varanasi). The school came to be known as Vasanta School. My grandfather decided to send my mother to that school. This was very unusual in Bihar at that time. Bihari girls did not go to school, much less to a boarding school far away from home. The conservative friends and relations of my grandfather advised him against this as that may cause problems for him in the future when arranging her marriage. My mother was happy to go to a boarding school and my grandfather ignored the advice of his friends.

After Jallianwala Bagh, Mahatma Gandhi gave the call for a Non-Cooperation and Non-Violent Movement. He advised the people to boycott British institutions like law courts or schools and colleges. He wanted Congressmen to give up wearing imported clothes and instead wear *Khadi*. He exhorted them to spin thread on the spinning wheel and make their own clothes. My grandfather gave up his lucrative practice at the Bar. He made a bonfire of all his English clothes and took to wearing *Khadi* (Pictures 4a and 4b). He also had a spinning wheel (*Charkha*) of his own on which he worked in his spare time. I never saw him in anything other than *Khadi* dress and of course the Gandhi cap. However, I saw pictures of him in European dress and in Barrister's gown. He became the President of the Gaya District Congress Committee. He was a prominent member of the Reception Committee for the famous 1923 national session of the Congress Party at Gaya. It was a momentous conference. The veteran Congress leader CR Das was the President of the Congress at this session, which was attended by Mahatma Gandhi who had just come out of jail. Girl volunteers presented a guard of honour to CR Das on his arrival at the Session for unfurling the Congress flag. My mother commanded this Guard of Honour. The Gaya Congress discussed the Montagu Chelmsford Act of 1919. CR Das favoured the Congress participating in the election to the Assemblies to pursue the agenda of self-rule from within, and if necessary force a deadlock.

Motilal Nehru supported CR Das. He had been an attorney of Maharaja of Tekari and the Nandkeolyars, being hereditary Dewans of Tekari, had been in touch with him. My maternal grandfather joined the CR Das–Motilal Nehru faction. The Mahatma was not in favour of the Congress joining the Assemblies and wanted to boycott them. The former were known as Changers and the latter as No Changers. Most of the delegates from Bihar, including Rajendra Prasad, were No Changers. My grandfather supported the Changers. Due to support from the Mahatma, the No Changers carried the day. The resolution of the Changers was defeated. CR Das resigned. Along with his supporters, he broke away from the Congress and formed the Swaraj Party. Later a compromise was reached with the Swarajists. They remained within the Congress, but were allowed to go ahead with their experiment and contest elections to the Assembly. My maternal grandfather now became a member of the Bihar legislature.

§

My maternal grandfather had three brothers and two cousins. They were fond of each other and lived as brothers in a joint family. The word cousin was frowned upon and not used. They were known as six brothers. My maternal grandfather being the eldest was highly regarded by the others. Three of them were Barristers, one a district Engineer, one an Advocate and the youngest held the hereditary appointment of Dewan of Tekari. Two among the six of them were in politics. My maternal grandfather opted for the Swaraj party which joined the State legislature and his brother joined the No Changers who boycotted the legislature. The two cousins practised law at the Patna High Court. They devoted themselves to their legal profession. One of them, Harinandan Nandkeolyar was doing very well in his profession and had a large practice. He was about to become a High Court Judge when he suddenly passed away. This was a great loss to the family. He was very fond of my father. I am told that when my father was preparing for the competitive examination for the Indian

Police, my paternal grandfather was Superintendent of Police at Monghyr (now Munger). My maternal granduncle, Harinandan insisted that my father come to Patna and stay with him and not in his own family house where he had his cousins and a large number of relations nearby to distract him. My granduncle's house was out of the city near the High Court. He took personal interest in my father's preparations for the examination. Since he was going for a holiday in Kashmir with his family for six weeks, my father lived alone in the house with my granduncle's butler and staff. They looked after him extremely well so he could devote all his time undisturbed, preparing for his examination. There used to be only one vacancy in the IP every year and one had to stand first to compete. My father used to say that preparing for the examination undisturbed in his uncle-in-law's house helped him to compete. This granduncle of mine died a few months after I was born and I have no recollections of him. However, for a long time I had a set of small silver utensils for a small child with my name inscribed on them. He had given these to me when I was born.

§

Joining the Indian Police had been my father's ambition from childhood. I have already mentioned his fascination for IP colours. In 1928, the Freedom Struggle had abated and my father unlike my grandfather did not face any mental conflict on deciding to join government service instead of joining the Freedom Movement like his friend Jayaprakash Narayan or his father-in-law and the latter's brother. That was also the time when General Thimayya serving as a young Army Officer had come in contact with Motilal Nehru in Allahabad. He had asked Motilal Nehru whether he should continue to serve in the Army or should resign and join the Congress. Motilal Nehru had advised him to continue serving in the Army so that when India became Independent, there would be Indian Officers in the Army to serve the country and we would not be dependent on British officers. The same consideration applied to Officers in Civil Services. It is relevant that in 1947 when India became Independent, both General Thimayya and my father were in key official positions to serve the nation at a time of great crisis. By then my grandfather's generation of Indian officers had all retired or passed away.

Although the six brothers including cousins of my maternal grandfather's generation pursued different careers in which some of them opposed each other, this in no way affected their warm personal relations. My grandfather and his one brother were in politics but the former was with the Changers and had joined the Swaraj faction while the other was with the No Changers. The latter and his wife had lived in the Mahatma's Ashram. Later he worked full time in the Congress office at Anand Bhavan in Allahabad. Subsequently the two factions of the Congress merged and the two brothers were now on the same page. His wife used to be fond of me and when she came to Gaya she would give me presents and sweets that she knew I liked. The Mahatma wrote a letter to her in his own hand on the occasion of the marriage of her son. He advised her on how to treat her daughter-in-law. This letter is still with the family. Text of that letter is included in this book (first letter on p 400). In 1946 when I was posted as a Captain in Delhi this granduncle of mine was Special Officer with Dr Rajendra Prasad who then held the Food portfolio. He returned to Gaya after Rajen Babu became President of the Constituent Assembly. He passed away not long after that.

§

Another interesting incident in the family was when my maternal grandfather as a member of the State Legislature raised a legal point in the Legislature on the functioning of the Governor. This was referred to his cousin who was then the government Advocate, for legal advice. It in a way brought them in confrontation with each other. I am told that this caused much amusement and the two would humorously discuss the point at issue with no bitterness. In fact, this became a joke in the family.

§

The Prince of Wales came on a visit to India in late 1921. The Congress party decided to boycott his visit. The heir apparent to the British throne was given a befitting official reception at the Gateway of India in Bombay, which had been constructed on the occasion of the visit of his father ten years earlier. The official reception at Delhi also had all the pomp and grandeur, but both at Bombay and Delhi there was little public participation. A large entourage accompanied the Prince on his tour to India. This included Mountbatten, a stunningly handsome young naval officer with royal connections. He had come out as the ADC of the Prince for his tour in India. A charming young lady, Edwina, the daughter of one of the richest men of England had also come along with the entourage. The Prince was then the most eligible bachelor in the world. The present Rashtrapati Bhavan was under construction at that time. The construction of New Delhi had got delayed due to the First World War and architectural controversy about the design for the residence of the Viceroy's House (present Rashtrapati Bhavan). Work on this building had just started. It got completed only in 1931. The Viceroy was then staying in Old Delhi in the present office of the Vice-Chancellor of Delhi University. The Prince and some of his staff stayed in the temporary Viceroy's House in Old Delhi. It was there that Mountbatten, during a social function, proposed to Edwina and she assented. Seventeen years later, the Mountbattens came to live in the Viceroy's House in New Delhi. Mountbatten became the last Viceroy of India. He had to wind up the British Empire in India.

§

The Prince of Wales proceeded to Allahabad from Delhi. Allahabad was the then capital of United Provinces (now Uttar Pradesh). Sir Spencer Harcourt Butler was the Governor of the province. He received the Prince at the railway station. The official reception was very impressive. The Prince drove in State in a horse-driven carriage with a cavalry escort in procession from the railway station to the Government House. The Congress party had called for a boycott of the Prince's visit. Jawaharlal Nehru had organised the boycott in Allahabad. The roads were completely deserted, all shops were closed and there were black flags on houses. This irked the Prince. He told the Governor that such a dead city did not deserve to be the capital of the province. In compliance with his imperial will, the capital of the province was shifted from Allahabad to Lucknow. The judiciary asserted its independence and the High Court remained in Allahabad. Even today the capital of Uttar Pradesh is Lucknow and the High Court is at Allahabad. Uttar Pradesh is the only State in the country whose capital and High Court are at different places other than the newly created several small States after Independence.

After his tour of United Provinces, the Prince was scheduled to visit Patna, the capital of Bihar. While the construction of New Delhi and the New Capital of the newly created province of Bihar and Orissa in Patna, had both started in 1911, the former got completed in 1931 and the latter in 1917. Of course the former is much larger in size than the latter. Moreover as mentioned earlier, the construction of New Delhi got delayed because of architectural controversies. New Capital at Patna emerged as the best planned provincial capital in the country. After what had happened at Allahabad, the Governor of Bihar was apprehensive of something similar happening at Patna. The Congress under the leadership of Dr Rajendra Prasad was organising the boycott of the Prince's visit to Patna. The Governor did not want to be asked to move out from the newly constructed provincial capital which had come up so well. A meeting was convened by him to discuss arrangements for the Prince's visit. A colleague of my grandfather, Mr Shahbuddin Khuda Baksh, was then officiating as Superintendent of Police, Patna. He was the son of the famous Khuda Baksh, the founder of the unique Khuda Baksh Oriental Public Library in Patna known for its rare collections of manuscripts of the medieval period. He was a very jovial person and so was his English wife. My grandfather and he had been good friends. After retirement they decided to move out of the city and settle in Danapur Cantonment, away from the hustle and bustle of the town. They bought houses fairly close to each other. He and his wife would often visit us and I liked going to his house to eat the excellent pastries his wife would make.

Mr Khuda Baksh would recall with gusto how he had ensured that the capital of Bihar was not shifted from Patna. At a meeting convened by the Governor to discuss arrangements for the visit of the Prince of Wales, he assured the Governor that he would organise a rousing reception for the Prince in Patna. While the Congress volunteers were making arrangements for a complete boycott in the city as had happened at Allahabad, he quietly sent his men to the neighbouring villages inviting them to the city for a big *Mela* (fair). The villagers were told that they would be given a free meal at the *Mela* and each person would get half a rupee in cash. This attracted villagers in large numbers who came in their bullock carts. They were each given a paper Union Jack and made to line the road for the Princes' Drive-in-State. They waved the Union Jack as the Prince went past. He was thrilled and told the Governor that it was the best welcome he had received anywhere in India. The Governor was mighty pleased and Mr Khuda Baksh was awarded a high title. He passed away a few years before Independence. Little could he have imagined that the art of collecting crowds pioneered by him will become the standard operating procedure for political parties in Independent India.

§

My paternal grandparents had gone on pilgrimage to Haridwar. They had a trusted servant with them whose family had served our family for generations. My grandmother once gave him a ₹100 note to get change and do some shopping. Those days ₹100 was a huge amount. The servant ran away and did not return. After a few years the servant came to Patna and went to see my grandmother wearing saffron clothes. He said that he had a sense of guilt for running away with the money she had given him and had come to return the amount. He had decided to pose as a saint living on a tree. He had spread the word that he was a Sadhu who had spent a long time meditating in the Himalayas and had acquired supernatural power to grant the wishes of people. Gradually he built a big following and many would come to him with offerings. He earned a lot of money. He now joined a Holy Order and became a Sadhu. This shows how one can use religion to exploit blind faith of the people and earn money. There is no shortage of such Godmen in our country today. Some among them have been found guilty of murder and rape.

§

My father was preparing for his BA examination at Patna University in 1923. In those days boys used to get married while still in school. According to the standard of those days his marriage had been much delayed. My grandmother insisted that it was high time he got married and my grandfather agreed. The family Pandit was asked to examine horoscopes and find a suitable match for him. My father's horoscope tallied with my mother's and their marriage was settled.

Considering that my father's family had been in government service, with my grandfather holding a senior appointment in Police, and my mother's family had been actively associated with the

Congress, eyebrows were raised in British circles. At a social gathering of Police officers one of my grandfather's British colleagues remarked, "Sinha is getting his son married into a family of agitators. I suppose he would now like to see the back of us." This upset my grandfather and he blurted out, "I pity the intelligence of an Englishman who believes that an Indian would like to be ruled forever and ever." The atmosphere became a little tense. He realised that he had perhaps over stepped the mark and should not have given such a harsh reply. He now said, "Queen Victoria on becoming Empress of India had said that it would be the policy of her government to prepare the people of India for self-rule. The difference between the agitators and others was that one wanted self-rule immediately and the others gradually as was being done. The difference between the two was of timing and not of principle. The agitators wanted this immediately and the others gradually as indeed was being done." One senior colleague said, "Of course." The tension disappeared and everyone relaxed. The marriage of my father to my mother, daughter of a leading Congressman, did not come in the way of my grandfather's official career or that of my father, when he competed into the Indian (Imperial) Police. I may mention that today a Chief Minister of West Bengal has set different norms. She has decreed that no member of her party should have any social contact with members of the Communist party who constitute the main 'opposition' in the Assembly nor should anyone from her party have a marriage alliance from his family with that of any member of the Opposition.

§

I was born in 1925 although as per normal practice those days my year of birth in school record was recorded as 1926. This was done to ensure that one did not become overage for government service after completing one's education. I inherited the traditions of both my father's and mother's families. During my army career, I always remained loyal to the government in power and remained totally apolitical even though I nursed a nationalist urge to serve my people. I did not allow this urge to come in the way of my official duties. During my post-army career, I took to public life without joining any political party. After I quit the Army, LK Advani, Chaudhary Charan Singh and Chandra Shekhar, leaders of different opposition parties, invited me to join their party. I declined to do so. Atal Bihari Vajpayee advised me that even if I did not join Rajniti (politics), I should take active part in Rashtraniti (public life). I have been following his advice. As time passed, I developed very friendly relations with both Vajpayee and Advani. The former is two weeks older than me and the latter two years younger.

§

Approaching Twilight: The Sun Past the Meridian

I was born at Gaya on 7 January 1925 but my school record shows that I was born on 7 January 1926. Neither was I responsible or even aware of this till much later that it was my official date of birth. In those days there were no Municipal or hospital records of births as children used to be born at their homes. As per Supreme Court ruling, the date of birth shown in the school records is the official date for the individual's birth date. The practice those days was to record a younger date of birth at school so that even if a person does not complete his education before the age of 25, he would still be eligible for government service. In Britain, after all, the Sovereign has two dates of birth, personal and official. Two Honours Lists of awards come out every year. The first is on New Year's day on 1 January and the second is on 1 June which is known as the Sovereign's Birth Day Honour List.

The tradition at the time was for the firstborn to be delivered in his or her mother's home. There was a small room with no windows in my mother's home for this purpose, called the 'Saurighar' meaning labour room. Gaya used to be one of the hottest places in the country surrounded by bare low hills. After extensive forestation by the Army, Gaya is now not so hot a place. Anyway, I am glad I was born in the peak of winter. If it had been summer, that would have been more tortuous for my mother. I was the first grandchild of my grandparents on both sides. Lavish celebrations were held to welcome my arrival. My mother passed away when I was a little over three years old. I am told that I called her *Didimaiyan*, a word that I had coined on my own. She was the eldest of her generation. All her brothers, sisters and cousins called her *Didi* and she was called *Maiyan* meaning girl child by her older generation. I combined the two into *Didimaiyan*. I had a brother three years younger to me. Soon after his birth, my mother suffered from tuberculosis. She had to be quarantined and taken to a sanatorium. As my mother had to go to a sanatorium when I was a little over three years old, I have no recollection of her. This has been my lifelong regret. She died in the sanatorium after a few months.

My first recollection goes back to living in a mud hut of four or five rooms, in an Adivasi village in Itki, a few miles out of Ranchi. It had a thatched roof with mud floor and mud walls which were kept spotlessly clean. Every day the walls and floors were given a mud wash. When it rained, the water flowing on the ground used to look pale red as the area had mud of light red hue. I liked seeing paper boats made for me floating on the water. The Tuberculosis Sanatorium was located close by. My mother was admitted there. My maternal grandparents wanted to be near her and had moved to Itki. They would visit her frequently but due to fear of contagion, children were not allowed to go to see her. Thus I do not have any recollection of my mother. My father was then a probationer under training at Police Training College, Hazaribagh, about 50 miles from Ranchi. He used to come to see us at the village. On one occasion, a leopard raced with his motorbike. He was driving at 60 miles per hour. The leopard overtook him. Luckily it did not attack him. It must be very tormenting for my mother to know that she was dying and her two sons were close by whom she could not see. Destiny can be very cruel and one has no option but put up with one's destiny.

I have faint recollections of everyone crying and looking sad one day. That must have been the day when my mother passed away. All of us now moved by car to Gaya and I vaguely remember that long road journey.

§

It was decided that my brother and I should be left for some time at Gaya to be brought up by our maternal grandparents. My mother's father and his brothers lived as a joint family in a large house at Gaya called Nand Villa. There were over half a dozen young children in the house. My mother was the eldest of her generation. She had three brothers all younger to her, the first two being much older than me and the youngest only three years older. Her younger sister was some eight years older to me and I remember her trying to look after me and my brother. Unfortunately, she died a year after my mother.

I have vague recollections of her. A few of my mother's cousins were of my age and some even younger. I had many playmates.

§

There used to be a British jail in Gaya town till the 1857 Uprising, on a large plot of land, leased by the Maharaja of Tekari. The British built a new jail a few miles out of the city. The plot of land on which the old jail stood reverted to the Maharaja. He gifted that land to my maternal great-grandfather, who was his Dewan. He owned plenty of land near his village and was landlord of several villages. The jail building was demolished and a large house was built at that site by my maternal great grandfather. This house was later named after him by his sons and called Nand Villas. Three quarters of a century later when I was a child and for long after, the house was still popularly known as Purana Jelkhana (Old Jail).

The sons of my maternal great-grandfather, except the youngest, chose different vocations on return from England where they had gone for higher education. My maternal grandfather, the eldest among them, became a Barrister. He practised at Gaya District Court. One brother chose to be an Engineer in Bhagalpur and the third also a Barrister joined the Congress Party. The youngest son, carrying out the family tradition, became the Dewan of Tekari.

§

To provide a glimpse of the way of life in Nand Villas, I would like to describe the layout of the house (Pictures 5a and 5b). It had a large front gate to allow elephants to enter the cemented forecourt. As one entered this gate, one saw a double-storey large building with the men's block on the Left. On the Right, were offices of clerks, class rooms for children, stables for elephants and horses, garage for the car and servants' quarters. There were no elephants when I grew up but we had horses and horse carriages. Two cars had also been acquired with folding canvas roofs. They were called tourers. Sedan body car with fixed roof came later.

The two-storey men's block on an elevation with a flight of few steps had a deep front veranda. There was a telephone fixed to the wall which was used by the elders. The telephone had to be rung manually holding the receiver in one hand while speaking into the mouth-piece fixed to the wall. One had to speak into the phone standing. I thought that the telephone was fixed high on the wall to keep it beyond the reach of children. There were two sitting rooms, one of Indian style and the other of Western style. The dining room with arrangement for both tables and chairs as also small wooden *pirhas* (low wooden planks), on which one could squat and eat from silver *thalis* (circular plates). There were also a couple of office rooms and a library full of law books in the almirahs. The latter was for my grandfather who practised in the District Court. All these rooms opened on the front veranda. Besides, the men's block had a few bed rooms for guests on both floors. This block was connected by an enclosed corridor *Deohri* on its flank, to the living apartments of the family. The latter was called the *Zenana* (ladies quarters) meant for ladies. The *Deohri* led to a large courtyard about half the size of a tennis court with deep veranda all round it. There were some several rooms on each of the two floors of this block opening on the veranda. Utility rooms like kitchen, store room, labour room and others were all on the ground floor. There were bed rooms on both floors. The verandas were used as sitting and eating place. During the summer, we slept in the veranda or on the courtyard. The latter was the lung of the house. The children played in the courtyard and on the open ground in the rear. We used the terrace on the top for flying kites. We ate in *thalis* squatting on the floor. Non-vegetarian food was cooked in a kitchen outside. Before I was born there used to be no electricity. There were old style *pankhas* (fans) with pulleys and holes in the wall for the pankha puller to pull the *pankha*. We had a virtual army of male and female servants, almost all from villages owned by the family. Only Indian meals, both vegetarian and non-vegetarian, were served. We did not have bread or eggs at breakfast. It was believed that bread was kneaded by feet and hence considered dirty. It was called *pauroti, pau* meaning feet. It also meant a quarter of a pound. Men had their meals first. The ladies sat down to eat after the men had fed. I was fond of eating food and sat down to eat first with my grandfather and later again with my grandmother. I once asked my grandfather a question which he found difficult to answer. I enquired that when God had given us two eyes, two ears, two hands and two legs why had he given us only one mouth. He replied that because He had given us only one stomach. I then asked why not two stomachs to which he replied that he would find out from God.

I recall an amusing incident. A close relative had come and had a meal with us. He was an old man and had false teeth. After the meal he got up to wash his hands and mouth in the courtyard. A servant with a jug full of water, soap, towel and a basin was in attendance. As the guest took out his denture before washing his mouth, the servant who had never seen a denture before, dropped the jug spilling water all over. He ran away screaming ghost.

§

Urdu was taught to boys in the family while the girls studied Hindi. Besides Urdu, we also had an English teacher. The normal age to start going to school was eight. School going children would also be given private tuition. When I was 5 years old, the *Maulvi* performed my *Makhtab,* a ritual marking a child's initiation for studies. I was taught to write the Urdu alphabets with chalk on a wooden slate. We spoke in Urdu with guests and in Magahi in the family and with the servants. Magahi is a dialect of Hindi, spoken in Magadh region comprising Patna and Gaya districts. Today it is fast becoming extinct. Even in the cities of Patna and Gaya, people have started speaking in Hindi instead of Magahi. The younger generations in my own family cannot speak in our native dialect. On the other hand, the other two local dialects of Bihar, Maithili and Bhojpuri, akin to Hindi, continue to be widely spoken. In fact, language status is now claimed for these dialects.

Mahatma Gandhi launched the Non-Cooperation Movement in 1920 and the Civil Disobedience Movement in 1930. The latter started with the long Dandi March and was called Salt Satyagrah. My maternal grandfather and his Barrister brother were active Congressmen. A number of Congressmen would come to see my maternal grandfather in our house at Gaya. Sometimes sitting on his lap, I would listen to their political discussions. I did not much understand what they discussed but I could make out that they revered Gandhiji. His long Dandi March was gaining momentum every day and was much admired. It was compared to an irresistible river torrent for which the British had no answer. Someone told the children that the Mahatma had supernatural powers. We believed him when he told us that the Mahatma could become a bird and fly out of jail at will, to organise the Civil Disobedience Movement and then return to the jail.

As children, we would play in the house carrying little sticks with paper Congress flags on them and shouting slogans like 'Inqilab Zindabad' (Long Live Revolution) and 'Mahatma Gandhi Ki Jai' (Victory to Mahatma Gandhi). We would pretend to draw salt from the sea. There would be water in a tub in which we would pour salt and then take out water with salt in our little pans. We would go up to the terrace and fly kites. Our kites would be in Congress colours. Some had kites with the colours of the British Union Jack. Our Congress kites would attack the Union Jack kites and cut their thread to our great delight. It was all good fun.

§

When we heard that Sardar Bhagat Singh had been hanged in Punjab some of us cried. We would talk amongst ourselves and say that when we grew up we would teach the British a lesson. We sang patriotic songs, the words of some, I still remember.

> *Azadi Ka Divana Tha Sardar Bhagat Singh, Kar Lia Phansi Gale Ka Har Bhagat Singh.*
>
> (Sardar Bhagat Singh was crazy for Independence. He made the hangman's rope a garland round his neck.)

The other song was,

> *Shaheedon Ke Mazaron Par Lagenge Har Varas Mele,*
> *Vatan Par Marne Walon Ka Yihi Namo Nishan Hoga.*
> *Ek Aisa Din Bhi Aega Jab Apni Hi Zamin Hogi, Aur Apna Asman Hoga*
>
> (There will be fairs held every year at the graves of the martyrs, in their honour. A day will come when this land will be ours and so will be the sky above.)

My maternal grandfather had a *Charkha* (spinning wheel) and would spin thread for making *Khadi* clothes. I tried my hand at it a few times but it was beyond me. As a child, I got imbued, good and proper, with the ethos and spirit of the Civil Disobedience Movement.

§

I have happy recollections of my childhood days in Gaya and of the way I was brought up. My mother's parents were over indulgent towards me. They showered me with much love and went out of their way to ensure that I did not feel that I did not have a mother. Yet in my quiet moments I missed my mother when I saw mothers coddling their children even though I had no recollection of my mother. I would hide this feeling from my grandparents and never mentioned it to them. I felt that it would hurt them. They would tell people that I was a tactful and a precocious child. I liked listening to my maternal grandmother when she talked to me about my mother.

§

One day, I was told that my paternal grandfather felt that I had to be brought up as a Sinha and not a Nandkeolyar. This meant that my younger brother and I had to be moved from Gaya to Patna and live there. An additional reason for our having to be moved to Patna was the fact that my younger brother had health problems which required better medical attention than what was available in Gaya. Anyway, I was most upset at the prospect of having to go away from my mother's family for what I felt on a journey to the unknown. My maternal grandmother was equally upset. My grandfather tried to explain things to me in his own way without showing emotion. He told me that in our society a person's identity is linked more to his father's family, though he is also part of his mother's family. He said he would personally take me to Patna. He assured me that it had been agreed that we would be allowed to spend time at Gaya during school holidays every year and he would be frequently visiting us in Patna. My maternal grandfather's cousin was a flourishing lawyer in Patna and my maternal grandfather used to go to him frequently. An old maid servant, who had been looking after my brother and me, would accompany us for a few months till we settled down in our new surroundings. My brother was too young to feel the change that was now taking place in our lives. When the day came for our departure from Gaya, I cried unashamedly and so did my maternal grandmother and my mother's youngest brother and her cousins who had been my playmates. I recall our departure from Gaya, as the most poignant moment of my childhood. My father had married again and was posted as Assistant Superintendent of Police in Patna City. I found my new mother always very considerate and kind to me. My parents would have a total of eleven children - six boys and five girls. My younger brothers and sisters showed me much respect and were very attached to me. We had brotherly feelings amongst us as in the *Ramayana*. Unfortunately, I lost two brothers and three sisters. Most of them at a young age.

My grandfather was Superintendent of Railway Police living in New Capital at Patna. I felt that I had been removed from my old moorings and taken to a different world. It was a traumatic feeling but I reconciled myself to accept the inevitable.

§

We arrived in Patna escorted by our maternal grandfather and he took us to our paternal grandfather's official house in New Capital. Our maternal grandfather stayed back for a couple of days with his cousin in Patna to see us settle down in our new surroundings. I found my paternal grandparents equally caring and affectionate. I became my paternal grandfather's favourite child. My paternal grandmother showered us with all her affection, particularly my younger brother who was a sickly child. I had two uncles and my two aunts, brothers and sisters of my father, who were older than me. I always showed them much respect. My aunt took special care of me and my younger uncle only a little older than me became my playmate. However, it took me some time to get over the vast change from Indian life style to a Western one in an official colonial environment.

§

New Capital was a recently built official colony, a few miles away from Patna town. It was much like New Delhi, some miles from Old Delhi. Lutyens was the architect who built both New Delhi and New Capital at Patna. There were four very imposing buildings in New Capital, the High Court, the Secretariat, the Legislature and the Government House. The latter was the residence of the Governor and is now called Raj Bhavan. Whereas officers' bungalows in New Delhi are single storey New Capital has double storey bungalows, both very big and not so big, with spacious compound and nice gardens, for senior officers serving in the Secretariat. Several bungalows had tennis courts. The roads were well-planned with well-maintained grass pathway on either side for riding horses and walkways for morning and evening walkers. Although every officer had a car, there was not much traffic on the roads. One would see few cars plying on the road, on an average not more than one every fifteen minutes by day and hardly any by night. The occasional horse-driven carriage could be seen bringing non-officials from the town to New Capital. In the city, horse carriages, bullock carts and very few cars would be seen on the roads. Patna had a total of some 300 cars at that time. There were no shops in New Capital and provisions had to be brought from the town, some three to four miles away. A colony for subordinate officers and clerks called Gardanibag was located a mile away across a railway line. There were small shops in this colony and fresh vegetables were also sold there. There were service lanes in New Capital behind the bungalows for servants to cycle or walk. Each bungalow had half a dozen servants' quarters, a garage for car and a stable for horses. There was no water-borne sanitation in those days. Bungalows had separate staircases to be used by the sweeper with a cane basket to carry the commode pot for cleaning. Unlike the house I grew up in Gaya, one heard no hustle and bustle of town nor did visitors come to the house all the time. New Capital was a very quiet area and its official residents, mostly British, led a much-disciplined life. It had a very colonial ambience, and was a haven for white rulers in an era of peace and plenty. Over 90% of officers living in New Capital were British. My grandfather was among the few Indians living in New Capital. His bungalow was only a few hundred yards from the Government House. Stray cows were not permitted inside New Capital. The milkman was allowed to bring his cow along the service lanes to deliver milk to officers' bungalows within a fixed time schedule. No cow was permitted to be kept in bungalows. I heard of an incident in which it was found that two cows were living in the servants' quarters of the British Chief Secretary who ranked only next to the Governor. He was the top civil servant of the Province. The Administrator of New Capital Municipal Committee was a young British ICS officer. The Chief Secretary had no knowledge of the presence of cows in his servants' quarters. Yet he was culpable and the Administrator had no hesitation in fining him for the lapse. He readily paid the fine and punished his servant for keeping the cows in the servants' quarters. The cows were sent away. That is how the British tried to uphold rules and enforce discipline. It would be unimaginable in India of today for a junior officer to fine or take action against a Chief Secretary, for whatever reason.

§

My grandfather's double-storey bungalow had a sitting room, a dining room, an office room and a guest room on the ground floor. The family lived in the four bedrooms on the first floor. We also had a large terrace above the kitchen complex connected to the house. This was another playground for the children apart from the lawn and open space on the ground. New Capital had a very official and exclusive atmosphere. Protocol was followed rigidly. On working days all officials would be in their home-office and available on the telephone for official work after breakfast from nine for an hour before proceeding for their offices in the Secretariat. They were expected to pick up their telephones themselves during working hours. At other times orderlies or *chaprasis* (peons) would pick up telephones. Telephone calls in offices were not put through PAs as happens nowadays. Perhaps at that time EPBAX facility was not available enabling a PA to transfer the call to the officer. At ten sharp all officers would be in their offices in the Secretariat. They would be home for one hour lunch break and back in their offices thereafter. They would return home soon after the office closed at five in the afternoon. Saturdays would be half days and Sundays holidays. The present-day culture of tea and snacks in offices was not in vogue in those days. Official visitors were generally received in offices and not at homes. Officers in the Secretariat hardly went out on tours. In the summer the whole secretariat with officers, clerks and files moved to Ranchi, the summer capital of the province for six months in a year. The same routine as in Patna was followed at Ranchi. Officers in the field spent half their time touring their areas of responsibility. They would visit villages, inspect subordinate offices, Police Stations, works being carried out in the field and so on. The saying was that a district officer should administer his district from the saddle of a horse so that the common man could get a prompt hearing. Most officers preferred serving in districts rather than in the secretariat. Secretariat officers were given secretariat allowance to compensate them for not serving in the field. The present culture of jostling for a job in the secretariat and serving for the minimum duration in the districts did not exist then. The judicial officers and the law courts were totally independent from the executive and zealously guarded their independence. Delay in disposal of cases or too many adjournments of cases in law courts were not the order of the day. There were no large backlogs of cases in law courts. Speedy and not very expensive justice was available to the people. The bureaucracy was manned at the top almost exclusively by the British. It was the steel frame of the Empire. It was considered more efficient in many ways than the bureaucracy in Britain. I have tried to describe the functioning of the administration as I observed from the routine followed by my father and grandfather as also on the basis of my own experience of interacting with bureaucrats in the closing years of British rule.

§

Although I stayed with my grandparents in New Capital, I often visited my parents living in Patna City some ten miles away. My father had a nice single storey official bungalow with a large compound in the heart of the city. He was an All India level Polo player. He used to come to play Polo in New Capital, once or twice a week. Only two other Indians, the Raja of Darbhanga, the heir apparent, of the Maharajadhiraj and a junior railway officer called Billy Badhwar, played polo in Bihar. A few years after Independence, Badhwar became Chairman of the Railway Board at Delhi. Mostly young British civil and army officers played polo in Bihar. The Governor was a polo enthusiast and often used to come to witness polo matches. He was very appreciative of my father's playing skill. My father was also a good tennis and bridge player. He used to be often invited to the Government House for tennis and social functions. Some of his Indian colleagues and even superiors became jealous of him. They would say that he was too Westernised and a blue-eyed boy of the British. Yet with all his Westernised way of life, both my grandfather and father observed Hindu orthodox rituals. They would have their breakfast only after a bath and morning prayers. They always wore the sacred thread (*Janeu*) under their clothes and would come out of their bath wearing wooden sandals for their morning *pooja* (prayers). My father often stayed with his British colleagues. The sound of his walking in wooden sandals would amuse them.

Once in a while my brother and I would go for the weekend or a short holiday to our parents in Patna City. My father's four Police orderlies had their peculiarities and we were friendly with them. Two of them Rehmat Shah and Babu Jan had served during the First World War in a cavalry unit and would tell us war stories. I had no idea that one day I would join the Army and serve in the Second World War. Chandraman Ram was the champion wrestler of the district but a little thick headed. When he received a telephone call from my father's boss MacNeilly, the Senior SP, he would put the receiver down and give a smart salute and then run to call my father. Naqi the car driver was a quiet orthodox man who did his Namaz five times a day.

On one occasion when I was with my father in Patna City, he was woken up in the middle of the night. A man had been murdered by the son of an influential landlord in the City. The scene of crime was in a narrow lane where a car could not go. My father went out on his horse and arrived at the scene before the officer in charge of the Police Station reached the spot. Immediate investigation was started, the accused was arrested and within three months the case was decided by the District Sessions Court. The accused was given a death sentence. His appeal in the High Court was dismissed and in about six months he was hanged. I am mentioning this incident because nowadays murder cases take several years to be decided. Even Police investigations take years to commence. Murder cases registered in Police Stations are kept pending for long, even years, before investigation starts. The Indian bureaucracy and dispensation of justice administration in those days were far superior to what one finds nowadays.

§

Social life of the *Bara Sahibs*, a term used for high civil officials, was very formal. Most of them were British with a small sprinkling of Indians among them like my grandfather and later even during the early years of my father's official career. At the gate of every house in New Capital there was the nameplate on one side and a small wooden box with a slit at the top on the other, to drop visiting cards. The box had the name of the lady of the house, with Not At Home written below it. The small box at our gate had Mrs Sinha Not At Home, even when my grandmother was at home. Bachelors dropped two cards to signify that they had called on both the gentleman and the lady. Married couples also dropped two cards one with only the gentleman's name and the other of both gentleman and his wife. This indicated that the lady had called on the lady of the house and the gentleman had called on both. New arrivals in the station were required to drop their cards in that box and not seek an appointment to come to the house. The person called upon had to similarly send his cards as a token of returning the call. It was incumbent on the person called upon to invite the caller to his house. This was all so formal. The dress code for being invited to lunch, drinks, tea/coffee or garden party was lounge suit. By day not only Scotsmen but some others also wore plus fours (half trousers down to the knee with long stockings up to the knees). For dinners, everyone dressed in dinner jacket with black tie. For very formal functions like investitures or special occasions at Government House, gentlemen wore tails and white tie. Ladies wore a long dress for dinner and formal occasions. Of course, Indian ladies would wear *Saris*. At informal dinners in Government House, dinner jacket with black tie was worn. All dinners at Government House would have printed cards with the menu, date and the seating plan as also the music being played by the band at the function. These cards were preserved by many people. Indians from the provincial services like Deputy Magistrates and Deputy Superintendents of Police would not be invited to dinner at Government House till they got into an All India Service. They would be invited only to afternoon tea (Reception). There used to be no social interaction with subordinate officials like Sub-Deputy Magistrates or Inspectors/ Sub-Inspectors of Police. Even at private formal parties protocol as laid down in the Warrant of Precedence (now called Table of Precedence) was followed. It used to be a very hierarchical official society following a strict protocol code. Eminent non-officials both British and Indian were included in the social circuit.

Private dinners at the house were generally formal affairs. No children came out for these dinners. Children were neither supposed to be seen nor heard. Most of the British officers in New Capital were senior officers and did not have small children. Their children would be in England for education. As a child, I would sometimes peep from the veranda or adjacent rooms to watch the proceedings of dinners at my grandfather's house. Guests arrived punctually at the appointed time and light drinks like sherry, port and so on were served before dinner. After a short session of these drinks, the dinner gong was sounded. Guests then trooped into the dining room and took their seats according to a seating plan with their names on cards displayed at the table. Wines would be served from decanters at the dining table while people were eating. Red wine was served with red meat and white wine with white meat like fish and chicken. There would be three or four courses. Plates were changed after every course. During dinner, there would be no loud talk or talking across the table. Guests were supposed to converse with people sitting next to them and not across the table. Talking about official matters was called talking shop and was discouraged during dinner parties. After dinner, ladies would move to the drawing room for a while, till the gentleman joined them. In polite language, it was said that ladies retired to powder their nose. The men could now relax, crack jokes and speak loudly at the table. They could also now smoke cigars and cigarettes. Liqueur and coffee were served. The gentlemen would then join the ladies in the drawing room. It was bad manners to leave immediately after dinner. Guests stayed on for some time. They now drank whisky or brandy. These were after dinner drinks and not pre-dinner drinks like we have nowadays. The following day the guests would write a letter of thanks to the hostess for the hospitality they had enjoyed.

§

All British officers were members of the European Club on the bank of the Ganga near the town. I learnt that there was great informality at the Club. I heard my father telling my grandfather an interesting incident that had taken place at the Club. My father's young colleague Churcher had had a few drinks and he told everybody that he would play the fool with his big boss the IG Police and the Chief Justice. They were playing Billiards in a large room. Churcher got on to his motorbike and barged into the Billiards room. Both the Chief Justice and the IG Police jumped on to the high chair along the walls of the Billiards room while Churcher on his motorbike did a couple of rounds of the Billiard table. He then switched off the engine of the motorbike and politely went up to the Chief Justice and IG saying "Sorry Sir, if I disturbed you. I just wanted to see how agile you were and I am very impressed by your quick reaction." This incident was not taken seriously by either the Chief Justice or the IG and they laughed it off.

Children were not permitted in the club. Indians were initially not allowed to become members of the Club. After the First World War, a few Indian officers from superior government services became members of the club. This included my grandfather and father. The former hardly ever went to the club but my father used to go frequently. He was even elected Secretary of the Club for a year. There was hardly any non-official member of the club. In North Bihar, British planters were members of European Clubs which were affiliated to the European Club in Patna. The *Bara Sahibs* in India had adopted the style of living of the nobility in Britain. The middle class or the common man in Britain did not observe such rigid social protocol. Much of this style of living changed under the pressure of the Second World War. Soon thereafter, the British departed from India. Hardly any British officer stayed back to live in India after retirement. The style of life of Europeans and senior Indian officials became a thing of the past after Independence. However, the Army was one institution where much of the old traditions continue to be observed.

§

On coming to Patna, I was admitted in St Joseph's Convent run for girls by German nuns. Boys up to the age of 10 were allowed to study in the Convent. I did not know any English but I soon picked up the language and learnt to recite English rhymes. I was determined to prove that though I had been earlier brought up in different surroundings in Gaya, I could do as well as my classmates brought up in a Westernised environment in Patna. The same feeling persisted with me when I joined the Army to prove myself as good, if not better, than my British colleagues. I worked hard at the Convent and managed to get two double promotions while studying there. Knowledge of English helped me to be pushed up to a higher class when I joined a government high school where the medium of instruction was in English from class 8 onwards. Thus, I could finish my school education at the age of 14 to join the University and graduated at the age of 18.

§

With all the official colonial environment that I was growing up in Patna, I also retained my link with the Indian style of living at my mother's place. I used to visit Gaya often during my holidays. My maternal grandfather visiting Patna would invariably come to see me or send for me while he was staying with his cousin. On one occasion, he asked me what I was studying at school. He was happy to learn that I would now be soon taught geometry. He told me an interesting incident about Motilal Nehru and geometry. Motilal Nehru was a leading lawyer of the country living at Allahabad. He was earning a tremendous lot and lived in Princely style in his palatial house, Anand Bhavan in Allahabad. It was said that his clothes used to be sent for washing to a laundry in Paris! He was friendly with Sir Harcourt Butler, the Governor of UP. He often entertained him in Anand Bhavan. When he used to go to Lucknow, the Governor would invite him to the Government House. Motilal and his son Jawaharlal joined the freedom movement under the leadership of Mahatma Gandhi. They were imprisoned. The Governor would send bottles of wine to Motilal in jail.

The Searchlight, a daily published from Patna, was very supportive of the Congress and highly critical of the government. The Editor had written an article criticising the government and making allegations against some senior British officials. The government sued the paper for libel. The case was being heard in the court of Chief Justice, Sir Courtney Terrel at the Patna High Court. He was a practising Barrister from London who had been directly appointed Chief Justice in Patna. He had earned a big name for his liberal views and legal acumen. Motilal Nehru was heading a team of lawyers which included my maternal grandfather, defending *The Searchlight*. The Chief Justice maintained that the two sections of the law quoted by Motilal were like circles which touched each other but were not contradictory. Motilal submitted, "My Lord, a circle is rounded by a line which has length but no breadth. Lines cannot touch each other. They either overlap or remain separate. I may also add that there is no law to say that a judge knows law but is always known to dispense justice." The Chief Justice smiled. His verdict went in favour of *The Searchlight*. My grandfather mentioned this incident to me giving me my first lesson in geometry of line having length but no breadth.

§

There were two marriages in the early 30s, one each in my mother's family and in my father's family. Some details of these weddings give a flavour of the style of marriages that used to take place in those times. They are worth recalling.

My maternal uncle had been in England for some years studying medicine. He was only two or three years younger to my mother. His marriage was arranged on the basis of horoscopes in a landlord family of Rasulpura, a village in Gaya district. The date chosen for the wedding clashed with his examination date at the medical college in Edinburgh. Travel by ship from England to India took nearly a month and my maternal grandfather wanted the date of the wedding postponed, so that he could come after taking his examination. The bride's parents were keen not to postpone the date of the wedding recommended by the astrologer. International air travel had just been introduced. KLM had pioneered this and ran a flight from London to Hong Kong via India. The bride's people bought an air ticket for my maternal uncle so that he could catch the flight from London after writing his Medical Examination and be in Gaya in time for the chosen date for the wedding. Being a Congressman my maternal grandfather was opposed to accepting any dowry but was persuaded to accept the proposal as buying an air ticket for travel was not dowry as such. The KLM airlines had small propeller aircrafts with seating capacity for about twenty passengers. There was no radar in those days and pilots flew by visual navigation. There was no flying by night or in bad weather. The normal flying time from England to India in those days was one week but one had to allow two to three days extra for bad weather. My maternal uncle was lucky. His flight did not get delayed due to bad weather en route. There were night halts at Amsterdam, Rome, Cairo, Basra, Karachi, Delhi and Allahabad. He took the train from Allahabad to Gaya and was well in time for his wedding. The airlines used to put up passengers in hotels for the night. There was no pantry service in the aircraft and no air hostess. Passengers picked up packed lunch from the hotel for the journey. My uncle told us of an amusing incident that happened at Cairo. A young lady travelling in that flight had left her shoes in the hotel. The pilot was very co-operative. The flight was delayed to allow her to go back to the hotel and collect her shoes. She sat next to my uncle in the plane and told him that she was going to Hong Kong. Her husband was in the Navy and his fleet, after a long sea journey, would be docking at Hong Kong port. She wanted to be in Hong Kong to receive him. Sailors were known to have a wife in every port. She wanted to ensure that her husband had his own wife in every port. My uncle had heard that she was the daughter of one of the richest men in England and had pots of money to travel all over the world. He asked her if she had been to India. She replied, "Oh Yes, quite a few times. I am emotionally attached to India." She then told him that she had travelled to India in 1920 with the entourage of the then Prince of Wales. Her husband a young naval officer was the ADC of the Prince for his India tour. He had proposed to her in the Viceroy's House at Delhi and she had readily accepted. A new Viceroy's House (now Rashtrapati Bhavan) was then under construction and the present office of the Vice-Chancellor of Delhi University was being used as the Viceroy's House. My uncle asked her the name of her husband and she replied, Louis Mountbatten.

§

I was awake till midnight to go with all the family to the railway station at Gaya to receive my uncle. I was duly rewarded when I saw the gift he had brought for me. It was a Leica camera with a leather cover of German make. It was a state of the art camera of those days. It was considered by everyone as being too expensive for a young boy like me but I clung on to it.

§

I was over 7 years old and had been told that I would be the *Sahwala* of my uncle during his wedding. *Sahwala* is the equivalent of the Best Man for a British bridegroom, with a difference. He is normally a young boy before teens or in early teens, generally a younger brother or a nephew of the bridegroom.

New clothes were given to all family members and servants going with the *Barat* (bridegroom's party) to the bride's place. Only men folk went in the *Barat*. Close relations and friends had been invited to accompany the *Barat*. My grandfather had many Muslim friends. Some of them also went with the *Barat*. After Partition, hardly any Muslim is now seen in a Hindu *Barat*, as most middle-class Muslims migrated to Pakistan. My uncle's *Barat* was about one hundred strong. We were the guests of the bride's family for three days for the wedding. As per custom, we carried clothes for the bride and her close relations and the servants of her household. We also carried toys for the children in the bride's family. The ladies from our side had stayed back in Gaya. They organised women-only song and dance in the house. They also made preparations for the reception of the bride when the *Barat* returned.

I was very excited because that was the first time I was going with a *Barat*. Normally small boys up to 4 or 5 years did not go in *Barat* as they required their mother to look after them. I travelled in a *howda* (a wooden chair like structure for sitting on an elephant) with the bridegroom. Ours was the leading elephant in the wedding procession. A *mehfil* (singing and dancing function) was organised for the entertainment of the *Barat*. Professional dancing girls had been brought for this from Benares (now Varanasi). Children were not supposed to be at the *mehfil*, which started after dinner and carried on almost all night. Along with other children, I kept awake one night and sneaked into the *mehfil*. To avoid being seen by the elders we hid ourselves behind some boxes from which we could manage to peep and witness the proceedings. I felt that the dances were obscene and vulgar. I remember that as part of the fun, the dancing girls would sing obscene and abusive songs, like the bridegroom's sister and mother being abducted and enjoying being molested, and so on. When we sat down for meals at the *Mandap* (decorated hut) in the courtyard of the bride's house, the ladies of the house would sing songs having a dig at the bridegroom's family members and even abuse them. The bridegroom's party had to listen to those songs sportingly and was not supposed to respond. It was all part of the fun in a wedding.

§

In Gaya there was a tradition among the Kayasthas to hold a quiz competition to test learning and general knowledge of boys from both bride's and bridegroom's sides. Perhaps this was because from time immemorial education was a high priority for Kayasthas. There were no illiterate Kayasthas in those days as indeed even now. Both sides would go all out to win this competition. One of us had found out that from the bride's side they would ask us the spelling of the word sister and the question would be directed at me as I was the youngest on our side. They thought that I would not know the answer. One of the elders briefed me to give a witty answer which he taught me. I promptly replied, "S I S T E R , sister, spell it together and give me Sir." This answer was a great hit and evoked much laughter among the elders from both sides. It was my turn to ask a question and I asked them the question, "Where is Timbuctoo?" My father often used this word and so did his British colleagues, to mean nowhere. He once told me that Timbuctoo is a town in Mali at the Southern edge of Sahara Desert in West Africa. The bride's side was stumped. No one knew the answer, not even the elders. We comfortably won the quiz and were given prizes.

§

We were a joint family and the use of the word cousin was frowned upon. Cousins were called and treated as brothers and sisters. My paternal granduncle was posted in Daltonganj, a remote district of Bihar. He had asked my father who was posted in Patna to arrange a match for his daughter. A promising young doctor from Bihar had just returned from England with a coveted degree of MRCP. He was perhaps the first Bihari doctor to have secured that degree. My father approached him for his cousin. He and his family agreed. There was a little hitch. He belonged to the Srivastava sub-caste while our sub-caste was Ambasht. Both my granduncle and grandfather readily agreed saying that an inter-sub-caste marriage would fulfil the wishes of their late father, who as President of the All-India Kayastha Sabha in 1898 had promoted inter-sub-caste marriages for the Kayasthas.

The wedding was to take place at Daltonganj. All the family including distant relations gathered at Daltonganj. I was seven years old and moved freely among the ladies. Many old ladies had come from our village. Some of them voiced their reservations about inter-sub-caste marriage enquiring what would be the sub-caste of the offspring of that marriage. My grandmother tried to explain to them that times had now changed and as decided at the All India Kayastha Mahasabha presided over by my great-grandfather, inter-sub-caste marriage was to be encouraged. This was for the good of the Kayasthas as a whole. It so happened that on the day of the marriage it started raining cats and dogs. Everyone was very concerned as the rains would upset arrangements for the wedding which was to be held outdoors. There was no adequate place for an indoor function in Daltonganj. Some of the old ladies started saying that perhaps inter-sub-caste marriage was not liked by the Gods. One of the ladies suggested that if the eldest son, and a first born of his parents born in his mother's house, went up naked to the terrace and lit an earthen lamp, the rain will stop. My grandmother said that I fully met all the requirements. I was not only the eldest son of my parents from both paternal and maternal sides but also the eldest grandson from both sides and born in my mother's house. I was asked to strip naked quickly and go up to the terrace. My protests were not heard. I had to go through that ordeal in front of everyone and light the earthen lamp on the terrace. Almost like a miracle, the rains stopped and the wedding functions were held smoothly. Inter-sub-caste wedding set a new trend in our family. It so happened that almost all the subsequent marriages including mine, was now inter-sub-caste. The younger generation in our family has been more progressive in our now globalised world. We have in our family, including my children, not only inter-caste and inter-State marriages but also international marriage alliances with foreign families in Europe and in the USA.

§

While I was in Patna, I used to go for my school holidays to Gaya. Having spent my early childhood there, I was happy to be in familiar surroundings again. On one of my visits to Gaya some of my mother's cousins teased me saying that I was a toady *bachcha* (child). They were referring to the fact that my father and grandfather were in the Police and serving the British. I stoutly defended them saying that they were not only serving the British but what is more also serving the people. Without the Police there would be chaos and anarchy in the society, with murderers and dacoits getting away with their crimes. We had heated arguments. My mother's youngest brother who was also our playmate was always protective of me. He defended my stand. When my maternal grandfather heard of this, he sent for all of us and explained to us that there were different ways of serving the Nation. An honest government servant was an asset to the society. He also said that if they teased me again, then he would send me back to Patna and I would not come again. All of them said in one voice that they did not want me to go. They were fond of me and liked playing with me. All was well thereafter and we did not get into this argument again. I used to tell them of life in Patna and about the Convent where I studied. They were impressed by the English I had picked up.

§

It is interesting that even as a child I could counter the argument used against people not joining the Freedom Movement and working for the government instead. In our own ways, my grandfather, father and I had taken a decision to serve the government in power without sacrificing our national loyalty. This brings out that on complex matters there can be no rigid division between Black and White. There are also shades of gray. At the appropriate place, I shall mention how my grandfather and father dealt with their predicament on this account. When I joined the Army under British Rule, I had my own reasons for doing so.

§

My paternal grandfather was posted from Patna to Chapra in 1936, as Superintendent of Police (SP) of the district. We were all expecting that he would be promoted to the rank of Deputy Inspector General (DIG) and were a little disappointed at this not happening. The reason given was that he had been away from district work serving as Superintendent Railway Police for five years. He had held charge of 5 districts for nearly twenty years. We feared that the British were side lining him because he was an Indian. We were mistaken. He was told that he had to go to Chapra for a few months as the Indian SP of the district had been placed under suspension for some wrong doings. They desired that the investigation of allegations against him be carried out by a senior Indian officer rather than a British officer so that in case he was found guilty, the people would not feel that he had been done down by the government because he was an Indian. My grandfather remained SP at Chapra for less than a year and thereafter, was brought back to Patna as DIG.

§

I remember our interesting journey from Patna to Chapra in 1935. There was no bridge over the Ganga in Patna. My grandfather's car was loaded on two country boats joined sideways together. At the farther end there was a Bamboo barrier to prevent the car slipping into the river. Loading the car on the two Boats appeared as a hazardous operation. On reaching the far bank, the car was off-loaded and driven first across the sand on a track made of dried grass and then on dirt track on firm ground to Sonepur and finally by a single-lane black-top bumpy road to Chapra.

At Chapra, I was admitted in Chapra Zila School. Dr Rajendra Prasad a contemporary of my grandfather had studied at that school forty years earlier. He had stood first in his Entrance Examination (later known as Matriculation) in Bengal Presidency comprising Burma, Bangladesh, West Bengal, the North-East States, Orissa, Jharkhand and Bihar. We were told that the bench on which he used to sit as a student was kept in the office of the Headmaster.

We lived in the SP's house at Chapra with a very large compound of a couple of acres. The original house had been reduced to rubble during the 1934 earthquake. We were accommodated in a temporary single-storey building with asbestos roof while work on a new permanent house was to begin soon. My grandfather was initially busy investigating the charges against the previous Indian SP. I learnt that he had three wives and when he used to go out on tours in the district, the Police used to arrange *Mehfils* of dancing girls for his entertainment. He was also very fond of drinking alcohol. There were no other charges against him and he had carried out his duties reasonably well. My grandfather recommended that he should not continue to be under suspension and he should be taken off suspension. He should be posted to another district and told to cut down on his lavish style of living. It may interest the present generation that he was only a Matriculate. He joined the Army during First World War as a Havildar in the Army Supply Corps. After the War, he was initially appointed a Sub-Deputy Magistrate. When the Indians were made eligible for Indian (Imperial) Police, there was one vacancy in Bihar for someone with war service. Being the only educated person, even though only a matriculate, he was taken into the IP cadre. During the 1930 Civil Disobedience Movement, it is said that he had consumed a lot of liquor and in the morning had gone to arrest Sri Krishna Sinha and started shedding tears. Sri Krishna Sinha appreciated his sentimental show of patriotism. In 1947 Sri Krishna Sinha became Chief Minister of Bihar and when the British left, appointed him IG Police of Bihar. He was the only Indian officer in the history of Indian Police who was not a graduate.

§

While I was with my grandfather at Chapra, my father was posted from Patna City to Samastipur as ASRP (Assistant Superintendent of Railway Police) BNW Railway which was then a metre gauge railway.

Although an ASRP, he held independent charge like SRP (Superintendent of Railway Police). My grandfather had been SRP at Patna on the broad gauge East Indian Railway. I used to like to travel with my grandfather in his saloon. I used to get very impressed by the Railway Guard. They used to wear spotlessly white uniforms with cross belts. They were almost all Anglo-Indians in those days. They would blow their whistle and waved red and green flags by day and those coloured lamps by night. The train would start moving or stop as per his direction. It was my ambition to become a railway guard. My grandfather would dissuade me saying that the Railway Guard was a subordinate rank and was not an officer. As ASRP, my father would also have a railway saloon and I looked forward to occasionally travel in his saloon. However, by now my fascination for becoming a railway guard had worn off.

I asked my grandfather as to why the BNW Railway which ran from Lucknow in UP to Katihar in Bihar was known as BNW Railway when it touched neither Bengal nor North-West Frontier. He explained that when that railway was started Katihar was in Bengal as Bihar was not a separate province and UP was known as North-Western Province. Punjab and North-West Frontier provinces were under Sikh rule. He also told me that this was a question asked in the General Knowledge paper for the ICS examination which had from the past few years started being held in India. He asked me to study hard so that when I grew up I could compete for the ICS which was the highest government service from which the bright and lucky few would become Governors. By the time I grew up, India would become Independent and I could become a Governor.

§

Lord Willingdon was the then Viceroy of India. The Maharajadhiraja of Darbhanga had invited the Viceroy to his Estate. Darbhanga was the richest landlord of India, richer than most of the 562 Feudatory Chiefs except the top dozen or so. The Feudatory Chiefs had treaty relationships with the British Sovereign under which they had acknowledged Britain as the Paramount Power. They had surrendered their Foreign and Defence policies to the Paramount Power but remained autonomous for administering their States. They had their own Judiciary, Laws and Police. These Feudatory rulers were addressed as His Highness. The Nizam of the Hyderabad, the richest and biggest amongst them was the only one who was addressed as His Exalted Highness. The Big landlords who owned vast estates were given the title of Maharajas, Rajas and Nawabs. They had neither any legal authority nor internal autonomy for administering their estates. The two richest landlords were Maharajadhiraj of Darbhanga and Maharajadhiraj of Burdwan. They were the only two who had the title of Maharajadhiraj. Darbhanga was the richer of the two and had the additional distinction of the heir apparent having the title of Raja. Maharajadhiraj of Darbhanga wanted to be made a Feudatory Chief and designated as His Highness with all the powers of a feudatory chief. He invited Lord Willingdon, the then Viceroy, to Darbhanga and the Viceroy accepted his invitation. The whole purpose of his inviting the Viceroy to his Estate was to get him to recommend his case to the British Government in London that he be made a Feudatory Chief.

The Viceroy travelled from Delhi to Darbhanga by the Viceroy's Special Train. My father had to arrange the security of the Viceroy for his rail travel in Bihar. I learnt from him that the Special Train was very luxurious and self-contained with a corridor from one end to the other. The General Manager of the Railway and my father travelled in a separate compartment of the corridor-train along with the Viceroy, the Vicereine and the Viceroy's staff. All the officers on the train used to have their main meals, lunch and dinner, in the dining room with the Viceroy and his wife. My father was the only Indian officer on the train. There was no racial distinction. The Viceroy and his wife were gracious hosts. The train stopped only at appointed railway stations for Their Excellencies to have their morning and evening walks on the platforms. All the railway stations on the route were spruced up for the Viceroy's tour. As the train passed a railway station, the Station Master and the staff stood in a line on the platform. They bowed and did their *salaam* as the train went past. Every kilometer, or so, of the railway track had a Chaukidar standing on the side of the railway track to bow and *salaam* as the train passed him. I wanted to have a glimpse of the Viceroy's special train as it went past the Chapra Railway Station. No one other than the railway staff and policemen on security duty were supposed to be on the platform when the train went past. I wanted to have a glimpse of the train and if possible see my father travelling in it. Because of my Police connection, I managed to be at the railway platform to see the train. It went past at a high speed and I couldn't see my father in the train. I was disappointed that I couldn't have a good view of the train. Strange are the ways of Providence. Over four decades later in 1947, during the Partition Holocaust, Mountbatten made the Viceroy's Special Train available to Lt Gen Sir Dudley Russell to have his mobile Headquarters on the train. I would be assigned, as a junior officer in the Army, to work under him. Russell had raised Delhi and East Punjab Command, replacing the old Northern Command at Rawalpindi, which was now not responsible for East Punjab and Delhi which fell in Indian Territory. The latter's area of responsibility till 1947 was from Peshawar to Delhi. Delhi and East Punjab Command now took over responsibility from Indo-Pak border to Delhi and also Rajasthan, from Bikaner to Ferozepur in Punjab. After a couple of months our Headquarters was re-designated Western Command. Our main task was to restore law and order in Delhi and Punjab. We were also responsible for escorting millions of refugees going from Refugee Camps in Delhi to Pakistan. Ours was a skeleton Headquarters with all facilities of internal telephone communication on the train with armed escort both in front and rear attached to the train. We also had our vehicles on flats with ramps so that they could be taken off the train wherever required. We travelled in this train for two months between Delhi and Lahore. Who could have thought that a young boy barely ten years old at Chapra Railway Station seeing the luxurious Viceroy's train going past will one day live on that train for two months.

The Maharajadhiraj of Darbhanga had made very elaborate and lavish arrangements for the visit of Lord and Lady Willingdon to Darbhanga. A special railway platform was made for the arrival and departure of the Viceroy. He was received with much ceremony. Long red carpets were laid for the Viceroy from his railway compartment on the platform. He was provided a guard of honour and after introduction with officers and dignitaries on the platform, he went in a procession of a couple of Rolls-Royce and other cars from the railway station to the palace of the Maharajadhiraj where he stayed during his visit to Darbhanga. A wing had been added to the Maharajadhiraj's palace for the Viceroy and his staff. A high tower was constructed with a lift inside to take the Viceroy to the top from where he could see his host's vast landed property. From the top of the tower to the horizon on all sides, he could see that all the land was owned by the Maharajadhiraj. Lavish entertainment was provided during the two days that the Viceroy was the guest of the Maharajadhiraj. Special trains from Calcutta to Darbhanga brought uncooked fresh items of food in refrigerated compartments. Top cooks from Calcutta hotels were also brought for cooking meals. At the end of the visit, Lady Willingdon was presented with the proverbial 9 lakh diamond necklace. Other lavish presents were also given to the staff and guests who had come with the Viceroy. I learnt all these details from my father who had attended all the functions, including the fireworks arranged during the visit. The Viceroy returned to Delhi, highly impressed by the lavish hospitality he received at Darbhanga.

On return, the Viceroy recommended to the British Government that the Maharajadhiraj should be given the status of a Feudatory Chief. The Secretary of State for India in London turned down the recommendation of the Viceroy. He wrote back that Feudatory Chiefs were a product of history when they allied themselves with the British Crown and accepted the latter as the Paramount Power. Feudatory Chiefs could not be created on the basis of wealth and property acquired by a person. However, the British Government agreed to give Maharajadhiraj of Darbhanga the highest title of GCSI (Grand Knight Commander of the Star of India). This title was normally given only to the Viceroy and Commander-in-Chief in India plus very few top princely rulers. Even Governors were not normally given this high title.

§

Another example of imperial splendour of British rule that I saw while in Chapra was during the annual Sonepur Fair held in Chapra district. It used to be the biggest fair in the world at which elephants, horses and cattle were sold. Attractive items for decoration and household goods were also sold from rows of tents in the bazaar. It had all the hustle and bustle of a fair with arrangements for food, entertainment and living in tented accommodation for visitors. The fair lasted for a month. Elaborate arrangements were made by the district administration of Chapra for this fair which was attended by lakhs of people. The District Magistrate and the SP camped in a secured area close to the fair. Elaborate security, medical cover and fire precaution arrangements were made. I stayed in the official camp with my grandparents. We lived in big tents with wooden floors and attached bathrooms. In the centre of this tented camp was a huge *shamiyana* with wooden floor, carpets and silk curtains for visiting VIPs who came to see the fair in large numbers. There used to be a holiday atmosphere during the fair held in good weather during October and November. I remember that the British Governor of Bihar with his family and high officials one day came to see the fair. They came across the Ganga from Patna in a luxury steamer and from the bank of the river in a procession of elephants. The Governor travelled on a richly decorated elephant on a *hauda*. I was much impressed by the imperial splendour I saw during the visit of the Governor. I told my grandfather that when I grew up I would like to be a Governor. He had replied Why Not, adding that I would have to first compete for the ICS. He also said that he was happy that I was now aiming high and had given up my old fancy for being a Railway Guard. Little could he have imagined, or could I, that without competing for the ICS, I would end up being Governor of two large States for eleven years. Destiny has its own ways.

§

My grandfather's tenure in Chapra finished in less than a year. Much to our delight, he was promoted DIG of Police and we returned to Patna. Hardly any Indian in the country held this senior appointment in the Police at that time. About the same time my father was promoted from ASP to SP and posted to Dhanbad.

§

I have recollections of our old ancestral house in Patna. The layout of the old house and living style was quite similar to what I had grown up in my childhood at my mother's home in Gaya. The old house had a large water pond for boating and fishing. A modern two-storey building with a large terrace above the top floor was built. The new house had marble floors and large Western style sitting and dining rooms. There were a dozen bed rooms with attached bathrooms. My grandfather named the house Gajadhar Mandir after his parents, Gajadhar being his father's name and Mandir his mother's. It was the first double-storey private house in the town and it became a landmark. The other private houses in the city at that time were mostly single-storey with tiled roofs.

I liked moving out of New Capital where we had to stay for a couple of months as our new house was under construction. Unlike New Capital, which I have described earlier, our house being in the city had an Indian ambience. One could see the hustle and bustle of living in a town. There was much informality in the house. Several relations and friends frequently dropped in and often stayed on for meals. Sometimes my grandfather's European colleagues would also come with prior notice or when invited.

In early 1937, my grandfather bought a big Philips radio which was then a novelty in Patna. Guests coming to the house admired the progress science had made. We could hear BBC News Broadcast from London and the chiming of the Big Ben. This was much before transistors or televisions had been invented. I recollect hearing the speech of King Edward VIII announcing his abdication. It started with, "At long last I have decided to abdicate so that I can marry a lady of my desire." The most eligible bachelor of the world, who on his father's death, a year earlier, had become the Sovereign of the largest empire in history, had decided to give-up his throne for the sake of his love. He wanted to marry an American divorcee, Mrs Simpson. This was not acceptable to Prime Minister Stanley Baldwin and his Council of Ministers or to the then conservative high society of England. Hence, the King Emperor decided to abdicate. We greatly sympathised with him and he became a hero in our eyes. Although by no means an Anglophile or a loyal subject of our imperial masters, I cried when I heard the King's abdication speech. A year earlier when his father had died, I had been indifferent. However, as required, at that time we had worn black bands on our arm with our Boy Scout uniform.

§

Patna Collegiate School, the leading government high school of Bihar, was less than a mile from our house. My great-grandfather had studied at that school in the 1860s. That was then the only English medium school in the whole of Bihar. My grandfather and father had also studied at that school. I was happy to be admitted to that elite school. My school tuition fee was only ₹3 per month. I got interested in studying history. The Kumhrar ruins were only a couple of miles from our house. A remnant of the hundred pillars hall of the palace of Chandragupta Maurya still exists there. One of the pillars is intact lying on the ground. The polish on the pillar still has its original shine after being exposed to the elements for over two millennia. Chandragupta Maurya was the first Emperor of India who had integrated the entire sub-continent in his Empire in the fourth century BC. He defeated a Greek invasion led by Seleucus Nicator in the battle of Indus in 310 BC. Seleucus was a leading General of Alexander the Great, a world conqueror who had invaded India in 323 BC. He had come up to the Beas river in Punjab, where his Army mutinied and forced him to return, leaving garrisons in the occupied territories of Afghanistan and Punjab. Guided by his mentor Chanakya, Chandragupta liberated Punjab and threw out the Greek garrisons left behind by Alexander. After Alexander's death, Seleucus succeeded him as the ruler of his Eastern Empire. He now invaded India to recover Punjab. Chandragupta Maurya defeated him in the battle of Indus in 310 BC forcing him to cede Kabul, Kandahar and Herat. He also married the daughter of Seleucus. Afghanistan became a part of the Mauryan Empire which was larger in size than the British Empire in India. Wandering in the Kumhrar ruins as a child, I would day dream of emulating Chandragupta when I grew up and throw the British out of India, freeing our country from foreign rule. Chandragupta, more than his world-renowned grandson, Ashoka the Great, was my childhood hero.

§

The Headmaster of Patna Collegiate School was Rai Bahadur Bechu Narayan. He was the first Indian to be appointed Headmaster of the school, a few years before I joined the school. Mr Spiller of the Indian Education Service was the Principal of Patna Training College located adjacent to our school. He was also the Inspector of High Schools in Bihar. He often visited our school. He would sit in the rear of the classrooms when one of the students of the Training College would be taking a class as part of their practical training. Our school decided to put up a play on Shivaji, and I was selected for the leading role. I memorised the English script and Spiller who attended the rehearsal patted me. Much to my disappointment, he later decided to cancel the play. This was because of our Assistant Headmaster Mr Hakim who, on return from leave, raised an objection to the play being staged. He said that it would hurt Muslim sentiments and may cause communal unrest. This incident made me aware of the virus of communalism which the British were only too happy to promote, as part of their Divide and Rule policy.

§

The Government of India Act 1935 provided for provincial autonomy. Elections were held in early 1937. Jawaharlal Nehru came to Patna on election tour. A crowd of several thousand kept waiting for him for hours. The crowd was in raptures when he mounted the rostrum, giving him a thunderous applause. He was the icon of the youth. I also heard people say they will eat the food that rich landlords contesting Congress candidates may provide and accept any gifts they may give, but they will cast their votes in Mahatma Gandhi's box. The Congress swept the polls and secured a clear majority in Bihar and six other provinces.

§

Sir Maurice Hallet was the Governor of Bihar. My grandfather had served with him as SP and DIG when he was District Magistrate and later Commissioner of a Division. In a rare gesture, he insisted that my grandfather should have my father serving under him in the CID. My father was thus posted as the SP in the CID working directly under my grandfather. He came to live in Gajadhar Mandir with us. They used to go to their offices in the Secretariat separately in their cars. They had their separate offices and separate telephones on different floors in the house. My grandfather's office was on the ground floor and my father's on the first floor. In those days manual telephones were in use. Dialling of numbers on the telephone had not started. When one picked up the telephone receiver, the operator would enquire 'Number Please' and on being given the number would connect the call. One of the telephone operators was Miss Bird. She was an Anglo-Indian as most telephone operators then were. We knew her. She used to come to our house for some time to teach my mother spoken English. My uncle who was a little older than me would sit in my grandfather's office and telephone me in my father's office, pretending to be my boss. He would hold long conversations with me and give me orders which I had to comply with. We used to play this game when my grandfather and father would be in their offices in the Secretariat. When Miss Bird would be on duty she would often join us in our conversation. It was all good fun.

In those days senior Police officers were authorised four Police Constables as orderlies in their house. One was the car driver. There used to be no staff cars for anyone. When an officer used his private car for official duties, he would claim mileage but this did not apply for attending office. The other orderlies were required to be on telephone duty, carry official files or messages, provide security for officers moving around on duty and receive visitors at the house. Orderlies were not required to do any household work. Things have changed so much nowadays. Senior officers now normally have not only many more than four orderlies but also use them for their household work which used to be done by private servants. They also now have the luxury of staff cars which they use not only for going to office but for also private work. Nowadays, their families also use staff cars. Both rules and value systems have changed.

§

I recall with much nostalgia my carefree young days in Gajadhar Mandir living with my grandparents and parents. I had a lot of friends at school which was easy walking distance from our house. They would often come to our house and enjoyed playing on the large open ground as also on the large terrace of the house on the third floor. Living inside a town was nice. Everything one wanted was available in shops nearby. One day my grandfather showed me the annual confidential report that he had written on my father who was his direct subordinate. His assessment of his work in his report was given in four words. He wrote, "He is my son."

§

Anticipating that the Congress may win elections to be held under Government of India Act 1935, Home Department of the Central Government decided to hold a high power meeting at Simla (now Shimla) to discuss the action to be taken by the provincial CIDs in the event of the Congress coming to power. The conference was inaugurated by the Viceroy and the Home Secretary at the Centre presided over the meeting. All IGs and DIGs, CID of the eleven provinces attended the conference. My grandfather was the only Indian at this conference. One of the officers attending the conference said that all confidential documents with the CID pertaining to the

Congress should be burnt before the Congress comes to power. Another view was that on Congress coming to power if any Minister sent for secret documents pertaining to them or their party, they should be told that those documents have been destroyed. It was also said that these documents should not be destroyed but preserved because they may be required later if and when the Congress went out of power. When my grandfather was asked his views, he said that the documents should be preserved and there was no need to state a falsehood about them not being available. He was confident that the Congress leaders would not be petty and ask for them. Even if they did, he felt that they should be persuaded not to insist on seeing them. Ultimately, it was decided that the Police leadership in the provinces should be left to decide what should be done in the event of such a contingency.

§

In the elections held in 1937 under the Government of India Act of 1935, the Congress Party won with a thumping majority in 9 out of the 11 provinces in the country. Initially there were some problems and the Congress did not agree to form the government. The Leader of the Opposition, Mohammad Yunus, was invited by the Governor to do so in Bihar. He became the Prime Minister of Bihar for a while, till differences were resolved and Congress agreed to form government. The designation of Prime Minister was used for the Provinces in those days. This was changed to Chief Minister after Independence. Yunus had studied at school with my grandfather and they were good friends. One day in the evening his nephew riding a bicycle without a lamp was going down the road near a Police Station. The traffic constable stopped him. He got into an argument with the constable and slapped him. He thought he could get away with this because he was the nephew of the Prime Minister. The constable caught hold of him and locked him up at the Police Station and also filed a case against him. He had to spend the night in the lockup despite his close relationship with the Prime Minister. Neither did the Prime Minister interfere nor did my grandfather. The next morning he got bail and came out of the lockup. The law was allowed to take its course and he ultimately ended paying a fine. Recently I read in a newspaper that in Calcutta, the Chief Minister on learning about her party workers being detained by the Police for rowdy behaviour and fracas in the street stormed the Police Station. She admonished the Police and had her party workers immediately released. This shows how the functioning of government has changed since the old days.

§

On Congress agreeing to form government after a couple of months, Dr Sri Krishna Sinha became the Prime Minister of Bihar. His son was in the same class with me at Patna Collegiate School. He failed at the annual examination and had to lose a year. We were all given our report cards, which we had to get signed by our father/guardian. He started crying in the classroom. Some of us tried to console him. We advised him that being the Prime Minister's son, he could ask his father to order the Head Master to promote him. He replied that knowing his father, he would never do that. His father had told the family never to take advantage of his official position. He said that he was crying not so much because he had failed but because he would get severe scolding from his father. In today's India it is unimaginable for a son of a Chief Minister to fail in a school examination. There are rumours in Bihar that a Chief Minister's wife, desirous of a PhD, had the degree presented to her by the Vice-Chancellor in ten days, without her having to write a thesis or to defend it.

§

Jagjivan Ram, then a young man in his 30s came to our house. He had just become a Parliamentary Secretary, counterpart of Minister of State. He had much regard for my grandfather and had come with sweets. I was with my grandfather and there were a few people in the room when he came. He distributed *rasgullas* to everyone. Most of the people took the *rasgullas* in their handkerchiefs and put them in their pockets. Some ate them. I took one and asked him for another, which he readily gave. After he left, some of the guests in the room said that they could not eat *rasgullas* given by a person of the Scheduled Caste. One of our close relations told us that soon after the First World War, Jagjivan Ram and he were in the same class at Ara Zila School. The classroom had benches with attached tables for two boys. No one would sit with Jagjivan Ram, because he was from a Scheduled Caste. This relation of ours had no inhibition and got Jagjivan Ram to share the bench with him. They became good friends.

However, there was a problem about drinking water at school. Each classroom had two earthen pitchers for drinking water. One was marked Hindu and the other Muslim. Both Hindus and Muslims protested against Jagjivan Ram having water from their pitcher. The Head Master had a separate pitcher marked Scheduled Caste for Jagjivan Ram, but the latter insisted that he would drink water from the pitcher meant for Hindus and broke the pitcher marked Scheduled Caste. Our relation found a compromise. He would take out the water from the Hindu pitcher and then share it with him. Such was caste orthodoxy of those days. Jagjivan Ram was a good student and he passed the Matriculation examination in the First Division. He got a scholarship and joined Benares Hindu University graduating with distinction. Thereafter he joined politics. Our relation also did well at school and took an Engineering Degree from Patna University. He became Chief Engineer of Bihar while Jagjivan Ram was a Cabinet Minister in Delhi. I remember that when Jagjivan Ram was Defence Minister at Delhi, and I was Major General serving at Army Headquarters, he invited me to a Holi function at his house in Delhi. He remembered me as a boy who had asked for an extra *rasgulla*. During that function, I was amused to see several Brahmins touch his feet. Times had certainly changed.

However, there was another incident which showed that for some people times have not changed. I had a barber named Chandgi Ram who had been with my Regiment at Abbottabad in Pakistan before 1947. He was very good at giving haircuts and body massage. He was choosy about his clientele. He would come to the house of officers of the rank of Generals only. Since I was from the same Regiment he had been coming to me even before I became Major General. When I was Director Military Intelligence, Mrs Jagjivan Ram mentioned to me that she wanted a good barber and masseur for her husband. I sent Chandgi Ram to Jagjivan Ram's house and he gave him a satisfying haircut and good massage. He was asked to come every fortnight on a Sunday. The next time he went, the Minister was busy in his office and he was asked to wait in his PA's room for a few minutes. The PA who was a Brahmin came out from the Minister's office with an empty glass in his hand. He put the glass on his table and said how have times changed, "I as a Brahmin have to hold a glass from which a *Chamar* had drunk water". The barber enquired from the PA if Jagjivan Ram was a *Chamar*. The PA replied, "Of course, didn't you know?" Chandgi Ram said, "No" and then ran away from the Minister's house. He never went there again.

§

I passed my Matriculation examination from Patna Collegiate School in 1939 and joined Patna College. There was a sea change in the atmosphere between school and college. I used to wear shorts in school. I had just entered my teens and was now a college student. I decided to wear trousers in college to appear more senior. Almost all students in the college wore either *Dhoti* or *Pajama*. I used to be dubbed a 'Sahib' by my colleagues because trousers were considered a dress of the Sahib, a word used for Europeans. Today trousers have become the most common dress not only for students in cities but also people living in villages. There were about half a dozen girl students in each class. They all wore sarees. Two or three in the whole college wore *Burqas*. The girls had a separate Common Room from where they used to be escorted to classrooms by the Professors. At the end of the class, they were escorted back by them to their Common Room. They sat in the class on a separate bench meant for them, a little away from the boys. No boy or girl was allowed to meet or talk to each other. Our society was very conservative at that time.

§

Europe was in turmoil with the rise of Hitler and his territorial ambitions. The British Prime Minister Neville Chamberlain had met Hitler at Munich and thought he had pacified him. He returned to London with his famous remark, 'Peace in our lifetime'. He was soon proved wrong. A few months later Hitler invaded Poland. Britain declared war against Germany on 3 September 1939. There was much excitement among students in the college. We would listen to radio broadcasts, particularly the propaganda from Berlin. We rejoiced over British defeats and felt that this provided a good opportunity for India to gain Independence. Winston Churchill now took over as Britain's Prime Minister. He was an arch imperialist and totally opposed to India getting independence. In the early years of the war, Germany was gaining a string of victories in Europe. British radio used to report that British forces were doing tactical withdrawals and would ultimately prevail over Germany. Chances of this appeared slender to us, particularly after the catastrophic defeat at Dunkirk.

France a major power was overrun despite its famed Maginot Line in a matter of weeks. The joke among the students used to be *Fateh Sarkar Ka Hota Hai, Qadam German Ka Badhta Hai.* (The British are winning but the Germans are advancing.)

§

The USA was giving aid under Lend-Lease Agreement to Britain. The Atlantic Charter, signed between US President Franklin Roosevelt and British Prime Minister Winston Churchill on board the HMS Battleship Prince of Wales, promised freedom for all countries after the war. Churchill issued a statement that the Atlantic Charter did not apply to India. This was much resented by us. The students used to discuss international developments and I was an active participant. Soon Japan joined the war and the defeat of the colonial powers in South-East Asia was hailed by us. The fall of Churchill's impregnable fortress of Singapore was a matter of much rejoicing for us. The invincible British Naval Power in the East based on two big battleships HMS Prince of Wales and HMS Repulse were both sunk by Japanese Zero fighter aircrafts. We felt that it was poetic justice from Indian point of view that the Prince of Wales now lay at the bottom of the sea because Churchill had stated that the Atlantic Charter would not apply to India. Incidently, Churchill was in New York when he received the news of the sinking of both HMS Prince of Wales and HMS Repulse. After getting this devastating news, Churchill suffered a heart attack. Churchill's doctor, Lord Moran, was with him and was asked to keep Churchill's illness a secret. It is amazing that Churchill even after this heart attack could continue with his gruelling schedule as Prime Minister of war-time UK. We used to call Churchill the Bull Dog in retaliation for his calling the Mahatma, a Half Naked Fakir. The warning of our teachers and elders that the victory of Fascism in the world will not be good for mankind sounded unconvincing to us. They told us that Japanese rule over India would be worse than British colonialism. Our reply would be that if we were doomed to be slaves let us shift the burden from one shoulder to the other. Our excitement reached fever pitch when we heard how Subhas Chandra Bose had escaped to Germany and from there to Japan. His forming the Azad Hind government and leading the Indian National Army was much hailed by us. Those were exciting days.

§

While at college I took a keen interest in debates and I used to win debating competitions both in my college and in the University. In 1940, I was selected to represent Patna University at an Inter-University Debate at Allahabad. In those days, as, even now, students of UP universities and Calcutta University used to consider themselves superior to students from Bihar. When I got up to speak at the Inter-University debate, I was heckled by some students referring to me as *Bihari Budhu* (Bihari Idiot). I did not get ruffled. I replied that my audience had got their pronunciation wrong. I was not a Bihari Budhu but a *Bihari Budha*. Everyone had a good laugh. This incident helped me to bag the top tier at the Inter-University debate.

§

My maternal grandfather had come on a short visit to Patna. He came to see us at Gajadhar Mandir. I got delayed by about half an hour cycling back home from college, while he waited for me. I apologised for the delay. I had to wait on the road as it had been temporarily closed near Khuda Baksh Library. Lord Linlithgow was visiting the library and I waited at a *paan* shop on the road from my college while my grandfather was waiting for me.

When I told my grandfather the reason why I got delayed he said that when he was in England he found that no traffic was ever stopped even for the King. He added that when India becomes independent traffic would not be stopped in that manner. It is strange that I had a similar experience in Patna in 1984 after I resigned from the Army. I was driving my car returning home when I was stopped at a road crossing. Rajiv Gandhi with his convoy of cars was passing that road junction. He was then holding no official post and was only the son of the Prime Minister. His convoy was like that of a Head of State with the Chief Minister in attendance accompanying him. There was a banner on the road junction with the following written on it, *"Samrat Ashoka ki nagri mein yuva samrat Rajiv Gandhi ka hardik swagat hai."* (Welcome to Rajiv Gandhi, the Emperor of Youth in the city of Emperor Ashoka.) I waited for about twenty minutes just as I had been made to do as a student for Lord Linlithgow's convoy. My grandfather was of course not alive to see that an independent India of his dreams would become like this.

§

The political scene in India was heating up. The Congress Governments in the Provinces resigned in protest against the Viceroy proclaiming that India was at war with Germany without any prior consultation with the Congress Governments in the Provinces or with top national political leaders of the country. Muhammad Ali Jinnah and his Muslim League celebrated the Congress going out of power in Provinces as a Day of Deliverance for the Muslims. He alleged that Muslims were being harassed by the Congress Governments. In March, 1940, the Muslim League adopted the resolution for establishing Pakistan comprising Muslim majority provinces, as a separate independent State. The communal virus started steadily spreading all over the country. His two-nation theory caught on with the Muslim middle class in a big way. In our college, we could see the communal divide among the Hindu and Muslim students becoming all pervasive. The parting of ways had started. Old family friends for generations now seemed to have reservations about each other. The cordiality that existed between the two communities appeared to be vanishing.

§

I remember Jinnah visiting Patna in 1940. I had gone to the railway station to see his arrival. There was a frenzied crowd of Muslims to receive him. He came out of his first-class compartment immaculately dressed in a three piece suit with brown and white shoes, known as co-respondent shoes. He had an aristocratic and aloof look with his monocle. I was impressed by his neatly folded hold-all, nice suitcase, and a brief case, all of matching colour. Later he delivered a speech in English at Gandhi Maidan in Patna. He received a tremendous ovation from the crowd, during and after his speech, even though over 90% of the audience did not know any English. I recall how he thundered that the plant of democracy as grown in the cold climate of Europe was unsuitable for tropical countries. He also said that Muslims were a separate nation with their own religion, culture, language and history. They must have their own country. Pakistan was the only solution for them. Every Muslim should be prepared to shed his last drop of blood for their legitimate demand. I could see that the stage had come when emotion was getting the better of reasoning. I often wondered how a whisky-sipping, ham-eating and English-speaking Muslim leader could garner such a tremendous mass following, while Maulana Abul Kalam Azad an erudite Islamic theologian and an Urdu scholar with ancestors connected with the Holy mosques at Mecca could get isolated from the Muslim masses.

§

There was a lot of political activity taking place in the country. Top political leaders like Mahatma Gandhi, Jawaharlal Nehru and Subhas Chandra Bose visited Patna. They addressed meetings of very large crowds in Gandhi Maidan. The Mahatma held prayer meetings at which he spoke on political and social issues. He was heard with great reverence in pin drop silence. Nehru and Bose were both highly regarded and received a great ovation. Nehru was an icon of the youth of my generation. I was struck by the handsome presence of both Nehru and Bose. It was interesting to see Subhas Chandra Bose driving in a car with large Congress flags flying on both mudguards of the car. It reminded me of Hitler and Goering's style of flying flags on their cars which one saw in the movies.

§

Under normal circumstances there were no prospects of my grandfather reaching the top position in the Police which had hitherto not been held by any Indian. Inscrutable are the ways of Providence. My grandfather started getting a bonanza periodically in his career which no one could have predicted. During the First World War, many of his senior colleagues went to the Army to fight in France. Most of them did not return because they became casualties in that war. This facilitated my grandfather becoming a SP out of turn and get absorbed in the IP after the war. With provincial autonomy being introduced under Government of India Act in 1935, two of his British seniors chose to put in their papers because they did not like to serve under Indian Ministers. And then in 1937, Orissa was detached from Bihar and became a separate Province. Thus there were now two vacancies in IG rank for Police Officers in Bihar cadre. This enabled my grandfather to become the first and only Indian to be appointed as IG Police in the country during British regime. Had it not been for these windfalls for him, there would have been no possibility of him becoming IG Police (Picture 6).

A host of officials both British and Indian came to our house to congratulate my grandfather. There was much celebration in the family. My grandfather used to say that when he joined the police, he never thought a day would come when he would get to the top of the tree. Hundreds of letters and telegrams of congratulations from all over the country came to him. He allowed me the pleasure of filing them and then giving them to his PA to whom he dictated replies. Each congratulatory message or letter was replied to.

As IG, my grandfather was now entitled to General Salute. I much liked the tune of General Salute on the bugle. My father used to say that he did not have any chance of reaching the top as there were several British officers senior to him and junior in age. Little did he then realise that India would become Independent in 1947 and all the British officers would quit overnight. Some ten years after my grandfather had held that appointment, my father became IG Police of Bihar. Having got this quick promotion at a comparatively young age, he remained IG of Bihar for a record time of seven years followed by IG on Special Duty for four years. He was now also getting General Salutes. Many years later in 1973, when I became a General Officer in the Army, I also started getting General salute. When I would hear the bugle playing General salute for me, my thoughts used to go back to my childhood when I first heard that played for my grandfather. My father was alive not only to see me get General Salute but also National Salute, accompanied by National Anthem, when I became a Governor. I wish my grandfather had lived to also see me take General Salute as he had seen my father. Destiny has its own ways.

§

My grandmother was a strong-willed lady with a lot of self confidence. Before I was born, my grandfather was SP of a district and she used to be in *Purda* (veil). One day on her own and without telling my grandfather, she came out of *Purda* and addressed a public meeting. She could not speak in English but could generally understand some English sentences.

When my grandfather became IG, my grandmother, as the wife of IG, got a high place at the dining table sitting next to the Governor, Sir Maurice Hallett in the Government House (now Raj Bhavan). During dinner, the Governor mentioned to her that she should now learn to speak in English. To the surprise of every one at the table she politely told the Governor, "Lat Sahib (Governor), I am in my own country and there is no need for me to learn any foreign language. You being in India should learn to speak better Hindi." Everyone at the table was taken aback. The Governor was gracious and in broken Hindi replied that she was right. This exchange of conversation became the talk of the town.

§

My grandfather retired in 1940 and decided to move to Danapur Cantonment, seven miles from Patna. He had acquired a very large house with a four-acre compound and preferred to spend his retirement in quiet surroundings, away from the hustle and bustle of the town. He now spent most of his time in prayers and reading religious books. He had a rich library of the latter. Our ancestral house in the city, Gajadhar Mandir, was rented out to the University as a hostel for students. My father was now posted as Senior SP of Patna, a coveted appointment. Some of his Indian colleagues were jealous of him because his British superiors were fond of him for his proficiency in sports. Moreover, some felt that he had enjoyed a privileged position because of his father being in top positions in the Police.

§

I now moved to live with my father in his official house on Gandhi Maidan. We had a nice tennis court in our house compound and I took to playing that game. Soon after he had taken over as Senior SP, Mahatma Gandhi started the individual Civil Disobedience Movement against the British to register protest against India being dragged into the war without the consent of the people. He did not want to launch a mass movement at that stage, because he felt that it may impede the British war effort. He was opposed to the fascist dictatorship of Hitler and Mussolini. Individual Congress leaders were asked to court arrest. My father received an order to arrest Dr Rajendra Prasad and put him in Bankipore Central Jail. As he arrived at Rajendra Babu's house early in the morning, he smiled and told him that he knew he would be coming to arrest him. He was prepared to go to jail straightaway, but inquired if he could be given a little time for his morning ablution and get ready to be taken to jail. My father had known him well and he was like an uncle to him as he and my grandfather had studied together in Calcutta and had been good friends. My father replied respectfully that he could take all the time he wanted to get ready and have his breakfast before he took him to the jail. He also said that he would wait for him on the veranda and would like to share breakfast with him before taking him to the jail. All this would have come to the knowledge of his British superiors and they would not have liked it.

After a little over one year, two other incidents took place, one after the other in a short time frame. One day my father was going in his car from Patna to Danapur along the Red Road, called by that name because it was a *Morang* road of light red hue and not tarmac. This road used to be deserted with no habitation on either side of the road. It was used primarily by British troops from Danapur Cantonment to commute to Patna. My father saw a couple of Anglo-Indian girls on bicycles being chased by two British soldiers. On seeing my father's car, the girls shouted for help. He immediately stopped his car. The British soldiers caught up with the girls and were trying to misbehave. My father had his orderly escort and orderly driver, both in uniform. He ordered the two to arrest the British soldiers. They were drunk and were shouting abuses. One of the two constables was the champion wrestler of the district. He took-off his turban and tied both the British soldiers with his turban and dumped them in the rear seat of the car, holding them tightly. My father drove straight to the house of the Adjutant of the British battalion in Danapur. As he approached the Cantonment several local people enjoyed seeing two white soldiers tied in a red turban. My father knew the British Adjutant both socially and on the Polo ground. He told him what had happened and asked him to take suitable action against the two British soldiers. The Adjutant appeared upset seeing his soldiers arrested by the Police and brought to him in that manner. However, he assured him that he would take necessary action against those soldiers.

The next incident took place a few months later. While my father had come to visit my grandfather, and was in our home, he got a report that an Indian had been killed by a British soldier on the main road in front of his Battalion Quarter Guard. He immediately rushed to the spot. The dead body was lying on the road and a few local people had assembled raising slogans. He found out that the Army had temporarily closed the road for traffic to allow the changing of the guard at the Quarter Guard. A Barber was walking down the road. The Regimental Policeman on duty was signalling him to stop which the barber misunderstood that he was asking him to come. The British soldier shouted in English asking him to stop. The Barber did not know English and misunderstood him, he kept approaching him. The soldier in a fit of rage gave him a couple of blows. The barber was a sickly man. He collapsed and died. To avoid any ugly incident between the British soldiers and the agitating crowd, my father ordered the arrest of the British soldier and took him to the Police Station and had the FIR registered. The soldier's statement was recorded and the barber's dead body was sent for post-mortem at a local hospital. While my father was at the Police Station, the Adjutant arrived. He said that the soldier was carrying out his duty and it was unfortunate that the barber had got killed accidentally. He also protested against the Police taking action against the soldier as he was covered under military law and had to be tried by the Army in a Court-Martial and not in a Civil Court. My father explained to him that the correct legal position was that in case of murder, culpable homicide not amounting to murder and rape, the Civil Court had the authority to try military personnel. He also told him that after the soldier's statement was recorded, he would be handed over to him for custody and not kept in the Police Station. The Adjutant was not happy about this.

Both these incidents were interpreted by some British officials as reflecting my father's anti-British attitude. The British Battalion at Danapur was very unhappy and took up the matter with higher military authorities. A British General from Kolkata came to Patna to represent against my father to the Governor. The latter sent for the British IG Police and my father. In the presence of the General, the Governor inquired what had happened. The General had complained against what he called Police high-handedness undermining British prestige. On listening to my father's version, the Governor explained to the General that what my father had done was legally correct. This should not be misconstrued as his being anti-British. The matter was closed.

Notwithstanding the Governor's decision, there was an undercurrent of resentment against my father in British circles. About six months later when my father had just completed two years as Senior SP of Patna, he was posted as SP of Purnea. The normal tenure for Senior SP of Patna was three years. This posting was viewed as a punishment posting. Purnea was a remote and most undeveloped district of Bihar. It had high incidence of malaria in those days. During Mughal days, Purnea was a penal settlement. In 1942 it had no electricity and no piped water. My father was upset at this posting. My grandfather told him that eighteen years earlier, he had been sent on posting as SP Purnea, which was then a dacoits-infested district. He had effectively brought dacoits under control. This had proved to be a turning point in his career. Seeing my father upset, he decided to go with him to Purnea for some time, leaving his house in Danapur vacant. I had to move to a hostel to continue my study at the University.

§

A few months later in August 1942, Mahatma Gandhi launched the Quit India Movement. In a way it was providential that my father was not in Patna when the Quit India Movement started. There was large scale disturbance in the town and he would have had to deal with the situation working under the nose of his British superiors. They would not have countenanced any leniency by the Police in dealing with the situation. Their attitude towards the movement was very hostile because after the fall of Burma in early 1942, the Japanese had advanced up to the Indian border with Burma. Andaman Islands had fallen to the Japanese. There had been Japanese stray air attacks over Calcutta. Japanese invasion of India appeared imminent. The war situation was very adverse for the British in the East, Middle-East and of course also in the West. It was a life and death situation for the British.

§

The students were in the vanguard of the Quit India Movement. They were very agitated and decided to take out a procession to Patna Secretariat to hoist the Congress flag on the main building. A few thousand slogan-shouting students proceeded towards the Secretariat. My closest friend and relation Bipin Bihari Sinha was active in politics and went with the procession. I also went along to see what happened. I was towards the rear of the procession. The head of the procession broke through a Police cordon and pushed towards the Secretariat despite the lathi-charge. A row of British troops immediately opened fire. Seven students in the forefront got killed and a few injured. The procession dispersed and I came back to the hostel. My friend Bipin was missing and I later discovered that he had been picked up by the Police and sent to jail. He continued to be active in Politics and a few years after Independence, he became a Cabinet Minister in Bihar. After Independence, a Statue of the seven students with Congress Flag in their hands was put up in front of the Secretariat where they had been killed in August 1942. The architecture of this Martyr's Memorial is very nice and it is now a landmark in Patna.

Curfew was clamped over the city and British soldiers started patrolling the streets. There were rumours that martial law would be declared in Patna and there was even talk of the British contemplating to drop bombs from the air over Kadam Kuan in the city, which was the hot bed of the movement. Students' hostels were closed and the students were asked to go to their homes. My younger brother Harinivas was also in the hostel at his school. The two of us decided to go to Purnea where my father was then posted. There used to be no bridge over the Ganga and we took a steamer to cross the river. On reaching the other bank, we found that all railway lines had been uprooted. Railway Stations and Railway Signals had been ransacked. There were quite a few students proceeding to various destinations in North Bihar along with other passengers. We decided to trek. Purnea is about 300 kms from Patna. It took us three weeks of walking to cover this long distance. Road communication in North Bihar was very poor. We decided to walk along the railway track. Monsoon was at its height with rivers and nullas in spate. I had only ₹15 with me after paying for our railway tickets. Carrying our essential baggage on our person, we started trekking. Crossing rivers and streams on culverts and bridges was frightening. We saw evidence of atrocities committed by British troops in the area. There were three instances of the Air Force machine gunning crowds from the air. On one occasion, an Air Force Plane flew low over us but seeing us carrying baggage realised that we were stranded passengers and took no action against us. We used to sleep in the open on railway platforms at night. The villagers would give us *Chura-Dahi*, the common cheap food in North Bihar. It was generous of them to feed us for free. After three weeks of a harrowing journey, my brother and I ultimately reached our father's house in Purnea. My grandparents and parents had no news of us and were very worried about what had happened to us. Telephone communication from Purnea to Patna was normally difficult. But after telephone wires had been cut, they had snapped. On reaching Purnea, I learnt that British troops had come to Purnea to restore order. Both the Indian District Magistrate and my father returned them saying that they could deal with the situation in the district without any military help. On two or three occasions, my father had been able to disperse agitating crowds after dialogue with them. Purnea was the only district in Bihar in which there had been no Police or Military firing during that movement. When my father was posted out from Purnea in 1943, the President of the District Congress Committee, with the approval of the Bihar Government, presented him with a Golf Set. My grandfather who had come to live with my father for sometime found himself homeless after the British Military authority decided to occupy our house in Danapur. The Commander of British troops in Patna, one Brigadier Richards had requisitioned his house to live in it himself. It now became the Flag Staff House. During the war, the Army had been given special powers to requisition private houses in Cantonments. It took us over two years to get back our house. My grandfather managed to do so by representing to the authorities in Delhi that my uncle was an Army Officer fighting the Japanese in Burma and his family was staying with my grandfather. They needed their house back for his family and for himself. Our case became stronger when I also joined the Army and proceeded to Burma. Ultimately, we got the house back in early 1945.

§

My father and Jayaprakash Narayan, popularly known as JP, had studied together in Patna College and they were good friends. JP boycotted the College when the Mahatma started the Non-Cooperation Movement. He went to the US for higher education while his wife, Smt Prabhavati Devi, the daughter of a leading Congressman of Bihar, Shri Brij Kishore Prasad, joined the Mahatma's *Ashram*. The Mahatma had no daughter and both he and his wife Kasturba brought up Prabhavati like their daughter and treated JP like a son-in-law.

On return to India after graduating in the US, JP joined active politics and became a member of the Congress Party. While JP was in politics, my father chose to join the Police. Despite this difference, their personal relations remained cordial. They would occasionally meet at our house and I had the privilege of intracting with him from my childhood. I used to call him uncle and as per our custom would touch his feet.

In 1942, JP made a dramatic escape from Hazaribagh Central Jail. After a few months, the Quit India Movement had run out of steam because all the Congress leaders were in jail. Schools and Colleges in Patna were re-opened and I returned to the hostel. The British had managed to quell the disturbances through brute force. I remember I was a Cadet in the University Officers Training Corps (earlier version of the present National Cadet Corps) and had attained the rank of Corporal. I had gone to Danapur Cantonment for our annual firing at the Ranges. There were two British Sergeants at the Ammunition Point. One of them had recently served in North Bihar in quelling the Quit India Movement. I overheard him talking to his colleague that 1943 was like 1858. They had quelled the 'Mutiny' in 1858. British rule over India continued thereafter for a century. In 1943 they had done the same in defeating the 1942 rebellion and the British would rule India for another century. That set me thinking and I felt that I should join the Army and weaken British military power from within. I decided to apply for a Commission in the Army.

I graduated with Honours from Patna University in 1943, securing a high place in the merit list. I applied for a Commission in the Army. My professors told me that I had a good academic record and I would be wasting my talent by joining the Army. I was not dissuaded. Both my grandfather and father did not raise any objection. The tide of war had changed and the fortune of the Axis powers was now on decline. Moreover, recruitment to the Civil Services had been suspended for the duration of the War and vacancies in the Civil Services were reserved for War service candidates after the War.

I got selected by both the District and Provincial Selection Boards. I received a letter that my name could not be forwarded to the Central Selection Boards for four months till I attained the minimum prescribed age of eighteen. I wrote a letter to the Commander-in-Chief of the Indian Army, Field Marshal Sir Claude Auchinleck, saying that I wanted to join the Army quickly and requested him to expedite the selection process, so that I could do so in January immediately after I attain the minimum prescribed age. I now realised what a childish request I had made. I was surprised that after a few weeks I received a reply to my letter from Lt Col Ridgway, the Private Secretary to the Commander-in-Chief. It said that my letter had been placed before His Excellency the Commander-in-Chief who appreciated my desire to join the Army quickly. He has issued instructions that my selection process be expedited. I wondered how the Commander-in-Chief of a 2 million-strong Army engaged in fighting a world war had the time to spare for my childish request and passed this order. I soon received instructions to appear before the Central Selection Board at Dehradun. The selection process was completed and I got selected by the Board, by the time I was eighteen years old. I was directed to report for training at Officers' Training School, Belgaum. I have mentioned my correspondence with the C-in-C to highlight the functioning of administration in those days. Today as a senior citizen in Independent India, when I write a letter to a Minister on issues like facilities for residents living in my colony in Delhi, no notice is taken of my letter. My letter is not even acknowledged.

After my selection for the Army, as per the prescribed procedure, enquiries about my loyalty and trustworthiness had to be made from the provincial CID. Johnston, SP-CID at Patna, cleared my name even though there was a CID report against me in 1942 saying that I had met Jayaprakash Narayan at my uncle's residence. Possibly being a colleague and friend of my father, he had given me the benefit of doubt. Jayaprakash Narayan had escaped from Hazari Bagh Central Jail, and spent one night with my uncle, Anirudh Sinha, a first cousin of my father, who lived in a house in Patna. I had been to his residence one evening and he told me that he was very busy and I should come some other day. Before leaving I got a glimpse of Jayaprakash Narayan who was in another room in my uncle's house. The next day, both JP and my uncle had gone underground. They operated from Nepal carrying out sabotage of communications in Bihar during the 1942 Quit India Movement. Forty years later in Independent India, when I was due to take over as Army Chief, intelligence report of my family's close association with Jayaprakash Narayan was held against me.

After retirement from the Police, my father renewed his old association with JP. He now started working as Director in an honorary capacity with an NGO started by JP, doing relief work during famine in Bihar. After JP's death, my father took over as President of that NGO. In view of my family's close association with JP, Indira Gandhi took the decision to supersede me for the top appointment in the Army in 1983. I resigned immediately without making an issue of it.

§

My grandfather had special *pooja* (worship) conducted for me at the house before I was to leave to join the Army. His parting words to me were that he had served under the British with a letter of resignation in his pocket. One should do one's duty faithfully but should never compromise on one's self respect. This had a big impact for me and I tried to live up to it throughout the 40 years that I served in the Army. At the end when I faced a crisis situation, I did not take even five minutes to resign irrespective of the consequences. I quit the Army immediately in 1983 when I learnt that Indira Gandhi, the then Prime Minister had decided to supersede me because of my association with JP. It is strange that in the British days this was ignored and I was cleared for joining the Army but in Independent India this was held against me.

§

In January 1944, I left Patna to pursue a career in the Army. I had a railway warrant to travel in Second Class. In those days there used to be four classes on railway trains. Officers travelled in First Class, British Soldiers and Indian Army Junior Commission Officers travelled in Second Class. Indian non-commissioned officers travelled in Intermediate Class and Sepoys travelled in Third Class. As an Officer Cadet, I was entitled to travel in Second Class. First and Second Class were very comfortable with the former having additional facilities. Intermediate Class had raxine covered benches with fans and third class had only wooden benches with no fans. During the war, separate bogies were earmarked for military personnel. I had a railway warrant but to make sure that I was not stopped from travelling in a compartment reserved for military only, I travelled in my University Training Corps (UTC) uniform.

I had a long journey ahead of me from Patna to Belgaum. It took three nights by train. I had to change trains at Mughal Sarai, Bombay (now Mumbai) and Poona (now Pune) before reaching Belgaum. As I entered the railway compartment at Patna, I saw a British Army Sergeant sitting inside. He was coming from Calcutta and was on his way to Itarsi and then Mhow. He was going on posting from his battalion. He had just returned from Burma. He had served during operations against the Japanese in Burma. He was a University student in England before he was conscripted for the Army. I found him an interesting companion with liberal ideas apart from talking about his war experiences. He referred to the Japanese as Jiffes. He told me that after what he had seen of the Bengal famine in Calcutta, he was convinced that Britain had forfeited the moral right to rule over India. He was all for India getting independence and the British to quit India after the war. I was very surprised to hear such liberal views from him. We became friendly and he was an interesting companion for the long journey to Itarsi.

I spent half a day and night in Bombay to catch my train to Poona. I was very impressed to see this modern metropolis. This was my first visit to Bombay. I proceeded to Poona by a morning train the following day. It was called, as it still is nowadays, the Deccan Queen. I had never seen such a luxurious chair-car compartment. We were served an excellent English breakfast on the train. At Poona, I had to wait the whole day to catch the connecting metre gauge train at night to Belgaum, which was an all night journey. I took advantage of my day's halt at Poona to go and see the Aga Khan Palace from outside. There was a British Army sentry at the gate of the palace. Mahatma Gandhi had been imprisoned and was kept there. I could not go inside and nor could I have a glimpse of the Mahatma from outside. I had a guilty conscience. I revered him and had wanted to follow his call for Independence. He wanted the people to boycott the war effort and here I was on my way to join the Army. I have already mentioned earlier how I decided to join the Army, after the Quit India Movement of 1942 had been crushed by the British. I felt that the Army could undermine British control over India as it was the mainstay of British Imperial Power. What Motilal Nehru had told General Thimayya at Allahabad in early 1930 equally applied to me. I have also mentioned earlier how as a child in my mother's ancestral home I had taken cudgels on behalf of my father and grandfather who were in the Police (Picture 7).

It so happened that in 1947 when India became Independent, I had a chance to see the justification for such views. I was then only a small cog in the wheel as a junior Army Officer. However, I happened to hold a key position in Delhi and could make a substantial contribution in my own little way in the service of the nation both during Partition riots and when Operation began in Kashmir three months after Independence. If Indian officers of my generation had not been in the Army, and with British officers suddenly going back to their homes, we would have found it extremely difficult to manage things.

At Poona, en route to Belgaum, I also went to see Shivaji's Singarh fort near the city. I wondered how his soldiers led by his famous General Tanaji Malusare had climbed the Dona precipice. They had done so using a rope tied to a Ghorpad (big lizard) and surprised the Mughal Garrison and captured the fort, which was supposed to be impregnable. I was a keen student of Shivaji's life and history. I found the visit to this fort very rewarding.

§

At Poona Railway Station on the metre gauge train going to Belgaum, I found that there were two or three special railway bogies. Both British and Indian Cadets going to Officers' Training School at Belgaum were travelling in the train. I met a Tamilian Brahmin with sandal paste on his forehead, wearing a tie and coat with a South Indian *lungi* instead of trousers. His name was Venkatswami and he was a highly qualified electronic engineer, recruited for the Army, and was going for a fortnight orientation course at Belgaum before joining a technical electronic Army unit in Madras (now Chennai). He and I travelled in the same compartment. We reached Belgaum the next morning. There was a reception centre for incoming Cadets at the railway platform. We reported at the centre. The Sergeant at the desk on seeing the Tamilian reporting to him exclaimed in surprise, "What egg did you come out from." He replied "A superior egg from which you came out from." There were trucks waiting for us and we were all told to get into them with our baggage. We then proceeded to the Officers' Training School (Picture 8).

On arrival, we were allotted rooms in an old two-storey barrack which had two-feet wide stone walls. Venkatswami and I were allotted the same room. There were two to three Cadets in every room. The British Cadets generally had separate rooms to themselves but in a few cases they had to share a room with Indian Cadets. We were issued our uniforms and a corporal showed us around our accommodation.

He briefed us about our daily routine. A servant was allotted for each room in the barrack. The Cadets living in that room had to pay the servant ₹15 each per month as salary. He told us that in the morning our servants would bring us our 'Gun-Fire Tea'. That was the British soldier's crude language for morning tea. We were showed our common toilet. It was a large room with commodes lined up on one side without any partition. There was no water borne sanitation. Wash basins were on the other side in the room. We were horrified to find such a lack of privacy but that was common among British soldiers. Of course, British officers would have separate toilets-cum-bathrooms. I was told that in the Indian Military Academy at Dehradun, living conditions for Cadets were much better. It was a peace-time establishment while our school was in British Soldiers' Barracks converted for the use of Officer Cadets. OTS Belgaum was meant exclusively for British Cadets. However, towards the end of the war three courses with Indian Cadets were also trained at Belgaum, ours being the first such course.

The ratio in the Company of British and Indian Cadets was fifty-fifty. There was a separate large room next to the toilet for our bath with a water pipe in the centre and attached bath showers running from one end to the other. The Corporal told us that we could have our bath in that room in our birthday suits. Venkat did not quite understand what a birthday suit meant. I explained to him that it stood for being naked. That very day he went to the market to buy himself swimming trunks.

§

All the Cadets had to hire a bicycle each for going to parades and classrooms. We had to learn how a platoon of Cadets had to follow the cycle drill with the platoon-leader leading and the others in a row of two. We had to go on roads in this formation. There was a drill for mounting bicycles with a command for ready to mount and dismount when asked to do so. One had to cycle in rows of two maintaining required distance. On seeing an officer, the Cadet platoon leader would give words of command like Eyes Right and Eyes Front to salute any officer we met on the road. Once we saw the Commandant's young daughter coming from the opposite direction on a bicycle. That day we had a British Cadet as our platoon leader. He gave the command Eyes Right and the young girl looked embarrassed. Our Company Sergeant Major saw this. He marched us up to the Company Commander and the latter gave us a punishment of three days extra drill. This meant running round the Parade Square with packs on our back for an hour for three days.

On our settling down in our quarters over the weekend, our Company Commander Major Thackeray of South Staffordshire Regiment gave us an introductory talk. He was a tall and fat person who had commanded a Battalion during operations in Burma. Due to some illness, he was placed in a Low Medical Category and had lost his acting rank of Lt Col. He had a good sense of humour. He told us what was expected of us as budding officers of the Army. I remember his mentioning that most of us would be going to Burma to fight the Japanese. He asked us not to worry because the Japanese were poor marksmen. They had fired several shots at him and despite his big body presenting a large target, all their shots had missed him. After his lecture, he got into his car but the car would not start. He asked us, if we knew how to drive a car. Half a dozen of us including me raised our hands, and he asked us to get his car started. He sat in the driver seat and asked us to push the car. The car started alright. He then told us that this should be our first lesson in the Army. One should never volunteer to do anything. He smiled and drove away.

§

We went through a very strenuous training schedule to learn the art of soldiering. Much emphasis was laid on physical training and weapon training. We were taught firing all infantry weapons. Our training included field craft which is the art of moving on the battle field under enemy fire, making use of terrain and foliage. We used to go out on self-contained long marches for a couple of days living in small bivouacs in the field by night. Everyone had to pass the prescribed swimming test with weapons and boots hung from our neck. There were also indoor classes where we were given training in various aspects of soldiering. Drill was another important subject of training requiring smart turnout and drill movements on parade. It was a long schedule from early morning to games in the evening every day except Sundays.

At the end of our training, a day before the passing out parade, the Sergeant Major announced that Siner had been selected for

Commandant's baton to be presented at the passing out parade by the Reviewing Officer. My friend Samir Chandra Sinha had the same surname and having come from Royal Indian Military College was very good at all the professional work, particularly physical training exercises. He raised his hand and Sergent Major called him to come up to him. When he saw that the Cadet No on his chest was 169, he said "Not You. The other Siner 175 has been selected." I then went up to him and he explained to me what was required of me at the parade next day. I think I got selected because of my better written work and elocution. Samir being a good friend and a great gentleman was delighted and hugged me.

As Samir and I progressed in our Army career and rose to the rank of Major General, there was often such confusion in regard to us, the initials SC and SK being almost similar. On one occasion even the Controller of Defence Accounts who used to send us our pay slips, made a mistake in this regard. It was interesting that in the early 1970s, Samir was DMT (Director of Military Training) at Army Headqurters and I was DMI (Director of Military Intelligence). This also caused confusion at times.

Samir retired as Major General and thereafter was Director of United Services Institution (USI) of India and instrumental in putting up the USI building at Rao Tula Ram Marg, Delhi Cantt. As Army Commander, I got the then vacant land allocated for USI. While he was the Director, I used to be a member of the Executive Committee for many years and we worked together. Alas, he passed away a few years later.

§

The war was raging furiously in different parts of the world. Europe, Africa and Asia were three theatres of war. The Japanese had launched a big offensive in Assam and Manipur. The fortunes of war seemed to be changing in favour of the Allies in all theatres. We used to maintain maps in the Information Room giving progress of operations on maps in different theatres. At the end of nine months of rigorous training, we were commissioned as Second Lieutenants. We got our posting orders and I was posted to the JAT Regiment. The Regimental Centre was at Bareilly.

The day after our passing out parade, two of us wearing a star on our shoulders were walking down the road. Our British Sergeant

Major, who used to be a terror on the parade ground shouting at us during drill parades, was coming from the opposite direction. We were now officers and as he approached us he smartly saluted us. We returned the salute in a casual manner. He came up to us and said, "Sir, I taught you drill for the last nine months. You have to return my salute smartly." He asked us to go back a few steps and this time when he marched up to us we returned his salute smartly. He now told us that it had taken him twenty years to earn the Sergeant Major badge of rank which he was wearing on his wrist, while we had got our lemon drop (one star) in nine months and were wearing it on our shoulders.

§

I reported to the JAT Regimental Centre at Bareilly. The JAT Regiment started having Indian officers from 1941 only, unlike a few other Regiments, like the Rajput Regiment, where the process of Indianisation had begun in 1919. There were some 60 officers at the Regimental Centre out of which there were about fifteen Indian officers. The senior most Indian officer with us was Capt Ahmad Ali Khan who had three years of service. The Majors, Lt Colonels and the Colonel were all British officers. We felt overawed before the senior British officers but were at ease with the junior British officers of our seniority. The Colonel Commanding the Regimental Centre was an officer with thirty years of service. He had fought both in the First and Second World Wars. He was a very amiable person and kind to us. Bareilly had a European Club. The Commissioner of the Division was the President of the Club. Other British Civil Officers, like DIG, District Magistrate, District Judge, District SP, Civil Surgeon and their British juniors were members of the Club. The JAT Regimental Centre had taken collective membership of the Club. Indian officers were not permitted to join the Club. The Colonel took a stand that since all officers of the Regiment had taken collective membership of the Club, Indian officers should also be allowed the use of the Club. If this was not acceptable, then the Centre would withdraw from collective membership of the Club. This would have meant much loss to the revenue to the Club because of our large numbers. The Commissioner reluctantly agreed. However, few Indian officers availed of this facility. I went to the Club one evening for the sake of curiosity. Compared to the life at Officers' Training School at Belgaum, there was more formality and rigid discipline in the Officers' Mess at Bareilly. At breakfast young officers were not supposed to talk except in whisper. It was said that senior officers after heavy drinking the previous evening wanted silence in the morning. Many of them would be reading newspapers or magazines while eating breakfast. For both breakfast and lunch, one could go into the dining room individually within the allocated timings and leave after finishing meals. Dinners were formal affairs. One had to assemble in the Mess half an hour earlier when the Officers Call was played on the bugle. There were four dinner nights every week and one went into the dining room in order of seniority. One had to be in uniform on dinner nights. After a formal dinner night, a toast was drunk to the health of the King Emperor with the band playing the British National Anthem. On non-dinner nights, one could wear lounge suits and come out of the dining room after the meal. The senior officers kept a distance from the junior officers. We had friendly and informal relations with British junior officers of our seniority. We were served Western dishes for meals in the Mess except on Sundays when we got curry and rice. The Indian officers naturally liked to have Indian meals. On non-dinner nights, or for lunch on holidays, we often went on bicycles or tongas to Bareilly Railway Station for Indian meals from the railway restaurant of Ballabhdas Ishwardas. At times, some of our British friends would accompany us to taste Indian food.

About this time the C-in-C Field Marshal Auchinleck issued orders that Indian meals would be served three times a week in Officers' Mess. Whereas Indian officers welcomed this order, British officers were not happy about this. Their point was that all officers paid for the food they ate in Officers' Mess and they should be allowed to have the food of their choice. It was clarified to them that in the field during operations officers would have to eat food with their soldiers. As part of their training for war, they should get used to eating Indian food.

§

After two months of exposure to Regimental ethos, culture and history, along with supervising the training of recruits at the Centre, I got my posting to jungle training division at Saharanpur. With a batch of 200 soldiers, we were given a ceremonial farewell from the Centre. We marched from our Regimental Lines to Bareilly Railway

Station with the Regimental Band playing. People knew that we were now on our way to Burma. Some street urchins were shouting *Bali Ka Bakra* (sacrificial goat). Possibly they were doing so because the Congress had given a call to boycott the war effort. We ignored the taunts of these urchins. On reaching the Railway Station, we boarded the Special Train for Saharanpur and were given a ceremonial send off by the Centre.

§

Our jungle training Battalion, 7 JAT was located in Badshahi Bagh. JAT Officers and soldiers going to Burma had to undergo training in jungle warfare for a couple of months before being assigned to an active battalion in Burma. The Divisional Headquarters of the Training Division was at Saharanpur. Major General WDA Lentaign was the Divisional Commander. He had commanded the Chindits in Burma after General Wingate had been killed in an air crash. He had a lot of experience in jungle warfare.

On arrival at Saharanpur we moved to Badshahi Bagh on the road from Saharanpur to Dehradun. This place had low hills covered with jungles. Not far from this location was the Yamuna river. For two months, we went through rigorous training in jungle warfare and in watermanship. We were trained to cross the river with improvised means. All this would come in handy for us in Burma. Jim Corbett, the legendary hunter of tigers, gave us an interesting lecture on jungle lore. My Company Commander was Major Turtle. He was quite a character and was fond of snakes. In his office, he would have snakes crawling on his table. I found that repulsive. As a part of jungle training we had to eat snakes' meat. I managed to avoid doing so.

Our Commanding Officer was an Indian, Lt Col Viseshwar Nauth Singh. He was more English than an Englishmen. It was very rare in those days to have an Indian Lt Col. He was one batch junior to General Cariappa who was the first Indian to be promoted to Lt Col in 1942 and again the first Indian to be promoted to the rank of Brigadier in 1944. We learnt that Viseshwar Nauth had been offered promotion to the rank of Brigadier in late 1944 and posting to Army Headquarters at Delhi. He declined saying that he did not want to become a pen pushing *Babu* at Army Headquarters. This was his contemptuous way of referring to a Staff Officer. The real reason was that he was an alcoholic and he did not want to work for more than fifteen minutes a day. The British ignored his weakness because he was more British than Indian.

Viseshwar Nauth (he liked "Nath" to be spelt and pronounced "Nauth") was the son of Col Bhola Nath who was in the Medical Services and had become a full Colonel during the First World War. Viseshwar Nauth was born and educated in the UK. He came to India as a Second Lieutenant in 1920. Initially posted to the GRENADIERS, he was transferred to the JATS during the Second World War. He spoke Hindi like an Englishman. I remember that a Company of Majhabi (Scheduled Caste) Sikhs was attached to our Battalion for jungle training. The senior Subedar of this Company had opened a Gurudwara in a Tent and had invited Viseshwar and all the officers to the Gurudwara. I recall that in his address, much to our amusement, the Colonel spoke, *"Hum Bahut Khushi Hai Ki Sikh Logon Ne Apna Girjaghar Khol Liya Hai."* (I am happy that the Sikhs have opened their (Christian) Church.)

§

Badshahi Bagh used to have a hunting lodge for Mughal Rulers to hunt tigers. Our Battalion was under tents close to the old hunting lodge. Visheshwar's daily routine was amazing. He used to get up at 10 in the morning, wash his mouth with Gin, come to the office at 11 and work for about half an hour and then go to the Mess for drinks and late lunch. After lunch he would retire to his tent and then come to the Mess in the evening. He would drink till midnight and then have his dinner. He liked to interact in the Mess with British officers only and ignored the Indian officers. On one occasion, the Divisional Commander had come to the Battalion in the evening. Dinner was held at the Mess in his honour. The Brigade Commander had also been invited. During the evening, Viseshwar interacted very well with both the British Brigade and Division Commanders. Major General Lentaign, the Divisional Commander, and Visheshwar had been Cadets at Sandhurst in UK at about the same time. He was calling him Bolo and the latter by his first name, Joe. Before they dispersed the General asked Visheshwar that he be shown the jungle lane in our Battalion which we had for jungle firing. He told him that the Adjutant, Tony Ofvenberg, would take him round and show him the jungle lane. The next morning we saw the General being driven around our training area in a Jeep by the Adjutant. Our Commanding Officer was in his tent and had not woken up. The General had his breakfast and departed thereafter. It is amazing how Visheshwar Nauth could get away with all this. I suppose even if Visheshwar had been sacked, he would not have bothered. He was the only child of his father and had inherited property in Lahore and agricultural land which got him more than double the amount of his salary in the Army. His English wife had divorced him and he had no child.

I had an interesting interaction with him. I received my posting orders to 6 JAT in Burma. The Adjutant took me to his office to say Goodbye to him. He got up and shook my hand saying, "Goodbye, Good Luck. By the way, what is your name?" All this may sound very strange and unbelievable. Facts can be stranger than fiction.

§

6 JAT had suffered heavy casualties and had been withdrawn from Burma to Gauhati (now Guwahati) in Assam for rest and refit before going back to Burma. Their advance party had already moved to Rangoon (now Yangoon). A draft of 200 Pathan soldiers of Frontier Force Regiment in our training division was going to 4 Frontier Force Regiment (FFR) in Burma. I was made the Draft Conducting Officer for this group of soldiers. Their Battalion was in Pegu where my Battalion was to fetch up. I reported with my draft to the Transit Camp at Calcutta. Rangoon had very recently been captured. I had to proceed with the draft by Ship to Rangoon and from there by road to Pegu.

We travelled by a troop-ship from Prinsep Ghat Calcutta to Rangoon. It took us three days to cover the distance. This was my first travel by sea. We sailed down the Hoogly River to Diamond harbour where the River joined the sea. Monsoon had just started. The Bay of Bengal was very rough and most of us were very sea sick. The war was still on, although the Japanese power was receding. We still practised anti-submarine drills on the ship to cater for submarine attack. We also practised anti-aircraft drills. On reaching Elephant Point on the mouth of the Rangoon River we found that mines laid by the Japanese were still there but a pathway had been cleared for ships to sail to Rangoon.

On arrival at Rangoon, I proceeded to Payaji, North of Pegu near the demolished bridge over the Sittang river on the border between Burma and Siam (now Thailand). The draft of 200 soldiers with me were to be conducted to 4/12 Frontier Force Regiment (now with Pakistan Army). I learnt that during the withdrawal of 17 Indian Division in February 1942, Maj Gen John Smyth, VC had prematurely ordered the blowing of the bridge when the bulk of the Division was on the far bank of the river. Our troops had to abandon their heavy equipment and swim across the river while under attack from the Japanese. This disaster opened the route to Rangoon which was speedily occupied by the Japanese. Smyth was removed from command and lost his acting rank of Maj Gen. This ended his Army career. One span of the Rail Bridge was still there. It reminded one of the disaster. I was told to stay with 4 FFR pending the arrival of my Battalion from India. The Brigade to which my Battalion was assigned was on the Eastern side of the Pegu Yoma range at Prome in the Irrawady Valley. The Brigade was also to come up to the Sittang Valley for the offensive across Sittang into Siam. The Japanese trapped in the Pegu Yoma were a starving lot in a desperate situation wanting to withdraw across the river into Siam. As per their practice, they would never surrender and would commit *Harakiri* (suicide) rather than surrender. Our patrols used to go to the Yoma, searching for Japanese soldiers. They had to be careful because even in that condition the Japanese would not give up and would throw grenades at our troops. Sometimes their dead bodies would be booby trapped. Patrols were warned to be very careful. I accompanied a few patrols and found quite a few decomposed bodies of Japanese soldiers in the jungles. Even in that desperate situation the Japanese would occasionally fire mortar bombs on our positions.

After a week, I learnt that our Battalion's advanced party had arrived in Rangoon Transit Camp and the main body was expected to follow soon. I reported to the Transit Camp and was told that due to difficulties in providing shipping, the arrival of the Battalion was further delayed. As directed, I proceeded in a convoy to the Brigade Headquarters at Prome. I met Brigadier PC Marindon from the West York Regiment who was commanding the Lushai Brigade of which my Battalion was a part. He was an old First World War veteran and a fatherly figure. He was indulgent and quite kind to me. I remember visiting 1 Bihar Regiment which was also at Prome. Lt Col Tweed was its Commanding Officer and Major Habibullah Khan Khattak was the Second in Command. I had known Tweed when he was a Major in Patna Commanding a Company of the University Training Corps in which I had been a Cadet while a student in Patna University. Both Tweed and Habibullah knew my uncle who had served in that Battalion for a few months when it was raised and had later been transferred to Hyderabad Regiment (now Kumaon Regiment). One evening when I was in the Officers' Mess of the Battalion, it was being discussed as to what should be the Regimental Crest of the Battalion. 1 BIHAR, which was raised during the war, had not till then a Regimental Crest. Being a student of history, I suggested that Ashoka Lion would be very appropriate for Bihar Regiment. Some Muslim officers felt that as there were then Muslim troops also serving in the Regiment, there should be something connected with Muslims. They wanted that the dome of the tomb of Sher Shah at Sasaram in Bihar should be included. The British officers felt that the Ashoka Lion mounted on top of the dome would be appropriate for this purpose. This ultimately became the crest of Bihar Regiment. The crest looks almost similar to what became our National Emblem after Independence. A close look of the Regimental Crest will show that the dome below the Ashoka Lion looks very much like the pedestal in our National Emblem.

§

While I was in Rangoon Officers Transit Camp, Atom Bombs were dropped over Hiroshima and Nagasaki and the Japanese surrendered. The VJ (Victory over Japan) Day was celebrated with great gusto in Rangoon. The British Governor Sir Dorman Smith who had been in exile at Simla in India had returned to Rangoon after its liberation in May 1945. He threw a Ball for all Officers of Allied Forces in Rangoon at the Government House (the palatial residence of the Governor). I was one of the many who enjoyed his hospitality. This was the first time that I had been inside a Government House. Everyone was in a jovial mood with drinks served on the house. The lavish display of Burmese Teak Wood in the building was very gorgeous.

My Battalion fetched up at last and I moved with the Battalion to Pegu. Soon after we settled down in our new location two incidents took place which showed how times were changing. The first was a tiff between two subalterns over music in the officers' mess. Salim had switched on the radio, he was listening to a Hindi song. Sheridan came in and switched off the radio saying such cattle drum music should not be heard in an officers' mess. The Standing Orders at our Regimental Centre at Bareilly had forbidden playing of Indian music in officers' mess. The two got into an argument and Salim in a fit of temper picked up the radio and threw it on the ground. The next morning the two officers were marched up before Col Newell, the Commanding Officer. The latter rebuked both saying that their conduct was not becoming of an officer. Sheridan was warned for having created this problem by switching off the radio and using the term "cattle drum" for Indian music. Salim was admonished for breaking the radio and was told to pay the cost of the radio. We were all told that we could play music of our choice after obtaining the permission of the senior officer present in the Mess. The second incident was even more serious. One night the Majors had retired and some young British and Indian officers got into a discussion about the Indian National Army (INA). A British officer said that the INA personnel were all traitors and deserved to be shot. The Indian officers argued that they had dedicated themselves to a noble cause and should not be treated like ordinary criminals. Heated discussion went on for some time. The next morning all the young officers were summoned by the Second-in-Command and told that mess rules did not permit discussion of any political issue in an officers' mess. Disciplinary action will be taken against officers who do so. This incident shows how Indian officers had begun to assert themselves with the British on equal terms.

§

After a few weeks, two companies of our Battalion were moved to Payaji where I had earlier been with 4 FFR for a couple of weeks. This was near the demolished Sittang Bridge. We were tasked to take over a Japanese Prisoner of War Camp. There were 8,000 Japanese prisoners in the Camp. I was appointed Adjutant of the Camp. It was a wonderful learning experience for me. I was very impressed by the discipline of the Japanese soldiers. The Emperor had ordered the Army to surrender and his orders were implemented scrupulously. Internal administration of the Camp was left to the Japanese and we provided perimeter defence of the Camp. In the morning Japanese soldiers would form up on open ground and take a deep bow facing the rising Sun as a token of their obeisance to the Emperor, supposed to be the descendent of the Sun God. The work culture of the Japanese soldier was unique. Anyone disobeying the Emperor's order to surrender would be sentenced to death. Thus, there was no question of any prisoner trying to escape. This made our task easy. However, there was a case of desertion one night of a Japanese soldier from the Camp. The following morning the Japanese General of his division reported to me in my office, "Your Excellency, I am ashamed to report that Private Yakamura has deserted. We immediately held a court martial last night sentencing him to death for disobeying Emperor Hirohito's order. His Battalion, Company, Platoon and Section Commanders have been given graduated duration of punishment. They have been given 3, 5, 10 and 15 days respectively of punishment of solitary confinement and half rations. The Section Commander got the longest duration, i.e 15 days." No other Army in the World gives out such punishment for desertion. I also noticed that slapping a junior, whether officer or soldier, for any mistake committed by the latter was a common form of punishment in the Japanese Army. General Patton of the US had slapped a soldier in Sicily during the war. The soldier was in a field hospital with battle casualties. There was nothing wrong with him and he wanted to remain in the hospital. The doctor said that the soldier was malingering as he did not want to go into battle. Patton during his visit asked the soldier as to why he was in hospital. The soldier cried and said that he was too scared to go to battle. In a fit of temper, Patton slapped the soldier and had him sent to the front line. This became a major national issue in the US. It was brought to the notice of the US President Roosevelt. He took a serious view of the slapping incident. Patton was removed from command and made to publicly apologise to the soldier for having slapped him at a parade. This incident resulted in Patton being superseded by his junior, General Bradley, who had served under him. How differently was slapping as a form of punishment in the Army treated in the Japanese and US Armies!

In India, the slapping of a soldier is not permitted. However, in Regimental Centres there used to be instances when a Havildar or Havildar Major, during lapse on parade, would slap a Recruit. People turned a blind eye to this form of punishment. However, I never came across an Officer resorting to slapping a soldier in our Army.

Another aspect of discipline in the Japanese Army was that orders were scrupulously carried out by its officers and men. The Allied command had ordered that all Japanese prisoners will salute Allied officers and come to attention while talking to an Allied soldier. This was done to humiliate them and was an act of revenge for the very harsh and brutal treatment meted out to Allied officers and men who had been taken prisoners by the Japanese during the early years of the war. I found the Japanese Generals comply with this order meticulously. I used to feel embarrassed when a Japanese General would salute me, take a deep bow and address me as Your Excellency. There were a few Generals in our Prisoner of War Camp. We had to maintain their war record. I found a few among them who had served during the First World War when Japan was an Ally of Britain. The career of one of the Generals in our Camp was interesting. He had earned the Military Cross, a British decoration of gallantry while serving alongside the British Army in the First World War. He had been a Military Attaché in the Japanese Embassy at Washington and done a course at National War College in the US. He had commanded a Regiment (equivalent of our Brigade) in China and later a Division in Burma. Inspite of his professional record, he never hesitated to treat me as a superior.

The work culture of the Japanese was also remarkable. We used them as labour for carrying out various tasks like clearing jungles, constructing roads, constructing *bashas* for our officers and men, and so on. The Japanese working parties would be given tasks for the day in the morning. When they completed their task and time was left, they would ask for more work to be assigned to them.

I found the Japanese particularly good in using jungle resources. All the living accommodation in the Camp was in *bashas* made of bamboos, large leaves and strings which were readily available in the jungle. I was most impressed by the *bashas* they made for our officers. Adjutant is called *Hukwang* in Japanese and is considered an important person. They took particular care in making a *bashas* for me. It was built on stilts to keep water away. There was a small bamboo stair case to the *bashas*. The room on stilts had a bamboo door and two bamboo windows. There was an attached bathroom with a bath tub made of bamboos covered by canvas. Half cut bamboos were provided for water to come from a slight height by pouring water from a tin. I also had bamboo chairs and tables made for me.

A few Indian prisoners of Subhash Chandra Bose's Indian National Army that had collaborated with the Japanese Army were also brought to our Camp. After some interrogation, they were immediately dispatched to a separate Camp at Rangoon. I recall some of them calling us lackeys of the British while they were patriots fighting for India's Independence. I must say that I felt embarrassed when they made that accusation.

The Japanese were given two scales of rations, sustenance scale for those not employed on work and a higher scale for those who were employed for manual labour. Sustenance scale was a starvation scale and not enough for a soldier. I tried to employ all the 8,000 prisoners for some work or the other so that they could all have enough to eat. This made me very popular with the Japanese prisoners. Although, serving in the Indian Army against the Japanese, I had a hidden admiration for Japan. I had learnt from my grandfather that Japanese victory in the Russo-Japanese War had inspired our national movement for freedom in the early twentieth century. I found that during the Second World War, Japanese victories against European colonial powers paved the way for the Independence of India. This was despite the fact that during the Japanese occupation, they had committed brutal atrocities against Allied prisoners with them and those Indians who had not collaborated with them.

After a couple of months, the winding-up of the prisoners of war camp at Payaji started. We were relieved by another unit and our Battalion proceeded to Toungoo in North Burma. Our Brigade had been earmarked to proceed to Siam and take the surrender of the Japanese there. I was given a farewell by the Japanese prisoners and presented a nice portrait of mine drawn in pencil showing me at my table working as an Adjutant of the camp. There was also a written memorandum presented to me expressing their gratitude for the compassionate manner in which I had treated the prisoners. The memorandum stated that one day they would repay the gratitude to me when I visited Japan. It added that Mount Fujiyama and the Sea of Japan will be anxiously awaiting my arrival. I have travelled all over the world but have not yet visited Japan. I wonder if Mount Fujiyama and Sea of Japan are still awaiting my arrival.

My tenure as Adjutant of the Japanese Prisoners of War Camps was very rewarding. It was my first appointment as a Staff Officer which stood me in good stead. The war had ended and Army officers were virtually in a holiday mood. British Officers and Soldiers conscripted during the war were looking forward to getting demobilised and going back to civilian life. A special war leave of two months had been sanctioned for all serving personnel and people were queuing up for their turn to go home on leave. As Adjutant of the Prisoners' camp, I had a heavy responsibility and I burnt the midnight oil to cope with all the work I was saddled with. It had its compensations. I learnt staff work on the job. The Camp Commandant was one of our senior Company Commanders, Major Ian Jack, a handsome and very amiable Scotsman. Another Company of the Battalion had been placed under his command for work at the Camp. The Battalion Commander and the Brigade Commander visited us. Ian Jack in conversation with them would always have a word of praise for me. This was a source of much encouragement to me. More than half a century later, I was Governor of Jammu and Kashmir. I was in touch with Ian Jack for some years after he had left the Army through exchange of Christmas Cards. After a few years, I had lost touch with him. I was surprised to receive a letter from Ian Jack in 2006. I had not met him after the Second World War. The JAT regimental Newsletter had a picture of mine as a Governor visiting 6 JAT, our old Battalion then located in Jammu Sector. Even the officers then serving with 6 JAT did not know that I had served with the Battalion during the Second World War. Ian Jack happened to see this Newsletter. About the same time a major earthquake took place in Kashmir in which over 1,000 people had been killed. This was reported in the World Press. I was surprised to receive a letter from Ian Jack saying how happy he was that I had done well in life. He also enquired whether our Battalion had suffered any casualty due to the earthquake. I immediately replied and told him that the earthquake had taken place in the Valley and 6 JAT being in Jammu was not affected. A year later I learnt that Ian Jack had passed away. I wrote a letter of condolence to his wife. She acknowledged my letter and wrote that her husband, in his will, had earmarked a large amount to be donated to the JAT Regiment for the welfare of troops. The following year during the Annual meet at JAT Regimental Centre at Bareilly, she and her daughter came all the way from the UK to gift the amount left by her husband for welfare of soldiers of the Regiment. I was requested to receive the cheque on behalf of the Regiment. That was the first time I met Mrs Jack and her grown-up daughter. I have narrated this incident to show how old loyalties survive despite political upheavals. The Regimental spirit built by the British in the Indian Army had been something unique and has survived the vicissitudes of time. In this connection, I may mention another such incident. In 1985, 1 BIHAR was celebrating their Golden Jubilee at their Regimental Centre in Danapur Cantt. I had quit the Army and I was then staying at our ancestral house at Danapur. My uncle had served in 1 BIHAR for a while with Habibulla (now in Pakistan); the latter was also there. It was nice meeting him and I was surprised how Military Intelligence at Delhi had cleared the visit of a retired officer of the Pakistan Army to a Regimental Centre in India. When I was Director Military Intelligence in 1975, there was total embargo on such a visit. My uncle knew Habibulla more intimately. I had met him at Jamshedpur in 1940 when the Second World War had just started and 1 BIHAR was earmarked to protect the TATA steel factory. He and my uncle were serving together in the Battalion at that time. Habibulla was a tall and handsome Pathan. His father was the Accountant General of NWFP and his family was friendly with Dr Khan Sahib, the then Congress Chief Minister of NWFP. He was from the Khattak tribe. I think Khan Abdul Gaffar Khan and his brother Dr Khan Sahib were also frcm the same tribe. Habibulla had two very pretty looking daughters 5 and 3 years old when Habibulla was at Jameshdpur. Next time I met Habibulla when he was the Second-in-Command of 1 BIHAR at Prome in Burma. I have mentioned him earlier in this book. A few months before Independence, Habibulla had been promoted to Lt Col and taken over command of 1 BIHAR. He was the first Indian Commanding Officer of the Battalion. I recall meeting him in 1947 at Delhi when he was leaving for Pakistan. He rose to the rank of Lt Gen in Pakistan Army. His elder daughter got married to the son of Field Marshal Ayub Khan, the President of Pakistan. After retirement from the Army he had set himself in business and was reported to be one of the twenty-two rich men of Pakistan. In view of his credentials and his association, our Military Intelligence made a special dispensation for him to visit 1 BIHAR. He told me that his wife had died in an air attack by Indian Air Force during the 1965 Indo-Pak war. He had married again and had come to Danapur with his second wife. During a conversation with her, I learnt that her brother had been Chief Secretary in East Pakistan during the 1971 Indo-Pak war. I told her that I knew him. He had been a Naval

Officer before Partition and we had lived in the same Officers' Mess on Wellesley Road (now Zakir Hussain Road, New Delhi). After Partition, he had joined the Civil Service in Pakistan and had surrendered in Dhaka. We had kept him in the Prisoner of War Camp at Bareilly. I was in-charge of all the Pakistani prisoners in 1972 and had met her brother a few times. We live in a small world. It is remarkable that despite India and Pakistan having fought three wars and Habibulla having lost his first wife in an air attack by the Indian Air Force, he had no bitterness towards India. He had come for what he called 'my battalion's function' and donated a couple of lakhs to the Regimental Funds of the Battalion. This is another example of the Regimental mystique built by the British in the Indian Army. Habibulla's son, Ali Quli Khan Khattak, was a serving senior Major-General in Pakistan Army. He was in line to become the Chief of Pakistan Army. Habibulla told me that his son becoming Chief was dependant on political bosses. He knew that I had been passed over to be Chief of the Indian Army for political reasons. He said that in Pakistan Punjabi Muslims dominated in politics and in government. They had a prejudice against Pathans. A few years later his fear came true. His son was superseded by Pervez Musharraf.

§

Going back to my narration of events during the Second World War, my tenure as Adjutant of a POW Camp, as mentioned earlier, had helped me. I had come to the notice of the Brigade Commander who had appreciated my work there. Later when we were at Mawchi near Toungoo, where Lushai Brigade Headquarters was located, Brigadier Marrindon asked my Commanding Officer to recommend an officer to serve as GSO-3 (General Staff Officer Grade 3 in the rank of Captain) at Brigade Headquarters. Col Newell recommended my name. I was promoted to the rank of Acting Captain and posted to Lushai Brigade Headquarters. Perhaps this was a reward for the work I had done in the Prisoner of War Camp. I superseded a British Lieutenant senior to me as also a couple of Indian Lieutenants. As a GSO-3, I got an additional amount of ₹150 per month as staff pay. In those days, very few Indians got an opportunity to serve on the staff, particularly on the General Staff. This set me on a course which in the wake of Partition got me an exposure to functioninag at the national level.

§

After a few months when we completed taking Japanese prisoners from different locations in Siam, we received orders for our Brigade Headquarters to move to Ranchi for being disbanded. The Brigade Commander was posted on promotion to command 19 Indian Division. My Battalion was to proceed to Wana in NWFP (North-West Frontier Province, now in Pakistan). I was asked to report to the Services Selection Board at Singapore for interview for a permanent commission in the Army. Hitherto, I had been a war time Emergency Commissioned Officer. I was happy that I would now have an opportunity to travel and see another foreign country.

I travelled by air from Rangoon to Singapore. On arrival, I learnt that the selection board was in recess for a week. I stayed at an Officers' Transit Camp in Singapore. I went around the city and I was impressed with this metropolis. It was then the capital of Malaya. It had a large Chinese population and also a fairly large Tamil population from Madras. Netaji Subhas Chandra Bose and the Azad Hind government functioned from Singapore during the war. I met a few Indians settled there. They showed me a documentary of a Japanese film. It showed the surrender parade held at Bikothima grounds where the British Governor-General Sir Shenton Thomas, and the British Army Chief General Percival had surrendered in January 1942. Japanese General Yamashita took their surrender along with that of 70,000 Allied troops, mostly Indians. I also saw the letter of Sir Shenton Thomas addressed to Yamashita kept on the wall in the foyer of Raffles Hotel. Yamashita had come to be known as the Tiger of Malaya. In a brilliant campaign of six weeks, he captured the impregnable Fortress Singapore. That spelt the death knell of the British Empire in Asia. We had as students rejoiced in Patna at the humiliation suffered by our imperial rulers.

§

There used to be a war memorial for the INA in Singapore. On re-occupation of Singapore after the war, British Army Engineers had dynamited this memorial. The Indian community of Singapore invited Jawaharlal Nehru to come to Singapore and lay the foundation of a new INA war memorial. Jawaharlal Nehru had accepted the invitation. He was expected to arrive at Singapore. On the day of his arrival, there was much excitement in Singapore. I learnt that the British Generals wanted to send Indian troops out of

Singapore for an exercise in the Jungles to prevent them from coming into contact with Nehru. The Supreme Commander Lord Mountbatten decided that this should not be done and Indian troops should continue with their normal activity. On the day of Nehru's arrival, I went to see the reception for him at Changi airport. There was a large crowd assembling at the airport. I was surprised to see some Army Trucks with Indian soldiers holding Congress Flag at the airport. This was something unimaginable in India. I realised that no one could now prevent India becoming independent soon. At the airport, I saw a British Colonel in uniform walk-up on the tarmac to the aircraft from which Nehru came out of the plane. He saluted Nehru and took him in a staff car from the airport. I could not believe my eyes. We learnt that Mountbatten and Nehru had studied at Harrow in England and wore the same school tie. Nehru was a few years senior to Mountbatten and they had not met before. Mountbatten switched on his charm on Nehru. He told him that India would soon become Independent and it was not in his interest to do anything that may undermine the discipline of the Indian Army. He urged that it would not be advisable for him to lay the foundation stone for the INA war memorial in Singapore or to go to Indonesia where he had been invited by Soekarno. The Indian Army at that time was engaged in a low intensity conflict with Soekarno's forces in that country. Nehru saw the point and accepted the advice of Mountbatten. During my return journey from Changi Airport, the taxi driver enquired from me the rank of Nehru. I could not make out what he meant. He then said that the Chinese leader Chiang Kai-shek was a Marshal. He asked if Nehru was also a Marshal. I thought it best to answer, Yes. The next day I saw Mountbatten with Nehru visiting the Army canteen for a cup of tea. Nehru was virtually mobbed by Indian troops at the canteen. I could not help feeling that I was witnessing history changing.

§

I appeared before the Service Selection Board for three days with a batch of 60 candidates. Only two of us got selected for a Permanent Commission. One evening, while still in Singapore, I visited the Tanglin Officers Club. I saw a British Colonel in uniform having a drink at the bar. I was then a Captain wearing the shoulder title of JAT Regiment. The Colonel beckoned me and invited me to have a drink with him. He told me that he was also from the same Regiment and enquired what I was doing in Singapore. I replied that I was from 6 JAT Regiment and had come from Burma to Singapore for selection for Permanent Commission. I had been selected and would now return to Wana in India where my Battalion had proceeded from Burma. I saw the ribbon of King's Police Medal on his chest and asked him whether he had served in the Police. He confirmed that he had served in the Police before the War and had earned the King's Police Medal. He added that normally everyone enquired what the ribbon he wore was and he was surprised that I had recognised that ribbon. I told him that both my grandfather and father were in the Police and wore that ribbon. He was impressed and became friendly. He asked me whether I would like to go to Indonesia where active operations were continuing. I answered in the affirmative. He then asked me to meet him in his office the next morning. He was serving in HQ ALFSEA (Allied Land Forces South-East Asia) at Changi in Singapore.

Next day I reported to him as directed. I discovered that he was in the Military Secretary Branch which dealt with postings of officers. He gave me my posting order as GSO-3 (Operations) at 15 Corps Headquarters in Batavia (now Jakarta). He also said that as I had dealt with Japanese Prisoners in Burma and had also been a GSO-3 in a Brigade Headquarters, I would be able to contribute in my new assignment. There were several thousand Japanese Prisoners of war in Indonesia who had to be sent back to Japan. It is indeed quite a coincidence that a chance meeting had a great impact on my future career in the Army. Strange are the ways of Providence.

§

I got an air ticket at the Transit Camp in Singapore to fly to Batavia in an Air Force Plane. Headquarters 15 Corps had been re-designated as Headquarters AFNEI (Allied Forces Netherlands East Indies). 5 Indian Infantry Division at Surabaya, 23 Infantry Division at Batavia and 26 Infantry Division in Sumatra were under command of the Corps. There was also a British Para Brigade in Semarang and an Indian Independent Brigade on Celebes Islands in the formation. Two Divisions of the Dutch Army were also under command of AFNEI.

Although, we had gone to Indonesia to take the surrender of nearly 1 lakh Japanese soldiers, we got embroiled in fighting the

Indonesian Revolutionary Army resisting the re-imposition of Dutch colonial rule in Indonesia. I felt uncomfortable at this role being thrust upon us. India was not herself independent and struggling for Independence from the British but here in Indonesia, we were being used to suppress the Independence Movement of the Indonesians. Quite a few Indian officers were uncomfortable being used as mercenaries to impose Dutch Imperialism. The Japanese before surrendering to us had given most of their weapons to the Indonesians. Two Dutch Divisions were in the process of getting re-organised after the Dutch Army had been routed by the Germans in Europe and the Japanese in Asia. During the war, Netherlands itself was under German rule until liberated by the Allies towards the end of the war. Its Army was being re-organised. The plan was that after we had taken the surrender of Japanese and dispatched Japanese Prisoners to Japan, Indian troops would withdraw and the Dutch troops would take over from us. Van Mook had returned as Governor-General to Batavia and General Spears as the Dutch Army Chief.

My name in the posting order received by signal at Headquarters AFNEI had been spelt as Sinner. When I reported to Colonel Stevens from the British Army, who was the GSO-1, he was surprised to see a brown man. Perhaps he thought that I was British. He had never served with an Indian officer and enquired if I was fluent in English. Every morning, I would be required to take my turn in briefing General Sir Montagu Stopford, the Commander-in-Chief and senior officers of the Headquarters in the Operations Room. There were two other GSO-3 who were British officers and would take their turn to do the briefing. I confirmed that I was confident of being able to do so. I took this as a challenge and would go to my office at 4 in the morning when it was my turn to do the briefing. By then all the situation reports of progress in operation on the previous day would have arrived. I would memorise all the details and do my briefing in the morning when the C-in-C and other senior officers would come to the Operation Room for briefing. I used to brief them with confidence and without notes. This would impress them. My two British colleagues, who had to do the briefing when their turn came, were not too happy with me, for doing so extempore. They would tell me that they were not bothered to follow my example and would do their briefing with notes as they had been doing. Both had been conscripted during the war and were looking forward to their release from the Army.

§

There were reports of clashes with the Indonesian forces every day, some of them were of a serious nature. Brigadier Mallaby was killed in an ambush at Sourabaya. Lt Col Surjeet Singh Kalha and two other officers were also killed in another encounter with the Indonesians. Kalha was commissioned from Dehradun, and had commanded a Battalion in Burma. Three other officers commissioned from Dehradun in that batch were Manekshaw, Musa Khan and Dun. It is a coincidence that all the three became Chiefs of their Armies, Manekshaw of Indian Army, Musa Khan of Pakistan Army and Dun of Burmese Army after the Independence of their contries. Kalha was the only one among them who got an opportunity to command a Battalion in the Second World War. The others got their promotions after the war. Kalha and Manekshaw had received gallantry awards in that war. Manekshaw was badly wounded and had got the MC (Military Cross). Kalha had won a higher gallantry award of Distinguished Service Order (DSO). There were four other Indian Officers who had also won the DSO but they were all more senior having been commissioned from Sandhurst before 1934. Destiny has its own ways. Had Kalha survived he would perhaps have been the Chief of the Indian Army in 1971 and Manekshaw would not have been the Army Chief and nor been promoted Field Marshal.

§

I had an occasion to see Mountbatten from close quarters. One day Mountbatten who was then the Supreme Commander at Singapore, walked into our Operation Room where I was on duty. I was taken completely by surprise. I had no prior information of his coming. Our C-in-C was with him and he wanted to show him something on the map. They were accompanied by some senior officers including BGS (Brigadier General Staff). During their conversation, Mountbatten said that he wanted to speak to General Robert Mansergh. He was the General Officer Commanding 5 Infantry Divisions at Sourabaya. We had a hotline direct to the Division's Operations Room. Captain Cunningham was the GSO-3 of the Division and I often used to talk to him on the hotline. I was asked by the BGS to get General Robert

Mansergh on the line for the Supreme Commander. When I spoke to Cunningham, he thought I was pulling his leg. After a few seconds, there was a gruff voice on the telephone saying, "Mansergh here." I told the BGS, "Sir, General Mansergh is on the line." The BGS handed over the receiver to Mountbatten who spoke, "Is that Robert" and the reply came, "If you are Mountbatten, I am Montgomery." Obviously Cunningham had thought that I was joking with him and he would get the better of me by giving that reply. Mountbatten with a smile said, "Let someone convince this fellow that I am Mountbatten." I thought I would get in to trouble but everyone laughed and the whole thing was taken as a joke. The British had a sense of humour otherwise I may well have got into serious trouble over this incident. Later my BGS told me that you must make things doubly sure before handing over the telephone to your superior.

That afternoon Mountbatten addressed all the officers at the Headquarters in a flamboyant manner. He told us that while the war is over in Europe, his Command was engaged in active operations both in French-Indo-China and Netherland East Indies where local Forces had risen in revolt aginst the French and the Dutch respectively. Being an ally of both France and Holland, his Command has got engaged in active operations in these two erstwhile Colonies. He gave us the broad political and international aspect of these operations and his aim and strategy. He added that his Command was larger in size than that of other Supreme Commands, and was facing more complex problems. I was much impressed with the way he spoke and how he talked about his interaction with the top world personalities of that time. I had other occasions to interact with Mountbatten from a very junior position which I shall narrate later in this book.

During the course of his talk, Mountbatten mentioned a very interesting anecdote of 1943 when he was appointed Supreme Commander of South-East Asia Command with General Stilwell of the US Army operating in China as the Deputy Supreme Commander. Mountbatten had gone to Cairo where he had to present his plans for offensive in South-East Asia to the Big Two, Roosevelt and Churchill. The Chiefs of Staff of both US and British forces were in attendance. Mountbatten presented what was then considered rather ambitious plans for offensive. The British Chief, General Alan Broke, remarked that it was dangerous to have Admirals on land. Mountbatten promptly replied "Not as dangerous as Generals at sea." Everyone had a big laugh. His plans were approved in principle and he had the satisfaction of executing that plan on the ground. He added that after having won the Second World War, his Command was still engaged in fighting a war in Indonesia and Indo-China. We were all very impressed by his talk.

I recall that Mohammed Nawaz, Staff Captain Supply and Transport, the only other Indian officer in our Headquarters was present in the audience. Nawaz quit the Army in 1947 and joined Pakistan Civil Service. He ultimately ended up in the top appointment of Civil Servant in Pakistan becoming the Cabinet Secretary of Pakistan. Some officers from local units had also been invited for this talk. I could see among them Lt Col Latif, Maj Moti Sagar and Capt Niazi of 4 RAJPUT located in Batavia. Latif as Maj Gen became Commandant of Staff College Quetta, Moti Sagar retired as Army Commander from Southern Command and Niazi who also became a Lt Gen, C-in-C in East Pakistan during the 1971 war and surrendered to us.

§

Bandung was the Summer capital of Java. It was some 60 miles from Batavia. It was largely under occupation of the Indonesians. It was decided to launch an operation to clear Bandung. I was sent as a Staff Officer to find a suitable location for our Tactical Headquarters near Bandung and also to report on progress of operations for clearing Bandung. I went with 1 PATIALA in a convoy via Soekabomi to Bandung. The convoy was ambushed but we broke through the ambush clearing the enemy entrenched there. Major Sukhdev Singh earned a Military Cross in that battle. We got to know each other well. The clearing operation of Bandung was successfully executed. In 1948, during the battle of Zojila in Kashmir, he was commanding 1 PATIALA and again as a Staff Officer of Command Headquarters. I had accompanied his Brigade Headquarters as Army Commander's Liaison Officer attached to the formation for the operations. We had walked across the Zojila Pass together in that battle. A couple of years later in 1950 when I was Brigade Major at Amritsar, Sukhdev Singh was one of our Battalion Commanders. Still later he became a Brigadier and my association with him continued. He would generously praise me for being a good Staff Officer and I in turn admired his qualities as a Commander.

Besides my work as an Operation Staff Officer in Indonesia, I was also given the task of arranging the repatriation of thousands of Japanese prisoners of war to Japan. This was in itself a full-time work. It required among other things to arrange for shipping for them and in consultation with the Headquarters of General MacArthur in Japan which was known as HQ SCALP (Supreme Command Allied Powers). A meeting was to be held in Tokyo at SCALP. Our BGS (Brigadier General Staff) was to attend this meeting and I had been detailed to accompany him. To my great regret that meeting was cancelled and I lost the opportunity to visit Japan. I recalled the address presented to me by Japanese prisoners at Payaji in Burma inviting me to Japan and saying that Mount Fujiyama and the sea of Japan would be awaiting my arrival.

My stay in Indonesia was both exciting and very fruitful. I learnt a lot and my work was perhaps appreciated more then I deserved. In fact at the time of my departure, I was told that I had been recommended for the award of MBE (Member of the British Empire). When I was born my grandfather had been awarded a higher grade of that order, OBE (Officer of the British Empire). My father was also in 1946 put up for the award of OBE. It so happened that neither did my father get the OBE nor did I get the MBE. The interim government came to power in late 1946 and decided that no Indian should be given any British award. Thus the recommendations for Indians to be given awards on New Year day of 1947 got cancelled.

§

I witnessed the changing political scenario of post-war developments in Asia. The awe of the old days for the White Man was vanishing. This also got reflected in the Army. Asian Nationalism was rising out of the ashes of European colonialism. Within a couple of years various Colonial Empires of European countries in Asia were dismantled. The British lost India, Burma and Malaya. The French lost Indo-China, the Dutch Indonesia, and Portugal Macao but the latter continued to hold on to Goa from where they were evicted by the Indian Army in 1961.

I found that the attitude of Indian soldiers serving in Indonesia was visibly changing. It was amusing to see Indian officers and soldiers walking hand in hand with white women who had been kept as prisoners by the Japanese and released by us. They were called RAPWI (Recovered Allied Prisoners of War and Internees).

Some Dutch officers were attached for training to a Maratha Battalion in Batavia. As per normal practice, the Battalion detailed some soldiers as Batman (Soldier attendant) to these officers. The Maratha soldiers so detailed, refused to serve as batman of Dutch officers. In the old days, they may not have raised any objection but after their exposure to changed conditions in South-East Asia they had become more assertive. Disobedience of orders is a serious offence in the Army but the British deliberately ignored this. They did not want this small incident to blow up and become something big. They tactfully withdrew the order and sent the Dutch officers to a Gorkha Battalion. The Gorkha soldiers had no inhibition and willingly worked as batman for these Dutch officers.

§

There was also a disturbing incident of communalism which showed how the political drama would unfold in India very shortly leading to Partition of the country. Indonesians tried to contact our Muslim soldiers serving in Indonesia. They found some of them sympathetic to them on grounds of religion. We had a Muslim Company of 8 PUNJAB attached to our Headquarters as our Defence and Employment company.

I was detailed as Duty Officer of the week and had to check the Quarter Guard at the Headquarters. I found that two Muslim soldiers were in the Cell at the Quarter Guard. I went up to check them and I asked them if they were getting their meals. Both broke down and said that the British officers on duty had not bothered to see them and I was the first officer to enquire about their welfare. I did not know that this would lead to my getting an additional task which I carried out diligently.

The two soldiers were on Guard Duty at the house of the C-in-C. One night the two deserted with their arms, as also of their colleagues who were sleeping, while they were on sentry duty. After a few months, they were captured in battle wearing the badges of rank of Captain of the Indonesian Revolutionary Army. They were facing a General Court Martial. They asked for me to be their Defending Officer at the Court Martial. My enquiring about their welfare while they were in the Cell had led to their asking for me to defend them. My boss told me that I should take on this additional responsibility.

I had never before been exposed to the working of a Court Martial, although I had acquired rudimentary knowledge of military law at Officers' Training School. Luckily I knew a legally qualified Indian officer at Batavia and I consulted him. He pointed out that the Summary of Evidence recorded by the Brigade Major of the Brigade that had captured these soldiers did not have the mandatory warning to them before recording their statements. This warning had to clarify that it was not incumbent on the accused to make any statement but should he do so that would be used as evidence against him during the Court Martial. They had both initially put up their defence which was very damaging for them. They had said that being Muslims they had joined the Indonesians to fight for Islam. If convicted of the charge against them of waging war against the king and of also deserting with arms in the field, they were liable to capital punishment. As advised by my friend, I pointed out to the Court that the Summary of Evidence was not legally valid in the absence of the required warning having been given to the accused. The Court accepted the plea and ordered fresh Summary of Evidence to be recorded. The accused now pleaded that some Indonesian women had given them drugged cigarettes on smoking which they had become unconscious. On gaining consciousness they found themselves in an Indonesian Camp. They decided to join the Indonesians and then try to get back to the unit during operation. This far-fetched defence did not convince the Court. However, it perhaps raised doubts and they got a light senctence of dismissal and eight years Regorious Imprisonment. This was in a way a relief for them otherwise they could have been given a death sentence. I am mentioning this incident to bring out that the communal virus was seeping into the Indian Army and this was a precursor to what happened in 1947 during Partition. I was told that a few hundred Muslim soldiers had deserted from the Indian Army and joined the Indonesians. They were not traced and had to be left behind when the Indian Army was moved out from Indonesia in September 1946 on the interim government under Nehru coming to power at Delhi.

The two soldiers whom I had defended at the General Court Martial in Indonesia were sent to a civil jail in Rawalpindi to serve their sentence of imprisonment. After partition they were released from jail and hailed as heroes in Pakistan, for having served the cause of Islam in Indonesia. They were released from jail and were promoted to JCO rank. I learnt this from one of them who was captured in battle in Kashmir in 1948 by the Indian Army. When the United Nations Commission for India and Pakistan came to the sub-continent in June 1948, Pakistan maintained that its Army had not gone to Kashmir and the raiders were tribesmen from NWFP. I was sent to the Prisoner of War Camp at Yole put up for Pakistani prisoners to collect evidence of Pakistan's participation in the Kashmir war. I met the Pakistani soldier whom I had defended in Indonesia. We recognised each other. I got a statement from him giving details of how Pakistan Army units had been deployed in Kashmir. There were other bits of irrefutable evidence of Pakistan Army's involvement in Kashmir that I managed to collect. All this effort proved unnecessary because Pakistan committed a volte-face and now accepted that regular soldiers had been sent to Kashmir as Indian Army's advance in Kashmir posed a threat to the defence of Pakistan.

§

I had to appear before a Civil Selection Board in India and I left Indonesia in August 1946. This was about a couple of weeks before the Interim Government came to power at Delhi. There were rumours that when the interim government came to power one of the first things they would do was to order withdrawal of Indian troops from Indonesia. It was embarrassing for us to be involved in fighting the Indonesian Army struggling for their Independence, when we were ourselves not Independent and seeking independence from British rule.

§

I returned to India by ship. After my Civil Selection Board at Bangalore, I received orders to report to Alipore Tranist Camp at Calcutta and await posting order. On Arrival at Alipore, I heard of Mohammed Ali Jinnah's declaration of Direct Action Day at Calcutta on 16 August 1946. He had now declared that he would resort to non-constitutional means including violence to achieve his political goal. He even said that he too had a pistol in his pocket. Bengal was the only province which had a Muslim League Ministry. Soon thereafter large scale communal violence started in the city. All officers and soldiers in Alipore Transit Camp were ordered to remain in the Camp and not to move out as large scale communal violence had broken out.

Suhrawardy was the Prime Minister of Bengal. He faithfully carried out the instructions of Jinnah. He let loose his party goons to attack non-Muslims in the city. The Police were made to turn a Nelson's eye to the violence unleashed by Muslim mobs. On the first two days about 2,000 non-Muslims were killed. By the third day Bihari labour and Sikh taxi drivers organised themselves and resorted to counter violence. By the fourth day, some 4,000 people had been killed in Calcutta. The Great Calcutta killings unnerved Suhrawardy and he now asked for the Army to restore order. It was surprising how Sir Frederick Burrows, the Governor of Bengal, had not intervened using his special power to dismiss the Provincial Government. The British obviously had their own agenda. All officers and soldiers who had been confined to the camp were now mobilised to go out on patrols in the city to restore law and order as widespread violence was raging in the city. The streets of Calcutta were littered with dead bodies. Units from Fort William, Ballyganj and Barrackpore were deployed all over the city and the situation brought under control.

I received my posting order to Military Operations Directorate at General Headquarters (India) in New Delhi, later designated Army Headquarters. I proceeded on a short leave to Patna before joining my appointment at Delhi.

Violence now spread from Calcutta to Noakhali region where Hindus were in a great minority. They were being attacked in the villages and many were forcibly converted to Islam. There was large scale killing, abduction and rapine of women. Mahatma Gandhi undertook a *pad yatra* in the rural areas to provide a healing touch and restore normalcy. Large numbers of Hindu Refugees seeking shelter came over to the neighbouring State of Bihar. Strong communal passions got aroused among Hindus in Bihar when they heard of the atrocities perpetrated on Hindus in East Bengal. Hindu mobs went on the rampage particularly in the rural areas where due to communication difficulties security forces found it difficult to restore order quickly. Some 20,000 Muslims were reported to have been killed in Bihar. The stage was now set for the Partition Holocaust which now commenced.

§

I reported for duty at GHQ(I) at South Block in New Delhi in September 1946. The interim government under Jawaharlal Nehru had come to power. Nehru had the designation of Vice-President and was supposed to function like a Prime Minister. Sardar Baldev Singh was the Defence Member of the Council and was to function as Defence Minister. Field Marshal Auchinleck was no longer Defence Member and was now only the Commander-in-Chief of the three Services. The Defence Secretary was now not to work under the C-in-C and was to function directly under the Defence Member.

Hitherto, the Military Operation Directorate had only British officers and clerks. Three Indian officers had been posted for the first time to this Directorate. These were Lt Col SHFJ Manekshaw who had just been promoted to that rank, Major Yahya Khan and me in the rank of Captain. Manekshaw and Yahya were pre-war regular officers and both had qualified from the Staff College which very few Indian officers had done in those days. Manekshaw had been severely wounded in Burma during the battle of Sittang when Indian forces were retreating in 1942. He had earned the gallantry award of Military Cross in that battle. He had just returned from a successful lecture tour of Australia. He later became a Field Marshal and earned legendary fame in 1971. Yahya had been a prisoner of war in Italy and had managed to escape from the camp. He later became the President of Pakistan. I am surprised how I had been selected for posting to the most important Directorate of GHQ(I). I was a war time officer without having qualified at Staff College. Possibly, I was picked up for this assignment because of the recommendation for good work on the General Staff in Indonesia for which I had been recommended for an award. Be that as it may, it was a great break for me to function in the Directorate and witness history changing radically at the highest level in those momentous days of 1946-47 when India emerged a fully Independent Nation after several centuries.

§

My first meeting with both Manekshaw and Yahya Khan was very interesting. I had not met them before but I had heard that they had been posted to MO Directorate and I was looking forward to meeting them. I met Manekshaw in the Car Park at South Block. He was on a small AJS 1.25 horse-power motorbike and I on my 3.5 horse-power Royal Enfield motorbike. Seeing an Indian Lt Col, so rare in those days, I guessed that he would be Manekshaw. I saluted him. He told me "Young man you must have got your fancy motorbike as a dowry." I replied that I was a bachelor. We then moved to our different sections in Military Operations Directorate. The next day I again met Manekshaw in the Car Park. This time he was driving a Riley Sports Car. He looked at me and said that he got that car as dowry and occasionally his wife permitted him to use that car. That was typical of Manekshaw's informality and humour. I will have occasion to refer to this later in the book. We served together in different appointments in the Army ending up to his being the Army Chief and getting the rank of Field Marshal.

Capt Yahya Khan was from the Baluch Regiment. He had been taken a Prisoner in the desert in 1942 and was for sometime in a Prisoners of War Camp in Italy. Capt PP Kumarmangalam from the Artillery was also taken a prisoner in North Africa and was in the same Prisoners of War Camp with Yahya in Italy. They had both picked up Italian and with the help of a local managed to evade the Italian guards and escaped from the Camp. The Allies had landed in Italy. That was the time when Mussolini was assassinated and the Germans had taken over control of operations in Italy. German patrols picked up Kumarmangalam from a village and he was put back in the Prisoners of War Camp. Yahya being a Pathan was fair looking and could pass off for an Italian while Kumarmangalam being from South India was of dark complexion and was easily spotted. When Yahya was in MO Directorate, Kumarmangalam was also in Delhi serving as a Major in Artillery Directorate. I lived in the Officers' Mess on Wellesley Road (now Zakir Hussain Road) near India Gate. Yahya was living with his family in temporary accommodation on the same road a few hundred yards from the Mess. Once when his motorbike was out of order I had given him a lift to South Block on my motorbike. Even in those days Yahya was very fond of his drinks and fast living. I had been to his house a couple of times. His wife was in *purdah*. It is interesting that in 1966 Yahya was Army Chief in Pakistan and Kumarmangalam was Army

Chief in India. In fact, Yahya came to Delhi for talks after the 1965 war and I was detailed as his Liaison Officer. We stayed in Ashoka Hotel. Yahya in a Presidential suite while I had an ordinary room adjacent to his. I had a bar with choicest drinks set up in my room. I was told that Yahya would not drink in public. This would have been much disapproved in Pakistan. He would drink in my room or at Kumarmangalam's house in privacy. One day we had to go for a reception at Rashtrapati Bhawan. Yahya knew that there would be no alcohol served there. Before going to the Reception, he was having a few drinks with me. Some one knocked on the door of my room and I told him to come in. They were a couple of Civil and Military Officers of his delegation who on being told that Yahya was in my room had come there. They were a little aghast to see Yahya having whisky. Yahya told them *"Ama Yar, Kafiron ka Sharab Pina Jayaj Hai. Tum Bhi Kuchchh Le Lo."* (Friends, drinking alcohol of infidels is permissible. You may also take drinks.)

During the 1971 Indo-Pak war Yahya was the President of Pakistan while Manekshaw was the Chief of the Indian Army. I heard a broadcast of Yahya on the radio and I could make out from his voice that he was drunk.

§

In 1946 New Delhi was a white-dominated colonial city of the British Empire in India. The city was confined to the limits of Lutyens Delhi with primarily an official ambience of mostly British officers. Connaught Place was the only shopping centre. It had big shops and there was very little traffic on the roads. Plenty of parking space was available in front of the shops. There were no hotels in New Delhi except the Imperial Hotel which was meant for the Princes. One had to go to Old Delhi to eat in a hotel. Maiden and Cecil were the two hotels which were frequented by Army officers. The only Indian restaurant in New Delhi was Madras Cafe which served South Indian food to the clerical staff of the Central Secretariat who was mostly from the South. In those days, hardly any North Indian ate *idly* and *dosa*. At that time, I had not even heard of these. How things have changed. Now these have become so popular all over North India.

§

I was overawed seeing the very quiet and spotlessly keen hub of Government of India in the massive buildings of North and South Blocks. The Military Operations Directorate was on the first floor of South Block. There was much order and discipline in the corridors of the building with people talking in whispers. Well over 90% Civil and Military officers were British. The senior ones had liveried *Chaprasi* (peon) who wore white turbans, red coat with golden *Kamarbandh* with a small dagger. All senior officers of both civil and military had quite a few decorations shown on their name plates.

Manekshaw, Yahya and I were assigned to different Sections of a large Directorate, Manekshaw to Future Planning, Yahya to Frontier Defence and me to Internal Security. The latter dealt with Aid to Civil Authority during civil disturbances to restore order. Never before or since has the Army been employed so extensively in this role. The INA trials at Red Fort had recently been concluded. The Naval mutiny at Bombay and Karachi had been brought under control. Normalcy was restored in both these cities. The British apprehended that the situation in the country was moving towards what had happened in 1857. The beginnings of the Partition Holocaust had already commenced in Calcutta. Many British officers had forebodings of a coming doom. I was destined to see big events taking place moulding the course of History. Along with this sombre environment there was also a feeling of 'could not careless' among junior war-time British Army officers, looking forward to return home and get back to civilian life.

I had to take over from Captain Henderson who was proceeding to the UK very shortly. He was looking forward to getting back to civilian life. He appeared a very happy-go-lucky person. He told me that he was doing the job both of a Major and his own as the former had gone home on leave. I would, therefore, have to hold the fort and do both Jobs. He welcomed me to what he called the mad house, the GHQ(I). In a lighter vein, he asked me if I knew what the GHQ(I) formation sign, which I was wearing on my Left arm, stood for. It was a shield with the top half Red and the lower deep blue with a golden five pointed star in the middle. I said I did not know. He then told me that it stood for the Star of India rising out of an ocean of Blue Ink into a sky of Red Tape. The present Army Headquarters formation sign is virtually the same except that the five pointed star has been replaced by the Dharma Chakra which is part of our National Emblem. The other flippant introduction he gave me was to enquire if I knew what the three trays on the table marked In, Out and Pending stood for. I said that as written on them the three trays were for incoming papers, outgoing papers and pending papers. He laughed and gave his own interpretation. He said that they stood for *Abhi Nahin, Kabhi Nahin* and *Fikar Nahin* (Not Now, Never, Not to Bother).

After such an informal and humorous introduction, he got down to explaining the various aspects of the duties that I would be performing. He said that he wanted to do all this within an hour or so before going to the Officers' Mess where he was staying. He had to pack up his entire belongings, say farewell to friends and depart for the UK, the next day. He now sent for the British Head Clerk and he asked him to bring the day's *Dak*. He advised me that the best course in GHQ(I) was to do as little work as possible and pass the buck to others. He briefed me about the Joint Operations Room that had been set up after the RIN Mutiny. The Operations Room had an officer each from Army, Navy and Air Force constantly on duty round the clock. Up to date maps of troops' locations and incidents had to be readily available in the Operations Room. I would be responsible to feed the required data from the Army and also act as a Staff Section officer to meet the requirements of the Operations Room. A map showing locations of Army combat units had also to be maintained in the office room of the C-in-C which was close to the Operations Room. This map had to be updated every morning before the Chief came to his office. It was my responsibility to do so. Thereafter he handed over the keys of the steel almirah in the office. He said that he had not checked the papers in the almirah before he had taken over and hence, there was no need for any signed handing /taking over papers between us. He now gave me a warm handshake and said good luck to me while he got ready to go home to what he called Blighty (UK).

§

I opened the almirah and found some Highly Secret and sensitive papers in it. One was called Assessment of Loyalty of the Indian Army. The other had the title Operation Gondola. Both had a security classification that I had not come across earlier. It was TOP SECRET

NOT FOR INDIAN EYES. This classification sounded very strange and of course made me very inquisitive. I got down to reading it on priority. The Assessment was written by Major-General O'Brien, the Director of Military Intelligence. It had been written in the wake of the Indian National Army (INA) trials at the Red Fort. A Hindu, a Sikh and a Muslim officer of the Indian Army who after surrendering to the Japanese Army in early 1942 in Malaya were put in a Prisoner of War Camp. Later they joined the INA. The INA had been raised from among Indian Prisoners of War with Japan who wanted to fight against the British for the Independence of India. After these officers had been captured by the British in Burma, they had been brought to India for a public trial on charges of treason against the government and for joining the enemy to wage war against the King. These were very serious charges calling for capital punishment. It was felt by the British that conducting their public trials in Delhi will disillusion the Indian people about the INA. These officers, along with the Japanese, were alleged to have committed atrocities against Indian officers and men who had remained loyal to the British and had not joined them for fighting for India's Independence. They were alleged to have killed some such Indian soldiers. The British hoped that the details of their atrocities would generate anger against them by the people. This would ensure that the INA did not get the sympathy of the Indian people. They were proved wrong. This did not happen. On the contrary a patriotic fervour swept the country. There was a tremendous support generated in the country for the INA. These officers being tried at Red Fort became national heroes. Thus these trials turned out to be very counterproductive for the British. The appreciation by the DMI was a highly professional analysis of the ground realities bringing out that the Indian Army could no longer be relied upon to uphold British rule over India. At the beginning of the Second World War there were about 450 Indian officers in the Army. By the end of the war their numbers had risen to 11,500. Among the 450 pre-war officers, there were two categories. Some 30 odd were King's Commissioned Indian Officers (KCIOs) who had been commissioned from England between 1920 and 1934. They were mostly in the rank of Lt Col with a sprinkling of about 4 or 5 Brigadiers. They were assessed to be very loyal. The second category was of some 400 pre-war permanent officers commissioned from Dehradun from 1934 to 1939. They were called Indian Commissioned

Officers (ICOs). They were considered as less loyal to the British as they had been discriminated against in their early career before the war compared to their British counterparts. They were given lower rates of pay than the latter. However, holding permanent jobs, they had more at stake and could be expected to be more loyal than the 11,000 non-permanent commissioned officers recruited during the war. The ECOs (Emergency Commissioned Officers) had been exposed to our national movement for freedom when they were students at schools and colleges. As Platoon and Company Commanders, they were in close contact with the soldiers working under them. Besides, the non-permanent officers faced an uncertain future after release from the Army. As far as the soldiers were concerned, the strength of the Army which had been 1.5 lakh in 1939 had drastically increased to about 22 lakh during the war years. The old concept of martial class and recruitment restricted to loyal families had given way to tremendous war-time expansion. After the war, the bulk of the Army running into several lakhs had to be disbanded. The INA trials had brought out a new fervour for Independence amongst the soldiers. Further, they knew about the mutinies that had taken place in the Navy at Bombay, the Army at Jabalpur and the Air Force at Karachi. An economically and militarily weak Britain was now in no position to maintain a large British military presence in India. The logical conclusion of all this was that sooner the British quit India, the better it would be for them. This view got confirmed in 1956 when Attlee was on a visit to India. He was the Prime Minister of Britain in 1946 when the decision to quit India was taken by the British Government. Attlee told Chatterjee, the then Governor of West Bengal, that the loss of trust in the loyalty of the Indian Army was the main factor behind the decision to Quit India in haste in 1947. I admired the logical and analytical recommendation made by Major General O'Brian in 1946.

The other Top Secret Not For Indian Eyes, document was Plan GONDOLA. It was a follow up of the previous paper by Maj Gen O'Brian. This was a plan for the evacuation of British civilian families in India and the repatriation of British Army troops to the UK. All British civilians from outlying locations in provinces had to be withdrawn to 1 or 2 KEEPS (Camps) in a province. These were temporary camps guarded by a mix of British, Gorkha and the Indian troops. The Gorkhas were considered more loyal than Indian troops.

The Gorkha units had only British officers and no Indian officers among them. Moreover, being mostly from Nepal they had hardly anything to do with the Indian Freedom Movement in India. From KEEPS in provinces, the British civilians with their families were to be moved to SAFES located near ports of Calcutta, Visakhapatnam, Madras, Cochin, Bombay and Karachi. They were guarded at the SAFES mostly by British troops awaiting repatriation to the UK depending upon the availability of required shipping. This Plan was also dovetailed to the repatriation Plans of the British Army Units.

§

I have mentioned the task entrusted to me for maintaining an up-to-date map of India showing locations of combat Army units in the country. Each category of unit had to be shown in pins of different colours—brown pins for Indian units, green pins for Gorkha units and red pins for British units. Obviously, the strategy was not to have too many brown pins in a location without some green and red pins in that location or nearby military stations. This was to guard against any repeat of what had happened in 1857.

§

The MO-2 Section of the Military Operations Directorate, worked under a British Lieutenant Colonel, a Major and a Captain in that Section. For a few months, I was doing the work of both the Major and the Captain because the Major had gone on Special End of War leave. We looked after the joint operations room of the three Services already referred to earlier. This room was later partitioned to provide accommodation for the office of the Foreign Secretary, his secretariat and a waiting room. It commanded a good view of Central Vista (now Vijay Chowk) and the road going up between the North Block and South Block to the Viceroy's House, now Rashtrapati Bhawan. A similar room close to the room towards the West had the office of the C-in-C, his Private Secretary and a Visitor's Room. This complex is now the office of the External Affairs Minister. MO-2 was the administrative section for looking after the requirements of the large staff working in the operations room. It also provided inputs of information regarding locations of units and details of violent incidents taking place in the country. In 1946-47, MO-2 was the hub of activities in the key Military Operations Directorate. Our Director was Major Gen WDA Lentaigne of Chindid fame in Burma. I have mentioned him earlier when he was commanding the Jungle Training Division at Saharanpur where I had been trained for jungle warfare prior to going to Burma. Later, he was Commandant of Staff College at Wellington where I was a student in 1952. Military Operations Directorate came under Lt Gen Sir Arthur Smith, the Chief of General Staff. He was the next ranking Army Officer in GHQ(I) after the C-in-C, Field Marshal Sir Claude Auchinleck. He had been his Chief of Staff in North Africa during 1942. Arthur Smith's younger brother was Sir Norman Smith, the then Director of Intelligence Bureau, a key top official of Government of India. As a very young and inexperienced Captain, I now had exposure to the very top key and awe-inspiring seniors. I also became witness to some historic events at the Capital taking place in those bygone days that were moulding the course of history of our country. Besides, I felt elevated and much inspired by my brief interactions with Civil and Military intellectuals who later attained international eminence. These were Mr Philip Mason, Joint Secretary (G) in Defence Department and Lt Col Masters. Mason had more service in the ICS than my age and was of the same vintage as my father. I interacted with him officially when on a few occasions I carried Top Secret files to be delivered to him. He was extremely polite and thanked me for doing so. On one or two occasions, he even asked me to sit on the chair opposite his table and made some personal enquires about me. He became the famous author of a two-volume book, *The Men Who Ruled India*. This book is an excellent history of the Indian Civil Service starting from its inception to 1947, when the British quit India. The title of the first volume is *FOUNDERS* and the second is *GUARDIANS*. He also wrote another master piece called *A Matter of Honour* which is a history of the India Army. The theme of the book is that the Indian soldiers served under the British to uphold their honour and were not mercenaries as such. This is a very fine record of the history of the Indian Army. Lt Col John Masters had been the GSO-1 in MO-2 before my then boss Lt Col FHB Ingal. I had read Master's first book, *Bugles and Tigers*. This is a delightful account of his regimental life at Bakloh, where the Fourth Gorkha Rifles Regimental Centre was located. He had acquired fame in military circles as the author of this book. He was from 4th Gurkha Rifles, the same Regiment as our Director, Maj Gen Lentaign. After the Second World War, he had been taking things easy while serving in Military Operations Directorate. I saw some hand-written manuscripts for his book *Road Past Mandalay*, a personal account of Operations in Burma. He visited us a couple of times in Military Operations Directorate. He had written a series of books on Military Service in India by his ancestors. There is a Col Savage in every book who was his ancestor. The books in this series represent different generations. *Coromandel Coast* covers the Arcot War, *Deceivers* the operations against Thugs, *Night Runners of Bengal* covers the 1857 rebellion and *Bhawani Junction*, the Quit India Movement of 1942. The Col Savage in the last book is an account of his own experience as a Battalion Commander. This book was filmed in Hollywood. This made him world famous and also earned him a lot of money. On retirement from the Army he had settled down in California.

§

One day in February 1947, I remember while standing in the projection of South Block from our Operations Room, a senior friend of mine, Maj Spittle and I saw a black limousine flying the Union Jack going up the slope between North Block and South Block. There was a cavalcade of cars following that car. Spittle remarked here goes the great-grandson of Queen Victoria, Mountbatten, who has come to hand over a big gift to the people of India and wind up the great empire which was the jewel in the British Crown. Being a little sensitive, I felt that I should give him a suitable reply. I told him, "Spittle, this is no gift to the people of India. They have earned it through a long struggle and Winston Churchill in his life time can see the liquidation of the British Empire." I reminded him of some of the remarks of Winston Churchill. He had referred with indignation to the half naked fakir having talks with Lord Irwin, the Viceroy of India. And also the other remark of Churchill, "I have not become the Prime Minister of His Majesty's Government to preside over the liquidation of the British Empire." Spittle appeared uncomfortable with what I had said. He told me that the majority of the people in Britain were not happy with what Churchill had said. I stated that he was correct and quoted the proclamation of Queen Victoria in 1858 when the East India Company was wound up and she became the Empress of India. I said the extract of her proclamation is inscribed on the entrance arch of North Block. It reads, "Democracy and freedom are gifts which have to be earned by people. It would be our endeavour to bring up the people of India to a stage in which they can earn these." Spittle was quite happy with what I said. He invited me to come inside our adjacent Operations Room and we had a cup of coffee together.

§

In early 1947, Sardar Patel sent for my father to work in the Intelligence Bureau at Delhi. Hitherto the Bureau had only British officers at its Headquarters and my father had been an exception even in the field because he had served as Central Intelligence Officer at Patna working for the Bureau. Sir Norman Smith was the Director. Sardar Patel, the Home and the States Member of the executive council, felt that it will not be prudent to share some sensitive intelligence information with any British officer. My father was the only Indian officer who had experience of working both in the Provincial CID and also as Central Intelligence Officer in the field. He wanted him to be brought to Delhi as the number two to Sir Norman Smith. Dr Sri Krishna Sinha, Chief Minister of Bihar, was reluctant to make the services of my father available to the Centre as he had earmarked him to take over as the Chief of Bihar Police after Independence. I was quite amused to read all this in Durga Das's book on the correspondence of Sardar Patel. A copy of the letter by Sardar Patel to the Chief Minister of Bihar is reproduced as Appendix 2.

My father arrived in Delhi to take over as the number two to Sir Norman Smith in March 1947. He was temporarily given accommodation at 10, Prithviraj Road. I shifted from the Officers' Mess to live with my parents. After a few months, we moved to 5, Duplex Road (now Kamraj Road) near South Block. While we were at 10, Prithviraj Road, Sardar Patel was a few houses away in 1, Prithviraj Road. He used to go for his morning walks in Lodhi Cardens while I was out jogging there. I would stop running when I would see him and wish him with reverence. Soon he would start giving me a smile of recognition. That was the nearest I ever got to him.Across the roundabout opposite Sardar Patel's residence was a double-storied palatial house at 10, Aurangzeb Road (now Dr APJ Abdul Kalam Road) in which Mohammed Ali Jinnah was living.

This house was owned by him besides another palatial house in Bombay. He was a flourishing Barrister with a very good income.

Close by was a double-storied building at 17 York (now Motilal Nehru Road) where Jawaharlal Nehru was living. Sometimes in the evening while passing this house, I used to see a light burning on the first floor with someone working in his office. That must have been Jawaharlal Nehru. Birla House is also in the vicinity of these houses where Gandhiji used to occasionally live. Living on Prithviraj Road, I felt that I was living close to an area in which the course of history of the country was being moulded. I may also mention that after Partition was announced, I often saw Muslim officers going to Pakistan visiting Jinnah at his house. Perhaps this was the beginning of the politicisation of Pakistan Army. I never saw any Indian Army Officer visiting the houses of Congress leaders in Delhi.

§

On 3 June 1947, the British government announced its decision to Partition India into two Dominions of India and Pakistan. There was much speculation regarding the future of the Indian Army which had served under the British for over two centuries. The war time Indian Army of over two million was in the process of being demobilized and reduced to the strength of 4 lakh. We heard that a Joint Defence Council will be set up with Mountbatten as Chairman and Jawaharlal Nehru and Mhammad Ali Jinnah as members. There were even rumours that the two Dominions will have a common Governor-General in Mountbatten. Auchinleck as the Commander-in-Chief would be in attendance at this Council. Two senior Indian Army officers, Brig Cariappa and Col Ayub Khan, had issued a statement that the Indian Army should not be partitioned and should serve under the Joint Defence Council. So far as a common Governor-General was concerned, Jinnah was totally opposed to this. He wanted himself to be the Governor-General of Pakistan. Jawaharlal Nehru invited Mountbatten to be the first Governor-General of India, which he readily accepted. Both Nehru and Jinnah rejected out of hand any proposal to have a common Army for the two Dominions. This meant that the Indian Army would have to be partitioned between India and Pakistan. This was to be done on the basis of a formula of 2/3rd and 1/3rd for India and Pakistan respectively. The undivided Army had to be vivisected. This applied not only to personnel but also to stores and equipment. The various Regiments of the Army were divided between the Indian and

Pakistan Army on the basis of the 2/3rd and 1/3rd formula. Muslim companies of Indian Regiments were transferred to Pakistan Regiments and non-Muslims in Pakistan Regiments to Indian Regiments. I had served with a Punjabi Muslim Company of 6 JAT Regiment before Partition during the war in Burma. When Muslim troops from my Regimental Centre at Bareilly were being sent to 8 PUNJAB Regiment in Pakistan, I had gone to the Centre to wish them good bye. This was a sentimental moment for both those going to Pakistan and others remaining in India. During the British regime there was no one class combat Regiment. Each Regiment had 50% Muslims and 50% non-Muslims. This was obviously because the British wanted to use one as counterpoise to the other. However, Gorkha Regiments with exclusively British Officers were one class Regiments because their loyalty was trusted more by the British. After Independence one class Regiments became the norm in both Indian and Pakistan Armies. The Jat Regiment got two companies of Jats from 15 Punjab Regiment which went to Pakistan. Thus after Independence, Jat Regiment like many other Regiments became a one class Regiment.

So far as officers were concerned, those from the majority community in India or Pakistan had no option but to stay with the Army of their country. Officers from the minority community had the option of serving in either country. As far as I know, no non-Muslim officer opted to serve with Pakistan Army. However, quite a few Muslim officers from India chose to continue serving in the Indian Army. Although the bulk of Muslim Officers opted to go to Pakistan, quite a few Muslim Officers chose to remain with the Indian Army. Brigadier Mohammed Usman, the Hero of Naushera was one of them. He stayed with the Indian Army.

§

After 3 June 1947 to impress a sense of urgency in Government of India to do all the ground work for partition, Mountbatten had a special wall calendar prepared. Apart from the date, this showed the number of days left for Partition to emphasise that all the work required in various offices had to be completed expeditiously and within the time frame. I also had one such calendar in my office. I was sent to Simla along with one Major Basir going to Pakistan to go through the old records of Military Operations Directorate containing a history of nearly two centuries. A British Army Head Clerk who was working in our Directorate was also with us to carry out this stupendous task. Thousands of files had to be sorted out within a week which was obviously an impossible task. However, we managed to do so on the basis of a formula. The title of the file could just be seen by us and those pertaining to areas earmarked for Pakistan were to be sent to Pakistan Army and the others retained by us. Files about which there was any doubt or dispute were destroyed. In the process, I confess we must be guilty of destroying important historical records.

One day the Defence Secretary, Mr Dundas of the ICS, rushed into the Operations Room. He had opted for Pakistan and was going as Defence Secretary to Karachi on Partition. All the records, furniture and other assets of the Army in Delhi were stacked up in hutments near South Block where the Sena Bhavan has now come up. Gen Lentaign, the DMO was also in the Operations Room at that time. Dundas said that Hindu and Sikh mobs comprising refugees who had come from Pakistan had assembled near the hutments with *mashals* threatening to burn the stores going to Pakistan. Lentaign said that he would ask the Joint Operations Room to send a mobile patrol to deal with this situation. It would take a little while for any patrol to fetch up. He asked me to collect a few Defence Security Corps men of the guard at the Defence Gate and go to the spot to take suitable action. In those days, we all used to come to offices armed with our pistols and the sentries had their rifles. I rushed to the spot with four armed Defence Security Corps personnel and found a threatening mob shouting Pakistan Murdabad with *mashals* in their hands near the site. The mob comprised Hindus and Sikhs and perhaps were all refugees from West Pakistan who had come to Delhi. I ordered the soldiers to fire overhead and the crowd started dispersing. After ten-fifteen minutes an Army patrol arrived and I arranged for a permanent armed picquette to be posted at that site. Dundas had accompanied me and was very happy with the way I had dealt with the situation. He asked me to accompany him to the office of Field Marshal Auchinleck. He told him of what had been done and Auchinleck complimented me.

§

I also recall that when Muslim officers of the Indian Army were departing for Pakistan, the Indian officers organised a function at the Delhi Gymkhana Club to bid them farewell. Being the senior most Indian officer, Brigadier KM Cariappa was the Chief Host. We presented a Silver Trophy to officers going to Pakistan. The Trophy showed two soldiers, one Muslim and the other non-Muslim wearing their different style turbans in kneeling position ready to fire against a common enemy. Lord Mountbatten, the then Viceroy, and Field Marshal Sir Claude Auchinleck, the Commander-in-Chief, also attended the function. In his farewell speech, Brigadier Cariappa said, "We have lived like brothers in war and peace. Many of our friends are now going to Pakistan. We shall always remain brothers." Alas, this did not happen. In a little over two months after Independence, Pakistan invaded Kashmir on 22 October 1947 and officers of the two armies were now fighting each other in battle.

On 15 August 1947, Auchinleck became the Supreme Commander with his Headquarters in South Block, New Delhi. General Sir Bob Lockhart became C-in-C Indian Army and our Army Headquarters moved to Red Fort, New Delhi. General Sir Frank Messervy became C-in-C Pakistan Army. The erstwhile Northern Command at Rawalpindi became GHQ Pakistan. The Supreme Commander had no operational role. He was required to supervise the Partition of assets and personnel of the undivided Indian Army and also arrange the repatriation of British Army Units from India to the UK. By October, he completed this task and his Headquarters was wound up. Our Army Headquarters returned from Red Fort to South Block.

As a tailpiece, I may add that Field Marshal Sir Claude Auchinleck was offered a peerage on return to UK in 1948. He declined saying that he had served the undivided Indian Army for forty-four years and now that the Army stood partitioned with some of its elements fighting each other in Kashmir, it was a sad moment for him and he would not like to be raised to peerage.

§

On 14 August 1947, I had come to South Block from my then office in Red Fort and met Spittle in our old Operations Room in South Block. We went out to the projection from where we saw the Union Jack fluttering over North Block. We could not see the Union Jack fluttering over South Block because it was concealed from our view from that place. Spittle remarked with a lump in his throat that we are witnessing the end of an era; today was the last day for the Union Jack to fly over the Indian Central Secretariat. I also had a lump in my throat and said tomorrow there would be a new Dawn when our National Flag will fly there and all over India.

§

Dawn and After: Sunshine and Cloud

On the night of 14-15 August 1947, all of us in the family including my grandparents living in my father's house listened to the mid-night speech of Jawaharlal Nehru in the Parliament that was broadcast by All India Radio. There were no transistors or televisions in those days. We heard Jawaharlal Nehru's soul-stirring speech. "Long years ago, we made a tryst with destiny and now the time comes, when we shall redeem our pledge, not wholly or in full measure, but very substantially. At the stroke of the midnight hour, when the world sleeps, India will awake to life and freedom. A moment comes but rarely in history, when we step from the old to the new, when an age ends, and when the soul of a nation long suppressed, finds utterance." All of us had a lump in our throats. I could well imagine the feelings of my grandfather who had seen British imperialism at its zenith in the nineteenth century and early twentieth century. He remarked, "I am glad that I have lived to see this momentous day." Next morning, he asked me if our National Flag will now be flying over the Secretariat. I told him that I had seen the British Union Jack over both North Block and South Block the previous afternoon and had learnt that from the next day the Indian National Flag will be flying over all official buildings. He wanted to be shown this. We were living in a house barely a few hundred yards from the Secretariat. I took him in my father's car and showed him our National Flag flying over North Block, South Block and the Parliament House. He was overwhelmed and I could see his wet eyes. Thereafter, I proceeded to my office in Red Fort. That day was a holiday for everyone, but the Army was deployed all over the city to maintain law and order, and I did not have a holiday. As mentioned in the previous chapter, after Partition was announced on 3 June 1947, Army Headquarters had moved from South Block to Red Fort. We had to work hard to put up our offices and new Operations Room in the barracks inside the Fort.

When I reached Red Fort on the morning of Independence Day, I found our National Flag flying over the Fort's rampart. I enquired as to who had hoisted our flag there. I was told that it had been done by the Havildar Guard Commander at the gate of the Fort. From subsequent years, the Prime Minister of India began to unfurl the flag at Red Fort and address the Nation from its rampart. Pakistan had got Independence a day earlier on 14 August 1947 because Lord Mountbatten, the Viceroy could not be at two capitals on the same day. He had been to Karachi on 14 August 1947 where the capital of Pakistan was then located. Jinnah took over as Governor-General on that date. The Pakistan flag was unfurled at a function in the presence of Mountbatten. In India, Mountbatten attended the Indian Independence Day function on 15 August 1947. He was now only the Governor-General of India and had shed his designation of Viceroy.

On the afternoon of 15 August 1947 there was to be an Independence Day Parade at India Gate. Lord Mountbatten as Governor-General was to unfurl the Indian National Flag on that occasion. Maj Gen Rajendra Sinhji, the General Officer Commanding Delhi Area, was to command the Parade. I had gone to witness the parade. There was tremendous enthusiasm among the people. We saw Mountbatten and Jawaharlal Nehru coming down in the Ceremonial Horse Carriage escorted by the Governor-General's mounted Body Guard. There was a large jostling crowd on either side of the King's Way (now Rajpath). As the cavalcade of Mountbatten and Nehru went down the road to the site of the parade at India Gate, the crowd was shouting the slogan *'Pandit Nehru ki Jai'*, *'Pandit Mountbatten ki Jai'*. At the site of the parade, as Mountbatten and Nehru mounted the dais to unfurl the National Flag and the Parade Commander gave the National Salute, the crowd broke the cordon and engulfed the Parade area. The Parade had to be cancelled but the unfurling of the flag was completed to the sound of 101 guns salute in the distance. Total confusion reigned. My friend Capt Hukam Singh Yadav who was the ADC of Mountbatten mentioned to me the interesting remark made by Mountbatten to Nehru that it was the best Parade he had seen in his long military career.

§

We got the welcome news in September 1947 that the Supreme Headquarters was now completing its task and was being wound up.

We would be moving back to South Block. Functioning from the Red Fort was not a very satisfactory arrangement. Apart from the distance to Ministry of Defence, and our wasting time travelling with escort to Red Fort, working conditions there were very poor. The open grounds in and around the Red Fort had a few lakhs Muslim refugees in temporary shelters living in very unhygienic conditions generating a swarm of flies. The other places where these refugees had been given shelter were, Purana Qila, the then open grounds up to the Yamuna and in Nizamuddin Railway Station Area where there was then plenty of open space. The Army not only had to protect these refugee camps from Hindu and Sikh mobs but also arrange for their evacuation by train to Wagah Border.

A thought occurred to me that in the medieval period, Mohammed Bin Tughlak had shifted the Capital of India from Delhi to Daulatabad in the South as that was in the centre of his Empire. He soon found that life was difficult in Daulatabad because of shortage of water. He brought back his Capital to Delhi. Our move back to South Block was something similar.

§

The Army had a very challenging task to restore law and order when the civil administration had virtually collapsed in Delhi and Punjab. In those days, all Army officers carried weapons on them to protect themselves from marauding mobs. While Indian officers had to do this, it was an irony to see that British officers of the Army could freely move around because neither Muslim nor non-Muslim mobs would attack them. I recall an incident in July when going to Red Fort, I came under sniper fire from the top of a building on the other side of the road near Faiz Bazar Police Station. The office of the pro-Muslim-League newspaper, *Dawn* used to be in that building and was shifting to Karachi, the then Capital of Pakistan. I had to get a platoon of the Army located at Faiz Bazar Police Station to clear the *Dawn* building before proceeding to my office at Red Fort.

Although it was a relief to get back to South Block, conditions on the sub-continent continued to deteriorate. I had to continue working round the clock because I was dealing with internal security in Military Operations Directorate of Army Headquarters. This move suited me very much because I was living with my father on Duplex

Road (now Kamraj Road). Our house was only about a thousand yards from South Block.

§

After Independence, Mountbatten had become a Constitutional Head of State and it was the job of the Cabinet under Jawaharlal Nehru to address problems of governance. Mountbatten had proceeded to Simla (now Shimla). With the situation deteriorating by the day and things getting out of hand, both Nehru and Patel decided to ask Mountbatten to return from Simla. With his vast military experience, they felt he would be of help in restoring law and order in the country. I had not heard of this till one evening when Col Manekshaw asked me to accompany him to the Governor-General's House (now Rashtrapati Bhavan) for setting up an Operations Room. I had to take a couple of clerks and draftsmen with me. Manekshaw briefed me about what had to be done and we worked together for a while. Thereafter, he left me to complete the task. He told me that he would be back early next morning to check that the task had been completed as directed by him. We had to put up two large maps of India on the wall. One map showed the location of all the combat units in North India and the other, the sites of various serious incidents of violence that had taken place in the recent weeks. Manekshaw himself went back to his office to prepare a detailed brief. Mountbatten was expected to return from Simla the next morning. He was to preside over a Cabinet meeting in that room the next morning at 10 o'clock. We worked all night against time and had the Operations Room ready as required. Throughout the night the Viceroy's staff was very considerate serving us rounds of coffee with excellent eats. Manekshaw came early in the morning and was satisfied with what we had done as per his instructions. By 9 o'clock in the morning, Mountbatten walked into the room dressed immaculately in his Admiral's uniform looking as fresh as ever after his night long journey from Simla to Delhi. This was the second time I was seeing Mountbatten from close quarters. The earlier occasion was also in an Operations Room at Batavia (now Jakarta) in Indonesia. Mountbatten was briefed by Manekshaw and he checked a few things on the map. He then turned around to his Military Secretary, Col Douglas Currie, and enquired if we had been well looked after during the night while we managed to complete the good work we had done. He replied that we had been given several rounds of coffee and eats. He smiled and told us, "Well done." He then went away. At 10 o'clock, the emergency meeting of the Cabinet was held in that room presided over by Mountbatten and attended by Nehru, Patel and others. Of course, we were not there because we left the Governor-General's House after Mountbatten had satisfied himself that a proper Operations Room had been got ready overnight for him.

There has been some controversy in recent times about Mountbatten presiding over meetings of the Cabinet. In a democracy, it is the Prime Minister who should preside over meetings of the Cabinet. Those were extraordinary days and I feel there was no harm in getting Mountbatten to do so. Some ultra nationalists like to maintain that this never happened as it hurts the sense of their National pride. Many years later, the authors of the famous book *Freedom at Midnight*, Larry Collins and Dominique Lapierre came to Delhi when Manekshaw was the Army Chief and I a Major-General on his staff. I was asked to show them around some important places in Delhi which had relevance to the events of 1947. Among other places, I showed them the Operations Room we had set up at Rashtrapati Bhavan where Cabinet Meetings presided over by Mountbatten used to be held. They wrote about Mountbatten presiding over Cabinet meetings in those days. I was criticized by some people for telling these authors about it. They felt that I should not have done so.

I later learnt that Mountbatten at that meeting of the Cabinet in early September 1947 had suggested that a new Command Headquarters be set up to undertake the gigantic task of restoring law and order in Delhi and Punjab and also evacuation of millions of Muslim refugees. He offered the Viceroy's luxurious Special Train to be used as the mobile Headquarters of the new Command. Pursuant to this decision about a Headquarters, Delhi and East Punjab Command (now Western Command) was set up on 20 September 1947. Lt Gen Sir Dudley Russell was appointed the Army Commander with a skeleton staff of about 12 officers who were all British officers except me. I was posted as General Staff Officer Operations in the rank of Major. Perhaps I had been selected because I had been dealing with internal security for the previous one year in the Military

Operations Directorate. My boss in that Directorate was Col FHB Ingall who had served as the Principal General Staff Officer under General Russell when he was commanding a Division in North Africa. He had also commanded an Armoured Brigade under Russell when he was Corps Commander in Italy. Soon after Partition, Ingall went to Pakistan and set up Pakistan Military Academy at Kakul on the same lines as Indian Military Academy, Dehradun. He was promoted Brigadier and served as Commandant of that Academy for nearly ten years.

§

Lt Gen Sir Dudley Russell, designated Army Commander of Delhi and East Punjab Command, was a highly decorated and experienced Senior Army Officer. He was of the same vintage as my grandfather. He had done well as a Regimental Officer in the First World War in France and had earned two gallantry awards in that war. Russell had commanded a Division during the famous and decisive battle of El Alamein in the desert working under Field Marshal Montgomery who was the Army Commander. He had also commanded a Corps in Italy while Montgomery was still the Army Commander. I was fortunate to get the experience of serving under such a senior and distinguished Army Officer. Recently he was commanding troops deployed in Bihar during the massive communal riots in that State in which over 20,000 people had been massacred. He had managed to restore law and order in a fairly short time. My father was then the Central Intelligence Officer of the Intelligence Bureau at Patna and had been deputed as the Liaison Officer between his Headquarters and the State Government.

On 20 September 1947, I reported to Russell at his residence on 8, Roberts Road (now Teen Murti Marg). I was carrying an Operation Instruction from Army Headquarters addressed to him along with my posting order on his staff. It was a hot and humid afternoon. I saw a pair of white legs of a person working under a Rolls Royce car in the portico of the building. I thought that the legs would be of a British soldier driver of the General. I enquired if the General was at home. I got a rather cheeky reply, "May be." I felt that this soldier was being insolent with me which British soldiers sometimes used to be with Indian officers. I was wondering what to say when that person came out from under the car. He was bare bodied wearing just a pair of khaki shorts. When I looked at him with his bald head and imposing long moustache, I realised that he was the General. He said, "So you are Sinha, Ingall told me about you. Give me a few minutes and I will wash up and then meet you." He asked me to wait in his sitting room. After a few minutes, he came out of the room in his full dress. I felt very overawed in his presence. I was a little nervous. He immediately put me at ease asking me to sit down while a cup of tea was being brought for me. He started the conversation by saying that Ingall who was his Staff Officer during the Second World War had spoken to him very favourably about me. Russell also told me that he had met my father in Bihar during the recent riots. He added that many years earlier he had been on deputation as Central Intelligence Officer at Peshawar in the Intelligence Bureau set up. I am sure he did all this to enable me to feel comfortable working under him. I would say that this was a good way for a senior officer to deal with someone so junior and to get the best out of him. Russell then asked me to set up his office in a hutment which had been allotted for his Headquarters, where the Sena Bhavan now stands.

To do justice to the task given by him, I went all out to set up his office. I virtually raided the furniture yard of the Chief Administrative Officer, Ministry of Defence to get necessary furniture for the Army Commander's office. By next morning when Russell came to the office he was happy to see a functional but an austere office ready for him. I had an office table with suitable chairs and sofa-set and a carpet in the room. The Army Signals had installed a telephone system overnight. He was pleased and complimented me for what I had done. I realised that what I had done was something very minimum and not in keeping with the high office that he held. Reflecting on this, I recalled that 36 years later when I held the same appointment and was Army Commander, Western Command, I had a luxurious office. Things in 1947 were so different.

§

Delhi and East Punjab Command had three subordinate Army formations. There were two Areas, Delhi Area under Maj Gen Rajendra Sinhji and East Punjab Area under Maj Gen KS Thimayya. Both these Generals later became Army Chiefs. Our third formation was Military Evacuation Organization at Lahore under Maj Gen BS Chimney, responsible for organising evacuation of non-Muslim refugees from West Pakistan. Apart from restoring law and order in North India, our Command was also responsible for protection and evacuation of millions of Muslim refugees from India to Pakistan. Besides, we put up a tented camp for 5 lakh non-Muslim refugees from Pakistan at Kurukshetra. This was a staging camp for them before they were dispersed by the civil administration to places vacated by Muslims who had left for Pakistan. All this was a gigantic task but with all the handicaps and hiccups, we managed to complete them fairly successfully. However, the fact remains that during the Partition Holocaust, millions were killed and millions uprooted. Perhaps this was the worst such tragedy in the history of mankind.

§

Our immediate problem in Command Headquarters was to ensure normalcy in Delhi. Communal violence had escalated considerably as non-Muslim refugees who came from Pakistan, narrated their harrowing tales of atrocities on them in West Pakistan. Hindu and Sikh mobs started increasingly to attack Muslims in Delhi. I remember that our old cook, Zahoor, who had worked for my father for many years was with us in Delhi. We were living in a house on Duplex (now Kamraj Road) close to the Central Secretariat. Sunehari Bagh Masjid (mosque) in a traffic roundabout was very near our house. This mosque is still there. Zahoor was not a staunch Muslim but would only occasionally go to that mosque. We asked him to stop going there till normalcy was restored. Hindu and Sikh mobs had attacked that mosque and damaged it. To ensure his safety, we changed Zahoor's name to Ram Prasad and got him to wear *Dhoti* instead of *Pajama*. My immediate boss, Lt Col MM Badshah, living in a bungalow on Prithviraj Road had changed his name plate at the gate so that he may not be mistaken for a Muslim. He now spelt his name in full, Lt Col Man Mohan Badshah. I am mentioning these facts to depict the situation in our national capital at that time. I was told that there were differences between Nehru and Patel over accommodation vacated by Muslims who had left for Pakistan. Nehru wanted such houses to be kept vacant for them in case they returned. Patel on the other hand insisted that non-Muslim refugees coming from West Pakistan should be accommodated in these houses. Patel had his way. This is being trotted out by some people to tarnish the image of Patel and accuse him of being communal.

A family friend of ours, Hakim Mohammad Saleh from Patna had gone for Haj and returned from Mecca. He had landed at Safdarjung Airport wearing white clothes normally worn by people going or coming from Haj. In those days of communal violence, it was highly dangerous for anyone to be seen on the roads in that dress. He had our telephone number and rang us up from the airport. My uncle who was also in the Army and I went to the Airport armed with our weapons and escorted him to the Railway Station for his journey to Patna under escort.

§

Army Sub-Units were deployed at each Police Station and sensitive areas to immediately deal with incidents of violence. There were also mobile reserves at important areas with Police guides for immediate action against rampaging mobs. At the Town Hall in Chandni Chowk in Old Delhi, we had a Joint Operations Room with the civil authorities functioning round the clock. It had representatives of the Magistracy, the Police, the Fire Brigade, the Telephone Department and Doctors with First Aid equipment and Ambulance. The Joint Operations Room was provided communication facilities. Each representative from different departments was in communication with his higher authorities. It was the hub of all activities dealing with widespread violence in the city. An Army Officer coordinated the functioning of this nerve centre. I often visited this place. It worked very effectively to control disturbances in the city and provided help to people in distress.

§

In September 1947, a train from Lahore steamed into Amritsar Railway Station. The train was littered with mutilated dead bodies of Hindus and Sikhs. This caused immediate reaction and large scale attacks started taking place against Muslim refugee-trains going from Delhi to Pakistan. The Prime Minister sent for the Army Commander and directed him to ensure that no Muslim refugee train going from Delhi to Pakistan was attacked by mobs anywhere in Indian territory. Russell came back and prepared a full proof plan for this. He gave us his broad plan on the basis of which we prepared detailed instructions. The windows of all Muslim refugee-trains had to have barbed wires to prevent bombs or burning *mashals* being thrown inside the compartments. Each train had three open flats one each in the front, middle and rear with light machine guns in sand bag bunkers on them to open fire against any mobs trying to attack the train. The Grand Trunk Road in Punjab runs parallel to the main railway line going from Delhi to Lahore. The entire route from Delhi to Lahore was divided into several sectors. A road patrol with armoured cars on this road would run parallel to the moving refugee train in that sector and take action against any mob assembling to attack the trains. Besides, an aircraft was to fly over the trains with ground communication to warn of sabotage on the railway tracks or approaching mobs. Curfew was enforced all along the railway tracks and at railway stations. No passenger or goods trains were permitted beyond Delhi in Punjab. With such detailed arrangements, we ensured that not a single Muslim refugee train was attacked between Delhi and the Indo-Pak border. Each train carried 10,000 refugees. Thus millions of Muslim refugees were safely transported in trains from Delhi to Pakistan.

§

Mountbatten had made his special train available to Russell to act as our mobile headquarters. This was a luxurious corridor-train with a large saloon for the Viceroy, a large sitting room, a large dining room and a large office. There were besides about a dozen cubicles with attached toilet for the staff officers. There was also a kitchen, a pantry and living quarters for the subordinate staff in the train. The Viceroy's saloon became the living accommodation for Russell and his wife. The sitting room was made into an Officers' Mess. There was also a large office compartment on the train which became our Operations Room with maps. We also had an internal telephone system. We added some bogies and flats for our Army escort and vehicles with ramps. Wireless communication to Army Headquarters in Delhi and to our subordinate formations was also made available. We could halt at any railway station, detrain our vehicles with escort and move around as required. This train was called the Command Train and was the only train running in Punjab besides refugee trains. We lived and travelled in this train for weeks together all over Punjab between Delhi and Lahore. I saw some very ghastly sites of brutality and massacre with dead bodies thrown all over which were much worse than dead bodies I had seen on the battle field.

§

The Military Evacuation Organisation under Maj Gen BS Chimney at Lahore was working under our Command Headquarters. It was required to facilitate the evacuation of Hindus and Sikhs from West Pakistan by air, train and road. This was a stupendous task. On our side we had put up a Staging Camp at Kurukshetra to accommodate 5 lakh Hindus and Sikh refugees. The Civil Administration would send these refugees from West Pakistan to various rural and urban locations on our side vacated by Muslims who had gone to Pakistan. This also was a gigantic task.

The civil administration had arranged with girl colleges in Delhi to cook food for our refugees coming in foot columns from Pakistan. The Army used to collect these food packets and deliver them to the Air Force at Palam to carry out food drops over non-Muslim refugee foot columns in Pakistan.

§

By October 1947, we were over the hump and things were getting under control. I recall that towards the middle of October, the Army Commander decided to tour areas around Delhi like Gurgaon, Faridabad and Rohtak by road visiting various units deployed to restore law and order. I had to accompany him in his staff car. On his first such road tour, the Army Commander had said that we should carry our packed lunch so that the units deployed in the field are not burdened with having to provide lunch for us. I decided to carry a sumptuous lunch in my father's elegant tiffin box. My mother had sandwiches, parathas, vegetables and fruit packed in the tiffin box. I also carried some chilled beer in an ice box. My father while holding field appointments in Bihar would carry his meals in that tiffin box. Brig Green, who was from the same Regiment as the Army Commander, and had served with him in North Africa during the Second World War, was commanding a Brigade in that sector. He accompanied us during the tour. After visiting a few units, we halted near a tree grove close to Gurgaon for lunch. A *durrie* and portable chairs were laid out for us in the grove. Both Russell and Green had brought their sandwiches in Army haversacks commonly used in the field. When I took out my elaborate lunch from the tiffin box and chilled beer from the ice box both Russell and Green smiled and looked at me. Russell said, "My boy you certainly have your lunch in style." My reply was that when in the field in Burma, I often carried austere meals in my haversack but today accompanying an Army Commander, I thought I should try and do better. I had enough food with me and I offered chilled beer and food to both Russell and Green. They replied jolly good and accepted my offer. The Army Commander said that he was reminded of meals in the North African desert. There used to be so much dust that one could not munch food and had to wash it down with beer. At that time Gurgaon and its neighbourhood was almost a desert with dusty tracks and camel carts. Local women covering half their face with *ghunghat* (veil) carrying pitchers used to move around then. Gurgaon today has become so entirely different. It is now like any flourishing city in the West. On return to Delhi, Russell's ADC came to me the following day with a case of 12 bottles of beer for the hospitality the Army Commander had received from me during lunch near Gurgaon. This showed the sense of values practised by senior Officers of not sponging on their juniors.

§

During this tour, I noticed that when a JCO saluted the Army Commander and said *'Ram Ram Sahib'* or *'Sat Sri Akal Sahib'*, the Army Commander would reply *'Walekum Salam'*. After a pause he would say, I am sorry *'Ram Ram Sahib'* or *'Sat Sri Akal Sahib'*. This was because he had served all his Regimental life with Pathan troops in the Frontier Force Rifles. His Regiment was now in Pakistan Army. After Independence, he had to adjust himself to greet Hindu and Sikh troops in their customary way. I shall later bring out that despite his early career, in a Regiment which is now in the Pakistan Army, he was one of the very few senior British officers after Independence in the Indian Army, totally loyal to India.

During this tour, we visited 1 SIKH Regiment near Gurgaon. Lt Col Dewan Ranjit Rai was commanding this Battalion. In those days, Indian officers with barely 6-7 years service had just got command of battalions replacing very senior experienced British officers with 20 or more years of service. One could see that these Indian Commanding

Officers were nervous during the visit of such a senior British General with a very high professional reputation. Dewan Rai appeared to be an exception showing much self-confidence. On the way back to Delhi during this tour, the Army Commander asked me as to what I thought of 1 SIKH. I replied that it appeared to be a good unit. He told me that a unit reflects the personality of its Commander. This was a remark pregnant with meaning. A week or so later, I saw how his visit to 1 SIKH influenced him in taking an important decision.

§

On the afternoon of 26 October 1947, we heard that something very important was afoot and the Prime Minister had sent for our Army Commander Lt Gen Sir Dudley Russell. We had no idea as to what it was about. On return after meeting the Prime Minister, Russell convened a meeting of all the twelve of us who were serving on his staff. He told us that Pakistani tribals had invaded Kashmir and were believed to be about 10,000 strong. They had reached Baramulla, only 30 miles from Srinagar. Maharaja Hari Singh had acceded to India. His Army had been overrun in the Valley by the invading forces. Srinagar lay defenceless. The Maharaja had fled from Srinagar with all his senior officials and had gone to Jammu. Our Command Headquarters was given the task of conducting operations in Kashmir and throwing out the enemy from the State. None of us in our wildest dreams had thought of such an operational role given to us at such short notice. We were thoroughly unprepared. For the last one year or more, the Army was totally pre-occupied in internal security duties. The odds appeared heavily loaded against us. The Army Commander said that the following morning at first light, 1 SIKH had to be flown to Srinagar. Many pro-Pakistan Western scholars have written that India launched a previously planned invasion of Kashmir on 27 October 1947. Some Indian troops, it was claimed, had gone to Kashmir even before the invasion launched by Pakistan. This is totally false and malicious. A book named *Operation Rescue* giving my personal account of the 1947-48 war in Kashmir shows what a great lie this propaganda is. Gen Russell, endorsing this book, fully supports the facts as mentioned by me. This is confirmed in his letter to me the extract of which is printed on the back cover of that book. This vindicates the Indian version on this point.

§

The Army Commander at the conference on the evening of 26th October 1947, gave us his directions on how the operation in Kashmir was to be conducted, starting from the following morning. He directed us that a Brigade group from Gurdaspur had to move to Jammu by road from Pathankot and another Brigade group from Delhi to Srinagar by air. The road from Pathankot to Jammu was a dirt track running along close to the border with Pakistan. There were no bridges on the Ravi, Ujh and Basantar. Vehicles had to cross Ravi in boats and ford through the other two rivers. Road convoys took two full days to cover the distance from Pathankot to Jammu. Nowadays we have a bridge over the Ravi and a tarmac road from Pathankot to Jammu with Irish bridges over Ujh and Basantar. Road convoys cover the distance between Pathankot and Jammu via Samba in about 4 hours. As for communication to Srinagar, whether by air or by road, we faced severe limitations. Srinagar had a grass air field which would become unserviceable by the middle of November due to snow and there were no night landing facilities. By road from Jammu to Srinagar, the convoy took two days. There were wooden bridges en route. The road would close in winter because there was then no tunnel at Banihal and the road went over the 9,000 feet high Banihal Pass which also used to close due to snow in winter starting from mid-November. Thus our window of opportunity for sending troops, stores and winter stocks was only about two weeks. From the point of view of road communications to Jammu and Kashmir, Pakistan was much better placed. They had two all-weather tarmac roads from Sialkot to Jammu and from Peshawar to Srinagar, besides several all-weather tracks from Pakistan to border locations in Western part of Jammu and Kashmir.

The Army Commander ordered that 1 SIKH would be the first unit to go by air to Srinagar. On the following morning, only 6 Air Force Dakotas would be available. Our Air Force had only one Squadron of transport aircraft, one third of which had gone to Pakistan. From the second day i.e 28 October 1947, all the Dakotas with private airlines would be made available to us. Russell also told us that the British Government, for obvious reasons, had laid down that no British officer then serving in either Indian or Pakistani Army would be allowed to go to the theatre of operations in Kashmir. He then said pointing towards me that since I was the only Indian officer on his staff he wanted me to go with the first lot of troops to Srinagar the following morning. He added that I had to act as his eyes and ears to keep him apprised of events in the theatre of operations.

Lt Col Mac Conachie, my immediate superior, prepared operation orders for the two Brigades going to Jammu and Srinagar. I assisted him in doing so. The first Battalion to go by air was 1 SIKH. On the first day, due to shortage of Dakotas we could send only the Battalion Headquarters and two Companies. The rest of the Battalion was to follow the next day. Lt Col Dewan Ranjit Rai, commanding 1 SIKH, was instructed that in case Srinagar airfield had been occupied by the raiders, he was not to land there but at Jammu and then proceed in civilian buses from Jammu to Srinagar. While 161 Brigade was to be flown from Delhi to Srinagar, 77 Para Brigade had to be moved by road from Gurdaspur to Jammu. We sent an Emergency signal to 1 SIKH to concentrate at the Airport by midnight for an operational mission. The Battalion was deployed in small sub-units in Gurgaon and it must have taken sometime to get them together and concentrate at the Airfield.

I had a host of other things to do which I had to complete that night. Never before had I worked all night against such heavy odds. Perhaps this was the most momentous night of my career which was of great national importance. Warm clothing, ammunition and defence stores had to be collected from Shakurbasti Ordnance Depot. They had to be brought to the Airport for issuing these to the troops being sent to Srinagar. Reception of troops at the Airfield, allotment of rest areas for them and a hot meal at the Airport had to be organised. Orders had to be delivered to the Commanding Officer and he had to be briefed. Load tables had also to be worked out in conjunction with the Air Force that night.

From the following day, we had 40 civil Dakotas available to us. Over 90% of these Dakotas had European pilots, some not very fluent in English and not amenable to military discipline. I had to handle them with much tact. It was a miracle that we managed to fly about 800 Dakota sorties from Safdarjung to Srinagar in a fortnight. The ceiling height of the Dakota unlike a modern air craft was limited and flying over Pir Panjal range used to be a little turbulent. Fortunately, we had no untoward incident during this massive airlift. This airlift to Srinagar saved the Valley. Mountbatten wrote, "In my long experience of war I have not come across another such massive air lift carried out at such short notice and so successfully." It may be amusing to people today that instead of getting any recognition in terms of award or appreciation, a couple of years later, I got into trouble over this airlift. My not getting any recognition for this was understandable because in those days India had decided to give up British titles and like Americans have no titles or awards recognising distinguished service. India had only instituted gallantry awards for battle. About 10 years later, the Bharat Ratna and Padma awards were introduced for civilians and Vishisht Seva Medal series for military officers. As for my getting into trouble, I may mention what happened. Three years later, our defence audit raised an objection on the unauthorized spending of a few hundred crores on this massive airlift to Srinagar in 1947 when private air companies had submitted their bills for our hiring of their Dakotas. There was no government letter authorising the use of these private aircrafts. Nor was there any specific record or sanction for each trip these aircrafts made. I would often not only send aircrafts to Srinagar but to various Ordnance Depots in the country like Allahabad, Jabalpur and Pune to pick up urgently required ammunition, clothing, defence stores and so on. I was not even aware of this requirement at that time and I had kept no record of verbal instructions that I used to give. It was not appreciated that in those very disturbed emergency conditions, it was difficult to do such account keeping. There was a suspicion that I may have received a cut from these companies and made money over the air lifts. The word scam had not been introduced then nor was there any investigative journalism. So there was no public focus on this transaction. However, an inquiry was instituted and my bankers told me that the CBI had asked to see my bank accounts. Fortunately for me, my accounts were in red because the banks used to provide up to one month's salary as overdraft for Army officers. After this inquiry was completed, a Government of India letter was issued saying that the President of India was pleased to write off the entire expenditure of crores on this air lift.

§

Reverting to the night of 26-27 October 1947, I must say that not only had I to work round the clock that night but also had to face numerous difficulties which I somehow managed to overcome. My immediate boss, Lt Col Mac Conachie, was of immense help and guidance even though he was getting ready to pack up his bags, quit the Indian Army and proceed to the UK, the following week. The last day in office he had worked till late at night and then told me that he had cleared his table and had left nothing pending. He handed over the keys of the Top Secret Almirah and wished me good luck. I was very taken by his sense of duty. Most of the British officers in the Gorkha Regiment were not very friendly with Indian officers because they led a secluded life in their Regiments in which there were no Indian officers. In some Regiments, British officers on the eve of their departure had drunk all the liquor in the Battalion Officers' Mess saying that the Regiment had bought those bottles in bulk and they did not want to leave them for their Indian successors. There was a case of a British Lt Col Commanding a Gorkha Battalion going to England taking away all the Regimental silver worth lakhs with him. He felt that the Regimental silver had been bought by British officers for the Regiment over the years. Now that there were all going away they could take the silver with them. When this came to the notice of higher authorities, they took a serious view. It was felt that no matter who had presented the silver pieces, they had become Regimental Property. Since the Regiment was continuing to stay in India, the silver had to remain with the Regiment. The British Col had to disembark from the ship at Bombay before it was due to leave for London. All the Regimental silver being taken by him were taken out from the hold of the ship and sent to the Regiment. Mac Conachie's conduct was in sharp contrast to that of this British Colonel.

§

On the night of 26-27 October 1947, I briefed Lt Col Dewan Ranjit Rai at the airport about the task assigned to him. He was quite confident and showed no nervousness at all. I told him that early in the morning the BGS (Brigadier General Staff), Brig Mellsop, will be coming to the airport to see them off and if he had any doubts, he would clarify that for him. He smilingly said, "No doubt whatsoever. I have not slept all night, let me go to sleep for half an hour on the sofa so that I wake up fresh when I have to go to battle in the morning. You complete all the arrangements for loading the aircraft and tie up details with my second-in-command." I much admired Ranjit Rai's self-confidence and composure. Anyone else in his position would have been on hot bricks trying to tie up knots before venturing out on such a dangerous task. Before dawn, Brig Mellsop, the BGS of our Headquarters, arrived to see off the troops and was happy to see that all the required arrangements had been duly completed. At the crack of dawn all the Dakotas took off from the airport for their hazardous mission. I heaved a sigh of relief. I felt that it was unbelievable how we managed to complete all the preparations that night. A couple of hours later, we received a signal from Srinagar that our first lot had landed at Srinagar airport safely. After emptying their load, the Dakotas returned to Delhi and were required to do a second sortie that day. I went to Srinagar in the second sortie reaching there at noon. When I arrived at Srinagar, I found that leaving one Company behind for guarding the airport, Dewan Ranjit Rai had proceeded to Baramulla with one Company to make contact with the enemy.

As Russell had asked me to serve as his eyes and ears, I had to constantly fly to Srinagar, sometimes spending the night there, to keep the General informed of developments on the ground. This was also necessary for me to do because I was in-charge of the air lift and I had to monitor progress on the ground. On the first day, I found the situation very tense. We were only 300 strong at the airfield when the enemy at Baramulla was 10,000 strong. Luckily foı us, the tribal leaders, who had never seen a modern town or city before, went totally berserk in Baramulla. They resorted to plunder and rapine for two days. They ransacked almost every house even pulling out doors and windows. Women were raped and tortured; and men brutally killed. Even the nuns in the convent or nurses in the hospitals were not spared. Baramulla was burning for two days. The Commander of the Pakistani invading force was Maj Gen Akbar Khan of Pakistan Army who had been given the pseudonym name of the Arab General, Tariq of medieval days who had conquered Spain. I knew Akbar Khan. He had a reputation of being a gallant and competent officer. He was one of the very few Indians who had won the high gallantry award of DSO commanding a battalion during the crossing of the Irrawaddy river in Burma. A little before Partition, I had met him in South Block at Delhi when he was Deputy Director (Weapons and Equipment) in General Headquarters. Obviously, he could not control the ill-disciplined tribesmen under him who had gone berserk. Thus, Pakistan lost a golden opportunity to capture Srinagar even before we could arrive there or secure the airfield and prevent our aircraft landing in Srinagar. Such are the ways of war. In retrospect, I may mention that instead of starting its invasion of Kashmir on 22 October 1947, if Pakistan had done so in November, the road and the airfield would have become unserviceable and India would not have been able to intervene in Kashmir that winter.

§

On arrival at Baramulla, Ranjit Rai occupied a small hill about a mile short of Baramulla. The next morning, the enemy advanced towards his position and with overwhelming numbers was likely to over run him. He encountered heavy fire from front and both flanks. He ordered a fighting withdrawal of his troops to Pattan, half way between Srinagar and Baramulla. Pattan had a suitable lay-back position on small ridges on both sides of the road. On the second day, we had the 40 civil Dakotas of private airlines available and we had started flying in 80 sorties a day to Srinagar. By the morning of 28 October, we had flown in the rest of 1 SIKH plus 1 KUMAON, the second battalion of the Brigade to Srinagar. Thus, on the second day we had nearly two Battalions holding defences at Pattan. Unfortunately, Ranjit Rai was killed that morning while withdrawing from Baramulla. He was posthumously awarded the Maha Vir Chakra for gallantry. Brig Jai Chand Katoch, Commander of 161 Infantry Brigade, with his Tactical Headquarters, had flown in on the second day. We now had two full Battalions in position at Pattan on either side of the road. The enemy now realised that the regular Indian Army was in the field against them. They moved cautiously approaching Pattan. Brig Jai Chand Katoch, had come up to Pattan to take stock of things. Unfortunately, that evening he was hit by a sniper bullet and had to be evacuated back to Delhi. I was told to remain at Srinagar to send a regular report on what was happening. It was a little disturbing that within the first 48 hours we had lost a Battalion Commander killed and the Brigade Commander wounded. There was no panic amongst the troops. The Brigade Major of 161 Brigade, Maj Dilbagh Singh, and I visited Pattan to see our defences there. Lt Col Pritam Singh, commanding 1 KUMAON became Officiating Brigade Commander. The next day, 4 KUMAON arrived and Lt Col Manmohan Khanna being the senior Commanding Officer became Officiating Brigade Commander. The following day we had yet another change of Officiating Brigade Commander when Lt Col GS Khullar, Commanding 1/2 PUNJAB arrived by road from Jammu. Thus in four days we had had different Officiating Brigade Commanders. The situation was rather fluid but the morale of troops was high and we were determined to beat back the enemy. I had stayed for three nights at Srinagar to give a helping hand to Major Dilbagh Singh, Brigade Major of 161 Infantry Brigade who had a difficult task with frequent changing of Officiating Brigade Commanders. The enemy with his large numbers had started out-flanking our position at Pattan. We decided to fall back to Shelatang on the outskirts of Srinagar, a short distance from the airfield. At that time, there was lots of water bodies at Shelatang which gave strength to our defences. It had been decided to hold compact defence at Shelatang with four Battalions blocking the route to Srinagar. Col LP Sen, DSO, who had successfully commanded a Baluch Battalion in the famous battle of Kangdaw in Burma during the Second World War, was Deputy Director Military Intelligence at Army Headquarters at Delhi. He was promoted Brigadier and sent to take over 161 Brigade in Srinagar. We were happy that the command situation of the Brigade had now stabilised. Sen with his war record inspired confidence. Soon after taking over the Brigade, he issued a statement that he would soon have the tribesmen swimming in the Jhelum. I remember that 3 November turned out to be a critical day. I was at Srinagar airfield with my friend Major Somnath Sharma of 4 KUMAON. I had known him for some time and we were having a mug of tea together. He had a hand in plaster due to a motorcycle accident in Delhi a week or so earlier. His Commanding Officer did not want him to come to Kashmir with the Battalion because of his injury. He insisted on coming with the Battalion and the Commanding Officer reluctantly allowed him to accompany the Battalion. Due to his injury, he was not allowed to go to the front with the Battalion which he wanted. Instead, he and his Company had been detailed to secure the Srinagar airfield. I was very relaxed that day because I had been to the city some 15 miles from the airfield. There was no habitation between the city and the airfield at that time. We had been too busy stabilising the situation on the front and had no time to worry about law and order in the city. I was sent to find out the situation in the city so that some troops could be sent there to maintain law and order, if necessary. To my very pleasant surprise, I found no communal tension or violence in the city. It was all very peaceful. I heard the slogan raised by the people, *'Hamalawar khabardar, Hum Kashmiri Hindu-Sikh-MuslimTaiyar'*. This was at a time when the whole sub-continent including the Jammu region of the State was engulfed in unprecedented communal violence during the Partition Holocaust. No wonder that later the Mahatma issued a statement, "I see a ray of light only in Kashmir." While I told Somnath about my visit to the city, he said that he was very unhappy to be left behind at Srinagar airfield on the rather passive task of securing it. He wanted a more active assignment for himself. I did not know that within a few hours his wish will get more than fulfilled. Third November turned out to be a critical day. The enemy completely outflanked our Pattan defences through a long route across the mountains with a column of 700 to raid the airfield. They had come up to Budgam, a little over a mile from the airfield. Somnath was immediately rushed to Budgam with his Company. It was an unequal fight with the enemy 700 strong and Somnath had only 100 soldiers with him. But Somnath held his ground. He personally manned light machine guns despite a fractured hand. He and two third of his Company were over run and killed. They held their ground till reinforcements arrived and restored the situation. His last message on the wireless was that I will fight till the last round and I will not yield. For his outstanding gallantry, Somnath was posthumously awarded the highest award for gallantry in war, the Param Vir Chakra. Fifty seven years later, I was Governor of Jammu and Kashmir. I had Somnath's statue put up at the entrance to the now modern Srinagar airport. This was to remind people that he had sacrificed his life to protect that airfield. Had we lost the airfield at that time our lifeline to the rest of the country would have been snapped for the next four to five months which would have been disastrous and we would have lost Kashmir during that winter. Besides having Somnath's statue at the Srinagar airport, I had a suitable Memorial put up under the tree at Budgam, under which Somnath had been killed.

Maj Gen Kulwant Singh arrived in Srinagar on 5 November 1947 and took over command of all forces in Jammu and Kashmir comprising a Brigade each in Kashmir and Jammu. Another Brigade was to be inducted in Jammu region. On 7 November, Brig Sen launched his well-planned offensive against the enemy at Shelatang.

He sent an armoured column from North of Dal Lake outflanking the enemy's position and hitting him from the rear while the main attack with the artillery and air support was launched from the front. Within a couple of hours, the enemy was completely routed leaving 369 dead bodies on the battle field and taking some dead bodies and wounded with them. Srinagar and the Valley were saved. Within 10 days we had virtually achieved the impossible. That is a part of the fortunes of war.

I returned to Delhi to brief the Army Commander about what had happened at Shelatang. I found Maj Gen Cariappa, who was then the General Staff Officer of the Commander-in-Chief at Army Headquarters, also present with Russell for my briefing. After having heard me, Cariappa said that he had to go to Mahatma Gandhi to apprise him of what had happened in the Valley. He asked me to accompany him. We went to the Harijan Colony in Delhi where the Mahatma was staying. This was the first and the last time I had an opportunity to see the Mahatma from close quarters. Cariappa briefed him of the details of the decisive victory we had achieved at Shelatang. It was the Mahatma's day of silence. After listening to Cariappa, he wrote on a slate, "I am proud of the Indian Army. Non-violence is the weapon of the brave and not of the coward." We saluted Mahatma and returned.

§

On a December evening, I was invited to dinner at Russell's house. Normally a Major is not invited for dinner with the Army Commander at his house with senior officers. This was not so in the old days when senior British officers would invite junior staff officers to their house. The Army culture was that the officer corps was a brotherhood in which all officers irrespective of rank were treated as brothers in arms. Of course, the junior officers always showed due respect for the senior officers. This dinner was an interesting experience for me. There were about a dozen people at the table. Lt Gen Sir Roy Boucher who was Chief of Staff at Army Headquarters was also present at that dinner. The other guests at the dinner included RK Nehru, a senior ICS officer who was then Additional Secretary, Ministry of External Affairs. Being a cousin of Jawaharlal Nehru and in a high position in the Ministry, he was an influential person in Delhi. I remember his wife making an innocent remark without any malice. She said that the other day a Major from Army Headquarters had rung up her house wanting to talk to her husband. She told him that her husband was in the bath and he should ring up his private secretary in his office. And then she expressed some surprise that a mere Major rings up and wants to talk to her husband. She added that the Army must observe norms. These remarks would have passed unnoticed. However, Russell being a good host realised that her mentioning this would make me uncomfortable. He very politely told Mrs Nehru that a Major is a senior officer in the Army. It took him 16 years to attain that rank. A Major is entitled to present arms from a Sentry while Captains and below get butt salute. I am sure, he said all this to put me at ease. Lady Russell was a charming hostess who was equally hospitable to everyone including me.

The other incident at the dinner party which I recall, was the conversation between Gen Russell and Gen Boucher. Russell complained that it was unfair on him and the troops he commanded in Kashmir to have an embargo on his visiting the field. Tomorrow if there was a critical situation in Kashmir, he would ignore the embargo and personally go to Kashmir to take stock of the situation. Boucher was being diplomatic and said that the British Government had rightly imposed this embargo because how could it permit British officers serving in the Indian and Pakistani Armies to confront each other in battle in Kashmir. Russell replied that in that case it is better for an Indian to be made an Army Commander rather than him. It so happened that after 10 days we suffered a reverse in Jammu and our troops were forced to withdraw from Jhanger and fall back on Naushera. Notwithstanding the order on the subject, Russell rushed to Kashmir to see what had happened. I accompanied him on that tour. There was commotion in Delhi when the top hierarchy heard that Russell had gone to the Operation Theatre in Kashmir. Messages were flying for Russell to return to Delhi immediately. After spending a day and reviewing the situation, Russell returned to Delhi and asked the government to appoint an Indian officer to replace him.

§

The appointment of Chief of Staff at Army Headquarters had been introduced for the first time in August 1947. This lasted only for five months. In view of the facts that Indian Generals were much junior in service and with no experience of serving at Army Headquarters earlier, the appointment of Chief of Staff had been introduced. At that time, Principal Staff Officers had been downgraded to the rank of Major-General and it was only after ten years in 1958 that these appointments again became tenable by Lt Gens.

§

In January 1948, Gen Boucher became the Army Chief replacing Gen Sir Rob Lockhart who was sacked. He had received information about Pakistanis preparing to launch invasion of Kashmir from Gen Sir Frank Messervy, his counterpart in Pakistan. Lockhart either deliberately or inadvertently had not informed the government about this, nor had he taken any preparatory action for that contingency.

§

Lt Gen KM Cariappa was posted as our new Army Commander and took over his appointment on 20 January 1948. Soon after his taking over, he was to be briefed in the Operations Room about the latest position in Jammu and Kashmir. Before the Briefing he told the Brigadier General Staff (BGS) that he did not like the designation of our Headquarters. Delhi and East Punjab was too much of a mouthful. Our designation should be Western Command. I was asked to issue the necessary orders for this change. Next day Brig Thorat, then Director Staff Duty, rang me up seeing my signature on the signal giving the new designation of our Headquarters. He sarcastically asked me how have you acquired the authority to change the name of your Headquarters. This has to be done with the approval of the government. I told him that I was only carrying out the orders of the Army Commander. He then said he would try and get ex-post facto sanction for this change. However, he also made a dig saying that the abbreviation of HQ Western Command could be HQ WC. Thus we now had a new name for our Command Headquarters.

§

Going back to the previous day when I briefed the Army Commander and senior officers, I may now continue my narrative. After my briefing, Cariappa asked me which was then the most threatened position in Kashmir. I replied, "Naushera, there are intelligence reports of the enemy massing 10,000 to 15,000 force to overrun

Naushera held by 50 Para Brigade under the command of Brig Usman." Cariappa said, "Let us then go to Naushera tomorrow morning." I made the arrangements and I flew with him to Jammu and from there in a light Auster plane to Naushera. We had no helicopters at that time and we used the three-seater Auster meant for directing artillery fire to go to Naushera. Brig Usman received Cariappa at the landing strip in Naushera and he took him in his jeep to show him the perimeter defence, he had organized at Naushera. With a long experience of fighting the tribes in North-West Frontier Province, Cariappa had a good eye for mountain warfare. He noticed that the Kot feature was unoccupied by us and it provided observation of our defences which the enemy could use to bring down artillery fire. Cariappa wanted that feature to be captured at once. Usman launched a night attack a day later and occupied that feature naming the operation as Op Kipper, using the Army commander's nick name. This proved of great help in the subsequent battle for Naushera a couple of weeks later. Cariappa was from Coorg (near Bengaluru) and he could not speak in Hindi fluently. Usman told him that after breaking the impending enemy attack in Naushera, he and his troops were very keen to advance to Jhanger and re-capture the position from which they had been forced to withdraw last December. Cariappa said that he would like to address the troops and explain things to them. Cariappa spoke Hindi like an Englishman, literally translating English words into Hindi. He mounted the bonnet of a jeep and addressed all the troops from a microphone in his hand. I reproduce his exact words which for long was a big joke in the Army. He said, *"50 Para Brigade ke afsaran, sardaran, jawanan. Aapka Brigade Commander Sahib ne bola ki aap aage jana mangta. Hum aapko tasvir ke andar dalna mangta. Aap abhi aage jana sakta nahin kyonki hamara bandobast ka dum bahut peeche hai. Aap is vakt dushman ko aankh maro."* (Officers, JCOs and men of 50 Para-Brigade, your Brigade Commander has spoken to me that you want to go forward to Jhanger. I want to put you in the picture. You cannot do so at present because our administrative tale is far behind. For the present, you keep an eye on the enemy.) His meaning was somewhat lost in his very literal translation into Hindi! After his address Cariappa asked me to find out the reaction of the troops to his address. I enquired from a Gorkha Subedar who had heard his address. The Subedar said, *"Saab General saab ka speech bahut achcha tha.*

Magar ek baat saab general saab angreji mein bola hum kuch samjha nahin." (The General's speech was very good but he spoke in English and I could not understand what he said.) After a couple of days of extensive battle field tour in Jammu and Srinagar we returned to Delhi.

§

After our decisive victory in the battle of Naushera, Cariappa approved of our advance to Jhanger. We recaptured Jhanger in March 1948. The British Army Chief at Delhi instructed Cariappa to refrain from further offensive operations saying that this may lead to direct confrontation with Pakistan Army. This must be avoided. I recalled how in November 1947, despite the then Army Commander Russell's recommendation, the Army had been stopped from pursuing the retreating Pakistani raiders to Muzaffarabad for the same reason. Cariappa was keen to liberate the territory inside Jammu and Kashmir which was under occupation of the enemy. Accordingly, we launched an operation to clear Thanamandi, now near the border with Pakistan. Thanamandi was on an approach to our vital Line of Communication to the Valley, the Jammu-Srinagar road. The enemy at Thanamandi could pose a threat to that key road. We sent a column with light tanks and cleared Thanamandi. Boucher was perhaps following a British agenda. He wrote a personal letter to Cariappa asking for his explanation for disobeying his orders. Cariappa replied that he had sent a fighting patrol and finding Thanamandi lightly held, occupied it because of its tactical importance. Boucher was not too happy about this.

§

The Pakistanis were targeting Brigadier Usman for being loyal to India. A Muslim being so was not acceptable to them. They had announced a reward of ₹50,000 to anyone who killed or captured Usman. One day we received a telephone call from Usman's younger brother Subhan who was a journalist in Delhi. He had heard rumours of Usman having been killed in Jhanger. We assured him that this could not be true because had it been so, we would have been immediately informed but, in any case, we would check and inform him soon. We sent a signal to Usman and he sent a reply, "I am still in the world of living." We duly informed Subhan of this. However, two days later the enemy shelled Jhanger heavily. There was only one casualty and that was Usman. While coming out of his bunker, he received a direct hit and was killed. After the battle of Naushera, Usman had become a National Hero. His body was flown to Delhi and he was given a military funeral at Jamia Millia. President Rajendra Prasad, Prime Minister Nehru and other top dignitaries attended the funeral.

§

When the summer of 1948 set in, with government approval, Cariappa launched an offensive from Uri to Muzaffarabad on 22 May that year. We had made progress in that offensive when on 1 June, the United Nations Commission for India and Pakistan (UNCIP) came to the Indian sub-continent to find a solution to the Kashmir problem. It appealed to both sides to refrain from offensive operation. Accordingly, our advance was halted on 1 June 1948. Although Pakistan had also accepted this appeal of UNCIP in August, its forces advanced to Skardu in Gilgit-Baltistan. The fort at Skardu, with a small State Force garrison and a large number of starving non-Muslim refugees, was forced to surrender. There after the enemy captured Kargil and reached Zojila Pass. They now threatened the Valley from the East and sent raiders towards Leh in the West where we had a small isolated garrison. We obtained government's approval for launching an offensive into Ladakh across the Zojila Pass to Kargil and thence to Leh. Our first two attempts to assault the features on either side of the 10,000 feet high, Zojila Pass failed. The enemy was holding formidable high features entailing difficult climb from our side. Our Artillery bombardment would not sufficiently soften the enemy position and our assaulting Infantry suffered heavy casualties without being able to reach the top. Cariappa much against the views of Boucher was determined to make a third attempt. We had unwittingly given the code name of DUCK to the earlier operation against Zojila. Cariappa told me that we had failed in Operations DUCK-1 and DUCK-2 because the code name was unfortunate. He said let us call the third attempt Operation BISON which is an offensive animal while DUCK is a peaceful bird. The term DUCK is often used to describe failure. He sent a personal signal to Gen Thimayya, Commanding the Division in the Srinagar Valley, "If you do not succeed try and try again, and then you are bound to succeed. Change the code name Operation DUCK to Operation BISON." Boucher had his reservations and was discouraging Cariappa from making a third attempt. Cariappa was not deterred.

We decided to bring up tanks to Zojila so that we could engage enemy bunkers on the hill tops with direct firing weapons. This posed a major problem. Tanks were in Jammu some 200 miles from Srinagar and the wooden bridges on the Jammu-Srinagar road were very frail which would have given way if we tried to take tanks over them. Only light tanks without their turrets could go across these bridges. We removed all the turrets and guns on the tank to be taken up to Baltal at the base of Zojila which is another 60 miles beyond Srinagar. We also decided to remove the engines of the tanks and winch the tanks across the bridge. Our next problem was to maintain secrecy of this move. If the enemy got to know of it, the whole operation would have got jeopardised. In mountainous terrain with no room for manoeuvre, a few antitank mines and antitank guns at Zojila could have foiled our attempt to use tanks in that terrain. It took us about ten days to complete this hazardous move of tanks in broken bits from Jammu to Baltal and reassemble them on arrival. We carried out this move only during night and at day time the tanks were kept covered with tarpaulin giving the look of stacked hay. We imposed curfew during the night when the column passed through built up areas. We managed to complete this task successfully. On 1 December when the third assault on Zojila with tanks took place, we had light snow fall which provided natural cover. Gen Thimayya was himself in the leading tank. The enemy was taken completely by surprise at tanks firing at their positions. Their forward unit reported to their Headquarters on the wireless that they were being heavily engaged by tank fire. We were able to get an intercept of this message as also the reply sent to them by their Headquarters that these must be camouflaged jeeps. The enemy defences were broken and we were able to get across Zojila and advanced another 12 miles to Matayan. We were held up by the enemy holding another 12,000 feet high Batkundi feature requiring to be cleared before we could advance to Dras and then to Kargil. For this operation, I was positioned at Baltal along with the Brigade Headquarters conducting this operation so that I could send direct reports to the Army Commander. I walked to Matayan along with the Brigade Major. We were now trying to construct a road in the mountains to bring up guns and ammunition for launching the attack. One late afternoon, I was summoned by the Army Commander to Delhi with instructions that I must report to him on the following morning. It was getting dark but undeterred I walked from Matayan back to Baltal, a distance of twelve miles during the night. It was terribly cold at those heights in a December night and in those days we did not have proper winter clothing. Notwithstanding this, I completed this tortuous walk crossing freezing water in streamlets, which made my my feet get totally numbed. On arrival at Baltal, a Doctor stopped me trying to warm myself by standing next to a burning *Bukhari* (improvised stove having burning logs of wood). He told me that I should apply mineral jelly to my hands and feet and bear the cold for a little while before going near the *Bukhari*. This helped me because I did not get frostbite. I then drove through the night to Srinagar airfield catching the first morning flight to Delhi. On arrival, I reported to Gen Cariappa in his office. He was waiting for me and after I briefed him, he asked me to go along with him. We went straight to the Prime Minister's office in South Block. I was very overawed when I entered that office behind Cariappa and saw Prime Minister Jawaharlal Nehru sitting at his desk. My first sight of him from such close quarter gave me a bit of a shock. I had always seen him from a distance or in pictures wearing a Gandhi cap and having a youthful look. Here he was a totally bald person looking very elderly. Cariappa briefed him about the progress of the operations at Zojila. Nehru emphasised the need for us to get to Kargil before the Zojila Pass got blocked due to snow in another few days. We had also to complete winter stocking across the Pass for the troops who had gone across. Cariappa said that we were working intensely to complete the 20 miles stretch of road from Baltal to Matayan to enable us to bring up guns and ammunition to clear the opposition ahead of Matayan. Road construction in the mountains is time consuming. Nehru interrupted saying that the distance from Baltal to Matayan was only 10 miles and not 20 miles. Cariappa then pointed towards me saying that I had walked that distance the previous night. Nehru looked towards me and I found that I had to provide an answer that would not be contrary to what Cariappa had said. I stated that the distance from Baltal to Matayan along the mountain track by foot or on horse was about 12 miles but the road for vehicles was very winding and was about 20 miles. Nehru was quite satisfied with this reply. After the meeting, Cariappa asked me to find out how the Prime Minister was so precise about the distance from Baltal to Matayan. I found out that in 1913, Jawaharlal Nehru had gone from Baltal to Matayan on his honeymoon with his wife, travelling on horses. They had stayed in Matayan Inspection Bungalow which we had been using for the Tactical Headquarters of 77 Para Brigade in that Operation.

The Operation across Zojila was a tremendous success. This was the first time in history that we had used tanks at that height. We reached Kargil and drove the enemy from that important location by 15 December. 1 PATIALA had decided to celebrate Guru Gobind Singh's Birthday in Kargil. This was on that date in 1948. A remarkable achievement at Kargil was that of Subedar Harka Bahadur Rana swimming across the icy cold water of the Shingo river, a tributary of Indus near Kargil, at the peak of winter. He and his men neutralised the enemy on the other side which enabled our forces to capture Kargil. A cement bridge has now come up at that site named after him. After the capture of Kargil, we sent a column to relieve our threatened isolated garrison at Leh. Thanks to the perseverance of Cariappa, we were able to win such a resounding victory. However, an incident thereafter in that theatre caused a lot of concern. We had mobilised 200 X 1-tonne trucks for winter stocking across Zojila. The road could not take 3-tonne lorries. One night there was suddenly very heavy snow fall and all our 1-tonne trucks got marooned in snow. The drivers managed to get out of the vehicles and get back to the Base. Many of them suffered from frost bite and in a few cases limbs had to be amputated. The fact that such a large number of these vehicles got stuck at Zojila for the winter gave an excuse to the Army Chief, General Boucher, to send a nasty letter to Cariappa saying that so many 1-tonne vehicles had been lost because as a senior Commander he had failed to appreciate and cater for this eventuality. This would affect the operational readiness of the Army till those vehicles could be replaced. Cariappa initialled the letter and handed it over to me to be filed saying, "ignore this." This only confirmed our feelings for long that we were fighting two wars in Kashmir, one against Pakistan and the other against our Army Headquarters. It is amazing that after a few months when the snow melted, we could recover all these vehicles without any damage to any vehicle. Our drivers had put anti-freeze mixture in the radiators of all the trucks. This ensured that no engine cracked.

While we launched a Brigade Operation in Zojila Sector to capture Kargil and relieve Leh, we also launched a Divisional size offensive to link up with our isolated and air maintained Poonch garrison in the South. This was also a tremendous success with our overcoming the resistance of approximately a Division of regular and 'Azad Kashmir' battalions. We were now in a commanding position occupying heights West of Poonch from where we had an excellent view of the plains around Kotli up to the International Border along the Jhelum and brought down heavy Artillery fire facilitating the capture of Kotli.

It was at this stage of our success in Battles both in the North and South that Pakistan agreed to accept the 13th of August 1948 Ceasefire Resolution of the United Nations. We had already accepted to abide by this resolution a few months earlier. Thus a ceasefire was declared in the whole of Jammu and Kashmir from 1 January 1949, bringing to end the first Indo-Pak War.

§

I may mention some incidents to show the high standard of integrity of General Cariappa and his punctiliousness about dress code. Cariappa had divorced his wife and he was bringing up his two young children Nanda and Nandini. Normally, when he used to go out on tour, he would leave his ADC behind at Delhi to keep an eye on his house hold and also his children. One day I was returning with him in his staff car after a visit to Kashmir. We drove from Palam to his house and as the car entered his gate, we saw his two children coming out with their school bags from the second staff car at the porch of the house. Cariappa was furious and asked his ADC why the staff car had been misused for unauthorized duty. The ADC said that the children had missed the school bus and the school authorities had rung up to collect the children from the school. The ADC had sent the staff car for that purpose as a taxi was not readily available nor was a tonga. He told the ADC that he was guilty of misusing the government staff car and had virtually stolen government petrol. He asked me to take disciplinary action against his ADC. I sent for the ADC and told him that knowing how strict a disciplinarian Cariappa was, he should not have used the staff car to get his children from school. However, I realised his predicament and told him not to do so in the future. Next morning when Cariappa came to the office he sent for me and enquired what action I had taken against his ADC. I told him that I gave the ADC a warning and he had assured me that he would not do so again. Cariappa was not satisfied and told me that what the ADC had done was a serious offence amounting to stealing government petrol. I then told him that we had found out that there were two rates for using government transport for unauthorised duty, the amenity rate and the penal rate. On the basis of the latter, we were going to deposit about ₹25 in government treasury. This mollified Cariappa and he told me that the amount should be debited from his personal account and the ADC was not to pay for it. This may sound strange nowadays when staff car whether in the military or in the civil are misused blatantly.

About Cariappa being a great stickler for dress, I may mention two incidents. One day we came back to Delhi from tour early and the General had no engagement that evening. He said that he wanted to go to see an English movie running at Regal Cinema after early dinner. I had to make the necessary arrangements. I rang up the Manager of Regal Cinema in Connaught Place requesting him to book two tickets in the Dress Circle, the term then used for the highest class. The manager was delighted to do so and said that he would personally receive the General on his arrival at the Foyer of the Cinema. At the appointed time after dinner, I went to pick up the General. I was dressed in a lounge suit while Cariappa was wearing a dinner jacket. He told me that the correct dress for an Army Officer attending a post-dinner function in public was dinner jacket and black tie.

The other incident pertaining to Cariappa being a stickler for dress pertained to a newly promoted Lt Col from EME. I had accompanied Cariappa to his workshop Company at Jammu where he was very impressed by the standard of maintenance. The Army Commander had even gone down to see how a 3-tonne vehicle in the workshop awaiting a new engine had been kept washed and clean and there was no grass under the vehicle. In the normal course, the officer got promoted to Lt Col and was selected for an assignment abroad. He thought he had been selected by the Army Commander on the basis of the good work done by him. He wanted to call on Cariappa to meet him before going abroad. I arranged an appointment for him one evening. He arrived at the Command House wearing a civilian bush shirt. Cariappa was furious at his dress. He asked him why he had come in a maternity jacket and enquired why he was neither in uniform nor wearing a lounge suit. The officer said that he had just dropped in to thank him for a foreign assignment given to him. He was told that his posting abroad would be cancelled because of his not being dressed properly while calling on the Army Commander. Word went down in the Army and the officers going to meet him were very particular about the dress they wore for meeting him.

§

On 30 January 1948, I was finishing my work in my office at about 5.30 in the evening. My civilian *chaprasi* (peon) came into my office and very gravely said that Mahatma Gandhi has been assassinated. I was shocked to hear that and could hardly believe that this could have happened. A few minutes thereafter the Army Commander Gen Cariappa walked into my office and confirmed the news. He was concerned that there would be a blood bath in the city and ordered me to have the Army deployed all over the city based on Police Stations as we used to have during the height of communal violence in 1947. With improving situation in Delhi by November-December 1947, troops had been withdrawn to their barracks in Delhi Cantonment and some had gone back to Meerut. I issued orders for immediate re-deployment of troops in the city and I had to report back to the Army Commander when this was completed. It took us almost the whole night to complete this task. There was, of course, some relief because the All India Radio was announcing that a Hindu and not a Muslim had killed Mahatma Gandhi. This implied that communal violence may not break out as it certainly would have, if a Muslim had assassinated the Mahatma. I later learnt that Mountbatten on his own, had told the press that it was a Hindu who had killed the Mahatma without even knowing who had killed him. This was certainly of help in ensuring that communal violence did not break out.

Having worked throughout the night, I returned home very tired. There was no question of my going to Birla House where the Mahatma had been assassinated. All the roads leading to that venue were blocked with crowds making it impossible to travel on the roads. My father, being in charge of the Intelligence Bureau, had already departed during the night and was at Birla House. My grandparents living with my father said that they wanted to pay their homage to the Mahatma's body. This was virtually impossible given the road conditions at that time. It struck me that a friend of mine Col Shukla lived on the first floor of the Army Officers' Mess on King Edward Road (now Maulana Azad Road) only a few hundred yards from my father's house. I decided to take my grandparents and my mother with me walking those few hundred yards through the crowd and reaching Shukla's house. Shukla took us to the terrace of the Mess at the junction of Queen's Way (now Janpath) with King Edward Road, along which the Mahatma's cortege was to go past on the way to the funeral site (now Rajghat). This Mess building has now been demolished and Air Force Headquarters has come up in its place opposite the National Museum. An hour later, we saw a sea of humanity passing down Queen's Way. The body of the Mahatma on a platform above an Army truck could clearly be seen. Jawaharlal Nehru and Sardar Patel were sitting on that platform at the feet of the Mahatma. We paid our homage to the Mahatma's body from the terrace. We now returned to my father's house walking in the opposite direction on the road. No sooner had I reached the house, I received a telephone call for my father from Patna. Ram Chandra Sinha, the Private Secretary to the Chief Minister of Bihar, whom I knew well as a family friend was on the line. I told him that my father had gone with the Mahatma's funeral procession. He said in that case he wanted me to do something important. The Chief Minister and two Cabinet Ministers of Bihar had flown in a special aircraft to Delhi and would be reaching Safdarjung Airport within a couple of hours. In those days there were no State Bhavans nor government staff cars. He wanted me to pick up the Bihar Chief Minister and two other Ministers from the Airport. I had no other option but to agree to do so. I took my father's car, a sturdy Ford, and drove through congestion on the roads to Safdarjung Airport. This took me more than an hour, normally one could cover this distance in 15-20 minutes. There was utter confusion at the airport with special planes from all over the country landing and crowding the place. I managed to reach in time to receive the Chief Minister and Ministers of Bihar. As they got into the car, they requested me to take them to the cremation site so that they could place flowers on Mahatma's funeral pyre. This was almost an impossible demand. I was wondering what I could do. Millions of people were on all roads leading to the funeral site and it was impossible for anyone to drive on the roads through that crowd.

It suddenly struck me that I could try driving cross country along the bank of the Yamuna river which had no habitation or roads at that time. I was familiar with that area because millions of Muslim refugees going to Pakistan had been accommodated in improvised shelters in that area. The Army was guarding them and I had on a few occasions visited those camps. This worked, but it took me nearly two hours of hard driving through crowds that had poured in from across the Yamuna. There was no Police anywhere for controlling traffic nor was there any vehicle in that area. I was in uniform and this helped me to drive through the crowd. I reached about 500 yards short of the funeral pyre. There was a ditch in front and I could not go any further. I saw Mountbatten, Nehru and Patel sitting on the ground. The funeral pyre had already been lit. I now realised that I may be in trouble if any one saw my car at that place. I was told that even Mountbatten had to walk nearly one mile to the cremation site because the road could not be cleared from the jostling crowd. The Ministers got down and managed to get to the site to place flowers below the pyre. As they were returning, I saw C Rajagopalachari, then Governor of West Bengal, shielded by his ADC and some others being brought towards my car. That was the first time that I saw Rajaji. He struck me as a frail old man who would have found it difficult to walk through that crowd. His ADC requested me to give Rajaji a lift in my car and drop him at his son-in-law's flat in Connaught Place. His son-in-law was Devdas Gandhi, the son of the Mahatma, who was then the Editor of *Hindustan Times*. I told the ADC that I could only accommodate Rajaji in the car because I had three Ministers from Bihar with me. The ADC said that he was happy to hand over Rajaji to me and he was sure that I would look after him. Rajaji sat in the front with me and the Ministers in the rear. Our return journey was faster because the crowd had begun to disperse. I reached Darbhanga House on Mansingh Road. This is now the office of the Intelligence Bureau. It took me nearly two hours to get there. When the crowd would see Rajaji in the car, they would shout 'Rajaji ki Jai'. Rajaji used to get angry saying that the greatest man of the world had been killed and that was not the time for anyone to raise slogans of 'Rajaji ki Jai'. I dropped the Bihar Ministers at Darbhanga House where they were to stay. They got out of the car and went inside without even saying thank you to me. Perhaps they were very emotional at that time and considering that I was a youngster, did not think it necessary to do so. I then dropped Rajaji at the flat in Connaught Place. I reached him up the stairs to his son-in-law's flat on the first floor. Before I left, Rajaji insisted on my having a cup of coffee. A steaming hot cup of South Indian coffee was brought for me which was most welcome because I had been under such physical strain for the past 24 hours. He profusely thanked me and I departed. A year later, Rajaji had become the Governor-General of India. Cariappa took over as the Army Chief on 15 January 1949. I had been his Staff Officer for a year and he invited me for the first Army Day Reception on 15 January 1949 where Rajaji was the Chief Guest. All of us were introduced to him. When it came to my turn, Rajaji shook hands with me and told Cariappa, "This young man had saved my life on a fateful day." I was surprised that he remembered me. He was in a good mood and made a humorous remark to Cariappa within my hearing that life in Governor-General's House was much too lavish for him. There was a huge tub in the bath room for bathing which he got removed saying that the tub was alright for Mountbatten who is a sailor but I prefer to have my bath from a shower.

§

Major Bunny Sen was an Artillery Officer whom I first met in Burma. He was Adjutant of a Field Regiment affiliated to our Brigade. In 1948, he was posted as GSO-2 (Artillery) in our Headquarters while I was GSO-2 (Operations). We became good friends. I discovered that he was much in love with Princess Kamla of Kapurthala. One day, the Army Commander, General Cariappa, sent for me and told me that the Governor-General Rajagopalachari had mentioned to him that the Maharaja of Kapurthala had spoken to him about his daughter being in love with Major Sen of the Army. He disapproved of this and he wanted Major Sen to break his friendship with his daughter. It was a delicate matter and Cariappa did not want to speak to Sen about it. Knowing that he was a friend of mine, he wanted me to tactfully dissuade Sen. I spoke to Sen telling him that in his own career interest he must cool off his relations with the Princess. As directed by Cariappa, I did not tell him that he had asked me to speak to him. Sen was very adamant and I realised that he could not be dissuaded. The authorities decided to post Sen out from Delhi to Srinagar which was then an operational area because of the ongoing war in Kashmir. I believe instructions had been issued to Brigadier Candeth, the Artillery Commander in Srinagar, not to allow any leave to Sen. It was hoped that by sending him away from Delhi, his relations with Princess Kamla may cool off. Sen continued to ring her up every day from Srinagar. He would even send Narcissus flowers from Srinagar by air and get me to deliver them to a contact of the Princess at Imperial Hotel in New Delhi. I knew that I was doing something which may affect me adversely, but I took the risk for the sake of a good friend. Somehow, it got known that flowers from Kashmir were being delivered to the Princess but fortunately my name did not figure. The authorities now decided to send Sen out of the country. He was posted to the Indian High Commission in London. He was given a few days casual leave to meet his mother in Darjeeling before proceeding to London. He came to Delhi and disappeared with Princess Kamla. There was a virtual man hunt launched to trace them. I was asked if I was aware where they had gone. He had not met me and I did not know where they were. A few days later before his casual leave finished, the couple surfaced and declared that they had got married. I was told the Maharaja was very unhappy. He laid down the condition that his daughter would not be addressed as Mrs Sen and she would always remain Princess Kamla. This was accepted by both. They lived happily as a married couple thereafter. Bunny Sen retired as a Brigadier from the Army. I am mentioning this incident because a Princess marrying a commoner was not acceptable to Maharajas in those days.

§

There were rumours about the Army Chief General Boucher relinquishing his appointment and being succeeded by an Indian General. According to convention, the senior Army Commander, that is General Cariappa should take over from him. There were also rumours that this may not happen as the government had Intelligence Reports about Cariappa being unduly friendly with Pakistan's Army Officers. Soon after Partition, General Raza, Adjutant General of Pakistan Army was coming to Delhi for a meeting in connection with Division of assets of the undivided Indian Army between the now two different Armies. Raza was from the Rajput Regiment and had served in the same Battalion for many years as a junior of Cariappa. There were no hotels in New Delhi in those days other than the

Imperial which was for the Princes. Hotels were only in Old Delhi. The Pakistan High Commission had not till then been fully set up. He wrote a personal letter to Cariappa enquiring if he could stay with him. Cariappa agreed to put him up. The second incident pertained to the Lahore Horse Show. General Iftikar Ahmed was the General Officer Commanding Lahore Area. He was an old friend of General Cariappa. He invited Cariappa for the Lahore Horse Show. Cariappa was at Amritsar and he drove down to Lahore which took a little over an hour. After attending the function and having drinks at Iftikar's house he returned to Amritsar the same evening. There was no Passport or Visa requirement at that time. Nor were there any orders for Army Officers to take prior permission for going to Lahore, next door from Amritsar. The Indo-Pak Border was marked at Wagha with only empty Oil Drums across the road. India and Pakistan's Army Guards stood on either side of the border. There was no Border Security Force or Indus Rangers at that time. A Staff Officer of General Iftikar was at the other side of the border to receive Cariappa and take him to the Horse Show. Both India and Pakistan's Guards turned out and presented arms to Cariappa. Yet another such incident pertained to Brig Nasar Ali Khan posted as Pakistan's Military Advisor in their High Commission at Delhi. In 1932, Nasar Ali Khan had been a Havildar Clerk at the Rajput Regimental Centre in Fatehgarh. Cariappa was then the Adjutant and he was working directly under him. Cariappa was impressed by his work and recommended him for a commission in the Army. He even coached him to qualify for the same. He got commissioned from Dehradun and was posted to the Rajput Regiment. Thus he could serve under Cariappa again in different Cantonments. After Partition, he had become a Brigadier and was posted at Delhi. He would frequently meet Cariappa and they were quite friendly. All these three incidents combined to create an impression that Cariappa was unduly friendly with Pakistanis. Sardar Patel had therefore reservations on Cariappa being made the Army Chief. In fact, at his instance, the Cabinet had decided to promote Lt Gen Rajendra Sinhji, the Southern Army Commander who was next in seniority to Cariappa. Sardar Patel had a soft corner for Rajendra Sinhji. As per the decision taken by the Sardar and communicated to him, he had very successfully conducted the Military Operations against Hyderabad. Another consideration was that he was the younger brother of Jam Saheb of Nawa Nagar who had been Chancellor of the Chamber of Princes and had been of much help to the Sardar in getting many Princely States to accede to the Indian Union. When Rajendra Sinhji heard of his being appointed Army Chief, he came up from Pune to Delhi and met the Prime Minister saying that he would resign if he was appointed Army Chief. He also said that there was no reason for the government to supersede Cariappa, a very capable General who had successfully conducted Operations in Kashmir for one year and was also senior to him. If the age old convention of appointing the senior Army Commander as Chief was broken, it could lead to dangerous consequences in the future. Generals may lobby for the appointment of Chief leading to politicising our apolitical Army. Nehru saw the point. The government now decided to appoint Gen Cariappa as the first Indian to become the C-in-C of the Indian Army. I may mention that the tradition of having the senior Army Commander appointed Army Chief has continued in our Army since then as it was also during British Rule. The only exception to this has been in my case in 1983. Subsequently, whenever there has been speculation about appointment of Army Chief, I get mentioned in this connection. I will enumerate my personal case on my supersession for Army Chief later in this book.

§

One afternoon as General Cariappa, still our Army Commander, was leaving his office at the end of the day, I saw him in the corridor in a very happy mood. He told me and the Brigadier Administration Sarda Nand Singh who was from his Regiment, "Listen to the All India Radio news bulletin tonight." That evening Lt Col Eric Sen in our Headquarters was celebrating his birthday and had invited us to the Delhi Gymkhana Club. We had a table near the dance floor and at 9 PM, all of us went to the Club office to hear the news bulletin on the Radio. It announced that Cariappa has been appointed C-in-C of the Indian Army and will take over this appointment on 15 January 1949. We were all very delighted. Maj Gen Thimayya was also at the Club that evening on a different table and we conveyed the good news to him. He was very delighted. A little later Gen Cariappa with the British High Commissioner came to the Club and we saw them in the alcove above the dance floor. We suggested to Sarda Nand Singh that since he was Cariappa's senior Staff Officer he should get the band to play 'He is a jolly good fellow'. Sarda Nand suggested that we should ask Thimayya to do that because he was the senior officer of the Army at the Club. When we approached Thimayya, he declined saying that the old man (referring to Cariappa) may not approve and consider it an act of indiscipline. Ultimately, the task was given to me as I was the junior most officer there that evening. I went to the band and asked them to play the desired tune. Cariappa stood up and smilingly waved his hand. This showed that he had not disapproved of what we had done.

Next morning, Cariappa sent for me in his office and told me that if I agreed, he would like to take me to Army Headquarters as his Military Assistant. I immediately replied that there could not be a greater honour for me. That posting to such a key appointment would have meant a promotion for me to the rank of Lt Col. Next day, Maj Gen Banerjee, the Military Secretary came to see Cariappa and told him that as per rules I could not be promoted to Lt Col at that time. I had to have a minimum of six and half years of service to be promoted to acting Lt Col but being the Chief, Cariappa could waive the rule and he would issue my posting order as desired by him. Cariappa said that he would not like to set a bad precedent and make an exception for me. That matter was now closed. However, Cariappa sent for me and explained his inability to take me with him. He was almost apologetic. I assured him that I fully realised the position and shall always remember that he had done me a great honour to think of taking me to Army Headquarters with him. The matter did not end there. Two months later, I received my posting order to go to the US in a newly created appointment as Assistant Military Attachee in our Embassy at Washington. This was obviously a gift to me from Cariappa to compensate me for not being his Military Assistant. Destiny willed it otherwise. The Prime Minister was on a tour to the US at that time. The Rupee had been devalued. The Embassy wanted the staff to be compensated for this while serving in the US. He enquired about the numbers affected and that was given to him also mentioning that one more was on his way. He told them to stop the latter coming. Thus ended this episode showing how even the wish of the Army Chief can be frustrated in regard to the posting of a junior officer in the rank of Major.

§

I continued to be GSO-2 (Operations) at Western Command for another year. After ceasefire coming into effect on 1 January 1949, United Nations Observers were deployed in Kashmir to report on any violations of the ceasefire. There were several instances of Pakistan violating the agreement on the Ceasefire Line and of their complaining that we had done so in different sectors. This kept us pre-occupied dealing with all these cases and getting verifications on the ground.

Lt Gen SM Shrinagesh succeeded Gen Cariappa as Western Army Commander. I was now serving under a third Army Commander at that Headquarters. I had met Shrinagesh when he was commanding 6/19 HYDERABAD Regiment (now 6 KUMAON) in our Brigade during Second World War in Burma. I was the GSO-3 in the Brigade Headquarters and the only Indian officer in that Headquarters. He would drop in at my office when he used to come to Brigade Headquarters. Before Partition, he had become a Brigadier. After Independence, he got quick promotions like other senior officers at that time. He became Maj Gen in 1947 taking over as Adjutant General which had been downgraded to that rank at that time. He then became a Lt Gen, Commanding a newly raised Corps in Kashmir in September, 1948 and our Army Commander in January 1949.

In the aftermath of Partition quick promotions were taking place for senior Army Officers. I served not only under three Army Commanders but also four Brigadier General Staff (BGS) and three General Staff Officers in the rank of Lt Col (GSO-1). In view of my long association with Operations in the Headquarters, Shrinagesh, with the approval of Cariappa, assigned me an important job. A delegation had to go to Karachi in Pakistan for talks with a Pakistani delegation to delineate the Ceasefire Line in Kashmir at a meeting convened by the UN. Lt Gen Shrinagesh was appointed the leader of the Indian delegation with two Civil and two Army members. The civilian members were Vishnu Sahay, Secretary, Kashmir Affairs and HM Patel, Defence Secretary. The Army members were Maj Gen KS Thimayya and Brig SHFJ Manekshaw. I was nominated as Secretary of this high-powered delegation. It is interesting that the stock of the Army was still high at that time. An Army Commander could be the leader of the delegation and the Defence Secretary one of its members. Today, a Defence Secretary would not accept being an ordinary member of a delegation led by a Service Chief, leave alone an Army Commander.

Our delegation was briefed by Sir Girija Shankar Bajpai, then the Secretary General of Ministry of External Affairs. Our last briefing was by the Prime Minister himself. We were ushered into his office and this was the second time when I as a Major had an opportunity to interact with Nehru. While we were leaving, Nehru told me that I had to be careful with Secret Papers at Karachi and should send daily reports on the progress of discussion.

It was a great experience to be the Secretary of the Indian delegation at an International Conference. The Pakistan delegation comprised Gen Cawhron, Chief of General Staff of Pakistan Army, Maj Gen Nazir Ahmed, Commanding a Division in Kashmir and Maj Gen Sher Khan, Director Military Operations of Pakistan Army. There were also two civilian members in the Pakistani delegation. There was much bonhomie between Indian and Pakistani Army Officers as only a little earlier we had served together in the undivided Indian Army. Thimayya and Nazir Ahmed were from the same batch at Sandhurst in UK and were now commanding Divisions opposite each other. I had known Sher Khan when he was a Colonel in General Headquarters (India) at Delhi. He had a Morris Car which I bought from him when he was leaving for Pakistan. In fact, he had sold his car to me at a concessional price, even when a business man from old Delhi was giving him a slightly higher price. His first question to me when we met at Karachi was to enquire as to how his old car was doing. In spite of all these old connections, our discussions during the formal conference used to be quite heated. There were opposite views which had to be reconciled and an agreement arrived at. It took us seven days of discussion to draw the 400 miles Ceasefire Line from Laleali near Chhamb to NJ 9842 beyond Kargil. It is a pity that we did not delineate the Line beyond NJ 9842 and left it as 'thence to the Glaciers'. The reason for this was that we were all too tired on the last day when the agreement was eventually signed late that night and the fact that no one could then visualise any military operations above the height of 20,000 feet. Moreover, a plebiscite was supposed to be held and after that the Ceasefire Line would lose significance. The dispute between India and Pakistan in Kashmir was expected to get resolved after plebiscite.

A significant success for us at the Conference was that the 200 sq mile of Tilel Valley in the North which was No Man's Land, was made inclusive to us. Our argument was that since Kashmir had legally acceded to India, No Man's Land, in which there was no presence of either Army should be made inclusive to India. Pakistan had bid for this Valley to be divided fifty-fifty between the two countries. On return to Delhi, the delegation was complimented by Sir Girija Shankar Bajpai. He told me that he could take me into the newly started Indian Foreign Service where I could become an Ambassador. I thanked him and declined the offer saying that I had chosen the Army as my career and I would like to remain in the Army. Destiny has its own ways. After I quit the Army, I was appointed Ambassador in Nepal. My son, Yashvardhan competed into the Indian Foreign Service and has been Ambassador in two countries so far.

Gen Shrinagesh asked me to tour all the major military stations in the Command including Jammu and Kashmir to deliver talks on the Ceasefire Agreement. This gave a boost to my image in the Army.

§

In 1949, I was posted as Brigade Major (BM) of 123 Infantry Brigade at Amritsar which was then commanded by Brig Sarda Nand Singh with whom I had served in Headquarters Western Command. Brigade Major used to be considered the best staff appointment for a Major in the Army. Normally officers who were among the top in their course at Staff College used to be posted as Brigade Major. I got this appointment even without being a Staff College graduate. I did my Staff College afterwards.

123 Brigade at Amritsar was a jumbo-sized Brigade with six battalions, an Armoured Regiment, an Artillery Regiment and a Squadron of Horse Cavalry besides administrative units. We also had a battalion of Punjab Armed Police under us deployed on the Border. There was no Border Security Force (BSF) at that time. Working under a Commander of great calibre like Sarda Nand Singh was a wonderful learning experience for me.

§

Sir Chandu Lal Trivedi, Governor of Punjab, suggested that the Army should have a mega function to show its competence in the wake of the chaos suffered in Punjab during Partition. Sarda Nand Singh volunteered to organise a ceremonial parade, a Tattoo and a Carnival at Amritsar. It was a gigantic task to organise three such mega functions at the same time. We also had to organise suitable accommodation for VVIPs including Defence Minister and the three Service Chiefs. There was no suitable hotel in Amritsar at that time nor did the Army have much accommodation. The Cantonment had catered for only one Company of British troops of the battalion located at Lahore.

It took us about six months to make all the arrangements. One of our COs was the son of the Military Secretary of the Maharaja of Patiala who got us half a dozen luxury tents from the Maharaja's *Toshkhana* (Maharaja's stores). These tents with wooden floors,beautiful carpets and velvet curtains were very luxurious, the likes of which I had never seen before. We put up these tents at Rambagh where there was plenty of open space. The Defence Minister took the salute at Brigade Ceremonial Parade commanded by the Brigadier himself and I marched behind him as the Brigade Major. The Tattoo had different interesting items like a Company of Marathas dressed in red coats and rifles of East India Company days performing old drills, Horse Show by Gwalior Lancers, Churchill tanks with flame throwers in a mock battle and so on. The Tattoo was much admired. Vice-Admiral Pizey and Air Marshal Elmhirst, the then Chiefs of the Indian Navy and Indian Air Force respectively, wrote to us later that they had seen Tattoos at Aldershot in the UK but the one at Amritsar surpassed them in originality and precision. This was indeed a great compliment. Our Carnival was equally successful. The star attraction at the Carnival was a 200 feet high See-Lahore-Tower put up by our Electrical and Mechanical Engineers. One could see the lights of Lahore in the distance from the top of this tower. The Carnival yielded a net profit of over ₹1 lakh which we deposited in our Brigade Welfare Fund. Brig BM Kaul commanding a Brigade at Jalandhar attended our 'Sainik Utsav'. He complemented Sarda Nand Singh and told him in my presence that he had a good Brigade Major. I could not imagine at that time that this may one day very significantly effect my career both for the good and also not so good.

§

Maj Gen JN Chaudhuri had commanded the Armed Division during the Hyderabad Operations and taken the surrender of the Turkish General El Adroos, commanding the Hyderabad Army. He was appointed Military Governor of Hyderabad for some time. He came to Amritsar to carry out reconnaissance of the border as his Division had an Operational role in our sector. I was detailed to accompany him. He took me to be a Bengali. He told me that Bengalis were considered non-martial and then said that initial plans for Defence of India after Independence was made by three Bengalis. Admiral Chatterjee from the Navy, Air Marshal Mukerjee from the Air Force and him from the Army. He enquired as to how the Bengali Company in 2 RAJPUT was doing. When General Cariappa visited Calcutta on taking over as Chief, some Bengali lawyers had protested to him about Bengalis not being recruited in combat arms. Cariappa had agreed to take Bengalis in his own Regiment, the Rajput Regiment. 2 RAJPUT has a Bengali Company and was part of our Brigade. I enquired from the General if he would like to visit 2 RAJPUT which was located at Khasa on the road to Wagha on the border. He replied in the affirmative and I sent a message to the Commanding Officer of that battalion. On arrival in the battalion, Chaudhuri was received by the Commanding Officer and the Subedar Major. After introduction, the General enquired from the Subedar Major as to how the Bengali Company was doing. The Subedar Major seeing Chaudhuri, a tall and well-built person, thought that he was a Jat because that is a common surname among Jats. He promptly replied, *"Bengali Company bilkul Ganda Hai Saheb, Fauj ke Layak nahin hai."* (The Bengali Company is no good and is not fit for the Army.)The General looked annoyed and said, "Saheb Hum Bengali Hain." Both the Commanding Officer and I felt uncomfortable with this exchange of conversation. The Subedar Major was an old veteran and a seasoned soldier. He was illiterate but his IQ was high. Without batting an eye lid, he promptly replied, *"Hum ko Malum hai Saheb ki aap Bengali Hain. Bengali Log General Bahut Achchhe hote Hain magar Achchhe sipahi nahin hote hain."* (I know Saheb that you are a Bengali.Bengalis make good Generals but not good Sepoys.)

§

Gen Russell, the Army Commander under whom I served had retired and settled on the Bahama Islands in the Atlantic Ocean. I used to exchange New-Year cards with him. While acknowledging my card, he advised me that I had been too long on Staff and to have a balanced career I should go back to Regimental soldiering. It is true that I had done a long spell on the Staff with a Brigade in Burma followed by a Corps in Indonesia, then GHQ(I) in Delhi, in Western Command and now at 123 Brigade. With the approval of Sarda Nand Singh, I requested for Regimental posting. I had by now been transferred from the Jat Regiment to the Gorkhas. I was posted to a Gorkha battalion in Kashmir beyond the Razadan Pass in Gurez Valley.

Before I finish with my highly fruitful tenure with 123 Brigade in Amritsar, I may mention two amusing incidents pertaining to two officers staying in the Brigade Mess with me. Capt Bachhitar Singh Sanga was the RTO (Railway Transport Officer) (now designated as MCO) at Amritsar Railway Station. He was attached to our Brigade. He had come up from the ranks and was an interesting individual. He believed in the superiority of man over woman. He had three wives who were all living in his village. His youngest wife had some medical problem and he brought her for treatment at Amritsar. The lady recovered. I met her one evening at a function and she told me that she lived in the village along with Bachhitar's other two wives and they were quite close to each other. Bachhitar lived away from them for most of the time because of his service in the Army. The three of them were good company for each other and they lived happily together. Bachhitar intervened and said to me, "Sir, I have trained my wives well and they live happily together." After the lady got cured, she went back to Bachhitar's village. He told me that he wanted to give a talk to all the officers of the Brigade on manhood versus womanhood. In a lighter vain, I agreed to his suggestion and we organised a lecture by him on the subject in the Officers' Mess. We had invited only junior officers below the rank of Lt Col for the lecture. Bachhitar started his lecture in all seriousness, saying, "Gentlemen, you need not take notes because I will give you a precis at the end of my talk." I must say he had done a lot of research to quote how in the past well-to-do men used to have several wives. He quoted from Hindu scripture, Islamic history and Greek mythology. The thrust of his argument was that if you want to have a good breed of men you should have successful and well-to-do people in life having more than one wife. In the context, he tried to prove that the recent plural marriage order issued in the Army that prohibited anyone from having more than one wife was not in the interest of the nation. He even quoted the name of a Maj Gen in our Army who used to marry every time he got a promotion. It was good fun for everybody and Bachhitar answered questions put to him by the audience. It so happened that after a couple of months his youngest wife died suddenly of illness in the village. I told everyone in the Mess that no one should raise the issue of plural marriage with him in view of this tragedy. A couple of months later Bachhitar came to me with an application that he wants permission to marry again. He wrote in his application that the plural marriage order did not apply to him because he had three wives before the order came into force and even after the death of one of them he still had more than one wife. His was a case of asking for a replacement issue rather than an initial issue. I showed his application to the Brigade Commander who had a big laugh and told me that I should forward his application through proper channel to Army Headquarters. He added that he did not want to deprive officers in the chain of having a good laugh after reading his application. As expected, the Army Headquarters turned down his application. I am told that after a year when he had retired from the Army, he made up his deficiency in the number of his wives.

The next amusing incident was of a young officer Capt Chawla who had just got his permanent commission. He advertised in the matrimonial column of the local newspaper seeking a bride for him. He received nearly a hundred offers. In the unsettled conditions in Punjab after Partition, a permanent commissioned officer of the Army was a big catch. He sought my help in selecting a bride for himself. I told him that we would constitute a board of three officers under my chairmanship to select a bride for him. He welcomed my suggestion. We devised a proforma allocating marks to various columns like looks, education, family background and any special qualification. Each of these qualities was allotted 100 marks. The board comprising me, the DAQMG and the Staff Captain at our Headquarters sat one afternoon and did the evaluation. We gave Chawla 10 selected names in order of merit. The person who topped the list was a lady doctor at Gurdaspur. Chawla went to meet her. He had a receding forehead bordering on baldness. He borrowed my Pork Pipe Felt Hat which in British days was invariably worn by officers in civvies. He went to

Gurdaspur and returned very disappointed. Apparently, when he met the lady doctor in the room he had not taken off the Hat that I had lent him. She told him that either he was bald or did not know manners that a hat should be taken off while sitting in a room. Soon after Chawla went to his home on Annual Leave. After 10 days, we received a telegram from him for permission to get married. The old convention from British days of officers seeking permission before getting married had continued. We sent the required approval. After his leave, Chawla returned to Amritsar with his bride. We welcomed the couple and there was a reception in their honour in the Officers' Mess. Chawla introduced me to his wife. She said, "I have heard of you, Major Sinha. I believe you had marked me number four in your selection list." I have never felt so embarrassed in all my life.

§

I joined my battalion at Kanzalwal in North Kashmir. I was detailed to take over a Company which was holding a 13,000 feet high piquet on the Ceasefire Line. My Company Officer, Lt Yograj Puri, had come down to our battalion Headquarters. He was a keen mountaineer and had done very well at the High Altitude Warfare School at Gulmarg getting an Instructor grading. He confessed to me later that he wanted to test my physical stamina thinking that coming from the Staff I may not be able to meet the challenge. He deliberately took me to the piquet on a track entailing steep climb rather than another easier but a little longer track. He was a good officer and I found him a good companion at the piquet. Living at that height particularly in winter months was very trying. Our piquet was fairly close to the base of 25,000 feet high Nanga Parbat. One had to sharply look up to see the top of the peak. During the morning and evening 'Stand to' we got a beautiful view of the peak when at dawn, the snow on it looked golden gradually changing to shining white and in the evening again golden due to the setting Sun before darkness descended. Puri would tell me that his ambition was to climb that peak which happened to be in Pakistan-occupied area. His ambition got fulfilled when an Italian expedition going up to the peak was permitted by Pakistan and it was allowed for Puri to go with them. On return, Puri was posted as Instructor at the High Altitude Warfare School. A few years later, I was Instructor at the Tactical

Wing of the Infantry School at Mhow. Puri came to do the Company Commander's Course and was allotted to my syndicate. He did extremely well on the Course. Again after a few years he qualified at the Staff College Entrance Examination and was supposed to come for the Course while I was now Instructor at Staff College. I was looking forward to having him in my syndicate. But God willed it otherwise. He was caught in an avalanche in the Himalayas and met a very untimely death. The Indian Army lost a very promising officer and I a good friend.

I may narrate a harrowing experience that I once had while serving on the piquet in Gurez Valley. It was early December and I was moving with a Platoon along a mountain track. We had four mules with us carrying stores. Suddenly, there was a snow blizzard. Everything went suddenly dark and in the high speed wind, snowflakes contacting the exposed portions of our body became like pins hurting us. The track became very slippery. We had to move very carefully, if we slipped we could go down a few hundred feet below. Two of our mules went down the hill side. We had no proper snow clothing in those days. The blizzard lasted for over 24 hours. We managed to get into an animal shelter without roof made by Bakarwals for their grazing animals. The walls of this shelter protected us from cold piercing winds. All of us remained huddled together having the benefit of each other's body warmth. The two remaining mules were accommodated inside the open shelter. When the blizzard lifted, the Sun was very strong and shining on the snow-covered terrain through which we plodded. There were some snow goggles with us and those who could not have one covered their eyes with cloth and could see through the cloth. Luckily we had only one case of snow blindness which got cured after some time. There was no case of frostbite. This was the most harrowing experience for all of us.

I recall an amusing incident. One of our mules appeared half dead. My Platoon Havildar said that he would revive the mule by giving it some rum. He poured half a bottle of rum in the mouth of the mule and the latter got up and appeared fully recovered.

§

I became very fond of Gorkha soldiers. Their loyalty and discipline are legendary. They carry out orders to the letter. I remember many interesting anecdotes. I was with the battalion near Jammu close to Ranbir Canal whose water is icy cold. We had no electricity and we were living in Bashas/tents. We used to put beer bottles in the canal for a while and get chilled beer for ourselves in the Officers' Mess. On one occasion the General Officer Commanding our Division was to come and have lunch in our Officers' Mess. I sent a few bottles of beer to be chilled in the canal instructing a Gorkha soldier to do the needful. He took over an hour to do this but when the General came we found that of the dozen bottles only one was chilled. I discovered the reason for this. He had sat on the bank of the canal and tried to chill the beer bottles one by one. After a few minutes, he would take out the bottle from the water and keep it on the ground. Thus those bottles ceased to be chilled. Only the last bottle was chilled which we served to the General. This shows that while giving orders to the soldier one has to explain things properly. This was a good lesson for me. Another amusing incident in the battalion pertained to Captain Maita Lal Gurung of our battalion. In 1947, when British officers left, it was decided that each Gorkha battalion will have three former Junior Commissioned Officers (JCOs) given direct commission as officers in the battalion without having to go to any training academy. Maita Lal was an old soldier who had won gallantry awards in Italy during Second World War. He was the Subedar Major of the battalion in 1947 and was overnight promoted to the rank of Second Lieutenant. Like other directly commissioned Gorkha officers he did not know any English. The authorities had appointed three directly commissioned officers from senior JCOs in every battalion to facilitate the takeover by Indian officers from British officers. After a Divisional Exercise, General Henderson Brooks gave a summing up of the exercise in English. Seeing Capt Maita Lal in the audience, he asked him, *"Saheb aap ko samajh aya."* Maita Lal with a straight face replied, *"Saheb ham ko samjh aata to main bhi aaj General hota."* Everyone in the audience laughed. This reminded me of what Field Marshal Slim wrote in his book, *Defeat into Victory*. Slim was a Gorkha Officer of long standing. During the retreat in Burma in 1942, he was the Corps Commander. As he was approaching a bridge, he came under heavy Japanese Artillery fire. He got out of the jeep deliberating what to do. Suddenly he heard peals of laughter from a young Gorkha soldier taking cover near a bush. He went up to the soldier and asked him why he was laughing. The soldier replied that he was laughing because it was for the first time he had seen a General not knowing what to do with himself. Slim has recorded in his book that he had commanded Gorkha, British, Indian and Sikh troops. Strangely he made a distinction between an Indian and the Sikh soldier. He realised that under those conditions a British soldier would have said, "For God sake Bloody Well take cover Sir." An Indian soldier would have pleadingly requested him to take cover. A Sikh soldier would have waited for him to get wounded so that he could cover him with his broad chest. Only a Gorkha soldier in those circumstances would laugh at him.

For the next six years, I served in the battalion in two spells as Company Commander of two different Companies. While with my Regiment, I did two training courses. The first was the Company Commander's course in which I stood first getting the rare grading of 'Distinguished' which used to be given perhaps once in two or three years. It entitled me to a special qualification pay of ₹50 per month. The other course was at Defence Services Staff College where also I topped the course. As a result of my performance on these courses, I subsequently did a tenure of three years each as Instructor on these courses at Mhow and Wellington.

§

In those days, only 30% of Majors used to get selected for Lt Col and one of the qualifications for becoming a Commanding Officer was a tenure as Second-in-Command of a battalion. I was earmarked to take over as Second-in-Command of my battalion when orders came from the blue posting me to Quarter Master General's Branch at Army Headquarters. For the first and only time I put up a representation to Army Headquarters that I have done enough of Staff and I should be left to do the mandatory tenure of Second-in-Command so that I did not miss out from being considered for promotion to Lt Col. My representation was turned down.

§

Lt Gen BM Kaul was the Quarter Master General at Army Headquarters. He had got his promotion and appointment against the recommendations of Gen Thimayya, the then Army Chief. Thimayya had resigned on this issue causing much consternation in the Army and controversy in the country. Nehru had persuaded him to withdraw his resignation in national interest. Thimayya withdrew his resignation. Later Nehru castigated him in the Parliament. Surprisingly, he took this lying down and continued to serve as Chief for the remaining part of his tenure. He was now sulking and had become virtually a lame duck Chief. Because of his proximity to Nehru, Kaul had become the most powerful General in the Army.

I was asked to report personally to General Kaul. When I went to meet him, he was visibly annoyed. He asked me if I knew the number of Majors in the Indian Army. I replied that I do not know the exact number but the figure could be around 1,000. He then said that he had personally selected me for his Staff and I had represented against that posting. I told him that I was not aware of this and now that he has told me about it, I considered it a great honour to serve under him. His remark ten years earlier after the Sainik Utsav at Amritsar appreciating my work, came back like a flash to me. I explained to him that the reason why I had represented against the posting was the fact that I had done a long spell on the Staff in the rank of Major and I was earmarked to take over as Second-in-Command of my battalion. In the absence of holding that appointment, I would miss the opportunity of becoming a Lt Col as that was a mandatory requirement. He saw the point and told me that he would ensure that I do not miss my promotion and if I worked hard for him, he would duly reward me. He sent for the Military Secretary in my presence asking him to bring my dossier. When the Military Secretary came, he wrote on my dossier, "This officer was brought to QMG's Branch to serve under me in the larger interest of the Army. The fact that he would not have held the appointment of Second-in-Command would be condoned for his promotion to the rank of Lt Col." Later, when my turn came for promotion, I was perhaps the only officer of my batch who had been promoted without having served as Second-in-Command.

I was assigned to what was then known as Q (Ops & Plans) which had only three officers, a Brigadier, a Lt Col and a Major. I was also given the additional task of working as the Staff Officer of the Quarter Master General, the all-powerful Gen Kaul. I recall that one day he picked up the RAX telephone and rang up the Prime Minister. He said, "Jawahar Bhai an Air Force Dakota has been shot down in Nagaland and the two pilots taken prisoner by the Naga rebels." He also said that he was leaving for Kohima to personally conduct operations there. He asked me to arrange a special plane of the Air Force to take him to Dimapur and thence to Kohima by helicopter. He also asked me to inform the Staff Officer of the Army Chief that he had gone to Kohima to oversee operations for recovering the Air Force Pilots. This was his style of working. As QMG he was not officially required to oversee operations but Kaul had his own ways.

There is no doubt that Kaul had a flair for logistics and administration. With his direct contact with the Prime Minister and using his name he could do anything that he wanted and even Cabinet Ministers deferred to him.

§

The Armoured Division was located at Jhansi-Babina and in event of war was required to move to its battle stations in Punjab. As per existing plans this move was to be completed in three weeks. At an operational conference in Shimla presided over by Thimayya, Kaul said that if the Armoured Division took three weeks to move from its present location to Punjab, the war would have been fought and may be lost while the Division was on the move. This planning had been done on the basis of adequate notice before commencement of hostilities. Kaul said that he would ensure that this move was completed in three to four days. Thimayya remarked that no one would be happier than him if this could be done. Kaul took on this challenge. For the next three months, we were working to ensure that this could be done. He arranged a meeting with Jagjivan Ram, the then Railway Minister, for organising the Rail move of the Armoured Division. He also sent a note to Thimayya informing him and saying that if he wanted he could also attend the meeting. Thimayya did not attend. Kaul had a very successful meeting with the Railway Minister who agreed to all his proposals. The rolling stock on the railways for this move had to be stabled at Jhansi-Babina so that the three days required to concentrate them could be saved. Similarly, all the preliminary work like raising overhead wires at Railway Stations to permit move of tanks mounted on rolling stock would be completed immediately. It was agreed that all the level crossings en route would have over bridges to permit simultaneous road and rail move. All civilian rail traffic on the route would be suspended for three days to permit special trains carrying the Armoured Division to move simultaneously on both UP and DOWN Railway Lines. Simultaneously, road convoys of the Division would also be moving. Rehearsals of entraining and detraining on special trains were carried out reducing the time allotted for this. Similarly, Road convoys were required to move faster and trained to do so. I have mentioned all these details to highlight Kaul's drive and vision. Concentration time for the Division was thus reduced from three weeks to four days.

§

While I was serving on the staff of Gen Kaul, I had two occasions to hear the vitriolic language the Defence Minister Krishna Menon could use. I had heard of his using sarcasm in his speeches. During the pre-Independence days while in London he was a Hyde Park orator. He would use phrases like, "The Sun never sets in the British Empire because even God could not trust the British during Dark" and "Britain rules the waves because it waives all the rules." One afternoon, Kaul had to attend a meeting in the Defence Minister's office on air maintenance in Ladakh. Since I dealt with the subject and had the statistics with me, he asked me to accompany him. We entered the Defence Minister's room which I was little familiar with because pre-Independence, Auchinleck used to have that as his office and I used to maintain the maps in that room.

The Defence Secretary, Pulla Reddy, the Air Chief, Air Marshal Engineer besides the Defence Minister were in the room. Kaul and I took our seats at the table. We had recently acquired Russian equipment from the Soviet Union at the initiative of Krishna Menon. Previously, we used to get all our military hardware from the Western countries. The AN-12 transport aircraft with high air lift capacity had been acquired from the USSR and was to be used for air maintenance in Ladakh. The meeting began with the Defence Secretary making some opening remarks. It appeared that Krishna Menon was not in a good mood. He cut short the Defence Secretary saying, "Pulla Reddy, you have neither any pull nor are you ever ready." The Air Chief now referred to the AN-12 saying that some checks had to be carried out before pressing them into service. This put off Krishna Menon. He said, "Air Chief, we sent Operational, Technical and all sorts of delegations to Moscow to acquire the AN-12 and it was now too late for him to have any philosophical doubts about its performance." The Air Chief persisted saying that flying to Ladakh was very hazardous. Krishna Menon replied, "I know that flying to Ladakh is hazardous but since when has service in the Air Force been equated with taking out a life insurance policy." Air Marshal Engineer persisted saying that the checks will not take more than a couple of days. That seems to have further irritated Menon and he let Engineer have the full blast of his vitriolic language, "Engineer, your mind is like a magnetic compass which reacts to every gravitational change on the Earth. You are like a typical English liberal who sees too many sides of a problem and loses sight of all sides. As Minister for Defence, I refuse to reconcile myself to the position of a gardener who plucks the plant every day to see what progress it has made." The meeting now proceeded on a subdued tone. I only passed statistics to Kaul who referred to them while outlining our requirements and the progress so far made in maintaining troops in Ladakh by air. After a while when other aspects pertaining to the Air Force started being discussed, Kaul stood up and told the Defence Minister, "Sir, I have another meeting to attend. I am leaving my Staff Officer behind who can furnish any details that may be required." I thought it strange for a General to leave the Defence Minister's meeting halfway and get away with it. Kaul could do so and even an abrasive Minister like Krishna Menon would accept that. This is all because of Kaul being known to be close to Jawaharlal Nehru. I carried on with the meeting and I was happy that I was not required to speak or give any clarification.

The second occasion when I saw Krishna Menon in action was in the Parliament. I had accompanied Kaul to the Parliament when the Defence debate was taking place. We sat in the official gallery in Lok Sabha. Krishna Menon was giving out whole lot of statistics on Defence production. The opposition was getting a little uneasy because Krishna Menon was taking a long time. Acharya Kripalani was in the Opposition and interrupted saying, "I did not get that." Krishna Menon was quick to react and turning around to the Speaker said, "Sir, I can only provide information to the Opposition, I cannot provide understanding." The house had a laugh. When it came to his turn, Kripalani was also quite scathing. He said, "Sir, during the tenure of the Honourable Defence Minister, India lost hundreds of square miles of her territory without the Indian Forces firing a single shot. Perhaps this is of no importance to our Honourable Defence

Minister." I am mentioning this exchange between the Minister and the Opposition to highlight the nature of Parliamentary debates in those days without attempts made to rush to the well of the House.

§

Kaul chose to reward me for all the hard work I had done for him. He rang me up one night at my residence to say that he would be taking over as Chief of General Staff (CGS) the next morning and I had to set up his new office in a room next to the Army Chief. Lt Gen LP Sen who was the CGS, was detailed for a while on a Study Group functioning from his house. After a couple of months or so, he would be taking over as Eastern Army Commander. He added that he wanted to take over his new appointment while Thimayya was still the Army Chief before he retires. This showed the power that Kaul wielded. He also told me that as I have worked hard for him, he had decided to reward me and send me on a course to the Joint Services Staff College in the UK. I never thought that I would get this big break in my career. This course had been started in the UK by Mountbatten when he was the Chief of Defence Staff. Only selected officers who had done their respective Staff College attended this course. India had one vacancy on this course every year which was rotated among the three Services and the Army got its turn once in three years. Normally, Brigadiers and Colonels or equivalent were selected for this course. At that time, I was only a Major coming up for promotion to Lt Col the following year.

Before leaving for London, I had to do two-weeks attachment with Defence Services Staff College at Wellington. I had done the course nine years earlier and it was felt that I should do short attachments with Naval and Air Wings. Kaul told me that this was being done for an officer going to Joint Services Staff College to ensure that he goes fully prepared for the course abroad. I thanked him for his kindness. Little did I know that this would land me in trouble and I would have to live with it for next ten years.

When I arrived at Wellington for my attachment I found that rumours had floated about my being "Kaul's man" sent to Wellington to report on what was happening at the Staff College. Manekshaw had known me well. We had worked together not only in Military Operations but also when I was Instructor at Mhow and he was the Commandant there. I found Manekshaw very cold towards me and he hardly took any notice of me. Kaul and Manekshaw were opposed to each other. Kaul being all powerful at Delhi, he had arranged a Court of Inquiry against Manekshaw for so-called anti-national activities. In one of his talks, Manekshaw had referred to Shivaji riding ponies instead of a horse as shown in the painting in the lecture hall. The other allegation was that he had the paintings of Robert Clive and Warren Hastings taken out from the godown and displayed prominently in his office. While I was in Wellington, Kaul sent a Lt Col from Delhi to collect information about Manekshaw from Instructors serving under him in the college. Surprisingly, two Colonels who had been close to Manekshaw agreed to give evidence against him. When I was approached, I said that I had not seen or heard anything and I could not give any evidence. The Colonel told me that in that case I may get into trouble. He even tried to put a telephone call to Delhi and asked me to speak to Kaul directly. I was happy that the telephone call did not materialise. When I returned to Delhi before proceeding to London, Kaul sent for me and even warned me that my name could be taken off from the course. Luckily, Kaul did not pursue this matter and two days later I proceeded by ship with my family from Bombay to UK. I was happy that I had not got involved in the Court of Inquiry against Manekshaw nor was I in India in 1962 serving on the Staff of Kaul. In fact, I did not meet Kaul again thereafter.

§

Whereas Kaul's forte was administration, Military Operations were not his cup of tea. He was the only officer from the administrative services of the Army to be given operational command appointments. To a large extent, this proved his nemesis in 1962. He used to get a whole lot of visitors in his office, many of whom were not connected with the Army. He attempted to project himself as a nationalist in his dress. Unlike other Army officers who normally wore suit and tie, he would wear buttoned up coat. He also tried to build a following amongst superseded Army officers championing their case. He had taken over as Chief of General Staff (CGS). This was the most important appointment after the Chief. He dealt with Military Operations, Military Intelligence and Military Training. People started talking that he was in line to become the Army Chief soon. After that he may even succeed Jawaharlal Nehru. In fact there was a book published at that time under the title *After Nehru Who?* by a foreign author, Welles Hangen. He mentions Kaul as a possible contender. Even as QMG, he would interfere in operational matters. At that time the Chinese claims for lines on the border with India in the Himalayas was called Shifting Lines because their versions kept changing. I heard talk about our adopting Forward Policy in the Himalayas. Rumours were that the Defence Minister, Krishna Menon, Intelligence Bureau Chief BN Mullik and Kaul were in the coterie, supporting this idea. I was in no way connected with this.

§

The sea journey for me and my family from Bombay to UK was a nice holiday. I had earlier been on a troop ship in the Bay of Bengal travelling from Calcutta to Rangoon and later while returning from Indonesia. Compared to troop ships, the first-class cabin allotted to us on the Anchor Line ship was really luxurious and the food on board the ship was fabulous. There were arrangements for entertainment and sports like swimming and deck tennis on the ship. We encountered rough weather on the Arabian Sea and again beyond Gibraltar on the Bay of Biscay. Sailing over the Mediterranean Sea was very smooth and the ship did not rock at all. After the invasion of British and French forces during the Suez crisis in 1956, the canal had been extensively mined. Later, a lane for ships in the canal was cleared but the remainder was still mined. This used to result in ships waiting on either side for their turn to cross the canal through the one-way cleared lane. It took our ship four days to cross the canal. My friend Colonel Hira was the Military Attache at Cairo. He had kindly sent a car to pick us up from Suez and take us to Cairo. We spent three days with him doing sightseeing including a moon light picnic near the Pyramids. We rejoined our ship at Port Said at the other end of the Canal. It is a pity that nowadays sea travel has become a thing of the past with people travelling by air. Time is now at a premium and fast air travel has converted the world into a global village. We had taken three weeks to go by sea from India to UK which is now covered by air in about seven hours. In the old days of sail before steam ships, it took six months for ships to travel from Britain to India around the Cape of Good Hope. The ships were dependent on favourable wind to cover the journey. In late eighteenth century, the Duke of Wellington had taken six months to reach India.

§

While I was at the Joint Services Staff College, Lord Mountbatten had come to address us. This was the second time I was hearing his address which was as fiamboyant as his address that I had heard in Indonesia. He started his talk, apologising for being five minutes late. He said it was because that morning he had got up and polished his shoes himself. He added that if his father Lord Battenberg had heard that an Admiral of the Fleet in Britain polished his shoes himself he would have thrown up his hand in horror saying that Britain had gone Communist. Britain has not gone Communist but occasionally he polished his shoes himself. I am sure all that talk was for creating an affect. He then went on to say that as a child he would often sit on his father's knee and ask him the secret of the supremacy of the Royal Navy. His father was the First Sea Lord, a designation for the Naval Chief in the UK. His father would reply, keep the Royal Navy toys as strong as any other Navy of the world. When Mountbatten became the First Sea Lord, his problem was how the Navy could pretend to be great when it was half the size of the major Navies of the world. Thereafter he talked to us about the jointmanship between the three Services in modern war. In that context, he told us that when he was Viceroy in India, he had started the National Defence Academy at Khadkwasla, near Pune, as a joint training institution for Cadets wanting to join the three Services. This was unique in the world. He also started the Defence Services Staff College at Wellington in India. This again was the first such institution in the world. He added in a lighter vain that there was a problem in getting the three Services whose duration of Staff training varied, to be on a common duration. The Navy used to have six months Staff course, the Air Force one year Staff course and the Army two years Staff course. Making all the three Services do their course together meant that the Army students could not get any weekends, the Air Force having all weekends and the Navy being on a week end all the time. This was a joke I had heard when I was a student at Wellington and it seems to have travelled to him. He then said that when he was Chief of Combined Operations attending a meeting of Chief of Staff Committee during the Second World War, the three Service Chiefs now working with him were in the rank of Lt Col or equivalent. Now when he proposed reforms in Defence organisation and functioning, the Naval Chief would quote the Spanish Armada and battle of Trafalgar, the Army battles of Blenheim and Waterloo, and the Air Force not to be left out, would quote the battle of Britain. He tried to get them all on board and talk about the 'Battle of Tomorrow'. In the evening, there was a cocktail party in the Mess in his honour. I wore a black *Sherwani* for the occasion. As he came into the room, he walked straight to me and said that I looked like Jawaharlal Nehru; this was because of my dress. I said, "But I do not have a red rose." He replied that in England they had a War of the Roses and he hoped that India will never have that.

§

The Joint Services Staff College in the UK was something unique in that it was a combined course meant for selected officers of the three Services who had already qualified at their Service Staff College and were hand-picked for a potential senior rank in their Service. There was a joke that at Service Staff College, Greenwich for the Royal Navy, Camberley for the Army and Bracknell for the Royal Air Force, the instructors asked questions and if the students did not know the answer, they were bowled out. At Joint Services Staff College the instructors asked questions and did not mind if the student did not know the answer. At the Imperial Defence College in London the instructors dare not ask any question because they were sure that the students did not know the answer.

§

I had several good friends among British officers at the course in Latimer. I may mention three of them. They were all senior Majors with 16 to 20 years of service like me due to be promoted shortly. Among them were Ronnie MacAlister, Bill Geoff Dockerill and Nigel Bagnall. During Second World War in Burma, Ronnie was the Adjutant of 2/3 Gorkha Rifles and relieved me as Adjutant of the Japanese Prisoners of War Camp at Payaji in Burma. He later became Major-General Brigade of Gorkhas at Hong Kong while I was President of the Gorkha Brigade in the Indian Army. Geoff Dockerill had been ADC to Field Marshal Montgomery in North Africa. At my request, he had arranged a meeting for me with the Field Marshal in London but that did not materialise. The reason was that the previous day the Field Marshal had been fined £ 10 for traffic violation. He had been driving his car down a no-entry road and the Police had given him a ticket (Chalan). His defence at the Old Bailey

(Court) that he had driven safely from El Alamen to Tunisia and from Normandy to Baltic causing harm only to the enemy was not accepted and he was convicted and fined. Nigel Bagnall was the brightest British Army Officer on the Course with me. He had won a gallantry award during Normandy Landings in France. He and I got the top grade in the Course. His later career and mine followed the same trajectory in our respective Armies. When he was Army Commander of the British Army of the Rhine, I was Western Army Commander. Field Marshal Sir Nigel Bagnall retired as British Army Chief. It is interesting that after I had resigned from the Army and had gone to my son posted in the Indian Embassy at Riyadh in Saudi Arabia, Bagnall had visited Riyadh a few days earlier and had heard of my going to Riyadh shortly. He had asked the British Military Attachee to convey his compliments to me.

§

I found in 1961 that British officers and ladies who had lived in India were quite friendly with me and my wife. Old British ladies would enquire if we still had Bearers, Khansamas, Dhobis and Ayahs in India. On one occasion, we had been for dinner to the house of a British Colonel who was the Deputy Commandant at the British School of Infantry at Warminster. After dinner, everyone got up and washed his plate in the sink. She would not allow us to do so saying she knew that in India we did not do that. When my wife asked her where she had been in India. She replied that she had been in India for a few years and had visited all important places in the country. My wife then enquired what her father was doing in India. She very modestly replied that her father was Lord Linlithgow. I was impressed by the fact that she had not in any way tried to show off that she had been in India as the daughter of the Viceroy of India.

§

The other interesting lecture we had at the college was by a junior British Minister who had returned from discussions at the United Nations on Goa. While I was at the college, the Goa crisis was building up. My friends would often ask me if India would take military action in Goa and I would tell them that we would not do so. In the past, when there was a freedom movement in Goa we had not intervened.

Being away from India for some time, I had no idea about what was happening over Goa. One evening when I switched on the TV at my house, to my surprise I saw the picture of my friend Lt Col Sucha Singh of the PARA Battalion, advancing into Goa with his battalion and of another friend Brig Sagat Singh commanding the PARA Brigade conducting operations in Goa. The next morning, Goa made the headlines in all British newspapers. One of them had a heading 'Nehru, the Sanctimonious Bully'. I knew that there would be fireworks in the college next morning. Portugal was the oldest ally of Britain and the British media was very pro-Portugal over the dispute regarding Goa. As I entered the lecture hall, many of my colleague who were already in the hall, shouted, "Welcome the new Imperialist and the new Aggressor." I did not want to get involved in any serious discussion. I went up on the stage and spoke, "Gentlemen, this comes from keeping bad company." This joke was well taken and everyone had a good laugh. The British have a good sense of humour and a remark like this goes down well with them.

A few weeks later, a British junior Minister who had been at the UN during discussions on Goa came to us to give a talk on the Problems of the United Nations. I knew that Goa would figure in the course of his speech. I had, therefore, gone well-prepared. He chose not to talk about Goa other than saying that for obvious reasons he would not discuss that issue. He must have been told that there was an Indian student in the audience. During question-hour, a US Naval Officer doing the course asked a provocative question. He enquired why the Minister had chosen to skip Goa which was an important issue affecting the functioning of the United Nations. He even said that what India had done in Goa was nothing short of International brigandage. The Minister in his reply mentioned that both Jawaharlal Nehru and Krishna Menon had written to the British Foreign Office on the subject but that did not make much sense to him. He even said that Nehru had mentioned that Goa was a pimple on the face of India which had to be removed. He then added that he would advise Nehru that what India had done was like scratching the pimple with nails which can be dangerous. I found most of the students looking towards me and I thought I must present my views on the subject. I said, "Sir, there are occasions when emotion gets the better of reasoning. Perhaps it was because of that you may not appreciate the Indian point of view. I confess that when I read about Goa in the British media I failed to understand the arguments brought out against India's action in Goa. A country can have the right to territory on the basis of legal, natural justice or military strength. The Portuguese Dictator, Salazar's contention about Goa being Portuguese metropolitan territory was too absurd to be accepted. The people of Goa had been struggling for years to throw out Portuguese colonial rule and merge with the rest of the country. Portugal lost its legal rights to Goa by repeatedly ignoring the resolutions of the United Nations calling for a peaceful settlement of the problem. As for her military ability to hold on to Goa, that got exploded within a dozen hours and with less than a dozen casualties." I realised that I had been very forthright in giving my views and I tried to sugar quote them. I added, "India has extended the boundaries of the British Commonwealth over which the Queen of England presides. Instead of appreciating this, much ill informed criticism of India has been taking place in this country." The audience had a good laugh and so did the Minister. He then proceeded to discuss other issues saying that he did not want to discuss Goa further. I wondered how my intervention on Goa had gone down with the authorities. That evening there was a cocktail party in the Officers' Mess at which the Minister was present. The Commandant of the college, Admiral Scatchord, sent for me and told the Minister that if he had been a student at a Staff College in India during the Suez crisis, he would not have been able to intervene like I had done. I was wondering whether this was meant to be a compliment or a mild reprimand. The Minister smiled and said let us have a drink together. It appears that the joke about extending the boundaries of Commonwealth was taken well. At the end of the course the report I earned showed that I had topped the course.

After completing the course and a fortnight's attachment with the British Army of the Rhine in Germany, I visited Bonn, the then capital of West Germany. Our Military Attache at that time was Brig Sharma who was married to the sister of my friend the late Major Som Nath Sharma, Param Vir Chakra. The Sharmas were a delighiful and hospitable couple who had picked up German very well and could fluently converse in that language. They took me to the Army Officers Club on the bank of the Rhine one evening and introduced me to some of their German friends. It was nice being introduced to a retired German General who had been the Chief of Staff of Field Marshal Rommel, Hans Speidel, who wrote the book, *We Defended Normandy*. I mentioned to him that I had read his book. He was happy to learn that his book had been read in India.

§

On completion of my course I got my promotion to the rank of Lt Col after a long wait of sixteen years in the rank of Major. I was posted as Instructor to Staff College in Wellington. Manekshaw was still the Commandant at the college and he still had reservations about me. The Court of Enquiry instituted against him at the instance of Kaul had completely exonerated him. Kaul was now in NEFA as a Corps Commander facing the Chinese. Soon after my return to India, the war against China commenced. After the debacle, Kaul resigned and Manekshaw was promoted to the rank of Lt Gen and took over command of 4 Corps from him. The Corps had suffered a disastrous defeat. On taking over the command of this Corps, Manekshaw's first statement was—"I would not allow any withdrawals." This gave a sense of confidence to the troops.

Maj Gen Som Dutt who succeeded Manekshaw was well-disposed towards me. He wanted me to carry out a Study Tour of the battle areas in NEFA to find out what changes we needed to make in our concept of Mountain Warfare in the light of what had happened in that disastrous war. On return from the tour apart from revising our Mountain Warfare Doctrine, I wrote a paper on the reasons for our debacle. I had come to the conclusion that there were three main reasons for what had happened. These were, first total mismatch between foreign policy and defence policy, second, marginalisation of the Military from the process of decision-making at the apex level and third, the loss of elan among Army Officers.

I carried out much research and study of India's Higher Defence Organisation. I wrote several articles on the subject and gave lectures at various Army Training Institutions. In 1977, when I was a Maj Gen I was invited to address the National Defence College on this subject. This continued for a few years. I have since been going to National Defence College almost every year for the last over thirty years. A monograph written by me on this subject was prescribed for study at National Defence College. After the Kargil War, the Defence

Working Group of the Kargil Review Committee was headed by Arun Singh, former Minister of State for Defence. He requested me for a draft on this subject for the report he was writing. He accepted this draft in toto recommending the appointment of Chief of Defence Staff and Integration of Ministry of Defence with the three Services Headquarters. This has continued to remain in limbo except for some cosmetic changes. In 2015, Manohar Parrikar, the Defence Minister announced that we will soon have a Chief of Defence Staff. Over a year has elapsed and there has been no progress in the matter.

§

It was most unfortunate that the golden period of the Nehru era ended with the disaster in the Himalayas which broke Jawaharlal Nehru and shattered his health. He died soon after in May 1964. Lal Bahadur Shastri succeeded him as Prime Minister and in a way the Nehru era continued for a while under the short tenure of his successor ending with his tragic death at Tashkent in January 1966.

There is no doubt that Jawaharlal Nehru was one of the great world leaders of his time but no human being can go through life without some failure. Despite all his greatness, Nehru's China policy proved to be disastrous for the Nation. C Rajagopalachari, the great Congress leader, had opposed Nehru on many issues but his moving tribute to Nehru did great justice to the latter:

> "Eleven years younger than me and eleven times more important to the Nation than me, eleven hundred times more beloved to the Nation than me Nehru has suddenly departed from our midst and I remain to hear the sad news and wear the shock. I have been fighting Nehru all these ten years over what I consider false in public policies. But I knew all along that he alone could get them corrected. No one else could dare to do it and he has gone leaving me weaker than before in my fights. But fighting apart, a loved friend has gone and the most civilised person amongst all. Not many amongst us are civilised yet. God save our country."

Starting with opposing views on the Cripps Mission of 1942, Nehru and Rajaji, as C Rajagopalachari was affectionately called, had opposing views on various matters of policy.

§

Our Second Prime Minister Lal Bahadur Shastri was a unique grass roots leader of our country. He was born into a very poor family and as a child had to swim across the river to attend his school. The fact that a person from such an humble beginning could end up as Prime Minister of India, providing excellent political leadership during a critical time in 1965, shows the strength of our vibrant democracy. I shall quote some incidents from his life to show his character.

Lal Bahadur Shstri joined the Freedom Movement started by Mahatma Gandhi in 1920. He was married and was given a small stipend of ₹30 a month as full time paid volunteer of the party, working in its Headquarters at Anand Bhavan, the residence of Motilal Nehru in Allahabad. After a few months, Shastri's wife told him that she could manage running their house on ₹20 a month and saved the remaining ₹10. Shastri took away her savings and deposited it in Party fund urging that thereafter his stipend be reduced to ₹20 per month. The same humble approach to life continued with him even when he became the Prime Minister of India. I learnt from his son that when he was Railway Minister, Jawaharlal Nehru had given him his old Sherwani as he didn't have one for formal wear. As Prime Minister, he was going to Russia and it was found that the old Sherwani had got torn near the collar. His family decided to get a new Sherwani tailored for him, despite his saying that the Sherwani should be darned and was quite alright for him to wear. The best tailor was summoned and Shastri was forced by his family to give his measurements to the tailor. As the tailor was leaving, Shastri quietly told him not to make a new Sherwani but repair the old one and have it dry cleaned to look like new. As Prime Minister when India faced food shortage he gave up eating one meal a day.

It is also in keeping with his character that as Railway Minister Lal Bahadur Shastri took moral responsibility for a major railway derailment in which a couple of hundred people had died. Such were the values practised by this great man.

He proved to be a great war leader in 1965 ordering an offensive into Pakistan when the situation in Jammu and Kashmir had become critical. This was at a time when Pakistan was flush with modern military hardware like Patton Tanks and Sabre Jet fighter aircrafts provided by the US while Indian forces were equipped with Second

World War vintage weapons. The war ended with blunting Pakistani military offensive and destroying their famous Patton Tanks in the battle of Asal Uttar near Tarn Taran in Amritsar. Shastri visited the battle field after the ceasefire and gave his famous slogan 'Jai Jawan, Jai Kisan'.

§

During the 1965 War, I was commanding my Battalion, 3/5 Gorkha Rifles (Frontier Force) at Kanchrapara near Calcutta. We were moved to the border at Bangaom and were supposed to be the Advanced Guard of the Division for the advance to Jessore in East Pakistan (now Bangladesh). Manekshaw visited my Battalion along with our Divisional Commander, Maj Gen PS Bhagat, Victoria Cross, a legendary General of our Army. Manekshaw continued to be cold towards me but wished the battalion good luck. The situation in the West was critical and a Pakistani Armoured Division had begun its advance to Khem Karan in Amritsar. It was feared that with its superiority of tanks, guns and combat aircraft, Pakistan may advance up to Beas leading to the loss of Amritsar. We were told to commence the advance before sunrise the following morning and were all teed up to go into battle. At midnight, we were told to stand down because in the West our forces had blunted the Pakistani Armoured offensive at Khem Karan which became a graveyard of Pakistan's Patton tanks. Government rightly decided not to extend the war to East Pakistan as that might alienate the people of that region. This was a wise decision which gave dividend in the 1971 War.

My Battalion had ninety families in ad hoc accommodation at Kalyani near Kanchrapara. The other two Battalions of the Brigade also had their families and they had been sent home. It was difficult to organise the dispatch of Gorkha families to remote areas in Nepal. It was decided that they should stay at Kalyani while the Battalion moved to the border for operations. My wife and children could easily have gone to my home in Patna but we decided that if the Battalion families were remaining behind, she should continue staying at Kanchrapara, much against the wishes of my father. Pakistan aircraft flew low over our positions and reached Barrackpore where the airfield was bombed. Kanchrapara is close to

Barrackpore and we had shelters dug against air attacks in which my wife and children took cover during the air attack. I am mentioning this to show that even the family of the Commanding Officer has responsibility for looking after the families of the Battalion. My wife's staying back at Kanchrapara and frequently visiting the soldiers' families was well-appreciated in the Battalion.

Soon after the 1965 War, my Battalion was moved to Ladakh. After a week's rail journey, we arrived at Pathankot and from there proceeded another 400 miles by road convoy from Pathankot to Ladakh. We spent a month travelling because we had to have a week's acclimatisation camp at Baltal and Leh. We were deployed at Kiari with holding defensive position at heights up to 15,000 feet. I remained in command of the Battalion for two winters. We had no electricity and were living in bunkers in Ladakh. During the winter the temperature used to go down to minus 30 degrees and everything used to freeze. The Indus nearby would have 20 feet of ice above water. We could with skid chains drive vehicles on the river. The flowing water of the river below the block of ice could be seen. I took the whole Battalion out on exercise and we moved up to Kimne Plateau at a height of 18,000 feet without any mishap. I am afraid my Divisional Commander was not too well-disposed towards me and this could have potentially harmed my career. The reason for this was that way back in 1948 both of us were Majors together on the staff in Western Command. While I was dealing with operations he had a less glamorous assignment on training, despite being senior to me. Subsequently, we were together as Instructors at Wellington and he felt that the Commandant, Maj Gen Som Dutt was well-disposed towards me and did not treat him well. Luckily, the Corps Commander was Lt Gen Candeth who was aware that people had lined up against me under the belief that this would please Manekshaw who was likely to be the next Chief. I had two direct interactions with Candeth. The first was during the visit of senior students from Royal College of Defence Studies in London to Kashmir led by an Air Marshal who was their Instructor. They were shown details of how the battle of Zojila was fought during December 1948. As I was closely connected with that battle, I had to organise a demonstration for them on the ground. Candeth, as a Brigadier commanding the Artillery, had taken part in this battle. This presentation had gone off well. The second occasion was during a

Telephone Battle at his Headquarters in which all Divisional Commanders including our Divisional Commander had taken part. As I used to conduct Telephone Battles as Instructor at Staff College, I had been summoned to write the Telephone Battle papers and help in its conduct. Both the Army Commander and the Corps Commander had appreciated my contribution and made special reference to it during the summing up of the exercise. This ensured that my Divisional Commander could do me no harm and I duly got my promotion as Brigadier.

§

As Manekshaw's fortune grew and he was going up the promotion ladder in the Army, I was in trouble because I was still being labelled as a Kaul man. Some of my immediate superiors tried to be more loyal than the king and even attempted to harm my career. I served as Battalion Commander for a short while in Calcutta when Manekshaw was the Eastern Army Commander, and again after a few years as Brigade Commander in Manipur while Manekshaw was still Eastern Army Commander. A close friend of mine from the same Regiment as me, Maj Gen ZC Bakshi, was my Divisional Commander. He was told by Manekshaw himself who was now Army Chief Designate that I may be a good Staff Officer, but perhaps not a good Commander. Bakshi stood up for me, otherwise my promotion to Maj Gen may well have not come about. Later as I shall mention in this book, Manekshaw changed his opinion about me.

§

On completing my three years tenure as Battalion Commander, I got my promotion and did another three years in Manipur as Brigade Commander. Manekshaw was still Eastern Army Commander and soon his promotion to Army Chief was announced. Both tenures in the field were rewarding but very strenuous. I commanded 71 Mountain Brigade in Manipur for nearly three years. It was a mega Brigade comprising five Infantry Battalions and four Para Military Battalions. We were employed in active counter insurgency operations. The Brigade was responsible for conducting operations in the whole of Manipur. We had some forty air maintained piquets in the jungle. We used to have frequent clashes with insurgents. The Brigade achieved good results both in terms of inflicting casualties on the insurgents and in recovery of weapons. I visited all my piquets travelling in a helicopter during the first month of my taking over the Brigade. Thereafter, I visited each piquet on foot trudging through the jungles which were leech infected. It was good for the morale of the troops to see a Brigade Commander walking up to piquets through the jungles facing all the hazards which the soldiers were facing constantly. I recall an amusing incident in Tamenlong Sector when I was climbing up to a mountain piquet. The *Gaon Burha* (Headman) had organised a reception for me in the nearby village. As I had climbed half way up, two Nagas came running down from the top with *Chhang* (rice wine) for me. What surprised me was their asking me the name of my son as desired by the *Gaon Burha*. I did not know the purpose for this. However, when I reached the top, I was ceremonially welcomed with shawls and dance in my honour. I heard the name of my son being mentioned in the song and learnt that they were saying that when my son grows up he should become a Champion Head Hunter. Head hunting used to be quite common among the Nagas. When one village attacked another village, they would bring back human heads and display the skulls as war trophies in the village. After I had danced and drunk with the Nagas, I was offered a special meal of snake barbecue and dog meat. Their sight was repulsive and I pretended to be a vegetarian.

§

Mowu Angami, the C-in-C of the underground Naga Army with 300 insurgents had gone to Yunan in China to get modern weapons and also training of his cadres. He was due to return to Nagaland. He could return crossing the Myanmar-Nagaland Border or across Myanmar-Manipur Border. My Brigade was responsible for guarding the Myanmar-Manipur Border. Mowu Angami split his returning gang into two groups. He himself tried coming through Myanmar-Nagaland Border. He and his group were nabbed by our flanking Brigade. My Brigade apprehended the second group under his Second-in-Command, Dosoi Chakasang. The performance of my Brigade had been very good and acknowledged by the Divisional Commander. I have already mentioned how despite Manekshaw's wishes my Divisional Commander Maj Gen ZC Bakshi stood by me. Army Headquarters had not issued any General Staff Training Pamphlet for counter insurgency operations. I was asked by Military

Training Directorate at Army Headquarters to draft such a pamphlet. I had experience of counter insurgency operations in Indonesia and as a Company Commander in Nagaland in the initial stages of Naga insurgency. My recent experience as Brigade Commander was very helpful. I did a close study of the British Military Operations in Malaya and the US in Vietnam to draw lessons from them. The draft that I sent was much appreciated by the Director of Military Training.

I now received the posting order to Adjutant General's Branch at Army Headquarters to head a newly instituted Pay Commission Cell. This came as a disappointment to me because it was not considered an important assignment. I had to reconcile myself to this realising that with Manekshaw as Army Chief, I could not be given a good appointment. My old friend Maj Gen BM Sarkar was Military Secretary at Army Headquarters. We had served in Indonesia together and in quite a few other appointments as Major in the 50s and 60s, including Instructor at Mhow and Wellington respectively. I expressed my disappointment to him saying that I had been side tracked. He corrected me saying that Manekshaw had specially selected me for this assignment to which he attached much importance. This was the first time that the Army case was to be put up before a Pay Commission. The first two Pay Commissions did not have the Defence Services in their terms of reference and it had been left to the Ministry of Defence to take a decision regarding the emoluments of the Defence Services. Manekshaw, being from the first batch at Dehradun in 1934, had suffered a pay cut like all officers commissioned between 1934 and 1946. Our pay had been drastically reduced. I remember that as a Brigadier Manekshaw's salary had been reduced to ₹1,450 per month in 1947 whereas Brigadier Chand Narayan Das commissioned in 1933 continued to have a salary of ₹2,500 per month. Both were working together at Army Headquarters in the same rank, Manekshaw as Director Military Operations and Chand Narayan Das as Director Military Intelligence. In those days, he often referred to how the ICOs had been treated unfairly compared to KCIOs. Manekshaw's term as Chief was due to expire soon. At that time, no one thought that we would go to war with Pakistan in 1971. Perhaps Manekshaw was keen that during his tenure as the Army Chief he could undo the injustice meted out to officers commissioned between 1934 and 1946. Sarkar told me that much would depend on my performance in the job for which Manekshaw had specially selected me. He also added that with Jagjivan Ram as Defence Minister there was no question of my not being given my due. Being an old friend, Sarkar knew very well my family association with Jagjivan Ram.

On taking over my appointment in the Pay Commission Cell, I represented to Manekshaw that we should send our report directly to the Pay Commission like all Service Associations on the civil side. Ministry of Defence wanted us to send our report to the Commissions through them so that they could vet it. I realised that the Ministry would tone down our recommendations and requested Manekshaw to take up the matter with the Defence Minister after evolving a consensus with the other two Chiefs. This was done and we had our way. I also got in touch with my counterparts in the Navy and the Air Force who were one rank junior to me. We formed a joint Committee under my Chairmanship so that the Services put up a united stand. There were differences between us on a few issues like Navy and Air Force having better scale of rations than the Army or Army having soldier batmen which the other two Services did not have. We decided not to take up any controversial matter between the three services as this will give a handle to civilian bureaucrats to weaken our case.

My staff and I carried out considerable research and prepared a 300-page printed document with statistics and arguments. The main thrust of our arguments for emoluments were on the basis of the following guidelines:

(a) The Pay Scale of Army Officers should be at par with those of the IAS who had the highest Scale among the Civil Services. This broadly conformed to what was in vogue during British Rule.

(b) Junior Commissioned Officers should be treated at par with Class II gazetted Officers in the Civil.

(c) The Infantry soldiers whose pay had been equated with unskilled workers on the civil side should be upgraded to Semi Skilled workers. The other tradesmen in the Army should be correspondingly upgraded.

(d) Non-combatants in the Army like Cooks, Washermen, Sweepers and others should be combatised and given higher scales of pay.

All the above four principals were accepted by the Pay Commission except that of parity of Army Officers with the IAS because it was said that latter were all graduates or post-graduates while almost all Army Officers were not graduates. However, they agreed to give Army Officers a higher scale of pay than Indian Police Service Officers, the next best Civil Service. Subsequently, we managed to get free rations for Army Officers. This gave us an edge.

Manekshaw was very happy with all that we had done and made me give a presentation of our proposal to the Army Commanders and subsequently to the three Chiefs. I could see a visible change in Manekshaw's attitude towards me. I was cleared for promotion to the rank of Major-General setting at rest my apprehension on that account. I happened to be the first Bihari Officer promoted to the rank of a General Officer in the Army. This had appeared prominently in Patna newspapers. Jagjivan Ram on a visit to Bihar in one of his speeches said that he was happy to have a Bihari promoted Major-General during his tenure as Defence Minister.

§

On 25 March 1971, Yahya Khan, the military dictator of Pakistan clamped Martial Law in East Pakistan reinforcing their Eastern Army with two Divisions. Sheikh Mujibur Rahman who had won a majority in Pakistan Parliament should have been asked to form the government, instead he was arrested and his followers taken into custody. The Pakistan Army let loose a reign of terror in East Pakistan (now Bangladesh). Atrocities were being committed on the local population in East Pakistan and some 1 crore refugees came over to India. Indira Gandhi and her Cabinet felt that immediate military action should be taken by India in East Pakistan to alleviate the suffering of the local population and reduce the burden on India of looking after 1 crore refugees. General Manekshaw was at the Cabinet meeting when it was conveyed to him to start the offensive in East Pakistan immediately. Manekshaw submitted that the Army would not be ready for the offensive before December. He gave his reasons for this. The Army was woefully short of military equipment and the shortages had to be made up. Indira Gandhi enquired as to why this had not been done earlier. Manekshaw's reply was that Sardar Swaran Singh, the Finance Minister, should be asked that question. He had not released funds for this despite the Army repeatedly asking for them. He then pointed out that soon Monsoon would start in East Pakistan and the ground would become very boggy. Our armour and vehicles would be confined to roads and would not be able to manoeuvre. Further, China may intervene because the Himalayan passes would be open. In winter, these would be blocked with snow and China would not be able to interfere. Indira Gandhi and the Cabinet were very unhappy at the stand taken by Manekshaw. He even offered to resign on this issue and the government could appoint another Chief who would agree to undertake operations during the Monsoon. The government ultimately agreed with the recommendations of Manekshaw. He had told the Prime Minister that if the offensive was launched during Monsoon defeat would be unavoidable, while if this was done in winter he would guarantee victory. It was good that this recommendation was accepted and time utilised for necessary preparation by the Army and at the same time the government managed to sign the Treaty of Friendship with the Soviet Union. This kept US gun-boat diplomacy at bay during the 1971 Indo-Pak War, while the US moved its Seventh feet including its Nuclear battleship enterprise to the Indian Ocean, the Soviet Nuclear Submarines moved in to neutralise this serious threat during that war. Thus India won a historic victory in 1971 in which 92,000 Pakistani prisoners of war surrendered and a new Independent nation of Bangladesh came into being.

§

By mid-1971, war clouds had begun to gather. I took the liberty of asking Manekshaw to send me to command a Division in the coming war. I even told him that the GSO-1 of the old days was going to war with the old GSO-2, and GSO-3 should not be left out of battle. My reference was to our positions in 1946 when Lt Col Manekshaw was the GSO-1, Major Yahya Khan was GSO-2 and I was GSO-3 in Military Operations Directorate before Partition. Manekshaw turned down my request saying that he needed me more at Delhi to see the Pay Commission recommendations through and do the Manpower Planning for the coming war.

I was promoted Maj Gen and appointed Deputy Adjutant General relieving Maj Gen TN Raina going on promotion to command a Corps in the East. Subsequently, Raina became the Army Chief.

For the next few months, Manekshaw worked meticulously preparing the Army for the coming war. He took weekly conferences with all Directors and higher level officers at Army Headquarters to monitor progress of preparations for the war. It was my task to ensure that no unit had any manpower deficiency and various war time units like Prisoner of War camps, transit camps and our medical plans for casualties was fully geared for their task. Of course, I had not catered for our having to look after 92,000 Prisoners of War. After the war, we organised several Prisoners of War Camps away from the borders. Manekshaw sent me as leader of the Indian delegation to UN Conference at San Remo in Italy to discuss the issue of Prisoners of War. India was the only country holding so many Prisoners of War. I was asked to make a presentation at the conference. I spoke for half an hour giving them details of how we were looking after the Prisoners of War. I assured them that all the provisions of the Geneva Convention on Prisoners of War were being duly followed by us. I quoted from history the incident when King Porus taken a prisoner was brought before Alexander who had been much impressed by his gallantry in battle. Though wounded when Alexander asked him how he would be like to be treated, Porus had replied, "Like a king." Alexander readily agreed and restored Porus back to his throne. It was in that spirit that we were looking after the prisoners of war, like soldiers, and this complied with all the requirements of Geneva Convention. Our policy was to look after these prisoners so well that when they returned to Pakistan, they would be ambassadors of durable peace on the sub-continent. The weight of each prisoner was regularly recorded and they were given full entitlement of rations. It was interesting that most of the Prisoners of War were putting on weight while in the camp with us. For their entertainment, we used to organise film shows and *mushairas* (Urdu songs) for them. We often used to organise games for them in the camp. I told them that on a visit to the Prisoners of War Camp at Meerut, I had played cricket with Pakistan Army Officers team in the Camp. I also mentioned that I had known some of the prisoners from pre-Partition days including the Commander-in-Chief in East Pakistan, Lt Gen AAK Niazi, whom I met at Ordnance Officers' Mess at Jabalpur which had been converted into a Prisoners of War Camp for Pakistani Generals. I concluded by mentioning how a team of US Press Correspondents had been allowed to visit a

Prisoners of War Camp. One of them wrote in *Los Angeles Times* that never in history had prisoners been treated as well as India had been treating the Pakistani Prisoners of War. On return to India, I submitted my report including the text of my address. Defence Minister, Jagjivan Ram and Manekshaw complimented me for this.

Apart from my other duties as Deputy Adjutant General, I remained very busy looking after the Pakistani Prisoners of War. I would frequently visit Prisoner of War Camps spread all over UP, Bihar and Madhya Pradesh. I recall, I was at Faizabad during Eid and I told the Camp Commandant to organise a Bara Khana for the Prisoners in which I would also participate. I sat with a Baluch Subedar next to me. He told me that he had put in twenty years service but had never sat with a General for a meal. He added that our Generals are too busy doing politics to spare the time for looking after their soldiers. And that is why they had lost the war. Another amusing incident was when I visited a camp at Bareilly where I met an old acquaintance Muzaffar Hussain. He had been a Naval Officer living in the same Officers' Mess on Wellesley Road (now Zakir Hussain Road). After Partition, he had joined the Civil Services in Pakistan and had risen to be the Chief Secretary of East Pakistan. To save himself from irate mobs in Bangladesh, he had sought protection from the Indian Army and we had accommodated him in a Prisoner of War Camp. He complained to me that he had been writing letters to his wife but had not been getting any reply saying that we were not allowing his letters to go to his wife. I assured him that we were strictly observing Geneva Convention and had allowed every prisoner to write home twice a week which we used to forward to Pakistan through the Egyptian Embassy in Delhi. I even offered to take his letter personally to Delhi and have it sent to the Egyptian Embassy. He wrote a letter and gave it to me and I did the needful. During my next visit to Bareilly after a few months, he complained that he had not received any reply from his wife. Thereby hangs an interesting tale. We found out from other prisoners and our intelligence sources that there was a reason behind this mystery. His wife had the name of Laila and was known to be pretty and social. Yahya Khan was friendly with her. He had posted Muzaffar as Chief Secretary of East Pakistan, like Jahangir had sent the husband of Noor Jahan to Dhaka. Laila refused to accompany her husband to Dhaka saying that the climate there did not suit her. She stayed back at Islamabad. After 1971 War when Yahya was in disgrace, she had run away to London with another man. In the circumstance, Muzaffar's letters to his wife always remained unanswered. It was a strange coincidence that Lt Gen Habibulla Khan's second wife was the sister of Muzaffar Hussain. As mentioned in the previous chapter of this book, I met Habibulla Khan and his wife in Bihar Regimental Centre at the Golden Jubilee Celebration function of 1 BIHAR at Danapur Cantt. During the course of conversation, I casually mentioned Laila and she burst out saying that she is the most wicked and characterless person who had ruined the life of her brother. During my visits to Prisoners of War camp, I met some senior officers who had served in the Undivided Indian Army before Partition. I found their attitude very different from the younger officers who had been indoctrinated as they grew up after Partition when religious fundamentalism and anti-India feelings had become strong. I have already mentioned earlier that I met Lt Gen AAK Niazi. I had known him well when we served at Batavia (now Jakarta) in Indonesia in 1946. We were both Captains at that time. He was very friendly when we met and that evening we had a drink together. We talked about the old days in a very friendly manner. He was very bitter about Bangladeshis saying that they had stabbed them in their back. He warned me that they would one day also stab us in the back. What he said then appeared to come true when fundamentalists were in power at Dhaka after the assassination of Sheikh Mujibur Rahman. The Finale of my last association with the Pakistani Prisoners was when on their return I received a letter from Nawaz Hussain, the Cabinet Secretary of Pakistan. He also had been a Captain with me in Indonesia staying in the same Officers' Mess and we had been quite friendly. He wrote that the prisoners on return had been very appreciative of the way I had taken care of them. He also mentioned that knowing me well he was not surprised that I had done so. This letter was a source of great personal satisfaction to me. However, the fact remains that our efforts to send back Pakistani prisoners as ambassadors of durable peace did not produce any positive results.

Pakistan used to raise the issue of Prisoners from time to time in the United Nations, particularly when any incident took place in a Prisoners of War Camp. There were a few occasions when our guards on duty at camps had to open fire when the prisoners would attack the guards. We used minimum force and in the melee some Pakistani prisoners had got killed. We had to send replies to our representative at the UN to put up our version of things. Most of the time the accusations against us were false or highly exaggerated.

§

Manekshaw's tenure as Chief was getting over. I have already mentioned that in the light of what work I had put in for presenting our case to the Pay Commission, he had become appreciative of my work and his attitude had changed. He was also happy at the manner in which I had dealt with the Prisoners of War. To my surprise, as a parting gift, Manekshaw recommended me for Param Vishishst Seva Medal (PVSM), the highest award in the Army for distinguished service. Normally, this award is given to Lt Generals on the eve of their retirement. I got this award as a Major-General when I still had about ten more years of service ahead of me.

§

While I was serving on the Staff of Manekshaw, Jagjivan Ram was the Defence Minister. Manekshaw was an outstanding Army Chief while Jagjivan Ram had been an outstanding Minister in various ministries, including Defence. Unfortunately, the personal relations between them were not too good primarily because Manekshaw had established a direct equation with Indira Gandhi particularly during the 1971 War and Jagjivan Ram felt that he was bypassing him. This had led to strained relations between them. My problem was that Jagjivan Ram knew me from my childhood. Both my grandfather and father had worked with him on different occasions. In 1938, Jagjivan Ram was appointed Parliamentary Secretary in Bihar government when my grandfather was the Police Chief of the Province. I had met him when he had come to my grandfather's house and I was a student at school. In 1946, Jagjivan Ram was the Labour Minister in Government of India. My father had come to Delhi on posting as a Deputy of Sir Norman Smith, the then Director of Intelligence Bureau, and on his departure in 1947, was looking after the Intelligence Bureau. He often interacted with Jagjivan Ram. In view of this family association my relations with Jagjivan Ram were close. There was no serving General Officer of Bihar Regiment at that time. The Senior Brigadier of the Regiment in the normal course should have taken over as the Colonel of the Regiment. Jagjivan Ram sent for me saying that he had met some JCOs of the Bihar Regiment who had told him that I should be made the Colonel of the Bihar Regiment. I thanked him but I said that it would be sending a wrong message in the Army. I had no credentials to be the Colonel of Bihar Regiment as I had not served in that Regiment. People would feel that regional parochialism had come into the Army and that would be undesirable. I further told him that I was likely to become Colonel of my Regiment, the Fifth Gorkha Rifles shortly. He asked me to think it over. I apprised Manekshaw about this and he emphatically told me that I must not compromise my stand. Of course, I did not tell Jagjivan Ram that Manekshaw did not like my being appointed Colonel of Bihar Regiment because that would have upset him. I merely told him that I had thought over the matter very carefully and would very earnestly request him that I should not be appointed Colonel of Bihar Regiment. He was unhappy but did not say anything. There was another occasion where I could be in the line of fire between the Minister and the Chief. I had sent to Ministry of Defence a list of officers commissioned from Indian Military Academy. The file came back to me with a query raised by Jagjivan Ram about the percentage of Scheduled Caste commissioned from the Academy. I replied that it was 1%. The file again came back with a minute signed by the Minister that the Parliament had laid down that 15% Schedule Caste should be recruited in all government services. He wanted to know why the Army had ignored this direction and wanted action to be taken against the person responsible for this lapse. Manekshaw sent for me and I could see that he was in a bad mood. He told me to draft a suitable reply for his signature that he was personally responsible for this and the Minister may take whatever action he likes against him. This was a bit of a hot potato and I told Manekshaw that I would draft a suitable reply which he could send to the Minister. He told me to put up a draft reply and not to omit to mention that he took responsibility for it and the Minister could take action against him. I pondered over how I could sugar coat the reply and started collecting statistics. I managed to dig out an old letter from Army Headquarters apprising the Ministry about the feasibility of reservation in officers cadre. The then Defence Minister had just initialled on this note and there was no further correspondence on this subject. I made out a case giving statistics that about 15% were Schedule Caste in the Army among personnel below officers rank. Apart from Mahar Regiment and Sikh Light Infantry, who were all Schedule Caste, every unit of the Army had people of different trades like Washerman, Equipment and Boot Repairer, Sweepers, Barbers, Tailors, Carpenters etc, who were all from Schedule Caste. They had recently been combatised as regular soldiers and the previous nomenclature of Non-Combatants Enrolled had been given up. This came to over 20%, well over the stipulated 15%. As regards officers, we had sought dispensation to make an exception in regard to them and the Ministry had accepted that. However, we had been making efforts to provide education facilities at our Military Schools to educate Schedule Caste students. As a result of our efforts, their percentage in the Army had risen to 1% and hopefully this would increase in the future. The Army had been fighting repeated wars after Independence and could not, in the interest of National security, compromise on the competence of its Officer Cadre. I thought that this was the best answer we could give to the Minister. Of course, I had no option but to include in the draft at the end that Manekshaw took full responsibility and the Minister could take any action that he liked. After the 1971 War, Manekshaw had become a national hero and it was not possible for any government to take action against him on this issue. Manekshaw read the draft with a twinkle in his eyes and approved it in toto saying that I had done a good job. After that in a light-hearted vein, he said that if the Minister has his way, the Indian Army will be full of Biharis and Bhangis. Of course, I laughed away this remark and there was no question of repeating this to anyone at that time because that would have raised a big storm. I remember that for a much less offensive remark to a Press correspondent on the eve of retirement, Manekshaw raised a controversy which echoed in the Parliament. A woman journalist interviewed him to cover his long career in the Army. In a light-hearted vein, he told her that in 1947 being from a minority community he had the choice to opt for either Indian Army or Pakistan Army, he opted to remain in India. And then added that had he gone to Pakistan, the results of 1971 War would have been different. This raised a lot of furore all over the country.

§

There were rumours all through 1972 that Manekshaw would be made a Field Marshal. However, in November 1972, we read in the paper that Jagjivan Ram had told the Press during his visit to Madras (now Chennai) that India will not have a Field Marshal or a five-star rank General. That put an end to this rumour. On 31 December 1972, when I switched on the Radio, I heard that government had decided to promote Manekshaw to the rank of Field Marshal. This was welcome news for all of us. Obviously, Indira Gandhi had overruled Jagjivan Ram. Next morning, I went to the office of Manekshaw and congratulated him. He was in a very good mood. He told me that he had got to know about his being elevated to Field Marshal. He was due to quit office in another fifteen days and a function was to be held on 3rd January 1973 at Rashtrapati Bhavan when the President would confer the rank on him. As Officiating Adjutant General, I had to make necessary arrangements. The first requirement was to have the badges of rank of a Field Marshal prepared. Manekshaw's personal staff had got Bastani Brothers, the Army Headquarters tailor in South Block to make cloth badges of rank for him. Manekshaw had this in his hand and showed it to me. I told him that the badge of rank made by the tailor was incorrect and in any case for the function at Rashtrapati Bhavan metal badges of rank would be required. He asked me how I could say that the badges of rank prepared by the tailor under his instructions were not correct. I reminded him that when we were in Military Operations Directorate, Field Marshal Auchinleck often used to come to the Operations Room and I used to observe his badge of rank. Manekshaw said that he also had been interacting with Auchinleck but he did not remember precisely what he wore. I explained that the badge of rank should be a wreath with cross baton inside and a miniature National Emblem (Ashoka Lions) at the top two lips of the wreath. Auchinleck used to have a crown at the top and we could have the Ashoka Lions in lieu. Manekshaw wanted me to show some written authority for this badge of rank. I looked at our old Defence Service Regulations going back to 1903 but there were badges of rank for all Army ranks except Field Marshal. I thought that may be the British Army Defence Regulations would have the Field Marshal's badge of rank as in the old days appointment of Field Marshal used to be made by the War Office in England. I tried to get in touch with the War Office through our Military Adviser in our High Commission in London. I spoke to him to get me the necessary authority from the War Office. He said that the War Office was closed for Christmas and New Year holidays.

He could get the information after some time when the War Office opens. My requirement was to get the information the same day to get it prepared for the investiture ceremony on 3rd January. It struck me to check the *Encyclopaedia Britannica* and to my pleasant surprise, I found the Field Marshal's badges of rank shown in colour in it. I took it to Manekshaw and he said that I had a better memory than him. Being from the Gorkhas, he wanted the badge of rank in black. I got the Army Workshop in Delhi Cantonment to fabricate the badge of rank overnight. They rose to the occasion and completed the task by next day. Manekshaw was quite satisfied.

I now had a big problem on my hand of getting government approval for the privileges to be sanctioned for Manekshaw on his elevation to Field Marshal. I drafted a letter asking for the following for him:

(a) Full salary for the rest of his life as per the practice in other countries. A Field Marshal never retires and continues to be a serving officer for the rest of his life. He should have all the privileges available to a serving officer.

(b) A Ceremonial Baton for the Field Marshal.

(c) An ADC and Secretarial Staff for the rest of his life.

(d) A high protocol status along with holders of Bharat Ratna Award.

A meeting was held in the office of the Home Secretary, Gobind Narayan, also attended by the Defence Secretary, KB Lal, and a few Joint Secretaries. As Adjutant General, I participated in this meeting. Knowing that the Defence Minister, Jagjivan Ram, was not too happy at the elevation of Manekshaw, the bureaucracy was well-prepared to raise hurdles and scuttle our proposals for Manekshaw's entitlements. They first started saying that we were a Republic and we should follow the pattern in the US for five-star Generals rather than the British practice of Field Marshals. Britain is a monarchy and British practice in this regard was not relevant for us. I insisted that the government had in its wisdom promoted Manekshaw Field Marshal and not General of the Army which is the designation for this rank used in the US. I pointed out that Republics like France and the Soviet Union, had Marshals. They reluctantly agreed but tried to deny the privileges that go with that rank. I had no problem in getting the badge of rank approved but there was long drawn discussion regarding a baton for Manekshaw. They argued that it was an unnecessary hang over from British Imperial days and our Field Marshal can do without a baton. Luckily, my knowledge of military history came useful and I gave them the background which they could not contest. I said that the rank of Field Marshal was introduced by Frederick the Great of Prussia (now Germany). The old practice was that a conquering General after a war could keep war booty for himself and distribute some of it to his Army. As part of reforms of the Army, he ordained that war booty will go to the State. The conquering General would be compensated for it and in case of outstanding victory in battle promoted to the rank of Field Marshal. It was decided that a Field Marshal would never retire, get full salary for the rest of his life and will be given a baton as a status symbol like the orb for a sovereign. In protocol the Field Marshal should rank next only to a Sovereign. Subsequently, all countries in Europe introduced the rank of Field Marshal in their Army. Britain was the last to do so. The Duke of Wellington had captured the baton of a French Marshal in Spain and sent it as a present to the British Sovereign. Thereafter Britain decided to introduce the rank of Field Marshal in its Army and the Duke was elevated to that rank. The bureaucrats reluctantly agreed on this point and a sum of ₹1,00,000 was sanctioned for a Field Marshal baton. As for our other recommendations, they said that they would take a decision after due consideration. The immediate requirement was sanction for the rank of Field Marshal, badges of rank for this appointment and baton. These were agreed to. After further discussion, they agreed to special pay of ₹400 only per month in addition to the pension of ₹1,200 authorised for Army Chief. As for protocol status, they later decided that the Marshal would rank with Service Chiefs and will remain junior to the Cabinet Secretary. As regards ADC and secretarial staff, they flatly turned down our recommendations. However, the Gorkha Regiment of Manekshaw on their own provided him with necessary secretarial support. It was a standing shame that the bureaucrats' commitment of fixing Manekshaw's salary in due course took 35 years to get settled. President Kalam on a visit to Wellington where Manekshaw was lying terminally ill in the local Military Hospital had gone to see him. Someone had told him that for the last 35 years Ministry of Defence had not given a decision on his salary as Field Marshal. On his return to Delhi, the President advised the government to expedite the decision before Manekshaw passed away. His arrears of pay amounting to over ₹2 crore were sanctioned. The Defence Secretary was sent to personally hand over a cheque to Manekshaw in the Military Hospital. A month later, when I was Governor of Jammu and Kashmir, I had gone to Wellington to give a talk. I had read in the newspaper about Manekshaw at long last having been given his arrears of pay. When I met him in the hospital, he still had his sense of humour. He told me that a *babu* (clerk) had come from Delhi to give him the cheque which he had sent to his bank. He was not sure if that cheque will be honoured. A month later Manekshaw passed away.

§

The investiture in Rashtrapati Bhavan on 3 January 1973 went off well. We converted the Army Day Parade of 15 January of that year as a farewell to Manekshaw who was demitting his office on that day. Unknown to Manekshaw, I got all the Regimental Colours from nearby Centres at Meerut and Dehradun for the Ceremonial Parade. It was for the first and only time that the Regimental Colours were on Parade at Delhi Cantt for Army Day Parade. As per Ceremonial Drill Regulations, the Regimental Colours dip in Salute to Heads of State and to Field Marshals. Even a Prime Minister is not entitled to this honour. As Manekshaw arrived at the Parade ground in Delhi Cantonment, I received him and told him that Regimental Colours were on Parade. In his usual way, he smiled and said that I had taken him by surprise. He asked me how he should return salute as a Field Marshal with a baton in his hand. I was not sure how a British Field Marshal does so. I recalled that I had seen in pictures the Reich Marshal Goering returning salute raising his Right baton above his head. I suggested that he may do so accordingly. Manekshaw adopted this way of returning salute and it became a standard practice in our Army.

After the Parade, I met Manekshaw at the MES Inspection Bungalow in Delhi Cantonment where he was temporarily staying prior to going to Coonoor near Staff College Wellington. On that occasion, I told him that I had annoyed General Kaul by declining to give evidence against him in the Court of Enquiry that had been instituted in 1961. His reaction was, "Why didn't you tell me this earlier? I was all along thinking otherwise." I told him that I had not done so while he was still serving in the Army because he may not believe me and may think that I was doing so to seek favours. He must have realised that while serving on the Staff of Kaul, I had been loyal to him in carrying out my duties but it had lead to an impression in the Army that I was a Kaul man. This had caused me problems for long. It was now a completely closed chapter.

It is a great pity that a National Hero like Field Marshal Manekshaw was not given due honour on his death. No Minister from Delhi or Chief Minister of Tamil Nadu was present for the funeral in Wellington. He was given a military funeral with the Vice-Chief of the Army attending it as the Army Chief at that time was in Moscow. The other two Chiefs were represented by two-star rank officers. I was in Srinagar in the process of winding up and could not go for the funeral because of the Amarnath Yatra controversy. There was much criticism at the neglect shown by the government. It may be mentioned that the funeral of Britain's first Field Marshal, the Duke of Wellington, was not only attended by the King and the Prime Minister but also all Heads of State in Europe.

A popular demand was raised in 2015, the Centenary year of Field Marshal Manekshaw, to award him Bharat Ratna. It is a pity that the government ignored this. In other democracies the services of a soldier with an outstanding war record and who has been a great achiever for the Nation are suitably recognised. In the US, there have been several Generals who have been the President of that country, the last being General Eisenhower. General De Gaulle became the President of France. In UK, their two top Generals, Marlborough and Wellington were made Dukes the highest peerage of the country which would be an equivalent of Bharat Ratna. Duke of Wellington also became Prime Minister of UK. In India, the military is ignored and while Film Stars, Singers, Musicians or Cricketers can get the Bharat Ratna, a Field Marshal who won the greatest military victory for the Nation in thousands of years of its history apparently cannot.

§

In 1974, I was transferred to command 23 Infantry Division then located in Assam. Field Marshal Slim had referred to command of a Division being like commanding an orchestra of war. I found that very true because as a Divisional Commander one's command is composite in that various arms and services comprise the Division. I enjoyed my command of the Division which was deployed in the Brahmaputra Valley. An added attraction was the fact that my own battalion was part of the Division at Tamulpur on Bhutan Border. We had an operational role in Bhutan when requested by Bhutan Government. This gave me an opportunity to tour in East Bhutan and see the famous Tashigong Monastery in East Bhutan. It is a multi-storied wooden building with no nails to join wooden pieces. The paintings inside were different colours which looked fresh withstanding centuries of time. Digme Singhe Wangchuk was then the new King of Bhutan. He visited my Division coming across the border at Tamulpur for a day. He was in his early 20s and was fond of playing football. We organised a Football match between his team and my Divisional team. The king was playing as Centre forward for his team and we allowed him to score a few goals. The king's team won and he was very happy and so was his sixteen-year old sister who was the Finance Minister of Bhutan.

My tenure was cut short and after a little over one year in command of a Division, I was posted as Director Military Intelligence. (DMI). I had half a mind to request that I be left with the Division for another year to complete my tenure but I was told that then Army Chief General Bewoor was keen that I should take over this appointment. I then decided not to represent.

§

I found the appointment of Director Military Intelligence very interesting. Soon after I took over, my old friend General Raina was appointed Army Chief. I had known him for a long time. In 1945, he was a Major in Indonesia and I a Captain. Thereafter we had been Majors together for a while at the Infantry School (now College of Combat) at Mhow. A DMI has to function closely with the Army Chief. Before he took over as Chief, I had to go to him at Shimla to give him an Intelligence briefing. He was then Western Army Commander and had his Headquarters at Shimla. I stayed with him and he was very hospitable. I looked forward to working under him. Within a month of his taking over as Army Chief, Indira Gandhi declared Emergency on 25 June 1975. People started talking that she had deliberately brought a Kashmiri Pandit as Army Chief who may be useful to her during the Emergency. I worked with Raina for two years and I can say emphatically that he was totally apolitical. However, Bansi Lal, the then Defence Minister was very co-operative with him because he thought that Raina was perhaps close to Indira Gandhi. There were occasions when he would himself come to the office of the Army Chief.

Jayaprakash Narayan (JP) was a good friend of my father. They had studied together at college. Whereas JP took to politics, my father joined the Police. This did not affect their personal relations. After my father retired from the Police, there was a virtual famine in Bihar. JP set up a Bihar Relief Committee which organised help for starving people. He got funds from various international and national organisations. He requested my father to join him as the Director in his Committee in an honorary capacity. The Relief Committee attracted volunteers from all over the country and even some foreigners from the West. The Committee put up a few hundred odd free kitchens all over the State. It also imported equipments to dig deep tube-wells for irrigation in the drought hit areas. The work of this Committee was much appreciated by the government. This Committee continued to function even after the drought was over to help in agricultural activities. On JP's death, my father took over as the President of Bihar Relief Committee.

Relations between Indira Gandhi and JP had been very cordial. JP had been a fan and colleague of Jawaharlal Nehru. After Sardar Patel's death, Nehru wanted JP to join his Cabinet as Deputy Prime Minister. In due course, he could have succeeded him as Prime Minister. JP declined saying that he did not want to remain in politics and wanted to be a social worker with Acharya Vinoba Bhave. JP's wife Smt Prabhavati Devi, who had lived in Mahatma Gandhi's Ashram for some years when JP had gone to the US for higher studies and was treated as their daughter, was very friendly with Kamala Nehru, the mother of Indira Gandhi. I remember that once when I was on leave, JP was in our house and talked to Indira Gandhi on the telephone. He was calling her Indu and I believe she used to call him uncle. A few years later a rift grew between them on the issue of corruption in government. Despite their earlier very close relationship, JP was forced to launch a movement against the government. My father had nothing to do with JP's political activities.

While I was DMI, the build up towards Emergency had started. JP was addressing huge gatherings at various places for strengthening the anti-government movement. I remember I was returning from Assam to Delhi. My plane transited through Patna. My father had come to Delhi and was staying with me. I did not break journey at Patna and there was a vacant seat in the front row adjacent to where I was sitting. At Patna, to my surprise JP boarded the plane and sat next to me. I wished him and he was happy to see me. He told me that he had heard about my becoming a General and enquired what I was doing. I told him that I was heading Military Intelligence at which he jokingly remarked that then he would have to be very careful with me. We talked for a while on different general and personal issues. No political matter was discussed between us. Most of the time JP had some papers with him which he was reading. On arrival at Delhi, we were getting out of the plane with JP holding his brief case in his hand. I requested him to hand over his brief case to me so that I can carry it for him. He mockingly said that I was a General and I should not be carrying his brief case. I replied that besides being a General, I was also a nephew and it was my duty to carry my uncle's brief case. He smiled and said you win and handed over his brief case to me. At the airport terminal building, there were thousands of people who had come to receive him. I handed over his brief case as directed by JP to someone who had come to receive him. I was in uniform and I saluted him before taking leave from him. The next morning when I went to see Raina in his office, he smiled and told me, "You are close to JP." I told him that Civil Intelligence at the airport, on the previous day, must have filed a report about my being with JP at the airport. I also explained to him my personal relations with JP. He said not to worry. He fully understood the position.

I was taken by surprise when I learnt about Emergency being declared. On that day no newspaper had been published and later I learnt that the previous night all newspaper offices had been closed. A strict censorship was imposed on all newspapers. I also learnt that JP and other senior political leaders had been taken into custody. That evening an acquaintance of mine from Patna came to see me at my house but seeing a lot of Army personnel and vehicles at my house had gone back and spread a canard that because of my association with JP, I had been placed under house arrest.

I continued to serve as DMI almost throughout the Emergency, primarily because I enjoyed the full confidence of General Raina. A sense of fear descended over the people during the Emergency because of the arbitrary manner the government had started functioning. Sanjay Gandhi had been given a long rope and virtually started running the government. I must give full credit to Raina for keeping the Army totally apolitical. I will mention a few instances to confirm this.

It was at the height of summer in June 1975 when a big Congress rally as a show of strength was organised in the open space on either side of Rajpath. The Rally was to be addressed by Indira Gandhi. The Defence Minister asked for Army Water Trucks to be made available for drinking water at the Rally. Raina took the view that this would affect the apolitical image of the Army and said that the orders be given in writing to the Army to provide Water Trucks at rallies of all political parties. It was suggested by the Ministers that the Water Trucks could be repainted and soldiers in civilian clothes could come with these trucks. We stood our ground saying that it would be bad for the discipline of the Army and its apolitical image. It would also send a wrong message to the soldiers. This was reluctantly accepted by the Ministry.

We also turned down the request of the Congress Party to provide Army tents for the Congress Session at Guwahati at which Sanjay Gandhi was to be anointed as the heir apparent. The Punjab Government had organised a big function at Ferozepur for inauguration of Anglo-Sikh War Memorial Museum by Sanjay Gandhi. All serving Generals had been invited for the function. With the approval of Raina, we issued orders that no serving General in uniform or even in civilian clothes should attend the function.

One day, I was asked by Raina to come over to his office. I found Professor PN Dhar, Principal Private Secretary of Indira Gandhi and R Mathur, the Director Intelligence Bureau were in Raina's room. I was told that an Ex-Serviceman from Rajput Regiment named Sundar had turned a dacoit and had threatened the life of Sanjay Gandhi. Apparently Civil Intelligence had information that he used to take shelter in Army units. I was asked to help in ensuring that he was apprehended. I asked Mathur to give me a copy of the photograph of Sundar which I could send to all Army units in and around Delhi.

After that almost every week, I would be asked about progress in tracing Sundar. A month or two later, I received a report from Brigadier Katoch of my Regiment who was commanding Jaipur Sub-Area that a Pakistani spy had been arrested by a Signal unit. He had come to buy stores from an Army Canteen. He was buying a vest which had the colours of the Signal Corps. The NCO at the Canteen asked him that his card showed that he was from the Rajput Regiment so why was he buying a Signal vest. Sundar replied that he liked the colours of the Signals. The NCO got suspicious. He asked him where he came from and the person replied that he was from Bulandshahr. The NCO said that Havildar Major of the signal unit was also from Bulandshahr and took him to meet the latter. While he was talking to the Havildar Major he put his hand in his pocket to show him something and a few pistol rounds fell from his pocket. He was immediately pounced upon and interrogated. He pretended to have come from Pakistan. The Sub-Area Commander asked me for orders to deal with the individual. I directed that he be handed over to the Civil Police and they would take necessary action against him as per the law. While he was in custody at the Police Station, a Deputy Superintendent of the Police from Delhi had gone to his home in Jaipur and had visited the Police Station. He recognised Sundar as he had escaped from an encounter with a Police party led by him. He was immediately brought to Delhi. Next morning the newspaper reported that Sundar had been nabbed by the Police after a very successful Intelligence Operation. By then, I had received reports from Jaipur about this. I informed Raina on the telephone as he was then out on tour. He asked me to also inform the Defence Minister. I went to Bansi Lal and gave him all the details regarding the arrest of Sundar. He stood up from his chair and thumping his chest told me that he would immediately inform *Bahanji* about this saying that it was because of the Army that he had been apprehended and the Police should not be allowed to take credit for it. He then asked me to write a detailed report in good English and also some questions and answers. I was perplexed about questions and answers and enquired what exactly was required. He told me to write possible questions which *Bahanji* would ask him and the reply that he should give to those questions. I had to do as directed. A few days later, I read in the newspaper that Sundar was being taken under a Police Escort to a Civil Court in UP across the Yamuna. On the way Sundar is supposed to have jumped into the river with his handcuffs and drowned. Thus ended the Sundar episode much to the relief of some people at the highest level in South Block.

§

I decided to visit our Military Attaches at Kabul, Baghdad and Tehran. This was a good experience to judge our relations with these Muslim countries. Our Attaches particularly Brig Chibber at Kabul had done exceptionally well and established very good relations with the host country. All the three capitals that I visited were of Muslim countries and we had good relations with those countries. We had established better relations with Iraq and Afghanistan compared to Pakistan's relations with them.

Daud was the President of Afghanistan when I went to Kabul. He had friendly relations with the Soviets. General Mustagnee was the Army Chief. Chibber had won Mustagnee's confidence to the extent that the former would discuss his operational plans with him. Chibber had been advising him on how to deal with the ongoing insurgency in North Afghanistan.

I was surprised to see the amount of food the Afghans ate. For breakfast, they would have a dozen hard boiled eggs and a big tumbler of Kandahar pomegranate juice besides other items. At main meals, they would each have a complete chicken plus half a dozen courses of meat. I remember the banquet hosted for me by the Afghan Army Chief, General Mustagnee. I sat next to him. While eating, he would take out some good pieces of meat from his plate and put them in my plate. He was only showing special consideration for me but that was something I had never come across earlier. I was also surprised when he said that it was a pity that India and Afghanistan had not worked together in 1971 otherwise the Armies of the two countries could have shaken hands across the Indus. Today the situation is so different. After the withdrawal of the Soviets from Afghanistan, that country has become radicalised and become very close to Pakistan.

I was given a briefing on the operational plans of Afghan Army in the event of Pakistan attacking Afghanistan. I was asked my comments. I suggested that while the Afghan Army planned to hold the Khyber Pass route in strength the other route via Bolan Pass was held weakly. The British had their main thrust from the Bolan Pass route in the Second Afghan War. My hosts even arranged for me to go to Jalalabad and thence to Khyber Pass from the Afghan side. Before 1947, I had been to Khyber Pass from the opposite side. In 1946 when my battalion was serving in NWFP, Jalalabad had the biggest Buddhist Vihar that I have seen anywhere. There were thousands of Buddha statues, big and small. Each one of them had been broken or disfigured by religious fanatics. I also visited Bamiyan and saw the huge Buddha Statue carved on the mountain side. This was the biggest Statue in the world. Later when the Taliban came to power in Afghanistan, this Statue was blown up by Artillery guns for a few days while the civilised world watched this in horror.

At Baghdad, I received an equally warm welcome. Saddam Hussain was the ruler at that time. He was, no doubt, a dictator but he was not a religious fundamentalist. He belonged to the Baath Party with communist leanings. He was friendly with India. General Shenshel was the Army Chief. He was a mountain gunner and discussed with me how mountain guns had faired during operations in Jammu and Kashmir. He made his personal aircraft available to me for going to Mosul and a historical site in its neighbourhood. The Divisional Commander at Mosul had been my student at our Staff College in Wellington. He took me to Hatra ruins where the Iraqis had halted the further Roman advance in Asia some 2,000 years ago. Of course, Baghdad with its hanging gardens and rich Museum is a treasure house of history.

My next port of call was Tehran, another city steeped in history. The Shahanshah ruled over Iran at that time. I found Tehran a very modern city with women folk dressed in modern European clothes driving expensive cars. All this changed after the Ayatollah's Revolution. The Chief of the Imperial Defence Forces was General Gulab Raza Azhari, a close relation of the Shahanshah. I presented him a Silver Khukari which he greatly admired and gave me a Silver Cigarette case which of course, was of no use to me because I am a non-smoker. Nevertheless, I much appreciated the gesture. In 1965, Iran had provided significant support to Pakistan during the Indo-Pak War of that year in terms of aircrafts and use of air bases. During the 1971 Indo-Pak War, Iran took a neutral stand. I was interested in ensuring that Iran does not adopt an anti-India and pro-Pakistan approach. I, on my own, suggested to Azhari that we would welcome his coming to India as a State Guest. He told me that he would welcome a visit to India. On return, I had a formal invitation sent to him by our Army Chief General Raina. A few months later Azhari came to India and we rolled out the red carpet for him. I took him to visit the Birla temple in Delhi and also have interaction with the Yoga expert Dhirendra Brahmachari. Raina was quite excited about this visit. He decided to deliver his speech at the banquette in Persian. I wrote that script in English in which I stressed the historical links between Iran and India when the capitals of the two countries were at Persepolis and Pataliputra respectively. During the Mughal period, this link continued particularly when Humayun was given refuge in Iran. Raina was very thorough in preparing his welcome address. A Professor from Jawaharlal Nehru University translated the English script into Persian and also got Raina to polish up his pronunciation of Persian words. Azhari and the Persian delegation was thrilled at this. This went a long way in building cordial relations with Iran. However, after the Revolution in Iran when the Shahanshah abdicated and left the country, Gulab Raza Azhari was assassinated. I may also mention that the Army Chief of Iran when I had been to Tehran was a Zoroastrian General. This showed that during the rule of Shahanshah Iran, was a liberal Muslim country. After the Revolution, it changed overnight and became a religious fundamentalist country.

During my trip to Iran, I was given the privilege of seeing the Crown Jewels that was most impressive. There were several large rooms showing Diamonds, Rubies, Pearls and Gold in glass Almirahs. I do not think that any other country in the world had such a rich collection of jewels. Compared to this, the British Crown Jewels on display in the Tower of London looked so pedestrian. I also visited Shiraz, an earlier capital of Iran. Two famous poets of Iran, Hafez and Saadi were from Shiraz. Shiraz is known as the city of poets, literature, wine and flowers. Not far from Shiraz is Persepolis, the ancient capital of Persia (now Iran). Darius the Great was the ruler of Persia in the fifth century BC and his empire extended from parts of Greece to Punjab in India. Alexander the Great invaded Persia conquering that country and coming up to the Beas river in Punjab. He had burnt the ancient city of Persepolis. I saw the ruins of Persepolis which are very impressive. The Shahanshah had held what was surely one of the most fabulous dinners in human history in tents near Persepolis to celebrate the 2,500th Anniversary of monarchy in Iran. The dining hall, in exclusively furnished tents, catered for a sit down dinner of 1,000 people. The table, the crockery and the cutlery were laid out and maintained for visitors to see. I was told that exotic flowers like Tulips from Holland, Daffodils from England, Roses from US and Orchids from Thailand and so on were brought for decorations of the dinner table. All the Heads of the States were invited for this dinner. There were roads named after continents with exactly similar accommodation for Heads of States of different countries. The Vice-President of India had attended this dinner. I was shown his accommodation. These were a beautifully furnished bed room, dressing room toilet, sitting room, dining room and a room for a Staff Officer all in tents with Persian Carpets and velvet curtains. This accommodation was on the road marked Asia and on its front was a sign board with India written on it. I also saw the accommodation for Shahanshah and Shah Banu, the Emperor and Empress of Iran. It was fabulous. The doors fitted inside the tent had gold handles and so had the taps in the wash basin. The Shah Banu's dressing table had a huge glass mirror set in a diamond frame. A whole Brigade of the Iranian Army was located at that place to guard the fabulous tented city. I was told that over a billion dollars were spent for that most lavish dinner in history. I do not know what happened to all that accommodation after the Revolution.

My visit to Capitals in Europe and in the USA was not as exciting as to the capitals in West Asia. However, in US, I saw the Walter Reed Military Hospital at Washington. This is a state of the Art such institution, the President of the US who is the Supreme Commander of the US Forces when requiring hospitalisation always goes to that hospital. We had no equivalents of such a hospital for the Military in India. Later when I became the Adjutant General, I along with the then DGAFMS started the project for a similar hospital where the President of India as the Supreme Commander could also be treated when required. We floated this proposal and ultimately got it sanctioned. Thus the Research and Referral Hospital came up in Delhi Cantt. All Presidents of India have since been going to this hospital when required. It is also a unique and a state of art institution serving Military personnel including retired individuals and their families.

Towards the end of the Emergency in 1977, I was doing the weekly Intelligence briefing of the three Service Chiefs. I covered Intelligence of interest in foreign countries particularly our two neighbours China and Pakistan. Along with this briefing, I used to cover information of activities within the country. In the course of my briefing, I mentioned that Jayaprakash Narayan then in detention had been moved from Chandigarh to Jaslok Hospital in Bombay for treatment. The Air Chief enquired, "Hasn't that old man died yet?" I got upset at the manner of his asking this question. I replied, "Thank God Sir, the greatest living Indian is alive." Raina who was the Chairman of the Chiefs Staff smiled and changed the conversation. Later, he told me that I had given a good reply. However, the rumour mills in South Block converted this incident into a major show down between the Air Chief and me. I was also labelled as a supporter of JP and as such anti-government. Those were Emergency days when such a person was liable to be proceeded against. It so happened that Raina had been telling me that I had served him well as Director Military Intelligence and he wanted that in my interest I should go back to commanding a Division again to complete a full tenure as Divisional Commander to make me eligible for promotion to Lt Gen. My earlier tenure in 23 Division had been cut short when I was brought to Delhi as DMI. I was happy to be posted to 10 Infantry Division in Jammu Sector. Maj Gen HN Kaul, a Kashmiri, succeeded me as DMI. This gave rise to the rumour that a Kashmiri Pandit had been especially selected to succeed me as I could not be trusted with my pro-JP feelings. The senior journalist Kuldip Nayar in his book *The Judgement*, published after the Emergency, has made a reference to this describing it as a move for political reasons.

§

I was happy to take over command of 10 Infantry Division and complete my remaining one year tenure as Divisional Commander. I participated in a big exercise in Northern Command under the Army Commander in which all the Generals commanding formations in Jammu and Kashmir took part. At the end of the exercise, I was required to make a presentation of how the battle of Chhamb was fought during the 1971 War in which Pakistan had got the better of us and how we lost Chhamb. I made an elaborate presentation on the ground with sound effects to show how the battle was fought. The view point was on top of a hill feature called Kachreal overlooking Chhamb, Munnabarwali Tawi and the battle area. I gave a historical background to operations that had taken place in the past. I started with the invasion of Alexander the Great going on to that of successive invaders down to Ahmad Shah Abdali and then how Chhamb had been changing hands between India and Pakistan since 1947. The presentation was much appreciated and the CD recording my voice called the voice of Kachreal is preserved in 10 Infantry Division. Thirty-eight years have elapsed and it is still being played for visitors to the Division. This was played for me, as Governor of Jammu and Kashmir, in 2004 and I was told that it continues to be played for VIPs visiting the Division or for officers on training courses like National Defence College, Higher Command and Staff College on their visit to Jammu and Kashmir.

§

In 1978, I was promoted to the rank of Lt Gen and posted as Adjutant General at Army Headquarters. I had already done a tenure as Deputy Adjutant General for a couple of years earlier and had often officiated as Adjutant General. I was, therefore, very familiar with the requirements of my new assignment. Adjutant Géneral is a key Principal Staff Officer dealing with a wide range of subjects as the Chief of Personnel of the Army. This covers Manpower Planning, Recruitment, Records, Discipline, Ceremonials and Welfare. My tenure as Adjutant General was very satisfying as I could execute a lot of welfare projects for the Army. I had the advantage in serving under a Chief with whom I had worked earlier. Gen OP Malhotra, the then Chief had commanded an Artillery Regiment in 123 Brigade at Amritsar in which I had been the Brigade Major. We had close and friendly relations. As Chief, he supported me in all projects started by me and was a source of great strength to me.

The four main welfare projects undertaken by me were Army Group Insurance, Army Welfare Housing Organisation, Army Welfare Education Society and Holiday Homes at hill stations. We made a small beginning in all these four areas which now have grown up into mega projects. I had read somewhere of the US Army running an Insurance Scheme for their troops serving in Vietnam to provide life coverage for casualties over and above their official entitlements. The Defence Service Regulations authorise Army Headquarters to impose a compulsory deduction in the salary of Army personnel for their welfare. Under this provision with the approval of the Chief, I decided that every soldier should pay ₹10 per month for Group Insurance and Junior Commissioner Officers (JCOs) and Commissioned Officers proportionately higher amounts. The officers had to pay ₹30 per month. This was a small beginning and in those days the salaries of Army personnel were much lower than what they are getting today. Nevertheless, the amount per month being collected was over a crore. As the amount increased various banks made a bid for handling our accounts of this scheme. We initially started with Syndicate Bank but as the Scheme grew, we invested in fixed deposits with various Public Sector Banks on a proportionate basis. We considered getting the Life Insurance Corporation to run the Scheme for us. We contacted them and they produced a Scheme in which they had Divisional and Branch offices of the Corporation whose overhead would cost almost our monthly subscriptions for this Scheme, thus making it not viable. Moreover, they declined to cover war risks. We decided to operate this scheme on our own. The Directorate General Defence Accounts was co-operative and he agreed to undertake the responsibility for making the collections. We got him to open a new column in individual ledger accounts showing collections. This could be done without having any additional staff. We also decided not to maintain any separate account and not issue any receipts. It was taken for granted that any one serving in the Army would have paid the required deduction and no checks were required for this purpose. Even if there was any error in accounting, the amount involved would be negligible and we decided to accept that risk. Another feature of this scheme was that the amount collected, with a slight deduction and with compound interest, would accrue to the individual on his retirement from the service. Thus unlike the US Scheme our Insurance Scheme catered both for casualties and saving. It also provided employment for retired personnel to man this project. I had a Cell in AG's Branch for this under a retired officer, Brigadier Narender Singh from Garhwal Rifles. He proved to be an accounts wizard and deserves full credit for making a success of this scheme. As the Scheme started growing, we increased subscription and added new features to it like giving loans to personnel on easy terms. The Ministry of Defence tried to get control of this Scheme but we kept them out of it arguing that it was a Regimental Fund and there was no government involvement in it.

We also started with Army Welfare Housing Organisation on a no profit no loss basis. The idea was that officers on retirement could have a flat constructed for them in various cities. Initially we started with the Som Vihar Project in New Delhi. I managed to get prime land near Delhi Public School (RK Puram) and constructed 400 flats. Maj Gen Soni, a retired Engineer was appointed as the Managing Director. Initially we decided to have a formula for allotment of flats for officers. Only the officers who had no house of their own were eligible to have a flat under this scheme and for allotment we gave them one point for every year of service in the Army. Officers selected for this Scheme had to deposit the required amount with AWHO to provide funds for construction. In 1978, officers had to pay ₹2 lakh in lump sum to get an allotment. Prices have escalated so much that these flats now cost ₹7-8 crore. I named the first lot of flats at RK Puram, Som Vihar, after my friend Major Som Nath Sharma, PVC. Encouraged by the success of this scheme, I decided to acquire several acres of barren land for ₹8 crore at NOIDA for 8,000 dwelling units for both officers and personnel below officers' rank. Initially our emphasis was for officers accommodation because soldiers in those days on retirement wanted to go back to their village rather than stay in cities. With changed living conditions, many soldiers had started wanting to live in cities after retirement. To cater for this, we extended this scheme to also cover them. General Malhotra felt that we were spending a big amount from AG's Welfare Fund for acquiring NOIDA land for ₹8 crore. We drove up to the War Memorial Pillar of 1803 Anglo-Maratha battle in NOIDA. It took us 22 minutes from South Block to NOIDA. There was hardly any traffic on the road in those days. The entire area was barren and dusty almost like a desert. One came across quite a few camel carts and there was not a single building to be seen in the vicinity. Despite this, I persuaded the Chief to approve the project which I felt had great future potential. I took General Malhotra to the view point and showed him the land that we proposed to buy and he approved of our doing so. We bought the required land for ₹8 crore. AWHO was the first to start construction in NOIDA. Soon others also started investing in land there and Delhi started expending phenomenally across the Yamuna to NOIDA. Today in a little over two decades

NOIDA is as thriving a city as New Delhi and is Part of the National Capital Region (NCR). We also acquired land in Calcutta, Pune and Bombay. Today the AWHO has expanded to cover most important cities in the country.

I found that Central Schools did not fulfil the requirements for schooling of Army children. I decided to set up an Army Welfare Education Society. The Navy had given the Army and the Air Force a share of the prize money collected by them during the 1971 War. According to International Law enemy merchant vessels with trading commodities captured in war was prize money for the victorious country. Keeping a major portion for itself, the Navy gave the Army ₹5 crore for our welfare funds. I decided to start Army Welfare Education Society with this money. Initially we decided to have one Army Public School each in all our Commands with the first school coming up at Delhi. We launched Army Public School at Dhaula Kuan as our first venture. The long-term scheme was to expand this to Army Public Schools in major cities and Army Schools in every cantonment. All the schools were to follow the Central Board of Secondary Education (CBSE) syllabus. The schools not only had a common syllabus but teaching of various subjects in a progressive manner in an academic year so that an Army child moving from one such school to another faced least disturbance. It was also laid down that Army children will be admitted in these schools as and when their father moves from one station to another without having to wait for the start of the academic year. This Scheme has also thrived a lot and has become a great success. The organisation of AWES provides ample scope for jobs for retired Army personnel. This scheme has expanded considerably over the years and now technical educational institutions like medical colleges, engineering colleges, law colleges and management institutions are being run for the welfare of Army families.

We also decided to have Holiday Homes for Army personnel both officers and personnel below officers' rank, at various hill stations. In my young days Army personnel taking leave would go to their homes rather than on holidays to other places. In the changed conditions, increasing numbers of Army personnel have started going on holidays to tourist places. These Holiday Homes met that requirement.

I found that Gorkha soldiers of our Army suffered from a handicap compared to Indian soldiers. For example, after the 1971 War, we found that war casualties and gallantry awardees were made eligible for various benefits like Cash Awards, Allotment of Petrol Pumps, Land and Jobs. Gorkha soldiers going back to Nepal did not have these facilities. The Leave Regulations for Gorkhas were different from Indian soldiers. They used to get four months leave after two years or six months leave after three years plus trekking time in Nepal which could be up to three to four weeks depending on the location of the home of the soldier. Moreover, whereas class X was made the minimum educational qualification for the Indian soldier, Gorkha soldiers had a special dispensation taking into account the lack of educational facilities in their villages. To cater for the special requirements for Gorkha soldiers, we started a Gorkha Cell in AG's Branch. We also organised Regimental teams to visit recruiting areas of these soldiers. These teams with medicines and doctors would be led by a Regimental officer and provided welfare funds to meet their expenditure. Their visits to Nepal were to be treated as temporary duty. As DMI, I had earlier also provided some Intelligence funds to these teams. We got Government of India to provide concessions to Gorkha soldiers like those given by State Governments to Awardees and War Casualties minus of course land allotments or government jobs. We set up a new unit at Raiwala near Haridwar called Gorkha Resettlement Training Unit. Before retirement, Gorkha soldiers could do three-months courses at this unit for various vocations like Motor Transport Drivers, Vehicle Mechanics, Agriculture, Medicines, Hygiene and so on to help them in rehabilitating themselves in Nepal. After prolonged negotiation, we managed to start a permanent pension paying office at Pokhra in West Nepal and in Darang in East Nepal. Our Embassy at Kathmandu acted in this regard for Central Nepal. Along with Pension Paying Offices we had Transit Camps and Recreational facilities at these places. The Indian Ambassador in Nepal inaugurated the Camp at Pokhra and I was the Chief Guest at the function. Later when I was Ambassador in Nepal, I inaugurated the Bharatiya Gorkha Sainik Niwas in the heart of Kathmandu. I had started work on this as Adjutant General and it took several years to complete it due to land hassles and financial and technical problems. This Niwas provides excellent accommodation for officers and JCOs as also a modern dormitory for soldiers. The kitchen is almost like that of a five star hotel with all modern facilities. Charges for accommodation are minimal compared to similar accommodation in the city. This Transit Camp is self supporting because the ground floor has been rented out to various banks and offices. Even officers from non-Gorkha Regiments can stay in this accommodation, if vacant. The British Army Chief visited this camp and told me that this was the best accommodation for Ex-Servicemen which he had seen anywhere in the world.

I also took up two other issues for the Army. One was in regard to up-gradation of ranks and the protocol status of the Army Commanders. As a result of Cadre review in the Civil Services and large scale proliferation of senior ranks, the Army was relatively badly off. There had been no cadre review for the Army. Paramilitary battalions had Commanding Officers wearing the badges of rank of full Colonel, and Section Commanders were wearing three stripes on their arm authorised for Havildars. Both in Kashmir and in North-East, para military battalions worked with the Army battalions in Army formations. This disparity in badges of rank caused natural resentment in the Army. We upgraded the rank of Commanding Officers to full Colonel and of Section Commanders to Havildars. Besides, as part of cadre review, we upgraded the ranks of Commandants and Instructors at various training institutions to provide better promotion opportunities for Army officers. The subsequent cadre reviews with wholesale upgrading of rank perhaps made the Army rank structure too top heavy. One often hears that at this rate we would have more Generals than soldiers. As regards the status of Army Commanders we wanted this rank to be upgraded to full General. An Army Commander had at least four Lt Generals working under him. He also had higher scale of pay. We recommended that the Army Commanders should be in four-star rank. The bureaucrats were averse to this because they felt we were preparing the ground for the Chiefs to be in five-star rank. Ultimately, government agreed to give Army Commanders higher protocol status ranking with Secretaries in Government of India while other Lt Generals continued to rank with Additional Secretary. There was also a change made in the uniform of the Army Commander by having a wreath under three stars on their Georgette patches.

§

One day in June 1979, the British Military Adviser (MA) in their High Commission in Delhi came to my office. He told me he had been asked to convey that Lord Mountbatten was very upset that his letter to Defence Minister Jagjivan Ram sent three months ago had not even been acknowledged, leave alone replied. I enquired about the subject of the letter. He told me that Lord Louis was planning his own funeral and wanted to know if the Armed Forces of India would participate in his funeral. Considering that as Supreme Commander in South-East Asia a few hundred thousands of India's Defence Forces had served under him during the Second World War and later he had served as Viceroy and Governor-General of India, he wanted to know if the three Defence Services would participate in his funeral. I told the MA that normally such a letter would come to me to put up a draft reply and I had not seen any such letter. I assured him that we would be sending an early reply. Mountbatten's letter could not be traced in the Defence Ministry despite a thorough search for two days. I informed the Defence Minister. He confirmed that he recalled having received such a letter from Mountbatten. The next day the letter was traced. It was lying in the drawer of a clerk's table in the Minister's Secretariat. Jagjivan Ram told me that he would make out a reply and send it to me that very day to pass it on to the British Military Advisor for onward dispatch to Mountbatten.

Jagjivan Ram's reply was amusing. He wrote that he had received Mountbatten's letter some time back and had delayed sending a reply because he felt emotional about such a sad eventuality. He added that in India it was considered bad omen to discuss or plan any living person's funeral. Mountbatten was very dear to all of us in India. However, since Mountbatten wanted to know about the participation of India's Armed forces in his funeral, Jagjivan Ram assured him that the Indian Defence Services would most certainly and suitably participate in his funeral. He added that we all hoped and prayed that the occasion for this would not arrive for a long-long time to come.

It so happened that within a few weeks of this reply being sent, Mountbatten was killed in a terrorist blast by IRA off the coast of Ireland. The Chief of Indian Navy with a suitable contingent of officers from the three Defence Services took part in the funeral procession in London. The belief that discussing a living person's funeral brings bad omen was strengthened.

§

On completion of my tenure as Adjutant General, I was given the privilege of commanding the strike Corps (2 Corps) of the Indian Army. My Headquarters was at Chandi Mandir near Chandigarh. I was Corps Commander for a year and a half during which I conducted two large scale formation exercises with an Armed Division and two Infantry Divisions. This was professionally a very satisfying experience.

§

In 1981, I was appointed Army Commander of Western Command. The Headquarters of Western Command was at Shimla at that time. This was of great sentimental value to me. Thirty-four years earlier I was among the first lot of officers posted to Western Command when it was raised on 15 September 1947. I was then a Major and was the only Indian officer posted to this newly raised skeleton Command Headquarters. I got married while serving at Headquarters Western Command. My son Yashvardhan who had joined the Indian Foreign Service got married while I was Army Commander, Western Command. We have two Silver Salvers from Headquarters Western Command officers, one given to me in 1949 when I was a Major and the other to my son in 1982 while I was the Army Commander.

My thoughts on becoming Army Commander were drawn to a point made by Field Marshal Lord Slim, who was a rare case of a British officer who had risen from the rank of a Private (Sepoy) to Field Marshal. The only other such example in the British Army was of Field Marshal Sir William Robertson. Slim's observations based on his experience at different levels of Commands are very interesting. The lowest command for an officer is that of a Platoon. That is his first command and he has about forty soldiers under him. He stated that a Platoon Commander should know his men better than their mothers do and care for them no less. According to him the next good command is that of a battalion Commander. Thereafter it is Divisional Commander where one has the complete orchestra of war under him. After that a good command is that of an Army Commander. His reason for saying so was based on his experience that in war an Army Commander shapes the course of history. The intervening commands of Company, Brigade and Corps though important are not so exciting. I did not have an opportunity of commanding an Army in war but as Western Army Commander, I felt that I could have influenced the course of our National history if we had dealt with the Akali problem as I wanted to do. I shall discuss this in detail.

As Western Army Commander, I was responsible for the defence of Punjab and Northern Rajasthan. I had three Corps comprising nine Infantry Divisions and one Armed Division under my command. Apart from defence of Punjab, I also had responsibility for conducting offensive operations in Pakistan during a war with that country. Bhindranwala had organised a violent agitation of Sikhs in Punjab and his demand was for a separate Khalistan. The situation was serious but till then the Civil administration had been handling the situation. I felt that the government should handle the problem with vision and not allow things to get out of hand. We were getting reports that Pakistan was helping the Sikh extremists.

The then Defence Minister came to Bathinda where one of my Corps Headquarters was located. I received him and took him around the Corps. He spent two days with us. At that time, he was heading the Groups of Ministers dealing with the Akali problem. The Defence Secretary Kaul had accompanied the Defence Minister. Towards the end of the Defence Minister's visit, I decided to raise the Akali problem with him. He told me that it was purely a political problem. The Defence Secretary added that Generals should not get involved in political issues. I abruptly told him that I was discussing the issue with the Minister and I should have my say. Though it was a political problem it also had Army dimensions. As Army Commander, I was interested in the Akali problem getting resolved quickly. There were three reasons for this. First, if a solution was not found, it may affect my operational plans for the defence of Punjab in the event of a war. I would have to be prepared to deal with internal violence. Second, even in peace time if the situation was beyond the control of the civil authorities, the Army would have to be deployed in aid of the civil power. Third, I had nearly a lakh of Sikh troops under my Command and continued Akali agitation could affect their discipline and morale. The Minister enquired from me as to what should be done. I replied that the sooner we resolve this problem politically the better. He then enquired as how that could be done. I repeated that my concern was a quick amicable settlement and I was not competent enough to advise him as to how that could be done. However, since he asked me my suggestions I would give him my views. The Akalis had made three demands. They want the train to Amritsar named Golden Temple Express. They also had two other demands namely Gurbani to be relayed on Doordarshan from Golden Temple and all cigarette shops in the proximity of Golden Temple to be moved out from its vicinity. There should be no difficulty in meeting these demands and giving owners of cigarette shops due compensation. The Minister replied that it was politics. You give an inch and you will have to give a yard. Today they had made innocuous demands, tomorrow they would want Amritsar to be declared a Vatican City. I replied that one should cross a bridge only when one gets to it. There is no demand for Vatican City status at present. If, and when, that demand is raised, the government can deal with it suitably. Our conversation on this subject now ended. I was not able to convince the Minister.

A month or so later, the Chief Secretary of Punjab Puri rang me up saying that Bhindranwala was in Mehta Chowk Gurudwara with 40 rifles. He was involved in the assassination of Lala Jagat Narain, Editor of *Punjab Kesari*, and he had to be arrested. He wanted us to lend a couple of tanks to the Police so that they could deal with his armed followers and arrest him. I replied that the Army does not lend its weapons to the Civil. Moreover, policemen were not trained to use tanks. The use of tanks inside a Gurudwara will have serious National and International implications. It may also affect the morale of Sikh soldiers. In view of this, I could not give the Punjab Government any tanks. Later, Chief Minister Darbara Singh rang me up saying that he wanted to meet me. I told him that I was going from Shimla by helicopter to Bikaner the following day and I would drop in at Chandigarh en route to meet him. When I met him, he told me that he realised that I could not loan some tanks to the Police. He wanted me to get the Army to arrest Bhindranwala. I explained to him that unlike the Police, the Army does not have legal powers to arrest anyone. I advised him that he had enough armed strength in Punjab Police and in Central Para Military forces to arrest Bhindranwala and his followers. However, if the situation went beyond the control of the Civil, Army assistance could be sought. He was not convinced of what I told him and said that I was not being helpful. I regretted my inability. Possibly, after meeting me he approached Indira Gandhi. The next day while I was on a helicopter recce of the Rajasthan Border, my Chief of Staff at my Headquarters in Shimla received orders from Army Headquarters in the afternoon to send the Army for arresting Bhindranwala the same night and report completion by next morning. He was also told that these were the personal orders of the Prime Minister. He told me that he had passed down these orders to the Corps at Jalandhar and the latter had done so to the Division at Amritsar. Mehta Chowk is about 30 miles from Amritsar and a Gorkha Battalion was moving that evening to carry out the task. I asked him to stop the Gorkha Battalion from moving that evening. He expressed surprise saying that we would not be complying with the orders of the Prime Minister. I told him that I will take responsibility for that and he should carry out my orders. I immediately rang up the Defence Minister as the Army Chief was on tour out of the country. The Defence Minister was taken by surprise at what I told him. It appears that he was not in the loop and did not know about the orders issued by the Prime Minister. It was so strange. However, he told me that I should not fail to carry out the orders of the Prime Minister. I explained to him that I would like my point of view presented to the Prime Minister requesting her to amend her orders. The arrest of Bhindranwala could not be affected the same night because that would involve troops going inside the Gurudwara without any day light reconnaissance leading to indiscriminate firing and avoidable casualties. This operation could be carried out the next night after due preparation, but I recommended that the Punjab Government should arrest Bhindranwala on their own for which they had sufficient resources. The Minister saw my point of view and told me that he would talk to the Prime Minister and let me know. After a while he rang me saying that the Prime Minister had accepted my recommendations and Punjab Government would do the needful on its own. Somehow this got leaked to the Press. The next morning the Chandigarh Edition of *Indian Express* had it on the front page that the Army Commander had refused to send troops to Mehta Chowk Gurudwara despite the orders of the Prime Minister. This was of course very misleading. The Police went to Mehta Chowk Gurudwara the next day and Bhindranwala agreed to come out after 24 hours, on concluding his *Ardaas* at the Gurudwara. The Police waited outside while a thousand armed *Nihang* Sikhs assembled at that place. When Bhindranwala came out, the *Nihangs* attacked the Police party which had to open fire. Eleven people were killed in this melee. Bhindranwala was arrested and taken to Ferozepur jail. After two days, he was released as it was found that there was not enough evidence to substantiate his involvement in the assassination of Lala Jagat Narain. When Bhindranwala was released from Ferozepur jail, there was a crowd of several thousands to welcome him and he became a great hero. He now moved in great style to the Golden Temple from where he conducted operations against Hindus, killing several innocent people. The situation was deteriorating by the day.

I felt that a day will soon come when the Army may be called upon to undertake operations to clear the Golden Temple and take Bhindranwala into custody. At this stage, ex-Major General Shabeg Singh had joined Bhindranwala and there were reports that he was fortifying Golden Temple against any Army onslaught. Shabeg had been an old friend of mine from our young days in Burma and we had served together at various places in different ranks. He had done good work in 1971 War with *Mukti Bahini* (Bangladeshi freedom fighters). There were allegations against him for misuse of funds while working with *Mukti Bahini*. Later he was General Officer Commanding of Uttar Pradesh Area at Bareilly. He was involved in a big scam of liquor from the Army Canteen. He was court-martialled and dismissed from Service. He was now not eligible for any pension. However, Supreme Court had given a ruling that the Provident Fund of a dismissed government servant could not be confiscated. He approached me to help him to get his Provident Fund which was a couple of lakhs. Ministry of Defence was opposed to this amount being released but I managed to persuade them to do so in view of the judgment of the Supreme Court. He had now joined Bhindranwala and he even wrote a personal letter to me from the Golden Temple.

I made out a Standing Operating Procedure for conducting operations in Golden Temple if and when the Army was called upon to undertake this task. The Army should have an effective double cordon around the Temple to prevent any one going in or coming out. Electricity and water supply to the Temple should be disconnected. Bhindranwala and the armed personnel with him should be repeatedly requested on loud speakers to come out announcing that they were committing sacrilege in a holy place and the Army did not want to enter the Temple. They were to be given time to do so for a couple of days or so. At the same time one could get the services of some Sikh leaders or holy man to negotiate with them and persuade them. Had I been the Army Commander at that time, I would have contacted Shabeg and tried to persuade him. This was not to be because when Operation Blue Star took place a year later I had quit the Army. My plans included establishing a Gurudwara outside the Temple where the Army would organise *Akhand Path*, praying that the task be carried out peacefully without the Army having to go inside the Temple. Full publicity to all this was to be given and some eminent Sikh civilians requested to witness what was being done. In spite of all this if the Army had to conduct operations inside the Temple, then soldiers should first offer prayers at the Ad hoc Gurudwara before entering the Temple and carry out the operations with minimum force. Both Sikh and non-Sikh troops should be used for the operation and soldiers should remove their shoes and cover their heads while entering the Golden Temple. After completing the operation, the assaulting troops should do *Kar Seva* to clean up the place and offer special prayers at the Holy Sanctum. Had Operation Blue Star been conducted in this manner, the Sikh people would not have been so deeply alienated and minimum damage would have been caused inside the Temple. Unfortunately, this plan was totally ignored. It was reported that the Akali extremists inside the temple would be declaring the independence of Khalistan from inside the Temple on 6 June 1984. Troops were ordered to complete the Operation that very night and sanction given to use tanks inside the Temple. The rest is history. There were large scale disturbances all over Punjab and ultimately Indira Gandhi was assassinated by her own Sikh guard.

§

Almost a year before Operation Blue Star I was posted out from Western Command to Delhi as Vice-Chief of Army Staff and given to understand that after four months when the tenure of the then Chief expired, I would be taking over as Army Chief. I had to understudy him while serving as Vice-Chief. Krishna Rao, the then Chief and I had been friends for many years having served together at various places. His father was in the Industries Department at Patna when my father was the Police Chief of Bihar. His sister and my sister were together in school and college. They had been good friends. Our families had known each other for a fairly long time. When I arrived in Delhi, Krishna and his wife asked us one evening while we were having dinner with them to go around and see the house where I would soon be living. I declined saying that I had known the layout of the house from the time General Cariappa had lived in it as an Army Commander and later as Army Chief. I had also been visiting the house during the tenure of several subsequent Chiefs.

As Vice-Chief, I had an interesting experience when I was officiating as Chief during Krishna Rao's visit to Vietnam. One morning General Hazare, the Director Military Operations, came to my house saying that the Cabinet Secretary had sent for him the previous evening and briefed the Naval Chief and him about sending a Brigade Group to Mauritius. The Prime Minister of Mauritius had very cordial relations with Indira Gandhi. The leader of the Opposition, Paul Bereger, was likely to stage a coup. The Prime Minister wanted to send a Brigade Group to Mauritius. Hazare could not contact me the previous night and had issued warning orders for a Brigade Group to concentrate at Bombay for onward move to Mauritius. The Naval Chief and I had to brief the Prime Minister of our plans in the Operations Room that afternoon. I was unhappy that he had not contacted me the previous night. However, he had prepared a detailed brief for me. The meeting took place in the Operations Room. The Prime Minister did not come but the Defence Minister was there. Senior Officials of Ministry of Defence, Ministry of External Affairs and RAW were also present for the meeting. The Naval Chief gave out the details of his plan. Troopships and Naval Escort for the convoy was to concentrate at Bombay Docks within 48 hours to take a Brigade Group from Bombay to Mauritius. The whole operation was to be kept a closely guarded secret. When my turn came to speak, I expressed my reservations both from the political and military points of view.

I stated that I was not competent to comment on the proposed operation from the political point of view. However, I would like to mention that India was the Chairman of the Non-Alignment Movement (NAM) and her seeming to interfere with internal developments in another country may not go down well. As regard the military aspect of the operation, we had to take note of certain important factors. The journey by sea of our convoy may take three to four days. The US has a military base at Diego Garcia not far from the route from Bombay to Mauritius. With Satellite communication, they will be able to pick up the move of our Convoy and we may encounter opposition when we land on the beaches in Mauritius. Amphibious operations are specialised operations and require appropriate landing craft assault and also troops had to be trained for such operation. Our troops had not done any training in this type of operation after the Second World War. We also did not have appropriate equipment and landing craft for assault on the beach. If Paul Bereger put up opposition to our landing in Mauritius with soldiers in the Mauritius Army, our Brigade may run into difficulty. Due to the time required for the movement we may not be able to send reinforcement for the Brigade which would have to fight it out on its own. In view of these considerations, this operation will be a hazardous undertaking. The Defence Minister said that he would discuss this with the Prime Minister. Krishna Rao on return to India fully agreed. Later we learnt that the government had decided to give up the idea of sending troops to Mauritius.

§

Krishna Rao had thrown a party at his house during the conference of Army Commanders. Indira Gandhi had also been invited for the dinner. Before the dinner, I saw her talking very amicably to my wife. I later learnt that she was admiring the colour combination of the Madras silk saree which my wife was wearing. On my wife telling her that the saree had recently been brought by me from Bangalore, she said that I had good taste for colours. She herself was wearing a Parsi saree which my wife said looked nice. She replied that it was her mother-in-law's saree which Sonia Gandhi had selected for her to wear that evening. At dinner, I sat next to her. She talked about my having selected a good saree. I was surprised that the Prime Minister had time for such small talk. I did not tell her that the saree had been selected for my wife by the wife of the local General at Bangalore when I had given her the money to do so. During dinner, Indira Gandhi was in a very good mood talking about her recent visit to Chile. When *Naan* (chapati) was served to us she noticed that my *Naan* was slightly burnt on the edges. She said that she liked burnt *Naans* and enquired if I would exchange the *Naan* served to me with what she had. I readily exchanged the *Naans*. The next day I found out the reason for all her affability to my wife and me.

The following day I was in the office of Krishna Rao where I had gone to discuss some files with him. While I was with him, he received a telephone call. I do not know who the caller was. I only heard him saying, "Has the decision been taken and can I tell him?" He then turned to me and said that the government had decided to appoint General Vaidya as the next Army Chief. Simultaneously, he asked his Military Assistant (MA) to get General Vaidya on the telephone. I was surprised that a person whom I considered such a good friend should behave in such a cold and matter of fact manner. I told him that I would like to put up my papers seeking premature retirement. He said that I need not be in such a hurry. In the meanwhile, the call to Vaidya came through and he warmly congratulated him. He asked me if I would also like to talk to him. I replied that I would do so from my office. We then discussed the files that I had taken with me to his office. On return to my office, I immediately put up my application for premature retirement. I then dictated a letter of congratulations to Vaidya and also spoke to him on the telephone.

That day my wife and I had been invited for lunch at the house of Major-General MS Chopra, a retired and very senior officer of my Regiment. There were quite a few guests at his house. The All India Radio in its afternoon news announced that General Vaidya had been appointed Army Chief superseding me. I told Chopra that I had been informed about it earlier. I tried to enliven the atmosphere by recounting some jokes.

The following day the newspapers carried the news about Vaidya being appointed Chief and my having been superseded. The Parliament was in session. A joint resolution was moved by former Prime Minister Chaudhary Charan Singh, former Deputy Prime Minister and Defence Minister Jagjivan Ram and former Information and Broadcasting Minister LK Advani enquiring reasons for my supersession. The Defence Minister replied that both General Vaidya and I were good Generals but government had decided to appoint Vaidya as the Chief and I had not been superseded. The Opposition pressed for a reply saying that I had obviously been superseded and they wanted to know the reasons for it. The Minister requested the Opposition not to press for a discussion of this matter because that may affect the morale of the Army and would not be in the interest of National Security.

In view of mounting controversy over my supersession in the media, the Defence Minister sent Brig Rama Rao, the Defence PRO (Public Relations Officer) requesting me to issue a statement to the Press to douse the growing controversy in newspapers and magazines. I told the PRO that it was for the government to issue any statement and I had nothing to say in the matter. While I was talking to him, a few Press Correspondents came into my office and took my pictures. They asked me for a statement. I found myself cornered and I felt that I must tell them something. I stated, "I do not question the decision of the government. I accept it. I have decided to fade away from the Army. General Vaidya chosen to be the Army Chief is a friend of mine and a capable General. I am confident that the Army will flourish under his leadership." I did not realise that this statement would virtually add fuel to the controversy. Another point that fuelled controversy was the reference in the Parliament by a member during the debate that I had been superseded because of my father's close association with Jayaprakash Narayan. For the next one month, several articles appeared in newspapers and magazines on my supersession. Never before had supersession in the Army became so controversial. Some of the headings of articles on me by top journalists were very flattering. Kuldip Nayar wrote, "Lt General Sinha's brilliance was his undoing." Prem Bhatia wrote, "Heads I win, tails you lose." Ashok Raina wrote, "The man who knew too much," and so on.

Indira Gandhi sent her 'Man Friday' RN Kao, RAW Chief, to me saying that my not being appointed Chief was not the end of my career. He advised me to withdraw my resignation and the Prime Minister was willing to appoint me as Ambassador or a Governor. I was determined not to do so recalling how in somewhat similar circumstances General Thimayya had withdrawn his resignation and that did not help him or the Army. Similar messages were conveyed to me by Brig Sailo, a friend of mine and then Chief Minister of Mizoram, as also a political leader from Bihar known to be close to Indira Gandhi. They advised me to pay a farewell call on Indira Gandhi and she was willing to give me an appointment of my choice. KP Singh Deo, then Minister of State in Defence Ministry, told me that he was in Orissa where he heard of my supersession and was shocked. He also asked me to withdraw my resignation and good care would be taken of me. He showed me a book that I had written *Of Matters Military* which he often referred to. He felt that the government needs to utilise my services. My stand was that I would certainly go to meet the Prime Minister if she sends for me officially, otherwise I had no plans to go to bid farewell to her. I was going to call on the President who was the Supreme Commander and also on Venkataraman, the Defence Minister, who was the Government of India for me. Indira Gandhi never sent for me and I did not go to meet her. When I called on the Defence Minister, he was rather cold to me and only told me that I was so much in the news and advised me not to join politics. I was amused by his unsolicited advice to me. President Zail Singh was very affable and warm when I went for my farewell call to him. He told me that everyone knew that I had been such a good General and my resignation was a great loss for the Army. He also told me that as Supreme Commander, the file appointing a Service Chief had to go to him for his approval. When the file on my supersession reached him, he raised a query asking what was the recommendation of the then Army Chief. The file came back to him with a note that Krishna Rao was also of the same view. As a Constitutional head, Zail Singh said that he had no option but to approve the recommendation.

I received some three hundred letters from various people, many of whom I did not know or had ever met. A large number of serving and retired Army officers wrote to me. An Army Commander wrote, "You have truly done the Army proud. Unfortunately, it was not your destiny to command the Army. But I think you earned more name for not becoming the Chief than some others could for becoming so." A Lt Gen wrote, "Yours has been a magnificent and unsurpassed contribution to an elite Army. The absence of your dynamic presence at the epics will be felt by us all from the lowliest jawan for whom you have done so much to the Commander of Field Forces such as I am for whom you have been a shining example in the sphere of leadership." A Maj Gen wrote, "We were stunned, shocked, surprised and highly disappointed to hear the news. What a way to leave the service after such a brilliant career and after having done so much for the Army and the Nation." A Captain wrote, "Not only I but I am sure the entire Indian Army would be losing a great soldier who throughout his career in the Army had strived for the betterment of the men and officers under his command." A retired Army Commander wrote, "The entire Army was looking forward to your appointment as its head, an honour that rightly belongs to you.

You have taken the set back with great dignity and grace, in keeping with the highest quality of an officer and gentlemen which you typify." A retired Colonel wrote, "It is a great surprise and shock that you have been overlooked for the post of COAS which you more than anyone else deserved." Surprisingly, I also received a large number of letters from civilians whom I had not known. A retired Cabinet Secretary wrote, "If the government's failure (not yours) had deprived you of the top Army post, it seems to be the machinations of the civilian bureaucracy. By putting in your papers, you earned the respect of many like me." A retired High Court Judge from Orissa wrote, "I am as happy and proud of your achievements as your father must have been. You must have noticed that the whole country is with you and has voiced what should have been done in your case." The most touching letter I received was from the mother of a soldier at Chandigarh, "Tears came to my eyes when I read in the papers of the touching farewell given to you. Mother India is still giving birth to such worthy sons who do not hesitate to give up their job with dignity and selflessness."

Dr Karan Singh associated with India International Centre offered me the job of Director of the Centre with a lot of perquisites. I told him that the Centre may be an autonomous body but the government had a hand in its functioning. It was no doubt a temptation offer particularly when my youngest child was studying in the final year for her BA in Delhi. I decided to leave her with my brother who was then in Delhi and chose to go back home to Patna to look after my father who was now past eighty.

As feelings ran high in the Army over my supersession, I decided not to have any formal farewell and quietly catch the morning flight from Palam to Patna. When I arrived at the Airport, I was surprised that the terminal building was virtually taken over by people in Olive Green. Almost all the Generals serving in Army Headquarters were there in their uniforms and so were many young officers particularly from my Regiment. My battalion was at Meerut and the Commanding Officer along with many officers, JCOs and soldiers had come from Meerut to wish me farewell. The Commanding Officer, Lt Col Anand Negi, had been my Quartermaster when I was commanding the battalion. He told me that knowing my views he had brought his officers and men in civil transport and had not used any government transport. There was a five-year old son of a Havildar who had also come. I picked him up in my lap and told him that he should not have missed his school to come to Palam to see me off. His reply moved me. He said that I was the father of the battalion and he wanted to see me and was happy to miss his class for one day. The Airport Staff was also very considerate. Contrary to rules, they insisted on my car going to the tarmac for me to board the plane. At the foot of the ladder of the aircraft there were two Air Hostess with a bouquet of flowers for me and my wife. On board the plane on my way to Patna old thoughts and events kept coming back to me. I remembered that when I joined the Army and was leaving home, my grandfather had given me a piece of advice. He told me to always serve with dignity and never compromise on my self respect. I wished he had been alive to see me act on his advice and quit the Army with dignity.

I was surprised to see a thousand or more people come to receive me at the Patna Airport with garlands and flowers. My supersession had made the headlines in the local Press and was seen as an injustice done to Bihar because I was the only Bihari General in the Army. I had been denied the top appointment because of my father's close association with Jayaprakash Narayan. My father was at the Airport to receive me. I was surprised to see Karpoori Thakur, former Chief Minister of Bihar and now the Leader of Opposition in the Bihar Assembly. I was also surprised to find Raj Narain at Patna airport. He had come from Lucknow. He had defeated Indira Gandhi in the election to the Parliament from Bareilly after the Emergency in 1977. He sprinkled perfume on me saying that like the perfume my fame will travel all over. There was also lot of slogan shouting. There were a few arches erected for me on the road to my house. I later learnt that my brother-in-law who had been the Mayor of Patna had organised this reception for me.

My forty years Army career had come to an end in a manner in which I could never have imagined earlier. One does not know how Destiny shapes one's career. It appeared that I was now all set for a post-Army career for myself by forces not under my control.

§

Lengthening Shadow: Diplomacy and Governance

I was happy to be back home after serving for forty years in the Army when I never had an opportunity to serve near home. Moreover, my father who had crossed 80 was living alone in the town in his large house with a large compound, which in the days of multi-storied buildings had become a rarity. My mother had passed away a few years earlier and he needed someone to manage his house. Our going to live with him was of assistance to him as also of help to us. In spite of his old age, he kept himself busy doing social work and also had a busy schedule of social engagements. He had taken over as President of Bihar Relief Committee after the death of Jayaprakash Narayan which kept him quite busy. He was also President of Hanuman Trust and was assisted by a dynamic young Police Officer Kunal who after serving as Senior Superintendent of Police of Patna had taken premature retirement to work on religious projects. He was the Secretary of the Hanuman Trust. A sum of ₹28 lakh was raised by the Trust for constructing a new temple at an old site near Patna Railway Station. The new temple is perhaps the tallest Hanuman temple in the country. With generous donations and offerings by devotees at the temple, large funds started being accumulated. The Trust now undertook two major social projects, a residential school for 1,200 boys and a Cancer Hospital with 200 beds. These institutions were running extremely well and my father as President used to take keen interest in their functioning.

My resignation from the Army and the manner in which I had accepted my supersession had attracted much notice among political leaders. The Presidents of all the three major Opposition political parties invited me to join their parties. These were Chaudhary Charan Singh of the Dalit Kisan Mazdoor Party (DKMP), Chandra Shekhar of Janata Party and LK Advani of Bharatiya Janata Party (BJP). I declined to join any political party. On arrival at Patna, as mentioned earlier, Karpoori Thakur, the former Chief Minister and now Leader of Opposition in Bihar, had come to receive me at Patna Airport. He was a very modest person and I developed very good personal relations with him. Two student leaders, Lalu Prasad Yadav and Nitish Kumar, were his followers. Karpoori Thakur would often visit me at my house. I was getting drawn towards politics but I was trying to keep away from it.

The Patna Municipal Corporation organised a welcome function for me. The Mayor Krishna Bahadur who had succeeded my brother-in-law presided over the function. I was taken by surprise when I was awarded the distinction of Bihar Ratna. I think I owed this largely due to the perception amongst the people that I had been superseded because of my father's close connection with Jayaprakash Narayan. I was also invited to give talks at Rotary Clubs, Lions Clubs and Universities. As a keen student of history, I often chose to speak on historical subjects. I was delighted to be invited as a Visiting Professor on Military History by the University of Pune. Government Service Conduct Rules demand that one should get sanction for accepting any job within two years of one's retirement. As a Visiting Professor, I was not to get any emoluments except travel expenses and free accommodation at University Guest House during my short visits to the University about once a quarter. Nevertheless, I sought government's permission to accept this offer. I was surprised that the bureaucracy at Delhi had the cheek to ask me to submit a list of subjects that I would be speaking on and also short brief of my talks. I wrote a rude reply stating that since I was not getting any remuneration for the assignment, it was not really necessary for me to obtain government sanction. As for sending briefs of the texts of my lectures that was too absurd a requirement to be acted upon. I concluded that I was going ahead and accepting this assignment and the government could take whatever action they liked against me. I never had a reply, and I took on this commitment in Pune University. I worked on two projects with students at the University. These were Military Leadership of Shivaji and the Military History of the Marathas.

Parliamentary elections were due in 1984. The Congress Party and its supporters had been projecting the likelihood of war with Pakistan in the near future. This was obviously because they wanted to cash in on the 1971 victory under Indira Gandhi, suggesting that her getting re-elected as Prime Minister was in our National interest. Advani rang me up requesting me to address Opposition Members of Parliament (MPs) on Threats to National Security at Mavlankar Hall at Constitution Club in Delhi. I accepted the invitation. Chaudhary Charan Singh and Atal Bihari Vajpayee jointly presided over the meeting at Mavlankar Hall. In my extempore talk for about an hour, I discussed the threats from China and Pakistan without giving any classified information. I shared my views that the threat of war from these countries was ever present but I saw no possibility of war breaking out in the near future. At the end of my talk, an MP from Bihar stood up and said that my supersession was an injustice done to Bihar. Vajpayee corrected him saying that it was injustice done to India. On the personal level, I found myself getting close to both Vajpayee and Advani. The former is two weeks older than me and the latter two years younger. They invited me to address the Annual Session of the BJP at Pune on Army and Politics. I hesitated saying that I was not a member of the BJP, and it would not be appropriate for me to address a party meeting. Advani pointed out that I was being invited as an expert and I did not have to be a member of the party. A few years earlier MC Chagla, former Chief Justice, Bombay High Court who had also held other appointments under the Congress Government, like Ambassador in US and Cabinet Minister, and never a member of BJP, had been invited to give a talk on Independence of Judiciary. He had delivered the address at a BJP Annual Convention. I agreed to go to Pune and my address was well-received. Although I never joined the BJP, in popular perception I started being seen as a member of BJP.

§

Madhu Mehta, a successful businessman from Bombay had started a movement called 'Hindustani Andolan' to promote clean politics in the country. It was a non-political organisation. He came to see me at my house at Patna and persuaded me to join his movement. He had a good political background. He had been General Secretary of the Swatantra Party founded by Rajagopalachari who had been Governor-General of India and one of the tallest leaders of the Congress during the Freedom Struggle. Rajaji had become fond of him and through him Madhu Mehta had wide contacts. He was a delightful person and I became fond of him. He also reciprocated this and we became good friends. I used to stay with him when I went to

Bombay. He introduced me to a number of leading personalities like Mrs Vijaya Lakshmi Pandit, BK Nehru, Minoo Masani, IK Gujral, Ram Krishna Hegde and some others. I accompanied Madhu Mehta in tours to various cities to propagate the idea of clean politics. I recall an amusing incident at a meeting in Delhi. Madhu Mehta was presiding and three of us Ram Krishna Hegde, Farooq Abdullah and I were invited to speak on Clean Politics. While introducing us Madhu Mehta said that all the three of us were 'Formers', the first two being former Chief Ministers and I, a former General, who were not favoured by Indira Gandhi. I was invited to speak first and I gave my views on the subject. Farooq Abdullah followed me. I had known him for long from the days of his father when he was a Medical Student in Rajasthan. He said, *"General Sahib ne siyasat ke baare main bari achchhi baten kahi magar baat ye hai ki siysat main jo safai siyasat karta hai uska safaya ho jaata hai."* (The General has said nice things about clean politics but those who try to practice clean politics get washed away in politics.) It was a good function which was well-reported in the Press. The following night while I was staying with my sister, I got a call from Andhra Pradesh Bhavan. The Secretary of NT Rama Rao was on the line. He told me that the Chief Minister would like to meet me at 5 in the morning in Andhra Bhavan. I told him that that was hardly a time at which I would like to meet any one. I did not fancy keeping an engagement at that unearthly hour on a winter morning. The Secretary, a senior IAS Officer, told me that in that case I would not be able to meet the Chief Minister. I replied that I had not asked for meeting with him and it was he who wanted to meet me. I then put the telephone down. A little later, he rang me up to enquire if it would suit me to come at 9 in the morning. I agreed to do so. I was wondering why NT Rama Rao wanted to meet me. Anyway, I arrived on time at Andhra Bhavan. There was a large crowd of people milling around the place as normally happens with Chief Ministers. I was received and taken straight to NT Rama Rao. I had never seen such a spectacle before. NT Rama Rao was wearing a saree to represent *Ardhanarishvara* (a half man and half woman deity). A couple of people were washing his feet with water in a utensil. I later discovered that they were Cabinet Ministers and the water was to be taken as *Charnaamrit* (holy water). NT Rama Rao could not speak much English nor much Hindi. In a very broken language he told me that he had formed *Bharat Desham* and he wanted me to head the Bihar

Branch of *Bharat Desham*. NT Rama Rao had Prime Ministerial ambition. I told him that I was not interested in politics and would not be able to do so. Thereafter, I took leave of him.

§

During my retirement at Patna, I received an offer from the Editor of the *Statesman* to write articles for that paper. I was told that General JN Chaudhuri even when he was serving as Army Chief used to write articles for that newspaper on security subjects under a pseudo name and later Lt Gen PS Bhagat had also written for the paper's columns. I readily accepted the invitation and I started sending my articles for that newspaper. This has become a hobby with me which I continue to pursue to till date. In a way, this has contributed to my name being in circulation in political circles.

§

One day when I was driving my car in Patna, I was held up for half an hour at a road crossing. Rajiv Gandhi was on a visit to the city and traffic had been closed for his convoy of cars. At that time, he had no official position, but, being the son of the Prime Minister, he was given all the honours. The Chief Minister accompanied him. There was a banner at the road crossing which attracted my attention. The banner had the following written in Hindi, *"Samrat Ashoka ke nagar main yuva samrat Rajiv Gandhi ka hardik swagat."* (In the city of Emperor Ashoka, a hearty welcome to the Emperor of the youth Rajiv Gandhi.) I felt such display of servility and sycophancy revolting. This reminded me of what had happened 40 years earlier when I was a student and was held up while cycling at a road crossing when Lord Linlithgow, the Viceroy of India, was on a visit to Patna. I was already under pressure from various people to contest the coming Parliamentary election in 1984. I decided to do so as an Independent candidate. The opposition parties did not put up a candidate from Patna. The BJP gave me active support. Madhu Mehta went all out to support me and did some fund raising for me. Patna Parliamentary Constituency was a large urban-cum-rural constituency of 11 lakh voters. The students of Patna gave me very active support. Normally people spend crores for Parliamentary elections. My total expense was about ₹2 lakh which I had received as donations. I campaigned on a bicycle along with my student supporters. I was surprised at the support wave in my favour. People were certain that I would emerge victorious. My campaigning on a bicycle was very unusual and attracted notice in both national and international media. Being a green horn in politics and without much financial resources it was no doubt a very difficult challenge for me. However, the support I received was also largely due to the fact that I had suffered because of my father's association with Jayaprakash Narayan. Indira Gandhi had been assassinated a few months earlier and understandably there was a great amount of sympathy wave for the Congress. My ancestral village Raipur Khajuri was within the Patna Parliamentary Constituency. The caste factor is all important during elections particularly in Bihar. The Congress candidate Dr CP Thakur contesting the election is from the Bhumihar caste. My village has almost 100% Bhumihar population. When Dr CP Thakur went to the village during his election campaign, the villagers told him that they would vote for me as I was from that village. When I went to the village I received an enthusiastic response. They showed me some wells in the village and neighbouring villages saying that they had been dug in the time of my great-grandfather who was still remembered as a very benevolent landlord. During counting of votes, I found that almost the entire village had voted for me instead of Dr Thakur who was from their caste.

A day after the polling, one of my student volunteers informed me that the Strong Room where the ballot boxes were kept had been opened by the District Magistrate and his Staff was working inside. I immediately went to the Chief Electoral Officer of Bihar at Bihar Secretariat and complained that the Strong Room had been opened without any prior information given to me. He told me that the District Magistrate should not have opened the Strong Room without obtaining his permission and if he had done so, it was a serious matter. He would personally go and see what had happened. I accompanied him. On reaching the Strong Room, he sent for the District Magistrate who admitted that he had issued orders to open the Strong Room because the ballot boxes had come late at night and details not recorded before putting them inside. This again was against specific orders on the subject. The Chief Electoral Officer expressed his displeasure. I sent a telegram to the Election Commission at Delhi. The next day counting of votes started and several malpractices came to light. Ballot papers marked in my favour in bundles had been collected from *Pan* shops nearby. The ballot boxes neatly stacked like currency notes were found all marked in favour of the Congress candidate. Despite these blatant irregularities, the District Magistrate declared the results showing Dr CP Thakur elected from the constituency. I had polled over 1 lakh votes despite all the irregularities. I was given to understand that orders had been issued from the highest level in Delhi to ensure that I was defeated. The Election Commission responded to my complaint saying that the District Magistrate should not have opened the Strong Room and Bihar Government had been instructed to ensure that this did not happen again. As regards giving redress to me, the Commission expressed its inability to do anything as the results had already been declared and only the High Court could take a view in the matter. I am sure if TN Seshan had been the Chief Election Commissioner, the election would have been set aside and fresh polls ordered in the constituency. He took over this appointment a few years later. As advised, I took up the matter in the Patna High Court and proceedings continued endlessly. Five years elapsed and other elections took place. I lost interest in the matter and realised that contesting elections under such conditions was beyond me.

§

Although I had not joined any Political Party, quite a few top leaders of opposition parties would come to see me in my house. Both Vajpayee and Advani were among them. My relations with them had become quite close. I was surprised that one day I received a telephone call asking when VP Singh could come to see me. He had resigned from the Cabinet and had formed a Jan Morcha. He came to see me and invited me to join his Morcha saying that it was a movement for clean politics and not a political party. He told me that he had read my articles in *The Statesman* against corruption and supportive of the stand taken by him against Rajiv Gandhi. I told VP Singh that I would not join his Morcha but would give him issue-based support. Later, he converted his Jan Morcha to a Political Party and announced that he would be contesting Parliamentary election from Allahabad. He again came to see me and asked me to support him. He also told me that he had seen in the papers how I had campaigned in Patna on a bicycle. He had decided to do so on Motorbikes and not use cars for campaigning. I agreed to canvass for him. I had to go to Saudi Arabia where my son was posted in the Embassy. My wife and I went to Riyadh where my grandchild (Ambuj) was born. After I had been in Riyadh, I received a message from VP Singh asking me to come to Allahabad as I had promised. Allahabad Constituency has nearly 1 lakh of Ex-Servicemen and also another 1 lakh civilians belonging to the Kayastha caste to which I belong. It was felt that my campaigning for VP Singh would be helpful for him. It was the height of summer in the month of June. As promised, I came back to India leaving my wife behind at Riyadh and campaigned in the summer heat of Allahabad. VP Singh was most appreciative of this. I recall that Sunil Shastri was the Congress candidate contesting from Allahabad. The Congress Party which had virtually ignored Lal Bahadur Shastri after his death wanted to cash in on his name during the election at Allahabad. The banners put up in the city had pictures of Lal Bahadur Shastri with his slogan of *Jai Jawan Jai Kisan* along with the picture of his son Sunil Shastri. Addressing an Election Rally, I said that I was very happy that the Congress had now remembered Lal Bahadur Shastri and the famous slogan that he had given to the Nation. I stated that it was now trying to exploit that slogan for electoral purpose. I also added that just as Congress had been promoting corruption it was corrupting that slogan by virtually making it *'Jai Jawan Jai Kisan Jai Santan'* (Victory to soldiers, farmers and progeny).This went down well with the audience and became a counter slogan for that election. VP Singh concentrated on the Bofors issue and this had a big impact on the voters. VP Singh won that election.

In 1989, Rajmohan Gandhi had come to Patna and was staying with me. VP Singh, Ram Krishna Hegde and Ajit Singh son of Chaudhary Charan Singh also happened to be in Patna. I invited them all for dinner at my house. We discussed as to who should be put up as a candidate against Rajiv Gandhi from Amethi Constituency for the Parliamentary elections in 1989. All these leaders were of the view that Rajmohan Gandhi should contest against Rajiv Gandhi. The former had an equally, if not better family background in politics as Rajiv Gandhi. Whereas Rajiv Gandhi was the grandson of Jawaharlal Nehru, Rajmohan Gandhi was the grandson of Mahatma Gandhi from his father's side and of C Rajagopalachari from his mother's side. He had been active in Moral Rearmament Movement and was a reputed author of books and articles. I suggested that it would be better that Rajmohan Gandhi contested from Champaran in Bihar. The Mahatma had launched his Freedom Movement in India from Champaran and his grandson contesting from there will have a big sentimental impact. The majority view was that Rajiv Gandhi was a sitting Prime Minister and no better heavyweight candidate than Rajmohan Gandhi could be put up against him. My wife's village home is close to Amethi and her brothers had local influence in that area. I was asked to canvass for Rajmohan Gandhi during the elections.

I camped at Amethi for a few days and addressed a few meetings. VP Singh also came to Amethi and I addressed a few rallies with him. I wondered what would be the reaction of the Mahatma and Jawaharlal Nehru in Heaven to their grandsons contesting against each other. Apart from the resources available to Rajiv Gandhi, the Muslims in the Constituency did not support Rajmohan Gandhi because in an article he had advocated that the Babri Masjid should be shifted using modern technology to another location and the site made available to the Hindus for constructing a Ram Temple. Be that as it may, Rajiv Gandhi won the election with a comfortable majority. However, the overall tally of his party was less than that of VP Singh's Janata Dal. Rajiv Gandhi resigned and VP Singh now became the Prime Minister.

§

I had come to Delhi for some personal work and was staying with my sister. I received a telephone call from the Prime Minister's office to meet VP Singh immediately. They had rung up my house at Patna and was given my telephone number at Delhi. I went and met VP Singh in his office and congratulated him on taking over as Prime Minister. He told me that he had two major problems on his hand, internally Kashmir and externally Nepal. He knew of my long and close association with the Kashmir problem from Day One on 27 October 1947. He also knew that for many years I had served with Gorkha troops, and had executed various welfare projects for Ex-Servicemen in Nepal. He said that Ministry of Home wanted me to go as Governor of Kashmir and Ministry of External Affairs was keen that I go as Ambassador to Nepal. He asked me where I would like to go. I replied that I was not looking for any job for myself but I would go wherever he wanted me to serve. He thought for a moment and then said that I should go to Kashmir. He enquired as to when I could go there. I told him that I could go within three to four days. Thereafter I came away and returned to Patna to pack to go to Kashmir. My father was very thrilled saying that as a young officer he had been for a short while ADC to a British Governor of Bihar and he would be happy to see his son installed as Governor. I received a telephone call next day from Inder Kumar Gujral who had taken over as External Affairs Minister. He mentioned that they have been able to find a Governor for Jammu and Kashmir in sending Jagmohan back to that State for a second tenure. They had no one to send to Nepal. He asked me if I would agree to go there. I replied that there was no problem. I had earlier left the choice to the Prime Minister and I would be only too happy to go to Nepal. It so happened that 13 years later in 2003, I had also to go as Governor to Jammu and Kashmir.

§

Ambassador to Nepal

Indo-Nepal relations had hit the Nadir in 1989 when the Trade and Transit Treaty between the two countries was allowed to lapse. It was said that this was due to personal misunderstanding between the King Birendra Bir Bikram Shah of Nepal and Rajiv Gandhi, the Prime Minister of India. Three specific incidents had occurred. During his official visit to Nepal, the wife of Rajiv Gandhi, Sonia Gandhi, wanted to visit Pashupatinath Temple. The Nepalese authorities declined to give her the necessary permission. Non-Hindus are not allowed inside the temple. Sonia Gandhi being a Christian could not go inside. Perhaps Rajiv Gandhi wanted special dispensation for her. The second incident took place in Islamabad during the conference of Heads of States of SAARC countries. Rajiv Gandhi sent word to the King to meet him at breakfast to discuss agenda points before going for the conference. The King felt that if he wanted to do so, he should have come to him for breakfast and discussed the matter. On the third occasion, I am told Rajiv Gandhi rang up the King at Kathmandu from Delhi. The King declined to take a call saying that Rajiv Gandhi should talk to his counterpart, the Prime Minister of Nepal. The King would take the call only from the President of India. Both Government of India and Nepal Government were in a belligerent mood. The Ministry of External Affairs wanted to tighten the economic screws to make Nepal feel the pinch. As per the Trade and Transit Treaty, there were twenty-two transit points on the Indo-Nepal Border through which export/import of goods used to take place. Once the treaty lapsed, India had the obligation to provide at least one trade and transit point as per International Law for a land locked country. Lateral East-West road communication was not developed in Nepal. Providing only one Trade and Transit point would cause much hardship particularly to the people of West Nepal. This is the area from which the bulk of soldiers come in the Indian Army. Government of Nepal felt that they could defy India and get their requirements from other countries. This would be very difficult because air supply from foreign countries was very uneconomical. Road communication from China by Tibet to Nepal had not developed. As a result, petrol had to be rationed to a few litres per day and there were long queues for vehicles at Petrol Pumps in Nepal. West Nepal faced acute shortage of salt and kerosene. The families of our serving soldiers and our Ex-Servicemen in West Nepal faced much hardship. Yet the Gorkha soldiers whether at Siachen or in Sri Lanka with the Indian Peace Keeping Force (IPKF) operations were carrying out their duties most loyally to India. I had started receiving complaints from retired Gorkha personnel to do something to help the families of Gorkha soldiers. As a retired officer, I was in no position to do anything in the matter.

There was also a security angle in Indo-Nepal relations. After our Air Force did bread bombing over Jaffna, violating Sri Lankan Air Space, the Nepalese became apprehensive that we may do something similar in Nepal. Hitherto the Nepal Army was dependent on India for its requirements of military hardware. India refused to give them anti-air craft guns saying that there was no requirement for these in Nepal. Thereupon the Nepalese Army approached the Chinese for these weapons. There were also reports that the Chinese Engineers were working in the *Tarai* area in South Nepal bordering UP and Bihar. India's international image had suffered as the breakdown of relations between India and Nepal was seen as a contest between Goliath and David. The International community had much sympathy for Nepal and India was getting a bad Press.

It was at this stage that Rajiv Gandhi's government was voted out of power and VP Singh took over as Prime Minister. Gujral, the then

External Affairs Minister, knowing my Gorkha background, was keen that I should go as Ambassador to Nepal to restore friendly relations between our two countries. Of course, the Ministry of External Affairs was not too happy as I was an outsider who would be taking over a senior job meant for the diplomatic service. Interestingly some Kathmandu newspapers on learning of my being posted as India's Ambassador to Nepal even mentioned that a General coming as Ambassador to Nepal indicated India's military ambitions. This was a very small minority. Most Nepalese who knew me welcomed my appointment because in my Army career I had been the President of Gorkha Brigade and had undertaken welfare projects for Gorkha Ex Servicemen in Nepal.

Internally Nepal was facing a political turmoil. There was royal autocracy in Nepal with the King exercising absolute authority. He nominated the Prime Minister and the Council of Ministers. The Royal Nepal Army owed loyalty to the King and the government had no control over the Army. All the political parties, the Nepali Congress, the Nepali Communist Party and some minor political parties had formed an alliance for movement to restore democracy. Ganesh Man Singh was appointed the Supreme Leader of this movement. He and all the top leaders of political parties had been locked up in jail by the King. There was growing unrest in the country. The Chinese were encouraging the King to deal with the situation very firmly. They had crushed a democratic movement of students at Tiananmen Square in Beijing. They had enough troops in Tibet to come to the aid of the King if required.

Before going to Nepal, I came to Delhi for briefing in Ministry of External Affairs. AP Venakateswaran, a former Foreign Secretary who had resigned because of Rajiv Gandhi's remarks about him, had joined the Hindustani Andolan Movement. We were both Vice-Presidents of this organisation and had become good friends. He wished me good luck in my diplomatic assignment and also cracked a joke. He said, "When a Lady says no, she means May Be, if she says May Be, she means Yes and when she says Yes, she is not a lady. When a diplomat says Yes, he means May Be, when he says May Be he means No, and if he says No, he is not a diplomat." I shot back and replied, "When a soldier says Yes, he means Yes, when he says No, he means No and when he says May Be, he is not a soldier." I adhered to my soldier's dictum as a diplomat and I found that I could achieve the desired results. My mind went back over half a century when on my return from Karachi where I had been Secretary of the Indian Delegation to a UN Conference on Kashmir, Sir Girija Shankar Bajpai, Secretary General of Ministry of External Affairs, had offered to take me to the much-coveted and newly-started Indian Foreign Service. I had declined saying that I had chosen soldiering as my profession and I did not want to change that. Providence gave me an assignment as Ambassador in my post-Army career. It was providential that my son competed for the Indian Foreign Service in the first attempt. He has now been a successful Ambassador in different countries and has earned a name for himself as a Senior Diplomat of our country.

§

I faced a very challenging task in Nepal but I had many advantages which normally an Ambassador does not have. I had old association with the political leaders of Nepal and with the Generals of the Nepal Army. Besides, I was a very popular figure among nearly 2 lakhs of serving and retired Indian Army Gorkha personnel of Nepal. However, I was not sure how the King would react to me. The Queen was close to the Chinese Ambassador and wielded a lot of influence over the King who was very fond of his drinks.

Normally Ambassadors are made to wait for days and weeks before presenting their credentials. In view of the acute economic situation in Nepal, the King decided to accept my credentials within 48 hours of my arrival in Kathmandu. My staff in the Embassy told me that much would depend on the relations that I manage to establish with the King who was all powerful.

After the formal presentation of credentials, the King invited me to have a drink with him. The Prime Minister and the Foreign Minister were also present. The King started the conversation in English. Being a graduate from Harvard, he spoke flawless English. He said, "Your Excellency, Mr Rajiv Gandhi started talking to us through the newspapers. Hence our relations soured. They say that Nepal is anti-India. How can that be? India is such a large country and Nepal is so small." I got a good opening and in my chaste Nepali I spoke, "Your Majesty, there is now a new government in Delhi which accords the highest importance to having the most cordial relations with Nepal. They have sent me here because of my long association with the people of Nepal. My coming here as Ambassador is a proof of their intentions. Your Majesty has mentioned that India is a large country and Nepal is a small country. That is a fact of geography. There is also another fact. Nepal is at the head of the sub-continent and the head is a small but most important part of the human body." This reply impressed the King and he had a big laugh. He then turned to the Prime Minister saying that for the first time he had an Ambassador who spoke their language. He told them that he would like to have a long conversation with me. The Prime Minister and the Foreign Minister took a deep bow and retreated leaving the King and me in the room. We talked for nearly an hour. He wanted to know my experience of trekking in Nepal in the early days and also my experience with Gorkha troops in war and peace. I told him that in the old days there were no roads in Nepal and I used to trek to our soldiers' homes which used to take a few days. I used to stay in the *bhatties* managed by Thakal women from North Nepal. They ran the *bhatties* which provided accommodation for the night and also food and drinks to the trekkers. He said that he had heard of them and Thakal women were very fair and managed *bhatties* very well. He himself had not seen *bhatties*. Over a few drinks our conversation became quite informal. I even gave him the words of Nepalese songs which, while marching long distances, Gorkha soldiers sang to the accompaniment of the *badal* (Nepalese drum). I gave him a popular Nepali song which the soldiers would sing on the line of march. This was, *"Thakhalni ko pailo galo, aunda jaunda Laure le mai khala."* (The Thakalni has yellow cheeks, the soldier going up and down kisses those cheeks.) He enjoyed the tune and made me repeat the song. This meeting and conversation with the King became a turning point in Indo-Nepal relations. The King told me that he would be very happy to give me an audience whenever I wanted. He would issue instructions to the Palace Chamberlain. Surprisingly, breaking protocol, he came out from the room to the verandah to bid me good bye. News of my long meeting with the King and his coming out of the Palace to see me off spread among the diplomatic corps. The US Ambassador once told me that I enjoyed unfair advantage over other Ambassadors because I spoke the Nepali language.

I had three priorities in mind for improving Indo-Nepal relations. The first was the restoration of the Trade and Transit Treaty. Second providing generous economic aid to Nepal whose economy had registered a negative growth due to what was called the blockade by India. This was in keeping with Gujral's thinking. He had initiated his Gujral doctrine of India giving aid to her small neighbours without expecting reciprocity. The third point of my agenda was to restore democracy in Nepal and work out a new Constitution. This was a very ambitious target but circumstances favoured me.

After a few months of interaction, I had managed to win the confidence of the King. The political leaders who were in jail were well-known to me. After the Rana regime of hereditary Prime Ministers, BP Koirala became the first democratic Prime Minister of Nepal. In 1942, he was in Patna living in a house adjacent to my uncle's house. I was then a student in Patna University and I often met him as also some Nepalese leaders of his party, the Nepali Congress, which had close ties with the Indian National Congress. Koirala had gone to jail during the Quit India Movement and was in Hazaribagh jail along with Jayaprakash Narayan. A family friend of ours, Devendra Prasad Singh, had also gone to jail with Koirala and was close to him. For sometime in the 50s he had done gun running for the Nepali Congress during their struggle with the Rana regime. He was a highly respected figure in Nepal. After I quit the Army, he and I had become close to each other in various social and political activities. Through him I had been in touch with Ganesh Man Singh, Krishna Prasad Bhattarai and GP Koirala, the younger brother of BP Koirala. Devendra Prasad would often come to my house and when Girija Koirala was staying with him would bring him along too. He was then the President of Nepali Congress and had once invited me to Nepal for a function which I had not been able to go to as I was going abroad to my children. Little did I then know that a couple of months later I would be going as India's Ambassador to Nepal. When I arrived at Kathmandu to take over my assignment, all the leaders of the Movement for Democracy were in jail. These included their Supreme Leader Ganesh Man Singh, Girija Koirala and Mohan Adhikari, President of the Nepal Communist Party. I established contact with them through Intelligence Agencies. Although the political leaders were in jail, protest rallies were taking place all over the country. I advised the King that he should come to terms with the democratic forces. At that time the movement was non-violent but over a period of time it could become an armed insurgency. We in

India with all our resources were finding it difficult to deal with insurgency in the North-East and in Kashmir. Nepal would find it more difficult to do so. The agitators could manage to get weapons from across the border and this may give an impetus to armed insurgency. The King would say that he would have to think over matters. The protest in Nepal continued to gather momentum. There was a complete strike of teachers and government servants. I also tried to put across my views on this score to the Generals of the Nepal Army. The Army Chief of Nepal and all the Principal Staff Officers and other senior officers at Royal Nepal Army Headquarters were well-known to me. They had all been my students at the Tactical Wing of Infantry School (later designated College of Combat) at Mhow or at Defence Services Staff College in Wellington. The Generals had regard for my professional views. All this was of great help to me in achieving my goal.

One day a large political meeting was allowed to be held at Kathmandu. The crowd became violent and tried to attack Singh Durbar (Secretariat) in Kathmandu and moved threateningly towards the Royal Palace. The Army and the Police opened fire and a large number of people got killed. From the Embassy, I could hear firing during the night and the siren of ambulance cars. No one knew the number of people killed but it was reported to be very large. I started getting telephone calls from some Indians in Kathmandu to get the Indian Army to Nepal. There was no question of my doing so because I did not want another fiasco of Indian soldiers getting involved in fighting in Nepal as had happened in Sri Lanka. Late that night the King sent his Foreign Minister, Pashupati Rana, to me for advice. I said that I did not want to be seen to be directly involved because later it would give a handle to anti-India elements to say that India had intervened in the internal affairs of Nepal. However, I suggested to him to convey to the King that it would be desirable to come to terms with the leaders of the Movement for Democracy. They should be immediately released from prison and invited to form an interim government like what the British had done in India in 1946. An Interim Combined Government of the Congress and Muslim League had been formed at Delhi with Jawaharlal Nehru as the Vice-President of the Viceroy's Executive Council. On the same lines a combined interim government of the Nepali Congress and Communist Party of Nepal could be formed. I also assured him that I would use my contacts to get a positive response from the leaders of the Movement for Democracy. The Foreign Minister went back to the King and early next morning all the political leaders in jail were released. Nepali Congress and the Communist Party of Nepal were invited to form an interim government and asked to prepare a new Constitution for Nepal. Complete peace was restored and there was much jubilation on the streets of Kathmandu. Krishna Prasad Bhattarai was sworn in as Prime Minister and a Communist leader Sadhana Pradhan as Deputy Prime Minister. Ganesh Man Singh, like Mahatma Gandhi in 1947, played the role of a father figure. Both GP Koirala and Mohan Adhikari remained out of government continuing as Presidents of their respective parties. I was on very good terms with Krishna Prasad Bhattarai who used to call me Kancha (younger brother) and I called him Daju (elder brother). This relationship went back to early 1940s when BP Koirala was staying in Patna. I was mobbed by a cheering crowd when I went to meet Bhattarai at his residence before he was sworn in as Prime Minister. He came out of his house and hugged me publicly with the crowd assembled there cheering us saying *'India-Nepal Guliyo maitri sambandh ko jai'* (victory to sweet India-Nepal friendly relations). Delhi was very happy with this development and Gujral rang me up to congratulate me for the key role that I had played. The King was also very happy with this development. He agreed to hand over power to the popular government with a proviso that the Royal Nepal Army will remain under his control.

My top agenda was now to ensure that the Trade and Transit Treaty should be immediately restored and all the 22 locations on the Indo-Nepal Border be opened. I was in communication with our Ministry of External Affairs and we had worked out the contours of a new Indo-Nepal Treaty which would allow free trade and transit across the border at 22 locations as before. In addition, I also got Delhi to agree to a generous economic aid package for Nepal whose economy had suffered a great deal when the Trade and Transit Treaty had been allowed to lapse. I argued that India had put up an Aid-Africa Fund providing quite a few crores. Nepal was of much greater importance to us than Africa and we should provide more funds for Nepal. All this was agreed upon by the authorities in Delhi. Gujral was of great help. This was in conformity with the policy which he was evolving, based on no reciprocity from the small neighbours for the generous aid being given to them. This came to be known as Gujral doctrine.

Having done all the spade work for a new Indo-Nepal Friendship Treaty with Ministry of External Affairs, and with their approval, I extended our Prime Minister's invitation to Bhattarai requesting him to visit Delhi when the Indo-Nepal Friendship Treaty could be signed. Bhattarai accepted the invitation and I accompanied him to Delhi. The Deputy Prime Minister Sadhana Pradhan also came along to Delhi with him. On arrival at Delhi, I was surprised that the bureaucracy in Delhi had second thoughts saying that we should not give everything to Nepal while the interim government was in power and keep back a substantial amount to be given when an elected government came to power in Nepal. I had kept Bhattarai in the picture about the details of the agreement and this would have put his back up. I did not want that to happen. I even said that if any change was made in the draft Treaty that we had worked on, I would be forced to tender my resignation. I met Gujral and he fully agreed with me in private and the change to the draft proposed by the bureaucrats was dropped. A slight hitch arose after the banquet at Rashtrapati Bhavan, when Sadhana Pradhan raised objections to the draft Treaty that had been worked out. Both Bhattarai and I persuaded her till late at night to accept the draft Treaty. Perhaps the fault lay with both Bhattarai and me because she was not kept in the loop when the draft Treaty had been worked out. Anyway, all the hurdles got removed and we were invited for breakfast with the Prime Minister at 3, Race Course Road in which I had stayed as Vice-Chief of Army Staff and in those days Indira Gandhi as Prime Minister lived in 1, Safdarjung Road nearby. After her assassination, her son and successor Rajiv Gandhi decided to occupy 3, Race Course Road, the official residence reserved for the Vice-Chief of the Army Staff, as the Prime Minister's official residence. The Vice-Chief was given an alternative accommodation.

In a very cordial environment, the Indo-Nepal Treaty was signed between the two Prime Ministers after breakfast.

We returned to Kathmandu the next day to a very rousing reception at the Airport to welcome Bhattarai seen to be returning triumphantly from Delhi with the Indo-Nepal Friendship Treaty duly concluded. There was a lot of slogan shouting about Indo-Nepal friendship. This gave me a great sense of achievement.

I now set about organizing the opening of Trade and Transit Points with due fanfare and ceremony. We had representatives of Nepal Government and of the adjacent State Governments in India at each of the 22 Trade and Transit Points. From the Indian side, we had convoys of trucks flying the Indian and Nepal flags, loaded with petrol, kerosene, salt and other items required in Nepal. Bhattarai and I went to Bhairwa on the Nepal UP border while Mulayam Singh Yadav, the then Chief Minister of UP, came from the other side. I also had the brass band of 11 Gorkha Regimental Centre brought to Bhairwa to play the Indian and Nepalese National Anthems along with other Nepali songs. I got a large number of Gorkha Ex-Servicemen in Nepal wearing their miniature medals to be present for the occasion. They lined up the road as the convoy of trucks drove in from the Indian side after Bhattarai and Mulayam Singh cut the tape at the border. This was followed by a largely attended public meeting which was addressed by Bhattarai, Mulayam Singh and me. This was shown live on Nepal TV. Overnight the old bitterness in Indo-Nepal relations had vanished and friendly relations between the two countries reached from nadir to zenith. It is pertinent that the film on Mahatma Gandhi produced by Attenborough had been shown all over the world duly dubbed in the language of various countries. Apart from seeing this film a couple of times in English, I had also seen the Spanish version when I was on a visit to my daughter in Spain. However, there were two countries in the world where this film had been banned. They were Pakistan and Nepal. While this being done in Pakistan was understandable, it being so in Nepal was strange. This was a direct result of the bitterness between our two countries in the wake of the Trade and Transit Treaty having lapsed and the economic hardships consequently being suffered by the people of Nepal. After this function, I was delighted to find that the film on the Mahatma was now running to capacity in all the cinema halls of Nepal.

There was one major hurdle that had to be crossed. This was the framing of a new Constitution for Nepal. This was a bit of a ticklish problem. The King wanted that Nepal should continue as a Hindu State. India having chosen to be a secular State, Nepal had been the only Hindu State in the world. On the other hand, both Nepali Congress and the Communist Party of Nepal who were in government wanted Nepal to become a secular State. I had received no instructions from Delhi on this point nor did I seek any instructions about this. I decided in my own way to support the King's view. This was not for any communal reasons. The King had co-operated so much and given up all the powers that he used to wield. Knowing the political trends in Kathmandu, I was of the view that the King was a cementing force to hold the country together and his desire should be respected. The Western Embassies in Kathmandu, particularly of the US and the UK, were very keen that Nepal should declare itself as a secular State. Christian Missionaries were trying to get a foothold in Nepal to convert the local people to Christianity. I knew from personal experience that in India they had succeeded in converting a number of people to Christianity particularly among our tribal population. Our North-Eastern States had become Christian majority States. Insurgency had first started in our country in these States. At my request, LM Singhvi, a Constitutional Expert, and a top lawyer was made available to the Nepal Government as Adviser for drafting their Constitution. I had long discussions with him and I put across my views on the subject which he much appreciated.

At my prompting, articles started being published in Kathmandu Newspapers about the need for Nepal remaining a Hindu State. It was pointed out that there had been no communal riots in Nepal which was a Hindu State while such riots were endemic in India, a secular State. As per Nepal Constitution, remaining a Hindu State had only three stipulations. First, the Sovereign must always be a Hindu; Second, Cow slaughter was banned and any one killing a cow had to be tried for man slaughter; Third, change of religion was illegal in Nepal. So far as the King being a Hindu was concerned, that was of no consequence when he was to be a Constitutional Monarch. The sovereign in the UK has to be a Protestant from the Church of England. From the time of King Henry VIII in the sixteenth century when he broke away from the Church of Rome, the monarch has the title of the Defender of the Faith. Though a Hindu State, Nepal had a government religious trust called Gothi. This gave out donations to all religious institutions including those of the minorities, Buddhists, Muslims and Christians. In France, Spain and Italy, government grants are given only to Catholic Churches and not to Protestants. As far the ban on cow slaughter, this is also in vogue in many States in India. There should be no objection to ban on cow slaughter continuing in Nepal. Lastly, about change of religions. The King was rightly concerned that in view of poverty in the country people should not be lured to change their religion for the sake of money and facilities as has been happening in tribal areas in India. In any case, there is free movement of people across the border between India and Nepal. Any one keen to change his religion could go across to India, get converted and return to Nepal. In view of all these facts, I felt that nothing would be gained by changing the *status quo* on Nepal continuing to remain a Hindu State.

I had sponsored articles on the above lines published in local Nepal Press. I also got Ex-Servicemen to influence the Ministers in Nepal. I told some of them to ask the Ministers when they tour their areas as to what secularism meant. Will Hindus in Nepal be required to eat beef. Ministers would try and explain that there would be no such compulsion or requirement if Nepal chose to be a secular State. When I met the Ministers in Kathmandu on their return from tour, I advised them not to disturb the status quo as that may result in their losing votes. The accumulative effect of all this was that the new Constitution provided for Nepal remaining a Hindu State.

§

In November 1990 after being Prime Minister for only eleven months, VP Singh was forced to resign as he had lost the majority in the Parliament. I was a political appointee and as per the practice in the US, I decided to tender my resignation. Chandra Shekhar became the new Prime Minister and, not being on good terms with VP Singh, readily accepted my resignation. Bhattarai was insistent that I should withdraw my resignation. The Koirala family and he were on very good personal terms with Chandra Shekhar for long. He made a special trip to Delhi to persuade Chandra Shekhar not to accept my resignation. He told me that some other political-appointee as Ambassadors during VP Singh government had not resigned and I should follow suit. The US example was not relevant for India. I stuck to my resignation and Chandra Shekhar did not change his mind on accepting my resignation.

The King and Queen of Nepal did us the rare honour of coming to the Embassy for a quiet dinner with us. Normally, a King or a Head of the State does not go on a private visit to an Ambassador's house. He broke this protocol in doing so to express his appreciation for what I had done in Nepal.

The Prime Minister of Nepal wrote to the Prime Minister of India saying, "General Sinha is a true friend of Nepal. He was as much India's Ambassador to Nepal as Nepal's Ambassador to India." For me it was a matter of great satisfaction that in a short tenure of one year we could restore the strained Indo-Nepal relations to a high level of cordiality. We ensured that instead of heading for chaos and anarchy, Nepal became a democracy and had a new Interim Constitution in such a short time. As India's Ambassador to Nepal, I had the satisfaction to be loyal to both my country of birth and the country of my profession. I am known in the Army as a Gorkha General.

On return to India, I had several engagements to give talks on Indo-Nepal relations from different platforms. Hindustani Andolan organised a public meeting at Delhi to felicitate me. Dharamvira from the ICS and a former Governor of Bengal, Justice Khanna, former Judge of the Supreme Court, AP Venkateswaram, former Foreign Secretary and Arun Shourie, the reputed journalist, spoke at that meeting praising my contribution as Ambassador in Nepal. Indian International Friendship Society at Calcutta chose me for the award of Vijay Shree of 1990 for enriching human life and outstanding attainments. This award was given to me at a function in Kolkata by Justice DD Thakur, Governor of Assam. Jyoti Basu, the then Chief Minister West Bengal, was also present at the function. I felt humbled at being generously felicitated. Destiny has its own ways.

§

Governor of Assam

On return from Nepal, I came back to Patna to live with my father and resume my old practice of writing articles, lecture tours and so on. I continued to be active in my own way while my father continued with his activities with two NGOs and his social life.

In 1997, I had been to the USA on a visit to my daughters, Mrinalini and Manisha. While I was with the former at Carbondale where she was a Professor at the University, I heard that there has been a change of government in India and IK Gujral had become the

Prime Minister. His son in the USA rang me up to say that his father would need to have some of his trusted friends to assist him. I did not quite understand what he was hinting at. I told him that I was shortly returning to India and would of course meet his father. On return to India, I broke journey for a day at Delhi to meet Gujral. He was not in town and had gone out on tour for four days. I therefore returned to Patna without meeting him. After a couple of weeks while I was at my home in Patna, I received a telephone call from the Prime Minister's Office saying that the Prime Minister would like to talk to me. Soon Gujral was on the line and he told me, "Assam is burning; I want you to go as Governor of Assam. Could you come over to Delhi immediately." I replied that it was a great honour for me to be selected for this assignment but I would like a little time before I could give him a reply. I said that I was looking after my 94 year old father and it would be difficult for me to leave Patna unless I could make some satisfactory arrangements. Gujral had met my father a few times when he had visited me at Patna. He said that I should take my father with me to Assam where he would be better looked after than in Patna. I hesitated saying that I would discuss the matter with my father. He then asked me to let him know soon and also added that people try hard to get appointed Governor and I was hesitating when that high appointment was being offered to me. I discussed this with my father. He was delighted and said that under no circumstances should I decline the offer. He told me that in his young days he had done a short spell as ADC to a British Governor and nothing would delight him more than to see his son installed as Governor. He agreed to go to Guwahati with me saying that he would continue his association with the two NGOs that he was looking after. He would periodically at least once in a quarter come over to Patna from Assam. My sister staying in Patna would look after him during his visits to that place. I confirmed my acceptance of the offer made to me by the Prime Minister and the next day I proceeded for Delhi.

On arrival at Delhi, I went to 3, Race Course Road where Gujral was residing. I had lunch with him and his wife. He told me that the situation in Assam was very grave and things had gone out of hand. Assam needed very careful handling. There was break down of law and order and many instances of violence. Insurgency was at its peak in the State and surface communication was getting frequently disrupted, cutting off the North-East from the rest of the country. He also mentioned that the Chief Minister was under a cloud as he was involved in a serious case of corruption. He had discussed my appointment with Atal Bihari Vajpayee, then Leader of Opposition, and also with Sitaram Kesri, then President of Indian National Congress. They knew me and had fully supported my going to Assam. He advised me to meet them. He also said that the Home Minister, Indrajit Gupta, and his staff would brief me about Assam. He added that I should on reaching Guwahati study the situation in the State and if I recommended dismissal of the State Government and imposition of President's Rule that would be immediately accepted by his government. The Leader of Opposition was also willing to support this.

During lunch, I mentioned to Mrs Gujral that I had lived in that house when I was Vice-Chief of Army Staff and Indira Gandhi was staying nearby at 1, Safdarjung Road. She told me that she would take me around the house to see what changes had been made. Basically the house was exactly the same as in my time but, behooving the residence of the Prime Minister, the furnishings had been done very well and wooden panelling put up in Drawing and Dining Rooms.

I paid courtesy calls on Vajpayee and Sita Ram Kesri. Vajpayee hugged me and said that I was the right man to go to Assam at that critical time. Sita Ram Kesri came from Danapur in Bihar close to our ancestral house. He knew both my grandfather and father. I had not met him but he had heard of me. He said that my going to Assam was a matter of pride for Bihar and for him. The Home Minister and his staff gave me a detailed briefing of the situation in Assam. I also had briefings in the Intelligence Bureau and RAW.

Surface communication to Assam and other North-Eastern States is through the narrow Siliguri corridor. There had been two major derailments of North-East Express and Brahmaputra Mail in each of which a few hundred people were killed. Road and Rail bridges would often be blown up. The Chief Minister and his convoy of vehicles had been ambushed in Guwahati. He miraculously escaped any harm. Two of his Cabinet Ministers had been killed by the insurgents. One Cabinet Minister had suffered injuries and was in hospital. An IG Police and a Brigadier had been killed in attacks in

Guwahati. A Lt Col had been killed inside the famous Kamakhya Temple at Guwahati. There was ethnic violence between Adivasis and Bodos in which seven hundred people were killed. Over a lakh each of these tribes were in refugee camps. Guwahati was in the grip of high tension with people not moving out of their houses after dark. In the remaining districts, the leading insurgent group in the State, United Liberation Front of Assam (ULFA), had become quite powerful. Insurgency was at its peak in the State. The Prime Minister was very right when he told me that Assam was burning. I faced a grave challenge but I was determined to do my best in the interest of the Nation.

§

After briefing at Delhi, I returned to Patna and packed up to go to Guwahati within two days. As there is not a direct flight from Patna to Guwahati, the Bihar Government had kindly made the State aircraft available to me. My son who was then first Secretary in our mission at Islamabad in Pakistan had taken a few days leave to attend my swearing in as Governor at Guwahati. My father, my wife and my son along with my personal staff flew directly from Patna to Guwahati. I was given a warm send off by my relations, friends and Army officers from Danapur at Patna airport. On arrival at Guwahati, there was a formal reception for me at the airport with a Police Guard of Honour. The Chief Minister, his Cabinet colleagues and senior officers received me at the airport.

We drove from the airport to Raj Bhavan in a convoy with my father and I in the first car and my wife and son in the second car. My father was very thrilled because he had not been to Assam before. He had been to all the most sacred pilgrimages in the country but had not been to the famous Kamakhya temple at Guwahati. He told me how happy he was that he would now have the good fortune of offering prayers at that temple. Although 94, he was both physically and mentally fit. He pointed out that the Guard of Honour at the airport gave me a General Salute while Governors were entitled to a National salute. I explained to him that technically I was still not a Governor as I had not yet taken the oath of office.

My father also told me that as an Officiating ADC to a British Governor he used to travel in the same car as the Governor in his car and it made him so proud to now travel with his own son as Governor in his car in a convoy. I also felt pensive and recalled how the wheel of fortune had changed. As a 10 year old boy, I was much impressed by the ostentatious arrangement for a British Governor's visit to Sonepur Fair at Chhapra in Bihar. I recalled my grandfather's advise about joining the ICS if I ever wanted to be Governor. Strange are the ways of Destiny. I wish my Grandfather was alive to see me as Governor.

§

I had a long association with Assam going back to early 1945. The Kokrajhar airport was not there in 1945. It is very close to the village of Palasbari where as a young subaltern I had stayed in a tent. I had crossed the Brahmaputra by steamer landing at Pandu in Guwahati. I had been picked up in a 3-tonne lorry and travelled to Parasbari standing in the rear of the vehicle on the same road on which I was now travelling in a convoy of cars as Governor designate. Due to security reasons the road was sanitised for me. I could not help but think of how life changes and unexpected developments take place in one's life. In 1945 my battalion which I had joined was bound for Burma where war was still raging. My subsequent tenures in Assam were as a Company Commander, Brigade Commander and Divisional Commander. Besides, as Director of Military Intelligence, I was closely connected with the insurgency developments in the North-East. We arrived at Raj Bhavan after a half hour drive and I was sworn in as Governor the same afternoon. This time after the function the Guard of Honour gave me the National Salute. My father had moist eyes.

After the Chief Justice had administered the oath of office to me, the Chief Minister gave a speech welcoming me and mentioned my long association with Assam. This normally does not happen at a swearing in function. Subsequently, half a dozen times, I was administered oath of office as Governor, for a second tenure in Assam, one in Jammu and Kashmir and two each in Arunachal Pradesh and West Bengal as caretaker Governor. I had to respond to the Chief Minister's welcome address for which I was not prepared. However, I made it a point to stress that I felt like an Assamese myself because of my long and friendly association with the people of Assam. I stressed that my mission in Assam would be to promote peace and prosperity and at the same time also the self-pride of the people of the State. The three icons of Assam namely Mahapurush Shankar Dev, Lachit Borphukan, and Gopinath Bordoloi were national icons whose contribution was not much known outside Assam. It would be my mission to promote awareness about them in the rest of the country (Picture 10a).

My arrival and swearing in was widely covered in all the newspapers but there was also a discordant note. Some mentioned that Delhi had sent an Army Officer to Assam as Governor to impose Military Rule in the State. The Army had become unpopular with the people because of military action against insurgents and in a few cases on account of human rights violations. I had a taste of people's disillusion with the Army in the very first fortnight of my taking over as Governor. There were floods in Tezpur and I had gone to see the situation. Some journalists asked me when the Army would be withdrawn from Assam. I told them that I had just travelled over the flood affected areas where the Army had been doing excellent relief work. I enquired whether they would like the Army to be withdrawn from flood relief operations. This highlighted the good work that the Army had been doing to help the people even when employed in dealing with armed insurgents. Some of the latter had been indulging in gross human rights violations. Only recently Sanjay Ghosh, a young graduate from Oxford University, had been doing excellent social work on Majhuli Island and was highly popular amongst the local people. The ULFA insurgents had abducted and killed him. There was much resentment among the local people on this account. The second incident during my first fortnight was of rape of an Assamese woman by an Army NCO along with an Assamese civilian. I ensured that disciplinary action against the NCO was completed within three weeks and he was dismissed from service and also given seven-years rigorous imprisonment. The wife of the local General on her own had visited the victim of the rape to console her and help her in recovering from the trauma. This had a favourable reaction among the people. The civilian accused involved in that rape case was tried in a civil court and his case lingered for a few years. We tried to make the people aware of these facts.

§

Within a few days of taking over as Governor, I attended a combined Annual meeting of Rotary Clubs of the East at Guwahati. I was the Chief Guest for the occasion. The person conducting the function introduced me giving a brief account of my career. At the same time, he also introduced my wife referring to her as Madam Governess. The audience broke into peals of laughter on his using the word Governess for my wife. He was later told that Governess is a person employed for looking after someone mostly children and the Governor's wife should be addressed as Her Excellency Lady Governor. This Governess joke became popular among my children who would refer to their mother as Dad's Governess.

§

I adopted the strategy evolved by Field Marshal Templer in Malaya in dealing with insurgency after the Second World War. He had a three-pronged strategy of unity of command, economic development and psychological warfare. I changed psychological warfare to psychological initiatives. I felt that the use of the word warfare while dealing with our own nationals was inappropriate.

It is surprising that despite our conducting counter insurgency operations in the North-East for over forty years, we had failed to establish unity of command. The Army, the Paramilitary and the Police all operated independently. They were virtually functioning as competing rather than complementary forces. We removed this lacuna by establishing a unified command with the Chief Secretary of Assam as Chairman and the Corps Commander in command of the operations group. Heads of Paramilitary forces, Police and heads of Central and State Intelligence agencies operating in Assam were made members of this unified command. Other civil officials from different departments of the government attended the meeting of this group as and when required. This arrangement worked very well. Between 2,500 and 3,000 insurgents surrendered to us with their weapons. This broke the military backbone of insurgency in Assam.

As for economic development, I found that Partition had badly affected the economy of Assam. Assam had lost the entrepot of Chittagong, in East Pakistan, and now Bangladesh. Assam and the North-East were now dependent on Calcutta Port which was a long haul via Siliguri corridor instead of the direct route of Pre-Partition days. I identified two main causes for the alienation of the people of Assam from the Central Government. These were total neglect of Assam's economy and exploitation of Assam resources, like the British colonial rulers in the past. During the 1962 debacle, the Chinese Army reached the foot hills. Tezpur was evacuated by both the Army and the civil administration. In his broadcast to the Nation, Jawaharlal Nehru mentioned that his heart went out to the people of Assam. This was misunderstood by the people of Assam and they felt that India had left them to their fate. Assam produced both oil and tea yet it was deprived of benefits from these commodities. The Oil Refinery for Assam oil was put up at Barauni in Bihar because of security reasons due to threat from China. The Assamese argued that if the oil wells and oil pipe lines were safe in Assam why would the refinery also not be safe. As regards tea, after the British left, the ownership of tea gardens was taken over by *Marwaris*. The head offices of their companies were located at Kolkata and they paid taxes to West Bengal Government and not to Assam Government. The labour in tea gardens was mostly from Bihar, Jharkhand and Madhya Pradesh. They sent their remittances to their homes. Thus Assam was deprived of any benefit from its tea wealth. On top of all this, Assam which has been the worst victim of floods and desperately needed power did not have any hydel project, while the Centre had put up major projects like Bhakra Nangal, Hira Kud, Damodar and others in the rest of India. This was considered a step motherly treatment towards Assam.

Apart from economic decline, Assam had become a rice-deficit State. Rice is the staple food of the people of Assam. The green revolution had not come to Assam. The State had only one crop a year during the monsoon and that used to get substantially destroyed during floods which is an annual occurrence in Assam during monsoon. In the winter months, cultivable land lay fallow. I decided to have 1 lakh shallow tube-wells dug (Picture 9). The water level in Brahmaputra Valley is very high and one can strike water on digging about 10-15 feet. Each shallow tube-well with cost of boring and water pump cost about ₹22,000. We decided to subsidise 70% of the cost of each tube-well from Central funds and have a village co-operative society of users in villages to share 30% of the cost. I felt that if the project was to be financed totally by the Centre, the users may not develop interest in maintaining these pumps. There were many Doubting Thomases who felt that my shallow tube-wells project was a harebrained idea. Funds were not available with the State Government and it would be difficult to find 1 lakh water pumps for the purpose in a short time. Moreover, the Assam farmers, known to be supposedly lazy would not be able to make use of these pumps. I organised a demonstration near Guwahati and got Yashwant Sinha, the then Union Finance Minister, to see a shallow tube-well functioning and how its captive area could be made productive. There was a nice paddy crop in winter in the demonstration-area when normally that area used to remain fallow due to lack of water for irrigation. I had known Yashwant Sinha for many years and his family was even distantly related to mine. I convinced him and he agreed to make ₹200 crore available to us from the Union Government. I also enlisted the support of KC Pant, then Deputy Chairman of the Planning Commission. With necessary funds at our disposal and a dynamic State Agriculture Minister, Chandra Mohan Patwari, we successfully completed this major project in a year and a half. I extensively toured the Valley to personally see progress in execution of the project. I also got the Army to monitor progress in completing this project. As a result of this major project, production of paddy increased by 11.53% and Rabi crops by 6.93%. Annual income generated for an individual farmer varied from ₹51,000 to ₹1,00,000 in a year. This was a great success story. I remember how happy the people in the villages were to have an additional crop in the non-monsoon season. During my tours to the interior it gave me much pride and satisfaction to see lush green crops in the fields at a time when those fields used to remain fallow. The villagers would organise warm welcomes for me expressing their gratitude for the success of this project. The Planning Commission wrote very favourably about this achievement in their Annual Report. The Prime Minister Atal Bihari Vajpayee spoke to me complementing us for the success achieved. Officials from different States came to Assam to see the functioning of shallow tube-wells.

The third prong of our strategy was psychological initiative. I tried to introduce an emotional content in it. Perhaps this was the first time that such an approach was taken. I went into the causes of insurgency in Assam, particularly the ULFA insurgency. The tribal insurgency in Assam of Bodos, and in other States of Nagas, Mizos and so on, were not as dangerous as ULFA insurgency. The latter affected a population more than twice of the combined total of all the tribal insurgencies in different States. Both strategically and economically it had a different dimension affecting our National interest. The Siliguri corridor could be blocked by insurgency in Brahmaputra Valley cutting the land link between Indian mainland and the entire land mass of the North-East. Economically Assam was a great asset for the Nation because of the oil and tea industry of the region. Tea and oil provided nearly ₹2,000 crore each to our National economy.

I found that apart from other grievances, the main reason for the people of Assam getting alienated from the rest of India was that Delhi had been encouraging unabated influx of illegal migration from Bangladesh to Assam. Initially after 1947, a number of Hindu refugees came into Assam from East Pakistan. They were mostly white collar workers who took over jobs denying the local population those jobs. This lay at the root of anti-Bengali riots. The Hindu refugees from East Pakistan had now stopped coming into Assam and got diverted to West Bengal and Tripura. However, the influx of Muslims from East Pakistan/Bangladesh continued unabated. There was a long history behind the movement of Muslim population from Mymensingh district of united Bengal and some other neighbouring districts into Assam. During the Second World War when Sir Mohammed Sanaullah of the Muslim League was Prime Minister of Assam, he had encouraged the migration of Muslims from Mymensingh in Bengal to Assam as part of 'Grow More Food' campaign during the Second World War. He used this as a pretext to settle them in Assam to clear jungles and put the area under cultivation. This was guided by a political motive to increase the population of Muslims in Assam and build his vote bank. Lord Wavell, the then Viceroy of India, in his book *Viceroy's Journal*, wrote that Sanaullah under the pretext of Grow More Food had launched a Grow More Muslims Campaign. After Independence, Mymensingh had become part of East Pakistan/Bangladesh. This influx continued unabated and now became an international issue. The Congress Party and the Communist Party of West Bengal encouraged this movement in Assam to boost their electoral chances. In fact, Ration Cards were being issued to these illegal migrants to get their names registered in the Voters' List of these States. Dev Kant Baruah, the President of Indian National Congress, who had coined the slogan of "India is

Indira and Indira is India," maintained that so long as "Alis" and "Coolies" were with the Congress, the Party would always continue to win elections in Assam. Alis stood for illegal migrants from Bangladesh and Coolies for tea garden labour from neighbouring States notably Bihar, Orissa and Madhya Pradesh. The indigenous people were getting increasingly isolated with many border districts of Assam with Bangladesh having Muslim majorities. Apart from the political angle, I felt that this posed a threat to our National Security and may bring about a Kashmir type of situation in Assam. In 1978, it was found that the voters' list of Mangaldai Assembly Constituency contained the names of 70,000 illegal migrants from Bangladesh. This sparked a wide spread unique students movement in Assam to identify illegal migrants from Bangladesh and deport them. At the same time a sister outfit of ULFA (United Liberation Front of Assam) was started which took up arms against the State. ULFA insurgency became wide spread in the Valley.

I extensively toured the Assam-Bangladesh border from one end to another covering the land and riverine sectors, the latter in speed boats on the Brahmaputra. I was amazed to see the large numbers of Bangladeshi Muslims on the border in Indian Territory. One could distinguish them from the Assamese as their dress and language were different.

I carried out research of the movement of population from North Bengal to Assam starting from early twentieth century. SC Mullan, ICS, Census Superintendent of Assam in 1931 wrote, "It is sad but by no means improbable that in another 30 years Sibsagar district will be the only part of Assam in which an Assamese will find himself at home." This prediction is increasingly moving towards becoming a reality. At a conference of State Chief Electoral Officers in 1978, the then Chief Election Commissioner SL Shakdhar expressed concern over the influx of illegal migrants from Bangladesh into Assam. He warned that a stage would be reached when the State would have to reckon with foreign nationals who may probably constitute a sizeable percentage, if not the majority of the population. In 1978, the discovery of the names of 70,000 illegal migrants in the voters list of Mangaldai constituency lit the fire of widespread students movement in Assam along with the commencement of arms insurgency of ULFA. By 1998, four districts of Assam had already come to have

Bangladeshi Muslim majority and another four were on the way to become so. I realised that this posed a serious threat to the culture, economy and politics of Assam. It may even result in Assam having a Bangladeshi illegal migrant as the Chief Minister of the State. Over 30% of the seats in the State Assembly were dominated by these illegal migrants. Apart from all this a Kashmir-like situation may develop in Assam with a demand for merger of Assam with Bangladesh.

In late 60s, BK Nehru was the Governor of Assam. He had clout in the Congress Party being a cousin of Jawaharlal Nehru. Bimal Prasad Chaliha, a veteran Congressman from the days of Freedom Struggle, was the Chief Minister of the State. Both the Governor and the Chief Minister took up the issue of illegal migration from then East Pakistan. They were told by Indira Gandhi not to raise this issue. The Party's policy in Assam was being controlled by three leaders from Assam who formed a coterie at Delhi. These were Dev Kant Barooah, President of the Party who had ingratiated himself with Indira Gandhi and was supporting illegal migration from East Pakistan for building a vote bank. The other two leaders from Assam in the Delhi coterie were Fakhruddin Ali Ahmed, then a Cabinet Minister (Later President of India) and Moinul Haque Choudhary, former Private Secretary of Muhammad Ali Jinnah and now a Cabinet Minister. BK Nehru and Chaliha were told not to pursue this serious matter. BK Nehru in his autobiography, *Nice Guys Finish Second* writes that, Chaliha, "from the days of the freedom struggle was governed by the values of that time. He placed the National Interest above those of the Party. But the high command thought otherwise. The Party's interests were paramount."

I chose to write a 42-page printed report to the President of India with a copy to the Prime Minister and the Chief Minister of Assam. The latter was in full agreement with my views but could not take up the matter himself because he was heading a coalition government in which one of his partners was not on the same page with him on this issue. I made 14 specific recommendations to check the influx of illegal migrants from Bangladesh. This included the repeal of Illegal Migration (Determined by tribunals) Act which was passed during the Congress regime both at the Centre and in the State to facilitate a legal migration rather than prevent it. Although BJP was now in power at Delhi, it did not have the support of its alliance partners on this issue nor a majority in the Rajya Sabha. Hence it was not in a position to repeal this act. However, this matter was taken up under Public Interest Litigation in the Supreme Court. The Apex court struck down this act quoting extensively from my report to the President. Unfortunately, the other 13 recommendations of mine including measures to prevent illegal migration, identifying illegal migrants and declaring them Stateless citizens without rights to vote or acquire immovable property have not so far been implemented. The situation today has worsened from what it was in 1998 when I had submitted my report to the President.

My report got leaked to the Press and every newspaper in Assam serialized this report publishing the full text. This had a tremendous impact all over Assam and I became virtually a popular hero. Newspapers in Editorials referred to me as 'A Friend of Assam' and as 'Our Man in Raj Bhavan'. I had identified the real cause for insurgency in Assam and I now proceeded to take other measures to win the hearts and minds of the people.

Interestingly my report had an adverse reaction amongst Congress MPs from Assam who wrote to the President complaining that I was interfering in the administration of Assam and I should be withdrawn from the State. The NDA government was in power at Delhi and there was no question of the BJP obliging the Congress on this issue.

My report on the subject became an authentic document which continues to be referred to both Nationally and Internationally in any discussion of illegal migration from Bangladesh into Assam.

§

Besides my report on Illegal Migrants from Bangladesh and the 1 lakh shallow tube-wells, there were several measures with high emotional content undertaken by me. I had documentary films prepared on the lives of Shrimant Shankar Dev, Lachit Borphukan and Gopinath Bordoloi. These were shown on Doordarshan to promote awareness about them throughout the country. In Raj Bhavan at Guwahati, I had a new wing constructed as an extension of the old building with a well-decorated Durbar Hall. Behind the stage in the Hall there was a large painting of Shrimant Shankar Dev. The swearing in of Governors, Chief Ministers, Chief Justice and so on started taking place against the backdrop of this painting. I carried out research and study of the military leadership of Lachit Borphukan and got a booklet printed on this. I established Lachit Borphukan Chair in Guwahati University for military studies and also introduced Lachit Borphukan Memorial Lecture every year at Guwahati University. I delivered the first Memorial Lecture at the University. In subsequent years eminent personalities like Dr APJ Abdul Kalam, later President of India, and Jaswant Singh, a Cabinet Minister in Central Government, delivered this Lecture. I was invited at Nehru Memorial Hall in Delhi to deliver a lecture on Lachit Borphukan. The Vice-President of India Krishan Kant presided over the function. I organised an annual function at Guwahati on Victory Day of Lachit Borphukan in battle of Sarai Ghat in 1670 defeating Aurangzeb's nearly 1,00,000 invading force, at a time when Mughal Imperial and Military power was at its zenith. This function was now organised with much fanfare and military Guard of Honour. I, followed by the Chief Minister and other dignitaries, laid wreaths at his statue. I also had a bronze statue of Lachit Borphukan put up at the National Defence Academy at Pune. I ceremonially unveiled that statue at the Academy and also delivered a lecture on his military leadership. Lachit Borphukan Gold Medal was instituted at the Academy to be given to the best passing out Cadet in Officer Like Qualities. As for Gopinath Bordoloi, I had the Guwahati airport named after him and with much difficulty persuaded the Central Government to give the Nation's highest award, Bharat Ratna to him, 40 years after his death (Picture 10b). His life-style bronze statue was installed in the Lok Sabha at Delhi which was unveiled by Prime Minister Atal Bihari Vajpayee. All these measures undertaken by me had high emotional content and virtually swept the people of Assam off their feet making them feel proud of their past.

The propaganda of the ULFA militants that Assam had never been part of India till British incorporated it in their Empire in early nineteenth century and Assamese were not Indians, was effectively contradicted. ULFA wanted to break away from India and make Assam a separate Nation. I countered this by various measures. I developed a large tree grove on the banks of a small river near Guwahati as a tourist spot. It is believed that Guru Vashishtha during the time of the *Ramayana* epic had his Ashram at this spot. I went on pilgrimage to Dwarka which was the capital of Lord Krishna. Before going to the main temple of the Lord, I chose to first go to the temple of his consort, Rukmini. As arranged, the Press correspondents enquired why I had chosen to do so. I replied that Rukmini came from Sadiya district of Assam and as Governor of Assam, it was my duty to pray at this temple before doing so at the main temple of Lord Krishna. Many in Assam were not aware about Rukmini being from Assam. I tried to underscore the fact that from the days of *Ramayana* and *Mahabharata,* Assam had been an integral part of India. Samudragupta's iron pillar at Allahabad mentions that Kamrup (modern Assam) was part of his empire in fifth century. Throughout the ancient period Assam was integrated with India. During the medieval period, Assam had defeated invasions of Muslim Armies while the rest of India had succumbed and became part of Muslim Empires for seven Centuries. Two major invasions of Muslim Armies were defeated in Assam. The first invasion was that of Bakhtiyar Khilji in early thirteenth century. He had conquered Bihar, burnt the famous Nalanda University, and then captured Bengal. He invaded Assam with 10,000 Turkish horses. King Prithu of Pragjyotishpur (modern Guwahati) ambushed Khilji's Army while it was crossing the Brahmaputra. His forces were completely decimated and Bakhtiyar Khilji died in Assam. It is interesting that the account of this big ambush as written by Minhas, the chronicler of Bakhtiyar Khilji, is corroborated by an inscription in stone written in Sanskrit at *Konai Bulso Sil,* South of Brahmaputra near Guwahati. I had this place with its stone inscription translated in Hindi, Assamese and English, put up at the site and developed a park at that location as a tourist spot. The second major invasion was of Aurangzeb's Army of nearly 1 lakh which, as mentioned earlier, was decisively defeated in the battle of Saraighat in 1671. As a result of Assam defeating these invasions, unlike the rest of India, it never came under Muslim rule. Whereas from Kashmir to Kanyakumari Muslim Rule was established for seven centuries and Persian became the official language, in Assam, Sanskrit remained the official language till the British conquered Assam in early nineteenth century. In this respect Assam was more Indian than the rest of India. I also emphasised that Mahapurush Shankar Dev in his writings often referred to Bharat Punya Bhumi. I highlighted these facts to bring out the fallacy of ULFA propaganda that Assamese were a separate Nation.

§

The cumulative effect of my three-prong strategy of Unified Command, Economic Development and Psychological Initiative resulted in the people of Assam getting back to the National Mainstream. ULFA militants who at one time were hailed as heroes in Assam started being viewed as criminals losing popular support. My psychological initiatives directed towards winning hearts and minds of the people of Assam had been very successful but in the process I myself had lost my heart and mind to the people of that State.

After six years as Governor of Assam, I was asked by Prime Minister Vajpayee to move to Jammu and Kashmir, then in a bad way to take over as Governor of that State. I accepted the challenge and left Assam with a wrench in my heart. The newspapers referred to me as 'A true son of the soil of Assam'. It was touching that even after a decade the people of Assam fondly remembered me. In 2012 when the Lachit Borphukan award was instituted, I was selected for this award for the services that I had rendered to highlight the greatness of Lachit as a military leader and for my services to the people of Assam. Besides mementos, including an Ahom General's robe and sword, I received a cash award of ₹55,555.

Before I conclude this section on Assam, I may mention that during my visit to our daughters in USA, I found that Dr Anna Simons of the Strategic Studies Institute of the US Army War College had written a monograph on counter insurgency operations. She describes my conduct of counter insurgency operations in Assam as one of the success stories for such operations in the twentieth century. She writes, "In Assam the main cause of insurgency was alienation from the Nation through misconceptions. This was duly addressed by highlighting past cultural, civilisational and historical links with rest of the Nation." She has further written about my conduct of counter insurgency in Assam saying, "Among his innovations was an emphasis on what he came to call psychological initiatives. In the case of Assam this meant paying homage to Assam's rich culture and history.... In his view highlighting Assamese history and culture was as important to achieving security as was providing physical security and promoting economic development. Indeed, he considered all three equally critical to re-incorporating the Assamese into India, and together they comprised his three-prong approach to counter insurgency."

I was impressed by the manner in which Dr Simons had analysed my conduct of counter insurgency referring to it as one of the success stories of counter insurgency operations in the twentieth century. Her Monograph was prepared for study at National War College, a premiere military institution in the USA. Unfortunately, there was not much recognition in India of what we had been able to achieve in Assam.

§

Governor of Jammu and Kashmir

During my Army career, I was associated with Jammu and Kashmir from Day One that is, 27 October 1947. I served for ten years in different ranks in Jammu and Kashmir.

After I quit the Army, I had gone on a holiday to my daughters in the USA in 1994. I was surprised to get an Invitation to address the Rand Corporation at Los Angeles in the USA. This is a leading think tank in that country financed by both the CIA and the State Department. I was invited to speak on India's Kashmir Policy. That was the time when large scale insurgency and violence were rampant in the Valley with numerous deaths. I obtained the approval of Siddhartha Shankar Ray who was then our Ambassador at Washington. He was enthusiastic about my going there as that would apprise the Americans of our point of view on Kashmir. He also said that it was the first time that an Indian had been invited to speak at that prestigious institution. After I completed my address at Los Angeles, I was asked several questions which I duly answered. One particular question and my answer went down very well with the audience. I was asked by an American Army Officer about the justification for India remaining in Kashmir when most of the population wanted to become part of Pakistan. Being a democratic country, India should respect the views of the people there as democracy is a game of numbers. My reply was that in a democracy, basic values are more important than numbers. Abraham Lincoln was one of the greatest democrats of all times. He believed that the basic value of freedom and equality applied to all citizens irrespective of the colour of their skin. He waged a long drawn civil war for the abolition of slavery in the Southern States when the majority there was in favour of slavery continuing. In the American Civil War, more

Americans were killed than the total figure of American soldiers in the First World War, Second World War and the War in Korea. On the same lines, we in India believe in Secularism and cannot allow some 3 million Muslim fundamentalists in the Valley to derail secularism and are not prepared to compromise on this. Our failure to uphold this will adversely affect over 150 million Muslims in the rest of India.

§

My being moved after a very successful tenure from Assam to Jammu and Kashmir received much publicity in the media. Mufti Mohammad Sayeed was the Chief Minister of the State and possibly felt that his position may get undermined with a pro-active Governor like me who had received such publicity. Moreover, he seemed to have a chip on his shoulder because he had done a tenure as Union Home Minister. I tried to build bridges with him and his daughter Mehbooba who was the President of his Party. I invited them for a quiet dinner. He kept trying to tell me that Kashmir was different from Assam and that my approach in Assam will not work in Jammu and Kashmir. He also said that the families of the militants in the State needed a healing touch. My view, of course, was that the families of victims of terrorism needed a healing touch. His daughter was constantly talking about the atrocities being committed by the Indian Army in the State. I realised that it would be difficult for me to get much cooperation from either of them. On the occasion of Eid, I sent greetings cards to all the separatist leaders. None of them bothered to reciprocate. I realised that I would face difficulties in dealing with them. However, the Army had a very large presence in the State and they were naturally very co-operative with me. All the senior Commanders had known me and had worked with me while I was in the Army. This was a great asset to me in getting things done even if the civil administration under Mufti was not going to co-operate with me.

§

State Assembly elections had been held in 2002. Foreign journalists had for the first time been allowed to observe this electoral process. They had been unanimous in commenting that the elections had been free and fair. A coalition government of the PDP and the Congress had been formed in the State with Mufti as Chief Minister. It had been agreed that half way through the coalition government, a Congress Chief Minister would take over from Mufti. I found the Congress leaders in the State not hostile to me. As time went on, they became very friendly particularly during the controversy in the wake of the duration of the Amarnath Yatra. Ghulam Nabi Azad, an important Congress leader at the Centre having good relations with the Gandhi-Nehru dynasty, called on me during his visit to Srinagar. I found him amiable and friendly. This was the beginning of subsequent very friendly relations between us, particularly when in 2005 he took over as Chief Minister from Mufti Mohammed Sayeed.

In 2003, when I took over as Governor of Jammu and Kashmir, insurgency continued to be at its peak in the State. On an average ten people were being killed every day and the annual arrival of tourists in the Valley was a mere 28,000. Tourism is the mainstay of the economy of the Valley.

On taking over as Governor, I had announced that I would attempt to promote the spirit of amity amongst all communities in the State and cordial feelings towards the rest of the country that I had seen in October 1947 when I had come to Kashmir for the first time. At a time when the entire sub-continent was in the throes of Partition Holocaust, complete amity amongst the people had reigned in Srinagar. I recalled the slogan I had heard at that time, *'Hamalawar Hoshiyar, Hum Kashmiri Hindu, Muslim, Sikh Taiyar'* as also Mahatma Gandhi's acknowledgement of the solace the Valley provided at a time when communal frenzy had taken over much of India.

I felt that the three-prong strategy of unity of command, economic development and psychological initiatives that had worked so well in Assam, could also succeed in Jammu and Kashmir with suitable modification. We had to take cognisance of factors that were not present in Assam. These were armed intervention promoted from across the border by a hostile neighbour, religious fundamentalism and diversity of the three regions in the State.

So far as unity of command was concerned, there was already unified command functioning in the State. As militancy had first started in the Valley, a unified command had been put up there. Subsequently, when it had spread to Jammu Province another unified command was set up there. Thus we had two separate unified commands in the State in Srinagar and Jammu. The Army Commander who was in overall command of the Army in the State was excluded from the set up in which his two subordinate commanders, the Corps Commanders in the two regions were included. Even at combined meetings of the two unified commands addressed by the Prime Minister or Home/Defence Minister from Delhi, the Army Commander was not invited. This made little sense and I wanted the Army Commander included in it with one unified command for the entire State. Surprisingly, Mufti opposed this. However, I managed to get this accepted through intervention from Delhi. The Army Commander, Lt Gen Rustam Nanavati who had left a few days before I took over as Governor met me at Delhi when I was transiting from Assam to Kashmir. He apprised me about the exclusion of the Army Commander in the unified command and also about Mufti being abrasive about any suggestions from the Army. Rustam had evolved the strategy of Artillery suppressive fire to silence the hostile fire coming from across the LOC. On taking over as Governor, I told the Army to continue with that arrangement and where possible intensify it to cause more damage to the other side. This was working well. In January 2004, Pervez Musharraf proposed a ceasefire on the LOC which was accepted by us. This worked for a few years and for all the time that I was Governor of the State. However, infiltration across the border continued and so did the level of violence in the State. We tried to change from cordon and search operations to surgical strikes against militants based on good intelligence. The former had caused much inconvenience to the local people and this change in tactical approach was generally welcomed. General NC Vij who had worked with me in Assam as a Corps Commander, was now the Army Chief. He proposed fencing of the LOC in the State. I gave him full support to get this tremendous task of fencing some 700 kilometres in most difficult terrain within a little over one year. Iron pickets and barbed wire bundles had to be carried on mules or by human labour. This remarkable measure was completed in record time. This further contributed to bringing down the daily rate of killing from ten to one. With improved security situation, tourist arrivals to the Valley increased from 28,000 a year to 6 lakhs by 2008, when I relinquished my appointment as Governor.

§

The second prong of our strategy was economic development. In Assam we had constructed 1 lakh shallow tube-wells. In Jammu and Kashmir, we decided to have 1,000 micro hydel projects on the mountains generating 5 to 8 kilowatts of electricity (Picture 11a, 11b and 11c). This provided 30 to 40 light points in villages where people had not seen electric bulbs before. I got this executed by the Army as part of Operation Sadbhavana. By day this power in the villages could be used for operating looms or grinding corns. This was highly popular among the beneficiary who were mostly Gujjars and Bakarwals. I recall that when I had been to inaugurate the last of the 1,000 projects, there was much enthusiasm among the local people. They had put up Indian National Flag fluttering in every village en route and villagers had lined up the road with paper National Flag to welcome me. Never before had I seen such enthusiastic response from the people identifying themselves with the rest of India. Of course, the people affected were Gujjars, Bakarwals and not Kashmiri speaking Muslims of the Valley. Separatism and terrorism is confined almost entirely to the latter.

Jammu and Kashmir has a very diverse population. Fifty-five per cent are Kashmiri Muslims, 15% other Muslims like Paharis, Gujjars, Bakarwals and Shias, and 30% Hindus, Buddhists and Sikhs. Each of these segments had its own problems. As mentioned earlier, the separatists and terrorists enjoyed maximum support amongst the Kashmiri Muslims. The strategy to win over the Kashmiri Muslim and others had to be crafted carefully. There was resentment among non-Kashmiri Muslims against being dominated by Kashmiri Muslims and denied their dues. We tried to address their grievances. The Dogra Hindus who constituted the bulk of Hindu population had ruled over Kashmir for more than a century and after 1947 had been marginalised. A martial class, the Dogras have been making a significant contribution in the Indian Army. I tried to cater for their sentiments by giving prominence to the contribution by the legendary Dogra General Zorawar Singh who had a unique record of military success. He conquered Gilgit and Baltistan enlarging the State to include these regions. He is the icon of the Dogras. I had two life style statues of Zorawar Singh put up one in the heart of Jammu City and other at Reasi. He had been the Governor at Reasi and had set out from there for the conquest of Ladakh, Gilgit and Baltistan. As Chairman of Shri Mata Vaishno Devi Shrine Board, I had several improved facilities provided for this pilgrimage. Helicopter service was introduced and the track improved to take electric cars for old and infirm pilgrims to the Shrine. On the route to the Shrine, we had medical and toilet facilities organised. A massive marble gate was provided at the base of the Shrine at Katra from where the climb starts. Suitable accommodation was provided for pilgrims both at the base in Katra and at the top of the mountain near the Holy Cave. We also had water and electricity provided for increasing number of pilgrims at the mountain top. As a result of these measures pilgrim traffic increased three times, to about 70,000 a year. In 2007, we decided to open a third tunnel to the Shrine increasing the capacity to 1 crore a year. We already had a fair amount of capital in our funds built up over the years and this now became considerably more due to increased donations and offerings at the Shrine. We decided to utilise the funds available to us in a productive manner for the society. Without any assistance from the State Government, we acquired land near Katra to put up Mata Vaishno Devi University and a Cancer Hospital with 200 beds to be eventually developed into a medical college as part of the University. We allocated ₹200 crore for a technical residential university for 1,200 students. President Dr APJ Abdul Kalam inaugurated this University in 2004. In 2008 Prime Minister Dr Manmohan Singh delivered the First Convocation address in a newly constructed artistic and air conditioned auditorium of 1,000 capacity. It was a record that we were able to do all this including residential accommodation for some 400 students at the Campus. The First batch graduating from the University in Management got 100% placement in business houses with very lucrative remuneration. The University's curriculum had only technical subjects like Management, Computer Science, Biology and so on. People of all communities joined the University on the basis of merit. However, the primary beneficiary from this University was the local Dogra population. I also tried to develop Jammu University taking much interest in its academic activities. As Chancellor of this University, I took special interest in its academic programme participating in seminars and lectures. We constructed a State of the Art Zorawar Stadium in the University which was a show piece comparing favourably with the best in the country. All these activities helped in removing the feeling of neglect among the Dogras. At a special function, the Dogra Sabha gave me the newly constituted Dogra Ratna award.

Ladakh and Kargil were taken care of by implementing the decision of local autonomy when we inaugurated District Councils for them, as also hydel projects. A Centre for Buddhist Studies was set up at Jammu in Jammu University which was welcomed by the Buddhist population. I had plans of having some departments of Jammu University put up at Leh but this could not materialise. A major project was to improve the economy of Ladakh through religious tourism. I proposed that we should approach the Chinese to allow pilgrims to go to Mansarovar in Tibet along the existing road from Leh via Dungti. This would be the easiest and shortest route to Mansarovar from India. Unfortunately, the Chinese did not agree to this proposal. I also wanted to have the Kargil-Skardu Road opened to enable the Shias in Kargil to contact their kins across the border. This also did not fructify because Pakistan refused to co-operate, even though we ill-advisably opened the Srinagar-Muzaffarabad Road for the benefit of Kashmiri Muslims, without insisting on Pakistan simultaneously opening the Kargil-Skardu Road.

The construction of micro hydel projects benefited the Gujjars and Bakarwals. Besides this we also built hostels and provided reservation for children of these tribes who go out for months to graze their animals on the mountains. Both the Army and the State Government co-operated in this. In 2005, there was a major earthquake in Kashmir with its epicentre at Muzaffarabad in Pakistan-Occupied Kashmir. On our side the casualties were less but we still lost 1,000 killed. Most of the victims were Gujjars and Bakarwals living on the mountains. There was hardly any casualty among the Kashmiri Muslims living on the floor of the Valley. I was in a helicopter which landed in the earthquake affected area just when the earthquake had started. The State Government's administrative machinery does not have much presence in these remote areas where the Army is deployed in strength to guard our borders with Pakistan. We immediately set into motion relief measures. Both the Army and the Air Force played a very major role. We used small helicopters to rescue people marooned in villages with mountain tracks obliterated due to landslides in the wake of the earthquake. Army ground patrols at great risk to themselves due to tremors and their consequences, also rescued villagers. In some cases, the troops even suffered casualties because loose boulders would come down the slopes during tremors which are common for some time after a major earthquake. The affected people were brought to Uri and Tithwal where we had put up field hospitals in tents and also relief camps providing shelter and food. From these bases, serious medical cases were evacuated in large Air Force Helicopters to Srinagar where they were treated at Army and Civil Hospitals. Very serious cases were evacuated in Air Force and civilian transport planes to All India Institute of Medical Sciences (AIIMS) at Delhi. As a result of these measures no victim of the earthquake died because of lack, neither of medical attention nor due to cold and lack of food. The Army also participated in rehabilitating the victims of the earthquake by putting up two model villages as a show piece. These villages had all modern facilities the like of which perhaps could not be found elsewhere in the country. There was a popular demand among the affected people that rehabilitation task be left to the Army because the civil administration was both lethargic and corrupt. It is interesting that while in the Valley often demands are made to get the Army to quit Kashmir, in the mountains they demand Army's presence for their survival.

§

So far as Kashmiri Muslims were concerned we crafted our psychological initiatives to wean them away from separatist leanings. I realised that this was our biggest challenge and one had to move imaginatively. In 1996, a great tragedy overtook pilgrims going to the Holy Amarnath Cave due to heavy snow and blizzard. Some 250 pilgrims perished and many suffered injuries. There was also a large number of pilgrims missing. Besides, there was constant threat of terrorists attacking the pilgrims. Several such incidents had taken place. During the tenure of Dr Farooq Abdullah, a committee was given the task of enquiring into the reasons for this disaster and submitting a report to the government on measures to be taken to prevent re-occurrence of such a tragedy. After much deliberation, the Committee recommended the setting up of Shri Amarnathji Shrine Board on the lines of Shri Mata Vaishno Devi Shrine Board, under the Chairmanship of the Governor. The State Legislative Assembly passed a bill for establishing such a Board. This Board came into existence in 2002. There were a lot of teething problems when I took over as Governor in 2003. Whereas the previous Chief Minister Dr Farooq Abdullah was known to be very co-operative, the same could not be said of his successor Mufti Mohammed Sayeed who was the Chief Minister in 2003. As Chairman of the Board, I took over responsibility for conducting this Yatra from 2003.

The first Yatra that I conducted took place within a few weeks of my arrival in Jammu and Kashmir. The previous couple of years, terrorists had been attacking the pilgrims on their way to Amarnath and had inflicted casualties on them. My first priority was to ensure full proof security for the pilgrims. I personally carried out a reconnaissance of both the routes from Baltal and Pahalgam covering a distance of 46 kms in the mountains. Pahalgam route was the longer traditional route with easy climb and camps en route at Sheshnag and Panchtarni for night halts. The Baltal route was much shorter but stiffer. Pilgrims could go to the Holy Cave from Baltal and return the same day. With the help of the Corps Commander at Baramulla who was also the Security Advisor to the State Government, I worked out a full proof security plan for the pilgrimage. The Army was given the task of dominating the heights and providing the outer ring for protection. The BSF was tasked to provide the inner ring for protecting the route and close protection of the pilgrims. The protection of pilgrim camps at Pahalgam, Sheshnag, Panchtarni, the Cave and Baltal was the responsibility of the CRPF. The Jammu and Kashmir State Police checked the identity of bonafide pilgrims before they were allowed to undertake the Yatra and enter the pilgrim camps. This security plan worked very successfully and there was not a single instance of terrorist's attack on the pilgrims.

After my first experience of conducting the Yatra, I worked out an elaborate plan for its organisation. I based it on the same lines as for Mata Vaishno Devi pilgrims. Dr Farooq Abdullah as Chief Minister had provided ₹2 crore to Shri Amarnathji Shrine Board as seed money for the Yatra and had promised to give ₹2 crore every year from the State Government. Mufti Mohammad Sayeed declined to give any seed money or annual grant for running the Yatra. I gave ₹2 crore interest-free long-term loan from Shri Mata Vaishno Devi Shrine Board till it became self-supporting. There was a requirement to extend the traditional duration of 15 days for the Yatra to cater for increasing rush of pilgrims. I found that even before the Yatra was opened pilgrims started going to the Cave on their own and continued to do so after the prescribed two weeks for the Yatra. Apart from making the pilgrimage safe and comfortable for the pilgrims, increasing number of pilgrims would bring more funds from offerings for providing facilities to the pilgrims during the Yatra. Taking all these aspects into consideration, I exercised my authority as provided in the Act to extend the duration of the yatra from two weeks to two months. I wrote two letters to the Chief Minister giving him the details and my plan for doing so. As he had gone out for a while from the State, I discussed the matter with the Deputy Chief Minister Mangat Ram Sharma. He was much appreciative of what I was doing. Besides extending the duration of the Yatra, I had established a cell in Raj Bhavan with my Principal Secretary as the Chief Executive Officer and a retired Chief Engineer of the State as the Manager with suitable subordinate staff to help me discharge my responsibility as the President of the Shri Amarnathji Shrine Board. We had put up model prefabricated huts with wooden flooring for the pilgrims and prefabricated toilets at Raj Bhavan Compound. The Deputy Chief Minister was shown these and he was very impressed by what was being done. He issued a Press statement saying the Yatra was being extended to two month with improved facilities for pilgrims.

§

In 2004, the NDA government fell and the UPA government led by the Congress came to power. All the NDA appointed Governors were being removed and I expected that I would also be asked to quit. Emboldened by the fact that the BJP was no longer in power, Mufti Mohammad Sayeed on his own without informing me issued a statement that the Yatra would be only for two weeks and got the State Police to stop prefabricated material going to Yatra Base Camps for putting up suitable toilets. When I asked him why he had done so even without informing me, his answer was that he had done so because I had extended the duration of the Yatra without consulting him. I told him that I had written two letters to him on the subject which had remained unacknowledged and, in his absence, I had briefed the Deputy Chief Minister who was in full agreement with me. He then said that he had not seen those letters and felt that I should have made the changes after getting his concurrence. He also maintained that Kashmir was different from Jammu and the Mata Vaishno Devi example was not relevant in the Valley. This was a strange argument. In any case, he was confident that the UPA government would be terminating my appointment in Jammu and Kashmir and he could have his way with my successor. In the meanwhile, some volunteers from Punjab who used to come to serve meals to pilgrims filed a case in Jammu and Kashmir High Court against the State Government for not allowing a two months Amarnath Yatra. A single Bench of the High Court directed that the Yatra be held for two-months as decided by me in my capacity as the President of the Board. The State Government appealed against this but even the Revision Bench of the High Court ruled in favour of my decision.

The differences between the Chief Minister and me now became a full blown National controversy. Four Hindu Congress Ministers in Mufti's Cabinet resigned protesting against Mufti interfering with the management of the Yatra. The Shiv Sena decided to send a *Jattha* of 20,000 Shiv Sainiks to Kashmir to protest against reduction of the duration of the Yatra. They also protested against registration of pilgrims going to Amarnath with a fee of ₹10 to be paid to Jammu and Kashmir State Bank. They called it *Jizya* (tax) as levied by Aurangzeb on Hindus. Feelings were running high on this issue and with elections to the Maharashtra Assembly due after a few months, the Congress did not want to be seen as anti-Hindu on a religious issue. Perhaps, this was the reason that though I had been appointed Governor of Jammu and Kashmir by the NDA government, I was the only BJP-appointed Governor to continue.

It is ironic to reflect that I owed my continuance as Governor to Amarnath controversy, but later all the progress we had made in winning over Kashmiri Muslims was also scuttled in the last week of my five-year tenure as Governor in June 2008 because of another unnecessary controversy over the Amarnath Yatra. While the controversy between Mufti and me was raging, I was surprised to receive a telephone call one afternoon from Ghulam Nabi Azad then a Cabinet Minister at Delhi and who was known to be in the Kitchen Cabinet of Sonia Gandhi. He told me that he fully agreed with the proposal for a two months Amarnath Yatra. Late that night, I got a call from the Union Home Minister, Shivraj Patil, that Kashmir was a sensitive State and this controversy was not desirable from National point of view. He advised me to have a meeting with Mufti Mohammad Sayeed and resolve the issue amicably. Next morning, I sent for Mufti and I found him accommodating. He agreed to the extension of the duration of the Yatra. I was, of course, very happy at this welcome development.

In 2005, Mufti's tenure as Chief Minister was to expire and as per the agreement arrived at by the two coalition partners, he was to be succeeded by a Congress Chief Minister for the remaining three years of the coalition government. There was much speculation till the last day about the possibility of the Congress forgoing its turn and Mufti being allowed to do the full term of six years. However, on the last day, I heard on the television that Ghulam Nabi Azad was to take over as Chief Minister of Jammu and Kashmir immediately. This was providential. I developed very close relations with Ghulam Nabi Azad and this helped me to continue with my efforts to win the hearts and minds of the people of the State. AK Antony, the then Defence Minister, on a visit to Kashmir, told us that he had been Chief Minister of his home State for a few years and he had not seen more cordial relations between a Governor and a Chief Minister as he found between Azad and me in Jammu and Kashmir.

Apart from virtually setting up Shri Amarnathji Shrine Board and organising facilities for pilgrims, I decided to use the Amarnath Yatra in my efforts to promote *Kashmiriyat* which stands for Amity and cordiality among different religions (Picture 12a, b and c). As Chairman of the Board, I would inaugurate the Yatra with the first *Poojan* at the Holy Cave. Immediately thereafter, I started the practice of flying by helicopter to Charar-e-Sharif to pay my homage at the shrine of the Patron Saint of Kashmir Sheikh Noor-ud-Din Noorani. Hindus revered him and referred to him as Nund Rishi. Laliteshwari, a Hindu priestess brought up Sheikh Noor-ud-Din Noorani during his childhood. She is equally revered by Muslims and was called Lal Deg.

Apart from paying homage at both the Holy Cave and the *Ziyarat* (tomb) of Sheikh Noor-ud-Din Noorani to mark the commencement of the Yatra, I started having three to five days Sufi Music Festival to mark the occasion. We got famous Indian *Qawwals* (Qawwali singers) for this function. For the first time in Kashmir after Partition, I also got *Qawwals* from Pakistan and other countries like Egypt, Syria and Uzbekistan. This became a highly popular event in Kashmir.

Further, as Chancellor of the Kashmir University, which has been and still is the hot bed of separatists' politics, I tried to build rapport by interacting with students in academic activities like lectures and seminars. I started an autonomous institute of Kashmir Studies within Kashmir University after obtaining a grant of ₹1 crore from the Central Government. A Muslim Professor of Kashmir who had studied Sanskrit and had specialised in Kashmiri history and culture was appointed Director of this institution. He had made a study of Kashmiri *Shaivism* (Lord Shiva's divine rule). We held a successful seminar on *Kashmiriyat* at Srinagar to which we invited Indian and foreign scholars. I discovered that Lahore University in Pakistan had a department for *Kashmiriyat*. I invited scholars from Pakistan and some Central Asian States. The Ambassador of Kazakhstan at Delhi was our Guest of Honour at this seminar. Kashmir has had strong ties with Kazakhstan which influenced Kashmiri art. For some time in the medieval period a ruler from Kazakhstan had ruled over Kashmir. During Soviet Rule, the Central Asian States had been under Communist influence and are liberal Muslims. They are unaffected by religious fundamentalism or terrorism. Kashmiri scholars could be influenced by interacting with these States. We worked out an exchange programme of students between Kashmir University and a University in Kazakhstan. My hope was that as a result of all this, one day people of Kashmir would go back to practising *Kashmiriyat* as they had been doing before Independence and eschew communalism and separatism.

I happened to meet Madanjeet Singh, UN Goodwill Ambassador based at Paris, then on a visit to Srinagar. His home was at Muzaffarabad in Kashmir. In October 1947, he was in Srinagar when Pakistan forces had reached Baramulla and posed a great threat to Srinagar. He mentioned the communal amity and peace that prevailed in Srinagar at that time and how an ordinary labourer would sing Kashmiri songs to boost the morale of the people in the city. I told him that I had visited Srinagar at that time and was much struck by the slogan in the city of *'Hamalewar Hoshiyar, Hum Kashmiri Hindu, Muslim, Sikh Taiyar'*. We talked about those days and developed close relations. He also told me that soon after Jawaharlal Nehru had visited Srinagar, he caught the Prime Minister's eye. Madanjeet had a good family background and was well-educated with a post-graduate degree from Banaras Hindu University. Later he met Nehru in Delhi and he selected him for the Indian Foreign Service. He served as a Diplomat for 30 odd years. He was our

Ambassador in various countries. He had a French wife and had settled in Paris. He was appointed UN Goodwill Ambassador based at Paris. He had started a South Asia Foundation for education of women and had been giving aid to universities in SAARC countries. He had given financial aid to Kashmir University and had heard about the Institute of Kashmir Studies at the University.

Madanjeet and I took to each other. I invited him and his wife to dinner at Raj Bhavan. I found that he had contacts at the highest political level in SAARC countries. I briefed him about our efforts to promote *Kashmiriyat* in the Valley. He offered to cooperate with us and suggested that we should hold an International Conference in Srinagar to promote *Kashmiriyat* in all SAARC countries. I readily agreed to do so. We planned to hold this conference at Srinagar in May 2008 before my tenure as Governor was to end in June that year. We also decided to invite the 'Junoon' pop music band from Pakistan to play Sufi songs on the occasion. He undertook to invite top representatives from SAARC countries to the conference while I was required to invite the President of India to preside over the function. We also decided that the conference be held in the auditorium of Kashmir University which I had managed to get completed with a lot of effort. The auditorium has a capacity for 2,500 audience. All this required plenty of ground work.

My efforts to promote *Kashmiriyat* were gaining momentum and were not much appreciated by the separatists. I was surprised that Mufti Mohammed Sayeed, no longer Chief Minister, continued to create difficulty in the smooth conduct of Amarnath Yatra. His party and co-travellers would keep raising the issue of environment degradation due to extending the duration of Amarnath Yatra. We continued to counter all this by saying that we were taking steps to ensure that ecological damage was not caused due to the extended period of Yatra. We had put up 2,000 prefabricated toilets in base camps and all around the Yatra route. Similarly, we launched a drive for disposal of garbage and ensured that the rivers were in no way polluted. We also pointed out that two months Yatra was of great benefit to the local people mostly Gujjars and Bakarwals. They provided ponies, *Dandies,* and potters for pilgrims. Local shop keepers at base camps also found the extended Yatra beneficial for their business. As for ecological damage, it is pertinent that as a result of persistent efforts by various political groups in the Valley, Supreme Court approval was obtained for making the 25 km Mughal route from Poonch to Shopiyan in the Valley motorable. This entailed the cutting of 10,000 trees and shifting of a wild life sanctuary. With vehicles plying on the road, there would be pollution caused by carbon emissions. There was already an all-weather road linking Poonch with the Valley via Jammu to Srinagar, but they wanted to cut down the distance between the two Muslim dominated areas of Poonch and the Valley. Government of India had sanctioned a huge amount for the construction of this road. Further, every effort was being made to increase tourist traffic to the Valley including Gulmarg. The pollution of the Dal Lake in Srinagar and of the ecology of Gulmarg region was ignored but much protest was raised to extending the duration of Amarnath Yatra. Obviously, the ecological issue in connection with Amarnath Yatra which had no vehicle movement on the Yatra route was based on political considerations and had nothing to do with damage to ecology. A local newspaper referred to the Yatra as a Hindu cultural invasion of the Valley.

The International Conference on *Kashmiriyat* was held on 26 May 2008 and was a resounding success. President Pratibha Patil inaugurated the Conference. We had high level representatives from all the SAARC countries. Chandrika Bandaranaike Kumaratunga, former President and Prime Minister of Sri Lanka, Dr Raja Ghazanfar, Senior Cabinet Minister from Afghanistan, Begum Salima Hashmi, daughter of the legendary Urdu poet Faiz Ahmad Faiz from Pakistan and other high dignitaries from Nepal, Bhutan, Bangladesh and Maldives representing their respective countries attended this Conference. After the inaugural address by the President, I addressed the Conference followed by Ghulam Nabi Azad, the then Chief Minister of Jammu and Kashmir. It was very encouraging that the first International Conference in Kashmir at such high level had been so successful. The large hall with 2,500 seating capacity was over-flowing despite the boycott call given by the separatists. It was very surprising that PDP Ministers of the State Government and Mufti Mohammed Sayeed did not attend this Conference when the President of India was presiding.

We issued a Souvenir on the occasion of this International Conference. Pakistan and the separatists have been wanting UN intervention to resolve the Kashmir issue. I thought it will be a good idea if I could get a message for the Souvenir from Director General of UNESCO. He sent a message appreciating our efforts and stated, "I hope that the new institute of Kashmir Study will help to reinforce the role of culture and education in ensuring a sustainable future for all peoples of the region."

In the evening, we had organised a Sufi Music Programme on the banks of the Dal Lake. The separatists had requested Pakistan not to send the 'Junoon' Band to Kashmir. The terrorists had even held out threats to their coming. Notwithstanding all this, the Junoon Band came and we organised a special security arrangement for them. Despite the boycott call of the separatists, several thousand young people gathered in the open ground near Dal Lake to hear this internationally popular band. The leader of the band from Pakistan, Salman Ali, in his opening remarks said that he had come from Pakistan to launch a musical jihad for peace. The leading English Daily of Pakistan, *Dawn* in its 28 May 2008 issue had an editorial under the heading "Breaking Barriers" stating, "Music knew no boundaries.... The people of Kashmir expressed their anger against religious militants and their violence."

This was the high-water mark of our success in promoting communal amity and peace in Kashmir. Little did I realise that the separatists would feel very marginalised. They would try to undo what we had been able to achieve as impressively demonstrated by the success of the International conference.

Some two years earlier, Shri Amarnathji Shrine Board had requested the State Government to give it the 100 acre of barren forest land at Baltal, traditionally used for putting up a base camp for pilgrims going to the Holy Cave. The High Court, despite the opposition of the State Government, had allowed the Board to put up temporary prefabricated shelters. Erecting these shelters for the Yatra every year and dismantling them after the Yatra led to avoidable losses in that process. Hence, the government was requested to give the Board 100 acres of the Baltal land for putting up prefabricated shelters with small guide bunds to prevent damage due to the shifting of snow in the winter. These shelters could remain in situ in winter and avoid the requirement of erecting and dismantling them every year. The State Government after examining the case for two years sanctioned the lease of the land to the Board on payment of ₹2 crore. The ownership of the land was to remain with the State Government and the Board was authorised to utilise the land only for prefabricated shelters in connection with Amarnath Yatra and no other purpose. The Forest Minister who processed this case was from the PDP. The State Cabinet unanimously approved of the proposal at a Cabinet meeting a day after the International Conference had concluded. A few days thereafter, I read reports in the Press that the separatists had issued the statement about what they call a sinister plan of the Shrine Board. They alleged that in accordance with RSS agenda, the departing Governor has given 100 acres of land at Baltal to the Shrine Board which was planning to develop a township of Amarnath Nagar at that site. It was further alleged that like Israel had done in Palestine, there was a plan to settle Hindus in this township to alter the demography of the Valley. I was in Jammu on my farewell visits when this canard was started. It was a totally absurd allegation. I got the Shrine Board to issue a contradiction saying that the land was at a height of 9,000 feet which was unapproachable and uninhabitable due to snow during the winter. It was to be used for prefabricated shelters only. This contradiction was blacked out in the Press and the false propaganda started spreading like wildfire among the masses. It was surprising that PDP ministers, as per direction of Mufti Mohammed Sayeed, joined in the protest against the lease of Baltal land when they had been a party to the Cabinet decision sanctioning the lease of the land to the Board. Concurrently forest land was also allotted for communication towers and other purposes but there was no objection raised about them. The State Government had no Public Relations Officer at that time. This appointment was vacant. Chief Minister Ghulam Nabi Azad was in Bombay as his wife was seriously ill. It was surprising how quickly the false propaganda of the separatists was spreading like wildfire. Protest rallies started being held but there was no violence at that stage. My relief was announced on 11 June 2008 and I left the Valley after about 10 days. Ghulam Nabi Azad returned from Bombay to organise a farewell for me. I left Srinagar on 25 June 2008 by which time one or two incidents had also taken place. At the airport when I was departing Ghulam Nabi Azad assured me that he would be holding a Press Conference on that day to clarify the matter. He was confident that the movement would lose its momentum.

Religious feelings had been aroused with a propaganda of 'Islam in Danger'. A mass movement had started in the Valley as it had done in 1963 when the Holy relic of the Prophet's hair was found missing from Hazratbal mosque in Srinagar. That movement had subsided after the Holy relic had been found. Unfortunately, Azad's Press Conference did not produce the desired result and the situation continued to worsen. The Police had to open fire on several occasions against mass rallies. The PDP withdrew its support to the government and the Congress Government led by Ghulam Nabi Azad had to resign. President's rule was imposed in Kashmir. My successor, presumably as directed by the Centre, revoked that land allotment order to Shri Amarnathji Shrine Board. The State was supposed to take over the management of the Yatra and the function of the Shrine Board was to be reduced to only overseeing the religious rituals at the Holy Cave. It is surprising that even a secular person like Omar Abdullah in an outburst in the Parliament stated, *"Jaan denge magar jamin nahin denge"* (we will give our lives but will not give land). A senior and respected journalist from Bihar wrote that the Shrine Board had plans to put up a 5-Star hotel at Baltal. I wish he had checked up that it was just not feasible to do so.

There was very sharp reaction in Jammu to the developments in the Valley. Rumours had been spread that the government was also taking over the Mata Vaishno Devi Shrine Board. This led to a spontaneous outburst in Jammu with demonstrators coming out on the streets with National flags in their hands and placards of 'Army is our friend'. The situation became very difficult. The demonstrators in Jammu burnt effigies of the Governor. The Police had to open fire and some demonstrators were also killed in Jammu. The agitation continued unabated for three months. In the process Jammu-Srinagar Road was blocked and the people in the Valley dependent on essential commodities coming along this road faced great hardship. This had never happened before. Government was forced to climb down and restore status quo ante. During this summer madness, a hundred people got killed and the economy of the State suffered a loss of a few thousand crores. Maulana Mahmood Madani, an MP, addressed a conference of a several hundred Muslim clerics at Hyderabad where he said, "Transferring of land from the Forest Department to the Board did not hurt Muslim interest in any way. There was nothing to oppose. It was unnecessarily made into a political issue by all sides." Dr Farooq Abdullah stated, "Mufti Mohammed Sayeed's politics had a hidden agenda to erode *Kashmiriyat*."

It was very unfortunate that our psychological initiative to win over Kashmiri people by promoting their old and valued traditions of *Kashmiriyat* got derailed. It was indeed a great pity that attempts to counter the absurd and forced propaganda for promoting communal animosity could not be effectively countered. All the success that had been achieved in reviving *Kashmiriyat* was nullified by a totally uncalled for communal frenzy. We have to learn from this experience and in future think of ways and means to achieve the objective we were striving to achieve. The Kashmir imbroglio has to be resolved not only through effectively countering violence and economic development but also through promoting *Kashmiriyat* which embodies peace and amity.

§

A New Dawn: Great Expectations

Retirement Projects

After I had resigned from the Army in 1983, I spent two interregnums of seven years each in retirement at my home in Patna before repeatedly undertaking assignments in service to the Nation. From 1983 to 1990, I lived in Patna working on my own with my writings of books and articles, and lecture tours. In 1990, I was given the assignment of Ambassador in Nepal. After my return from Nepal, I had another spell of retirement for seven years before being sent as Governor of Assam followed by a tenure as Governor of Jammu and Kashmir. After 11 years of continuous service as Governor in the two most sensitive States of India from the point of view of security, I hung my boots in 2008 and settled down in Delhi where I had acquired a house. My father was no more and I had lost almost all my old friends in Patna. I now decided to settle down in Delhi where the best possible medical attention was available for both my wife and me from Army and Civil medical sources. Delhi had attractions for me because of my many contacts and scope for intellectual activity. This also suited my children, all living abroad, because they required a house in Delhi when they came to India. However, I maintained my contact with Patna where we have our ancestral house.

Although reaching my mid-80s and realising that I was now in my final retirement, I was determined to remain both physically and mentally active. There were two issues to which I wanted to devote myself. My top priority was to dispel all the misinformation spread by separatists in Kashmir about Amarnath controversy. Secular intellectuals and secular media were more inclined to support the separatists over this controversy. My next priority was to glorify the history of Patna, my home town. At the same time, I continued playing Golf regularly. In fact, it was a record that at the advanced age in mid-80s, I got a hole in one. The best of players miss getting a hole in one. To get this one needs 90% good luck and only 10% good play.

§

I briefed LK Advani in detail about the unnecessary controversy on Amarnath Yatra based on total and blatant falsehood. He arranged for the top leaders of his party to come to a meeting at his house at which I explained the Amarnath issue in great detail. I met Atal Bihari Vajpayee but I was sorry to see his poor state of health. Although he recognised me, I realised that one could not have any meaningful conversation with him. One felt so sad to see him in that state of health.

The counter agitation in Jammu for three months was a major issue prominently being reported in the media. I also appeared on TV channels and gave my point of view. Further, I gave interviews to Press correspondents and wrote articles which were published in the Press.

I accepted invitations to address meetings at Delhi and other places to explain developments in Kashmir. I went to Ahmedabad to address a meeting there. I called on the then Chief Minister of the State Narendra Modi. I was immediately taken to his office without having to wait as normally happens when one goes to meet a Chief Minister. I found him very courteous and he inspired confidence. He had heard of me and showed a lot of interest on the whole controversy regarding Amarnath Yatra. Narendra Modi fully agreed with my views. He requested me to set up a defence university in Gujarat and offered me the chancellorship of that university. I thanked him but declined saying that I was now too old to take on any assignment. The next time I met him was in January 2015 when he was Prime Minister and also subsequently.

On return from Kashmir in 2008, I had paid a farewell call on Home Minister Shiv Raj Patil. He was courteous but was not interested in my views on Kashmir particularly at a time when separatists' agitation in Jammu and Kashmir was at its peak. I could have called on Prime Minister Dr Manmohan Singh but seeing the attitude of the Congress Party towards me, I thought there was no point in my doing so. The situation in Kashmir was steadily worsening and a strong counter movement in Jammu region had erupted. I happened to meet AK Antony at a memorial function for Field Marshal Manekshaw in Delhi Cantt. Antony was presiding at the function and I had been invited as the main speaker. In his concluding address, as President at the meeting, he praised me for my photographic mind. Over tea, after the meeting, he told me that he would like to meet me and discuss some matters. I told him that I would be happy to come over whenever he wanted. But I did not hear from him nor did I make any effort to meet him.

The spread of misinformation on the Amarnath land-controvesy is some indication of the disastrous media policy of the Governement of India both in the Valley and beyond. My aim in contributing articles to the Press on Kashmir has been both to correct the specific misinformation about the Amarnath land-deal and to put the on-going problem in Kashmir in proper perspective.*

There have, no doubt, been costly mistakes made by the Government of India and its security forces in Kashmir. The Armed Forces (Special Powers) Act (AFSPA) has become especially controversial. While no one should condone atrocities committed by security personnel, it should also be remembered that the Indian Army's record of human rights in Kashmir has been far superior to that of Pakistan's Army in the erstwhile East Pakistan and Baluchistan or the Chinese Army's in Tibet and at Tianamen Square and the US Army's in Vietnam and Iraq. Whereas these countries have been using offensive air support, artillery and tanks, India has never used these weapons during counter insurgency operations in Jammu and Kashmir. She has been using only small arms.

There are two specific examples that highlight the difference between India's policy in Kashmir and Pakistan's in Baluchistan. In 2006, an Indian Army Major was caught by the local people of Handwara in the house of a woman when her daughter raised a hue and cry. The Valley was on the boil for over a month demanding that the Army should be withdrawn from the State. The Major was tried by court martial with its proceedings open to public. Rape was not proved. It was found that the Major had illicit relations with the woman and used to frequently visit her at night. When her daughter found him in her mother's room, she raised an alarm. The woman alleged that she was being raped. The Court Martial acquitted him of the charge of rape but he was convicted for an act unbecoming of an officer. He was discharged from the Army. About the same time, a

---

***Editor's Note:** The author had occasion to discuss his views on Kashmir, as well as other issues of national importance, with Prime Minister Narendra Modi, members of the administration, and various political leaders.

Pakistan Army Major was accused of raping a lady doctor in the hospital. There were violent disturbances against this in Baluchistan but no action whatsoever was taken against the Major. The Lady Doctor and her husband migrated to Canada. Pervez Musharraf was on a visit to the US. He was asked about this incident by a journalist and he dismissed the matter saying "Get raped and get a visa to Canada."

Pervez Musharraf ordered an air strike on the hide out of Nawab Ali Bugti Khan, the 79 year old veteran leader of Baluch insurgency. The Khan was killed. By contrast, the 80 year old Kashmiri separatist leader, Sayed Ali Shah Geelani who was in prison at Ranchi was provided State Government plane to fly him to Mumbai for treatment. In 2007 he was reported to be suffering from cancer of the liver. He wanted to go to US for treatment but was denied visa by the US because of his terrorist connection. All treatment facility was provided for him in Mumbai and a successful miraculous operation was performed by a Kashmiri Pandit surgeon whose family had been evicted from the Valley. Syed Ali Shah Geelani has all the freedom to visit Pakistan High Commission at Delhi. He continues to propagate sedition and continue anti-India activities.

The contrast between Kashmir and Balcuhistan deserves to be far better known than it is at present. Kashmir is considered an international flash point, happenings in Baluchistan are ignored. There is little awareness of Baluchistan problem in the world.

Although Kashmir has throughout recorded history been an integral part of India, Baluchistan was never so till the British acquired that region in 1876. The British had entered into a treaty with the Khan of Kalat in the same year. The British got the right of passage to Bolan Pass and to garrison Quetta. During the Second Afghan War the British invaded Afghanistan along this axis and won a great victory at Kandahar capturing Kabul thereafter. Baluchistan was not a Princely State within the British Empire or a member of the Chamber of Princes. It was also not a British administered province.

Muhammad Ali Jinnah was the Solicitor of the Khan of Kalat. Mountbatten the then Viceroy of India, Muhammad Ali Jinnah, the Governor General designate of Pakistan, and the Khan of Kalat, signed a tripartite agreement at Delhi on 4 August 1947 providing for Baluchistan to revert to its 1876 status. Thus Baluchistan became

Independent on 11 August 1947. Baluchistan remained Independent till 11 March 1948 when the Pakistan Army invaded Baluchistan and forced the Khan to accede to Pakistan. The people of Baluchistan immediately rose in revolt. Insurgency in Baluchistan with varying intensity has continued to this day. Pakistan Army using offensive Air power and Artillery has been perpetrating horrendous human rights violations. Pakistan was a favoured ally of the West during the Cold War. Till its withdrawal from Afghanistan, the US was dependent on Pakistan for surface communications. Thus, Pakistan's aggression and atrocities in Baluchistan were internationally ignored.

Whereas Pakistan's legal claim to Baluchistan has been dubious, Kashmir's accession to India was perfectly legal as per the Independence Act of 1947 passed by the British Parliament. Maharaja Hari Singh signed the Instrument of Accession on 26 October 1947 when Pakistan invaded his State violating the Standstill Agreement. Pakistan has always been violating all agreements it has entered into since 1947.

The Rulers of Princely States in India had signed a treaty with the British, ceding Foreign Affairs, Defence and Communication. On withdrawal of the British from the sub-continent, this treaty lapsed. The Ruler had to decide the Dominion to which he would accede. There was no provision in the Act for any State to become Independent. The provisions of this Act conformed to the demand of Jinnah and the Muslim League. Jinnah hoped that on this basis Hyderabad, the richest and largest State, will accede to Pakistan. As regards, Jammu and Kashmir, he was confident that on account of geographical compulsions and being a Muslim majority State, Kashmir will fall like a ripe plum in his lap. In the event, he got neither Hyderabad nor Kashmir.

The legality of Jammu and Kashmir's accession to India was accepted by the UN. Its Ceasefire Resolution of 13 August 1948 required Pakistan to withdraw all its forces from Jammu and Kashmir before Plebiscite while Indian Forces were to remain in the State till Plebiscite. The 200-square mile Tilel Valley which was No Man's land was made inclusive to India despite Pakistan's demand to have this Valley.

Unlike Baluchistan where insurgency erupted from the day when it was occupied by Pakistan Army, peace prevailed in Kashmir with a functioning democratic polity for the first 42 years after the State acceded to the Indian Union. Baluchistan constitutes 44% of the land space of Pakistan. The Kashmir Valley on the other hand is only 10% of the land space of Jammu and Kashmir and not even 1% of India's land mass. Insurgency in Jammu and Kashmir is confined largely to Kashmiri speaking Sunni Muslims in the Valley. The remaining population of the State under Indian administration, comprising Shia Muslims, Gujjars, Bakkarwals, Hindus, Buddhists, and Christians constitute a majority. They are happy to remain as part of India. Yet our approach to the Kashmir problem has been Valley-centric, ignoring other stakeholders in the state. In the case of Baluchistan almost all Baluch people want to separate from Pakistan. Pakistan has been using maximum force to crush insurgency in Baluchistan employing mass destruction weapons like aerial bombing, artillery strikes and machine guns. India has never used such weapons against insurgents in Kashmir.

No doubt anti-India feelings have now become very high in the Valley. Despite all the stone-pelting and curfew in the Valley for over three months, all is not lost. While stone-pelting was continuing, 25,000 candidates came forward to be appointed Special Police Officers. Similarly, 2,200 Kashmiri Muslims in the Valley came for the Army Recruitment Rally in July 2016. The composition of battalions of Jammu and Kashmir Light Infantry is 50% Kashmiri Muslims and 50% Dogras. India has never faced shortage of Kashmiri Muslims recruits. On the other hand, the Baluch Regiment of Pakistan Army which used to be 50% Baluch at the time of Independence has very few Baluchs volunteering to join the Army. The current strength of Baluchs in this Regiment is now down to 3%.

While Pakistan has inserted itself in Kashmir from Day One, going on to promote cross-border terrorism in the region, India has maintained a strict policy of non-intereference in the POK and Baluchistan, refusing even moral support to the insurgents. Gilgit-Baltistan region is virtually a colony of Pakistan. Its predominantly Shia population is denied basic democratic and human rights. Punjabis and Pathans from mainland Pakistan are being settled there altering the demography of the region. The local population has been agitating against this and the Pakistan Army has been crushing their agitation. We have never given any assistance to the separatist leaders, not even any moral support to them. Our High Commission in Islamabad does not maintain any contact with the separatist leaders of Gilgit-Baltistan as that may ruffle feathers. We even agreed to open Srinagar-Muzaffrabad Road even though Pakistan refused to open Kargil-Skardu Road. Our supporting insurgency in Gilgit-Baltistan would have been a fitting reply to Pakistan's cross-border terrorism in Jammu and Kashmir.

Despite India's non-interference in Gilgit-Baltistan, Pakistan has been accusing her of promoting terrorism in Baluchistan for long. India has no common border with Baluchistan and cannot promote cross-border terrorism like Pakistan does in Kashmir or India could do in Gilgit-Baltistan. There has never been a shred of concrete evidence to establish India's support of insurgency in Baluchistan. Possibly Pakistan has been making this accusation to establish moral equivalence with India for all its own nefarious activities in Kashmir. By contrast, India has done little to bring attention to the insurgency in Baluchistan.

It was very appropriate for the Prime Minister in a shift in direction to refer to the Baluchistan issue in his Independence Day Address from Red Fort in 2016. A mirror was shown to Pakistan of its Baluchistan hubris. Concurrently world attention was also drawn to this festering problem. It was a great morale booster for the Baluch people and they have expressed their deep gratitude to the Prime Minister.

We have to find a solution to the wide spread alienation in the Valley. We need to think out of the box solutions to win over the people of the State so that they can live a life of dignity and prosperity as part of the great Indian Nation upholding modern secular values.

§

I have mentioned earlier that as a child in my early teens, I used to cycle to Kumhrar ruins which were close to my ancestral house in Patna and admired the polish on one of the one hundred pillars still extant lying in the open for over two millennia. I used to day dream that one day when I grew up I would expel the British like Chandragupta Maurya had expelled the Greeks from Punjab. As I grew older and became a college student, I nurtured a desire that on India becoming Independent we would get the name of Patna changed to its ancient and glorious name of Pataliputra.

I joined the Army in 1944 and in 1945 I was serving in Burma, (now Myanmar) during the Second World War. After the atom bombs were dropped over Hiroshima and Nagasaki in August 1945, the Japanese surrendered. I was then a Captain serving on tne staff of a British Brigadier. I accompanied him to Chengmai in Siam (now Thailand) to take the surrender of Japanese soldiers. A Japanese General with a few thousand soldiers surrendered at a parade organised in the compound of a local school. The Principal of the school was a lady called Thaptim. She asked me where my home was in India. I replied, Patna. She enquired where is Patna? I was surprised that she had not heard of Patna. Knowing that she was Buddhist, I replied that Patna is ancient Pataliputra. Her face lit up and she said that Pataliputra was one of the leading cities of the world in its time. Lord Buddha had himself blessed the city when it was being constructed. This exchange of conversation reinforced my desire to get the ancient and glorious name of my home town restored.

Forty years later when I resigned from the Army and returned home, I worked with zeal to get the name of Pataliputra restored. I found that Bihar had hit the bottom as a most backward State. Law and order had broken down and the economy was in terrible state. The State had become a laughing stock and dubbed a basket case. I decided to invoke Bihari Self Pride by reviving the memory of the State's glorious past. I delivered lectures at educational institutions on Bihar's history. My talk on Bihar's Martial Traditions was well-researched and was much appreciated. I traced the military exploits of Magadh which extended to the whole of present Bihar and beyond to the rest of the country. It emerged as a leading military power reaching its zenith under Chandragupta Maurya and continuing under the Gupta dynasty, followed by Sher Shah Suri in the medieval period. The unique military exploits of the eighty-years old Veer Kunwar Singh during our first War of Independence in 1857 were also highlighted. After that war the British had declared Biharis as non-martial and had stopped their recruitment into the Army from Bihar. My aim in stressing the martial traditions of Bihar was to restore Bihari Self Pride.

I also decided to launch a movement for restoring Patna's ancient and glorious name of Pataliputra. I obtained signatures of 1 lakh citizens of the city supporting this demand. The Mayor of Patna requested me to write the history of Pataliputra from ancient to modern times. I complied with his request. Both the English and Hindi version of what I wrote was compiled in one book and published by the Patna Municipal Corporation. This book was distributed free of cost to all educational institutions in Patna.

I submitted a memorandum with 1 lakh signatures to Bindeshwari Dubey the then Chief Minister of Bihar. He enthusiastically supported my submission and his Congress Government strongly recommended the proposal to Government of India. I contacted Rajiv Gandhi, the then Prime Minister. He reacted positively. At this stage, some Muslim and Communist historians raised objections to the proposal on the plea that this change of name will promote Hindu fundamentalism and Patna was a more glorious name than Pataliputra. It was strange that they came out with totally untenable arguments. Pataliputra was connected more with Buddhism than with Hinduism. In fact, the name Patna has a Hindu religious association because it is derived from the name of an ancient pre-historic temple called Patan Devi. As regards, Patna having a more glorious history than Pataliputra, it may be pointed out that in the 500 years of its history for most of the time Patna was not even a provincial capital while Pataliputra had been the capital of India for 700 years. Some Muslim historians wanted that Patna should be given the name of Azimabad after the name of Prince Azim-us-Shan (popularly known as Azim Shah), grandson of Aurangzeb who became Governor of Bihar in 1704. During his rule, Patna was given the name of Azimabad for a few years and thereafter it reverted to the name of Patna. With all this controversy and the fear of losing Muslim votes, successive governments both at Delhi and Patna decided to allow the status quo to continue and the proposal for restoring the name of Pataliputra was kept pending. After 20 years when NDA government came to power both at Delhi and Patna, I was then Governor of Jammu and Kashmir. Nitish Kumar was now the Chief Minister of the NDA government in Bihar. I had known him from his student days. Both LK Advani and I urged him to support the pending proposal for renaming Patna as Pataliputra. Along with the proposal to change the name of Patna to Pataliputra, I had submitted other recommendations like putting up a Civilisation Gate to depict how knowledge and learning travelled from the river port of Pataliputra to different parts of the world during the ancient era (Picture 13). Besides there were recommendations like having a river front road in Patna along the bank of the Ganga like Marine Drive in Mumbai, Small Boat transport service in Ganga to ease traffic congestion in the very linear city. Nitish Kumar accepted my proposal for a Civilisation Gate on the banks of Ganga near Mahendru Ghat in Patna. Mahendru Ghat has special significance because it was from this Ghat that Prince Mahendra, son of Emperor Ashoka, had travelled as a Buddhist Monk and gone to Sri Lanka. On arrival, he had converted the people of Sri Lanka to Buddhism and the day of his arrival in Sri Lanka is observed as a major national holiday in that country till this day.

For the last three years or more, I have been working with a leading firm of Architects based at Delhi on the design for the proposed Civilisation Gate. It took quite some time to get possession of land for this project and to start work on it. The structure is now about 40% complete and hopefully it will be ready by early next year. This Gate has a huge dome with Ashoka Lions on top and arches in Mauryan architectural design. This Gate will have the symbols of all major religions associated with Patna namely Hinduism, Jainism, Buddhism, Islam, Sikhism and Christianity. The secular message of two great rulers of Bihar namely Ashoka the Great and Sher Shah Suri will be inscribed on the Gate. This Gate will be facing all the four sides and will have pathways leading to it with a water channel and small fountains in its middle. A landscape with Ashoka trees will also be there along with an amphitheatre for sound and light shows. The Civilisation Gate will be grandeur than India Gate in New Delhi, Gateway of India in Mumbai and Arc-de-Triumph in Paris. With its unique landscaping and Ganga flowing close to it, this Gate will be a land mark in the world.

Nitish Kumar has also put up a huge Pataliputra Karuna Stupa on a prime large plot of land adjacent to Patna Junction Railway Station. This Stupa was inaugurated by His Holiness the Dalai Lama. Fairly close to this site is the place where Lord Buddha in 487 BC had blessed the Fort under construction around which grew the city of Pataliputra. A second road-cum-rail bridge over the Ganga is under construction in Patna and the railway station for it has been named Pataliputra.

It is surprising that having approved these projects recalling the memory of Pataliputra, Nitish Kumar continues to have reservation about changing the name of Patna to Pataliputra when so many cities in the country have had a name changed including Gurgaon to Gurugram. No city in the country or for that matter in the world has a better claim than Patna to get back its ancient name. Hopefully, Nitish Kumar will ultimately agree to this change of name and even if he does not, I am sure his successor will do so.

§

Political Reflections

Indian democracy has a long history. Vaishali in fifth century BC was the first Republic in the history of mankind. India had also developed the Panchayat system in the villages which was another manifestation of democratic functioning. However, Parliamentary democracy as India has adopted is based on our British connection of two centuries during the days of the British Empire. It is pertinent to mention that in the Third World India is unique in that, she has remained a functioning democracy served by a totally apolitical Army.

§

Our first War of Independence was led mostly by the upper class, our Freedom Struggle was led by the middle class and the present day politics of India is dominated by the lower class. This progression from upper to lower class is nothing wrong and should be welcomed. However, the problem arises when people in the lower class lacking the required background dominate politics for self aggrandisement promoting family interest and exploiting caste structure for their personal interest. Our leaders of the Freedom Struggle under the Mahatma had made great personal sacrifice giving up their paying vocations and personal interest to serve the Nation. These leaders were erudite professionals and on Independence they occupied the seats of power at the Centre and in the States. They continued to serve the Nation with the same spirit of sacrifice and devotion as they had done during the Freedom Struggle. They believed in simple living and high thinking. For the first decade or so after Independence, as desired by the Mahatma, they drew a salary of ₹500 per month and lived an unostentatious life while officials working under them were drawing maximum salaries of ₹3,000 in the States and ₹4,000 at the Centre. All that changed radically in the post-Nehru era.

§

C Rajagopalachari wrote in 1922, "We all ought to know that Swaraj will not at once or I think even in a long time to come, be better government or greater happiness for the people. Elections and their corruption, injustice and tyranny of wealth and inefficiency of administration will make a hell of life as soon as freedom is given to us. Men will look regretfully back to the old regime of comparative justice and efficient, peaceful and more or less honest administration." Rajaji was indeed a very far sighted person. Although what he wrote at the beginning of the Freedom Movement did not apply during the Nehru era, his views of 1922 proved to be very relevant starting from the time when Indian democracy got debased during the Black Emergency and after.

There was a very perceptive view on democracy given by Dr BR Ambedkar in his speech at the Constituent Assembly on 23 March 1949. He said, "*Bhakti* in religion may be road to the salvation of the soul. But in politics *Bhakti* or hero worship is a sure road to degeneration and eventual dictatorship." Jawaharlal Nehru was too great a democrat to allow his adulation by the people to abandon his commitment to democracy. Unfortunately, in the post-Nehru era, modern political leaders have sullied Indian democracy with a pronounced feudal culture. Political parties like the Congress and regional parties particularly in Bihar and UP have become family concerns, reminiscent of oriental court in the medieval period. Our political leaders, whether Ministers or even Bureaucrats, have an attitude of superiority and of rulers instead of the humility required of them to serve the people of the country over their own interests. They like to strut about as rulers treating the common man with disdain and demanding special privileges for themselves and their families. Family members of ruling parties are given political posts as a matter of right even when they are not qualified for that. We had the case of a Chief Minister in Bihar who had no formal education and could hardly read and write. School dropouts are accommodated as Deputy Chief Ministers and Cabinet Ministers. The mental attitude of political leaders and bureaucrats is demonstrated by the fact that they all want to have flags and Red Lights on their cars. Any number of incidents get reported of their taking law into their hands and misbehaving with officials and the common man. This is one aspect of the degradation of our democracy, the other being rampant corruption at all levels. Politics has become the most paying career for an individual and his family. The number of crorepatis among our political leaders is staggering.

A political leader during the Nehru era used to be looked up to for his sacrifice, integrity and leadership qualities. The political class with very few exceptions is today looked down upon. I may be accused of being very harsh in my views of the political scenario of our country. There are of course exceptions but they are very very few. I may mention some individual political leaders in this category. LK Advani has been perhaps a national leader with a longest record in that capacity. He never took advantage of his position to help the members of his family in politics. In this respect, he has been like the Congress leaders of the Nehru era who never promoted their family members in politics. Despite all his greatness, Jawaharlal Nehru tried to promote his daughter in politics by appointing her President of the Party and after his death she became the Prime Minister on the demise of Lal Bahadur Shastri. There was once an allegation of corruption against Advani in the Hawala case. He immediately resigned from the Parliament and refused to continue in politics till the matter was investigated and he was fully exonerated.

Dr Manmohan Singh is rightly known and respected for his erudition and unimpeachable integrity. If he had retired from politics after completing his first term as Prime Minister, he would have gone down in history as one of our great Prime Ministers. However, during his Second term as Prime Minister he became a pathetic figure by presiding over a government accused of repeated mind-boggling scams without taking any action in the matter. His excuse for justifying inaction because of Coalition Dharma does not do justice to him. During UPA-2 regime, he started being seen as a puppet Prime Minister being dictated to by his Party President.

I would like to mention a not so well-known Congress leader in Bihar whom I admired greatly for his integrity. Rajendra Singh had been PWD Minister for two terms in the State. PWD is a notoriously corrupt department and it is a well-known fact that PWD Ministers make a lot of money. However, Rajendra Singh was known for his personal integrity. After I returned to Bihar on quitting the Army, I had started a movement to put up the statue of Jayaprakash Narayan at a prime location in Patna. The Bihar Cabinet approved of giving a plot of government land for this purpose. Before written orders could be issued rumours started that differences had arisen between President Zail Singh and Prime Minister Rajiv Gandhi. It was said that the President was thinking of dismissing the Prime Minister. I had invited the President to unveil the statue but the Chief Minister wanted this done by the Prime Minister. The formal orders for allotment of land to us for the statue had not yet been issued. I wanted to have written land allotment orders before the government changed its mind. I went to Rajendra Singh in his office and found him extremely polite and courteous. He obviously knew that the decision about the allotment of land could get changed. On my request, and despite his IAS Secretary having reservations, he showed his strength by immediately issuing written orders. If the government changed its decision, we could now go to the Court seeking redress. Some years later after he had seized to be a Minister, one day he came to my house on pillion seat of a scooter to make a personal request. He recommended the name of a young boy of his village for recruitment to the Army who had qualified at the test for it but apprehended that he may not get selected by the Recruiting Office. I immediately responded and I am glad that the young boy got duly recruited. I am mentioning this that I doubt very much if another former PWD Minister would have come to me on the pillion of a scooter. Perhaps he would have come in a Mercedes. This only showed his personal integrity.

§

Winston Churchill the arch imperialist who was always opposed to Independence of India, wrote, "Power will go into the hands of rascals, refugees and freebooters. Not a bottle of water, or a half of bread will escape taxation. Only the air will be free.... They (Indians) will fight among themselves and India will be lost in political squabbles." This gloomy view was proved totally wrong during the first one and half decade of Independence when we had political power in the hands of our erstwhile Freedom Fighters. However, after the demise of Lal Bahadur Shastri, particularly with the Black Emergency and after, Churchill's prediction has come true. Democracy has been debased and become a feudal anarchy. The temples of democracy have started witnessing violent exchanges between the law makers. Legislators have become crorepatis and the entire government machinery seems to be badly corroded. Political leaders have begun using the vulgar language of the fish market and attacking each other in unbecoming language.

§

India got her Independence as a result of a unique non-violent freedom struggle launched by Mahatma Gandhi. He was a saint in politics firmly believing in high values. The leaders, chosen from all over the country, accepted his philosophy and were devoted to his concept. It is pertinent that in 1920 when the Non-Cooperation Movement was at its peak, with success appearing to be around the corner, a Congress procession at Chauri Chaura was fired upon by the Police from the Police Station. A few processionists were killed. They retaliated by attacking the Police Station and burning it down in which some 22 Policemen were burnt alive. The Mahatma to the dismay of some Congressmen, called off the National Movement in the entire country because he did not approve of violence by Congressmen under any circumstance. He emphasised that both the end and means had to be noble. Wrong means for even a noble end were not acceptable to him.

Political leaders from all Provinces of India were carefully chosen by the Mahatma each one of whom believed in high values. Never before has such a galaxy of highly educated, individuals totally devoted to high principles gathered together for such a noble cause. They made great personal sacrifice, going to jails and with no lust for any personal gain. After Independence, these leaders were installed in offices of power as Prime Minister, Ministers at the Centre and Chief Ministers and Ministers in their Provinces (now called States). The British used to say that agitators cannot be good administrators. These leaders proved that wrong. The high standard of public life in India was fully maintained during the Nehru era.

§

Prime Minister Dr Manmohan Singh was at his best in striking a civil nuclear deal with President Bush. Although the BJP was opposed to it, I personally supported it. Notwithstanding the opposition of the Communist Party on whose support the government was dependent, Dr Manmohan Singh stuck to his stand even when the Communists withdrew support. Like liberalisation of the economy in early 90s, when he was the Finance Minister, the Nuclear Deal with the US was a great achievement.

In 2009 elections to the Parliament were held as scheduled. LK Advani was projected as the Prime Ministerial candidate by the BJP. I owed it to my close and warm personal relationship with him to campaign for him at that election. However, I chose not to address meetings from party platforms of the BJP as I was not a member of the Party. I did so from non-party platforms. I also toured many places in the country for this purpose. Unfortunately, the BJP lost the election and the UPA returned to power with a comfortable majority. The Congress had won the 2004 elections primarily because of the leadership of Smt Sonia Gandhi. I feel they won the 2009 election on the basis of the clean image of Dr Manmohan Singh and his record as Prime Minister in UPA-1 government.

Whereas Dr Manmohan Singh had been a very successful Prime Minister in UPA-1 government, in UPA-2 he completely failed falling a victim to what he himself called 'Coalition Dharma'. During his second tenure as Prime Minister he was seen as a puppet Prime Minister with reins of power in the hands of Smt Sonia Gandhi. An Ordnance permitting convicted politicians to participate in elections was approved by the Cabinet and had been sent to the President of India for his consent. Rahul Gandhi at a Press Conference tore off a copy of the Ordnance calling it 'Nonsense'. Dr Manmohan Singh was abroad and on his return took the whole thing lying down. He even praised Rahul Gandhi and declared that he would be happy to serve under Rahul Gandhi as Prime Minister. Thereafter the Ordnance was withdrawn and scrapped.

The other thing which went drastically wrong for Dr Manmohan Singh and the UPA-2 government was major scams after scams. There was the 2G Spectrum Scam, Commonwealth Games Scam, Coalgate Scam and so on. The situation had virtually become one of a scam a day. Though no one doubted the personal integrity of Dr Manmohan Singh, he was seen as one who had shut his eyes to the scams and would not assert his position as Prime Minister.

Apart from rampant corruption, the government's image was badly tarnished by paralysis of decision-making, rising prices and economic crisis. Rahul Gandhi was nominated Vice-President of the Congress Party and was being projected as the future Prime Minister.

He was found totally wanting in leadership qualities. His 40 minutes interview on 'Times Now' was disastrous for his image.

The growing middle class in the country was sick and tired of dynastic rule in the country. In previous elections the middle class avoided voting and taking the trouble of going to polling booths to cast their votes. In 2014 the middle class turned out in large numbers to exercise their franchise. All this worked to the disadvantage of the Congress Party. This proved to be disastrous for the Grand Old Party. The Congress was reduced to an all time low of mere 44 seats out of 543 in the Lok Sabha.

§

New Dawn

As the 2014 Parliamentary elections were approaching there was much speculation as to who would be projected as the Prime Ministerial candidate from BJP. I felt that LK Advani should be the Party candidate for the top job. However, the party chose Narendra Modi. He had been vilified for long for the 2002 communal carnage in Gujarat both internationally and within the country. The Courts had absolved him of any guilt but that was not considered enough by the secularists and most of the media. The US and some other countries were not prepared to give Modi a Visa for visiting their countries. Notwithstanding this, the BJP nominated him as the campaign manager and he was projected as the party's Prime Ministerial candidate. I heard his speech at Shri Ram College of Commerce at Delhi on TV kicking off the BJP election campaign. I was swept off my feet at his mesmerising oratory. Thereafter, I made it a point to listen to his speeches on TV at election rallies all over the country. His vigorous and very effective campaigning was the biggest single factor in BJP's sweeping victory in 2014 elections.

Narendra Modi was now our Prime Minister and I had a feeling that I was witnessing a second Dawn with his coming to power, the first one having been on 15 August 1947. Modi embodied a new hope for young aspirational India and deliverance from dynastic feudalism, unlimited corruption and non-functional administration. His swearing in as Prime Minister in May 2014 was an unprecedented event. Heads of Governments of all neighbouring countries including

Pakistan were invited for the function. Till the last minute there were doubts whether the Prime Minister of Pakistan would come for the function as the Pakistani Army was not inclined to agree to his doing so. Anyway, he did turn up and the stage was set for Saree Diplomacy with Sarees being exchanged for the mothers of the two Prime Ministers. Nevertheless, Pakistan organised terrorist attack on Indian Consulate at Kandahar which synchronised with this event, showing no abatement to the anti-India attitude in Pakistan.

§

Narendra Modi had established his reputation as an excellent administrator as Chief Minister of Gujarat. The economic development in that State had been remarkable and was duly recognised internationally. However, he had no experience of functioning at the National level from Delhi. He was new to foreign diplomacy. One wondered how he would do in this field. Surprisingly, foreign policy has become his forte. In two years as Prime Minister, he has been on State visits to about 45 countries. Similarly, there has been a flood of foreign Heads of Governments visiting Delhi during his tenure. The US President Barack Obama visited India twice in a year including being the first US President to be the Chief Guest at our Republic Day Parade in 2015. When Britain was at its zenith of power in the nineteenth century, Heads of Governments from countries all over the world used to visit London which was regarded as the Centre of the world. It was said that school students were made to locate on the Atlas the not so well-known countries whose Heads of Governments were visiting London. Similarly, one has to look up the map to locate some of the not so well-known countries that Modi had been visiting or when visitors from the countries come to Delhi. He has tried to pioneer two new approaches in his foreign tours. The first is to establish personal chemistry with Heads of foreign countries whom he hugs when he meets and secondly to reach out to the growing and flourishing Indian diaspora all over the world. One of his early achievements was the use of soft power to get the United Nations to declare a Yoga International Day. This was approved with the support of 177 votes out of 193 in the world body. Soft power is a term coined by a Harvard University professor for achieving political objective without military threat or economic pressure. Most countries of the world started observing this with their people participating in Yoga Exercises. Pakistan did not do so. Except for Congress-ruled States, other States in India observed the Yoga Day with enthusiasm and mass participation.

Narendra Modi gave priority to neighbouring countries while starting his whirlwind foreign tours. I remember his visit to Nepal soon after taking over as Prime Minister was breath taking. Having been long associated with that country and also being India's Ambassador there, I found that no Head of Government visiting Nepal has had such a tremendous impact in that country as Modi had during his first visit. His starting that visit with offering prayers at Pashupatinath Temple followed by his address to the Nepal Parliament mesmerised the people of that country. I heard his address on the TV and his choice of words was remarkable. He touched the religious sentiments of the people by saying that he had come from Somnath via Vishwanath to Pashupatinath, all different names of Lord Shiva. Somnath is in Modi's home State of Gujarat, Vishwanath is in his Parliamentary Constituency and Pashupatinath is in Nepal. He also mentioned that Nepal was the birth place of Lord Buddha, who is the embodiment of peace. He complemented the Communists for having done something unique in terms of giving up arms and joining the democratic process. As he put it, they had given up *Shastra* (weapons) to adopt *Shaastra* (discourse) by giving up arms and joining the Parliamentary process. He also assured Nepal that India will provide all possible help to Nepal as desired by that country without in any way imposing her will over them. He also assured them that India will never interfere in the internal matters of Nepal. I not only heard his address to Nepal Parliament on the TV but got feedback from various sources about the most favourable reaction to his Nepal visit. Not long after, Nepal suffered a severe earthquake and Modi personally ensured most speedy response and most generous aid in this calamity. Unfortunately, subsequent events have undone all the good results personally achieved by the Prime Minister. Our handling of the Madhesis agitation in Nepal left much to be desired. It is widely believed that in view of elections in Bihar, from where the bulk of Madhesi population in Nepal come from, our Nepal Policy was influenced by the State elections in Bihar in 2015. In the process, the BJP not only lost the election in Bihar but there has been a sea change in Indo-Nepal relations. The Communists with their well-known leanings towards China have been making accusations against India and Indo-Nepal relations seem to have hit the nadir.

§

Pakistan with its visceral hatred of India has been a problem State for us. Having made a good beginning with Pakistan's Prime Minister attending the swearing in function of Narendra Modi, our relations with them have continued to be more hostile despite efforts on our part to improve the relations. It was decided soon after Modi government came to power that Foreign Secretary level talks will be started between the two countries. India had to call off the talk in 2014 when Pakistan High Commissioner, defying the Indian Foreign Secretary's advice, held meetings with Kashmiri separatist leaders prior to the scheduled talk. This was followed by increased cross border/LOC firing in Jammu and Kashmir. India retaliated with heavy firing over targets in Pakistan. After sometime normalcy was restored on the border/LOC, while stray incidents of infiltration and cross-border terrorism continued. Narendra Modi and Nawaz Sharif met on the sidelines at FIFA in Russia and at Paris in France. As a result fruitful NSA-level talks were held between the two countries at Bangkok. Foreign Secretary level talks were now to follow. Narendra Modi took everyone by surprise by dropping in at Lahore on his way back from Kabul on Christmas day of 2015 to wish Nawaz Sharif happy birthday and also attend the wedding of his granddaughter. This is in keeping with his attempts to establish cordial personal relations with Heads of all Governments. There was much bonhomie between the two Prime Ministers at Lahore and one hoped that a new chapter may begin in Indo-Pak relations. This was not to be. The ISI and the hard-liners had their way and Jaish-e-Mohammed launched an attack on Pathankot airbase within a week of the meeting at Lahore. Seven Indian security personnel were killed before the terrorists were eliminated. Luckily no damage was caused to any of our aircrafts.

Initially, Pakistan for the first time showed a soft attitude towards India. Unlike in the past they did not deny that terrorists from Pakistan had attacked the Pathankot airbase and also did not allege that the attack was carried out by terrorist elements within India. India allowed a joint investigating team from Pakistan to visit Pathankot airbase. We had allowed this for the first time. It was presumed that an Indian investigating team will be allowed to visit the Jaish-e-Mohammed Camp in Pakistan. There was evidence of the attack having been carried out by Jaish-e-Mohammed and of involvement of its leader Masood Azhar. The Pakistan High Commissioner at Delhi declared that no reciprocity in visit of investigating team had been agreed to. At the instance of Pakistan, China prevented Masood Azhar, the master mind of the attack on Pathankot airbase, declared a terrorist by the UN. A retired Naval Officer on a private business trip to Iran was kidnapped by terrorists and brought to Baluchistan. Pakistan authorities arrested him alleging that he was a Research and Analysis Wing (RAW) spy. The Indian Consulate has been denied access to him. The Foreign Adviser of Pakistan issued a statement gloating over India not being given entry to the Nuclear Supply Group. China had stipulated that if India was allowed into this Group so should Pakistan be allowed. With India's impeccable record on nuclear proliferation and Pakistan's known record of stealing nuclear material and selling it to clients like North Korea, it was ridiculous to equate Pakistan with India. China for its own reasons opposed India's admission into the Nuclear Supply Group at Seoul.

All this shows that how even good-intentioned and unique efforts to establish personal chemistry with his counterpart in Pakistan to promote friendly relations between India and Pakistan gets wrecked because Pakistan cannot get over its congenital hatred for India. Narendra Modi's good intentions to develop friendly relations with Pakistan is stymied by the latter's encouraging the crisis of pelting stones in the Valley. A young terrorist Burhan Wani, guilty of killing security personnel, had become a hero and his legitimate killing by Security Forces was exploited by Pakistan and separatists in the Valley to create a widespread stone-pelting popular movement. One may parody what the Mahatma had said during the Non-Cooperation Movement, namely—"On bended knees I begged for bread and got a stone." Narendra Modi had made an unprecedented friendly gesture. He dropped-in at Lahore on his way back from Kabul to break bread with Nawaz Sharif. Pakistan reciprocated by assisting stone-pelting by the youth against Security Forces in the Valley. A leopard does not change its spots.

Much has been made in our own media of the suffering of young boys due to pellet rounds by our Security Forces in which many such attackers have suffered. There has been a widely circulated picture in our Press of a man holding a five-year old boy in his arms who has lost his eye sight and become blind. No doubt it is heart rending to see this picture but it is important to appreciate that the parents of the child are perhaps more blameworthy than the Security Forces firing pellet rounds in self defence. The parents were negligent in allowing this child to come out on the streets instead of keeping him indoors in their house. No one in the Press has reported that stone-throwing at Security Forces is confined primarily to the southern districts of Kashmir Valley. The Gujjars and Bakarwals living on the mountains in the Valley, the Muslims in Jammu, Rajouri and Poonch regions and of course, the Shia Muslims in Kargil have kept away from this so-called *intifada*. Press reports suggest that the entire Kashmir Valley is up in arms against India. Burhan Wani, the young terrorist responsible for attacks on Security Forces causing casualties, is being made into a martyr by Pakistan and its cronies in the Valley.

Stone-pelting has continued in the Valley for over four months with approximately 65 stone-pelting youths killed, over 6,000 suffering injuries and 100 blinded from pellet bullets. Security Forces have also suffered many casualties. The crisis continues in the Valley while the rest of the State is unaffected. Pakistan declared its Independence Day on 14 August 2016 devoted to the liberation of Kashmir. On 15 August 2016, Narendra Modi in his address to the Nation has drawn world attention to the massive human rights violations being committed by Pakistan in Baluchistan. He also highlighted the popular movement against Pakistan in POK and Gilgit-Baltistan which is being suppressed by Pakistan Army. Narendra Modi's conciliatory efforts to establish friendly relations with traditional enemies does not mean that he is soft on any attack on our nation. This can be verified by his quick reaction to the treacherous Uri attack on September 18, 2016. Eleven days later India responded with surgical strikes on 200-kilometer front and seven terrorist staging camps were targeted inflicting heavy casualties on the enemy while Indian forces returned unscathed. The success of this operation depend both on impeachable intelligence and the Army's professonalism in carrying out the task. However, it is the political leadership, in this case Prime Minister Modi, who makes the decision to go ahead. Those who tried to undermine Modi's role failed to appreciate the crucial decision he took.

§

While Pakistan has been making much of stone-pelting in Kahsmir, it is interesting that large-scale violence has broken out in Pakistan-occupied Kashmir due to rigging of elections in that area. Baroness Emma Nicholson, a member of both the House of Lords and European Union Parliament was commissioned by the latter to carry out a study tour of Jammu and Kashmir State and submit her findings to the European Union Parliament. Her report stated that the people of Pakistan-occupied Gilgit-Baltistan region are denied basic democratic rights and also human rights. That region is now the only surviving colony in the world. The Pakistan-occupied Kashmir (POK) from Muzaffarabad to Mirpur has a controlled democracy with levers of powers at Islamabad. Jammu and Kashmir has been enjoying full democratic rights and there has been much development in this area. Pakistan tried to scuttle this report but the European Union Parliament endorsed it by 400 votes against 9. This highly favourable report was totally ignored even in our own Indian media.

Narendra Modi's government has promoted good relations with other neighbouring countries like Bhutan, Bangladesh and Sri Lanka. The long pending land deal was successfully concluded with Bangladesh.

§

The Kashmir problem has defied solution from day one due to successive blunders on the part of India. It all started with conditional accession by a desperate ruler which he was in no position to stipulate. Whereas all the remaining 561 Princely States acceded to India unconditionally and were fully integrated with the Indian Union. Jammu and Kashmir accession was only for Defence, Foreign Policy, Communications and Currency. This lay at the root of the present Article 370 giving Jammu and Kashmir a special status. We compounded matters by halting our pursuit of the enemy at Uri on 14 November 1947 and not advancing to Muzaffarabad in pursuit of the enemy in disarray and clearing the whole of Kashmir. We took up the case of Kashmir in the UN asking for the latter to resolve the Kashmir situation. This internationalised the Kashmir issue. During the Cold War, the West was supporting Pakistan's illegal stand on Kashmir. It was only the Soviet Veto which came to our rescue on Kashmir in the Security Council.

We have been, as I have mentioned, neglecting Gilgit-Baltistan region. We have not even provided moral support to the people's Uprising even though we claim that Gilgit-Baltistan is an integral part of India. We have ignored the agitation by the people of Gilgit-Baltistan against Pakistan's anti-Shia policy and the colonising of the region through trying to change its demography by settling Sunni Punjabi Muslims and Pathans in that region, like Israel had done in Palestine. The Pakistan Army has been brutally suppressing their agitation. For the first time now, India has spoken out for the oppressed people of that region with Narendra Modi drawing world attention to their plight in his Independence Day Address on 15 August 2016. Hitherto we had never provided moral support. China with its 'One Belt One Road' policy from Karakoram through this region to Gwadar Port in Pakistan has virtually become a third party in the Jammu and Kashmir dispute. We dismissed Sheikh Abdullah, then Prime Minister of Kashmir in 1953 for treason and kept him in house arrest for nearly 20 years in South India. The separatist leaders of Kashmir, like Syed Ali Shah Geelani, Mirwaiz Umar Farooq, Yasin Malik and others, are allowed to spit venom against India and guide separatist/terrorist activities even when they are occasionally under house arrest and receive Hawala money from Pakistan. I have already referred to our disastrous media policy not only in the Valley but also nationally and internationally. It is not realised that the Kashmir problem is really a Jammu and Kashmir problem and is not only Valley centric, covering 10% of our land space in Jammu and Kashmir, with the Valley-population constituting barely a majority or near majority in the entire state of Jammu and Kashmir.

Although we have been repeatedly asserting that Jammu and Kashmir is an integral part of India, we have not pursued a road map to ensure this. Musharraf at least had a four-point formula for resolving the Kashmir issue. The first point was recognizing the LOC as an International Border. I also believe we need to focus on making our case to the media. Through proper media policy the world at large should be apprised of the ground realities in Jammu and Kashmir. With the entire civilised world suffering from jihadi terrorism, international opinion should be mobilised to isolate Pakistan and have it declared a terrorist State. Dialogue with Pakistan should continue but this must be on our terms and from a position of military strength within the State, for which we should take measures to win over the people. There are various ways of doing so. No doubt this will take time. Our Security Forces must ensure peace within the State through firm measures but at the same time use minimum force.

In 1947 the people of the Valley were rescued from a brutal invasion and barbarous massacre. Today our brethren in the Valley have to be rescued from intolerance and fanaticism to lead a life of honour and dignity as part of a prosperous Nation. Their precious heritage of *Kashmiriyat* must be revived.

§

PV Narasimha Rao as Prime Minister had started the "Look East" Foreign Policy. The UPA government under Dr Manmohan Singh further pursued this policy. Narendra Modi has converted Look East to a policy of Act East. He has reached out to Japan and Vietnam establishing close relations with these countries. He has also supported the Policy of free navigation in South China Sea. The strategic interest of US and India coincide in this region to allow maritime movements for trade in this area. This will counter China's expansionist design.

§

Despite Jawaharlal Nehru going out of his way to befriend China, the latter showed little recognition of this. India was the first country outside the Communist block to recognise Communist China after the Communist Revolution in that country. She advocated China's entry into the United Nations and even decided to forego the offer of permanent membership of the UN Security Council in favour of China. Ignoring these facts, China in pursuit of its Policy of Hegemony, overran Tibet and stabbed India in the back in 1962. Its befriending Pakistan is primarily in pursuit of its anti-India policy. Its strategy of a string of pearls is designed to keep India bottled in South Asia. India is developing the Chabahar Port and surface communication to Afghanistan and Central Asia as a response to China's 'One Belt One Road' to Gwadar. China has been generously providing military hardware to Pakistan. Narendra Modi has very rightly provided Brahmos missile to Vietnam.

Narendra Modi's attempts to befriend China have not worked. Although 38 out of 48 countries supported India's admission into the

Nuclear Supply Group at the Conference at Seoul in June 2016, this proposal was scuttled primarily by China. India has to be prepared to deal with a hostile China.

§

The US is the leading world power and China is fast trying to catch up with it. India has the potential to be one of the leading world powers after US and China. It is as much in India's interest as in that of the US, that these two democracies have close friendly relations. Without joining any bloc or signing any treaty, India has developed most cordial relations with the US. This should stand her in good stead. Never before have Indo-US relations reached such a high level of cordiality as during the Obama-Modi regimes. Modi got a rock star welcome at Madison Square in New York during his first visit to that country as Prime Minister. His address to the American Congress in June 2016 received a tumultuous welcome. No Head of Government or State in the recent past has received such an ovation on Capitol Hill. The US has agreed to provide modern military equipment to India and at the same time seems to be holding back in providing that to Pakistan which for long had been a beneficiary of US generosity.

It is remarkable that Narendra Modi has been able to have close friendly relations with all countries, big or small in the world except of course, China and Pakistan.

§

Besides foreign policy, Narendra Modi has taken many bold and new initiatives for making administration responsive to the people and developing the economy of the country and providing a corruption-free government.

He drives himself very hard working 16 to 18 hours a day. He has a remarkable stamina for doing so. He insisted that offices of government in the Central Secretariat open punctually at 9 AM and offices be kept scrupulously clean. Visiting a few government of India offices, I was very impressed to see how these instructions have been duly implemented.

Some of the wide-ranging schemes initiated by him have shown remarkable progress. He has shown concern for the welfare of "What is there for the last man." He started a Pradhan Mantri Jan-Dhan Yojana (PMJDY) of opening bank accounts for the poor man without the individual having to deposit any money to do so. A total of 22.12 crores new bank accounts have been opened since the starting of this scheme. Account holders who did not have any money in the bank of their own have a total of nearly 40,000 crore in the bank. The government funds and subsidies are being paid to the individuals concerned through their bank transfer ensuring that there is no leakage from funds to grease the palm of corrupt petty officials. Another such scheme is Pradhan Mantri Ujjwala Yojana (PMUY). Five crore LPG connections costing ₹8,000 crore have been provisioned for poor consumers. At Prime Minister's appeal, 10 lakh well-off consumers have voluntarily decided to forgo subsidy for LPG connections. Similarly another imaginative scheme has been Pradhan Mantri Fasal Bima Yojana (PMFBY) which would alleviate the distress of farmers. Yet other innovative schemes have been the Swachh Bharat Abhiyan (Clean India Mission), Skill India, Make in India and so on. Till August 2015, 80 lakh toilets have been constructed under Swachh Bharat Abhiyan. The aim is to totally eliminate open defecation in the country.

All these schemes seem to be doing well but there are lacunas which need to be addressed. For example, in the National capital garbage can be seen stacked on roads sides and no attempt made to clean them.

Being an old veteran of the Army, I have been keenly watching military affairs. Despite the Prime Minister identifying himself with the military and visiting difficult areas like Siachen and so on, not much has been done to address the legitimate grievances of serving and retired military personnel. Unless a rational Higher Defence Organisation is provided and a Chief of Defence Staff installed, the deliberate neglect of the military by the civil bureaucracy will continue.

§

My Regimental Centre at Shillong has put up a General Sinha Museum with my various mementos, documents and artifacts covering my Army career, my tenure as Ambassador in Nepal followed by the two assignments as Governor in two different States, Assam and Jammu and Kashmir. This Museum was inaugurated by the Army Chief General Dalbir Singh Suhag of my Regiment. There is also a Museum at Headquarters Western Command with a Sinha Wing which has some mementos and the books written by me. Adjacent to it is a Railway Engine and the Saloon converted into an Operations Room to depict the Viceroy's Special Corridor Train which Lord Mountbatten had made available to the then Army Commander Lt Gen Sir Dudley Russell who had raised the Command on 15 September 1947. The Saloon with all the requirement of an Operations Room inside it has been put up. I used to work from this Saloon during those hectic days. During the Partition Holocaust we functioned as a mobile self contained Headquarters from this train, travelling between Delhi and Lahore. I was the first officer to join the Headquarters in the rank of Major as General Staff Officer Grade 2 (Operations). Later, about ten British officers joined on the Staff of the Headquarters and I remained the only Indian officer serving in that Mobile Headquarters. My voice has been recorded of the events of that time to be played at the Museum for posterity. This recording covers both the Partition riots and movement of refugees as also details of the first Indo-Pak war fought in Jammu and Kashmir in 1947-48.

I feel very humbled and honoured at such recognition being given to me for what I did in course of duty in service of the Nation while holding different appointments assigned to me at different stages of my life.

§

Although I have been getting on in years approaching 90, and now gone beyond, I have kept myself fully occupied. I continue to write a column every fortnight in the *Asian Age/Deccan Chronicle* on mostly security and political matters. These are widely read and I often get calls from individuals appreciative of my views. *Deccan Chronicle* has a wide circulation in South India and I am sometimes surprised to get calls from strangers in the South. Besides, being regular in writing these articles, I have written two books during this period and the current one is the third. So far I have authorship of 10 books published from my early career. I have also been delivering Convocation addresses at different Universities, Memorial lectures and attending Seminars and so on. I have been for long on the Executive Committees of two think tanks, the United Services Institution of India and Vivekananda International Foundation.

§

I may mention that I over-strained myself in December 2014 as a result of which I suffered a heart episode. I was fortunate to get over it but I have now to maintain a relaxed work schedule. We had organised a combined wedding reception for our granddaughter and our grandson, Anjali and Rahul. They are the children of my eldest daughter Meena. They had got married in Europe and the reception function for them was held at Delhi on 7 January 2015 coinciding with my birthday. The family of the bridegroom had come to Delhi from Germany and of the bride from Brazil. My children had decided to cancel the function because of my illness but I insisted that this be revoked. Despite reservations of my doctors, I was able to persuade them to allow me to attend the reception. I came straight from the hospital for the reception with my team of doctors with me. It gave me great personal satisfaction to be able to go through the programme as scheduled and then get back to my house that night to lead a very restful life on release from hospital that very day.

§

I shall conclude this chapter with an account of my soul satisfying visit to Varanasi in March 2016 to attend the Centenary function of Vasant Kanya Mahavidyalaya College at Kamachha. This was my first visit to that institution, founded in 1916 by Dr Annie Besant as a Theosophical School for Girls which has now grown into a full-fledged girl's college. Some 15 years ago, I had donated a corpus of ₹50,000 which I subsequently raised to ₹1 lakh to this institution. The annual interest earned from this corpus provides a scholarship to the best passing out student in academic and extracurricular activities every year. The selection is made by the college authorities. The scholarship is called Shrimati Radha Sinha Memorial Merit Scholarship named after my mother. She was one of the early students of that Institution who had studied there for three to four years from 1919. My wife Premini also studied at that Institution for 16 years from 1933 to 1949 when we got married. She was made the Guest of Honour for the function. A very impressive function of a few hours was organised by the Principal Dr Kusum Mishra and her staff. The students put up an excellent musical and dance programme for the occasion. It was also their Annual Prize Distribution function. I was requested to give away the prizes, the first being a Memento for the winner of Shrimati Radha Sinha Memorial Merit Scholarship. A framed picture of Dr Annie Besant and my mother were put up on the wall and we paid our floral tribute to both. It was a sentimental occasion for both my wife and me. The college authorities have put up my mother's picture prominently on the wall in the Assembly Hall of the college where students meet every morning and sing the morning prayers.

Attending the centenary function of my mother's school/college has been one of the memorable moments of my life. I also feel a sense of achievement and great satisfaction that I have been able to complete this book which is dedicated to the memory of my mother.

§

Epilogue

Past a Memory and Future in Crystal Ball

Introduction

This book is a compilation of first-hand account of events and anecdotes of earlier generations and also of my own. With failing health and physical faculties, it has taken me unduly long to complete writing this book from memory. I have enjoyed recalling old memories. I hope the readers of this book find it interesting. Research scholars may even find some material for research in it. Starting from the High Noon of the British Empire to a totally changed world of today, this book covers a period of a century and a half. It concludes with crystal gazing the future in the coming centuries.

Life is synonymous with change and Death defies change. The extent and degree of change in all aspects of life that has taken place in the last hundred and fifty years is staggering. These have been ever so much more stupendous than in several past millennia of the history of mankind. Sometimes when in a pensive mood recalling the old days that I have seen and heard of, I feel like a Man from the Moon who has descended in the strange world of today.

§

There were two devastating World Wars during the twentieth century. After the First World War, four major Empires collapsed the German Empire, the Czarist Empire, the Turkish Empire and the Austro-Hungarian Empire. Post Second World War, the colonial empires of Britain, France, Netherlands, Portugal and Belgium in Asia and Africa became extinct, ushering the end of the Imperial Age. India emerged as an Independent country. I had a grand stand view of the change and the political upheaval in 1947 when our country attained Independence. After the Second World War, I also saw Asian nationalism rising from the ashes of European colonialism in countries of South-East Asia.

Having lost the Jewel of the Crown, Britain which was once the centre of the World, became just an island off the shores of the European Continent. After BREXIT referendum, England may get reduced to a truncated island, if Scotland decides to break away. Coinciding with the result of the referendum to quit the European Union, Sadiq Khan of Indian Sub-Continental origin, has taken over as Mayor of London. In a light-hearted vein a friend mentioned to me that England should now consider merging with India and become her Union Territory. There will be some poetic justice in this. Be that as it may, things have now changed so much. When Jamshedji Tata was trying to set up Asia's first steel mill at Jamshedpur at the turn of the twentieth century, the President of the British Board of Steel had remarked that he would eat each pound of steel produced in India. He did not live to see Tata's Corus Group not only buy British Steel but become the largest steel producer in Europe.

§

British Rule Over India

Britain ruled over India for nearly two centuries. It impoverished India and looted much of India's wealth. India's GDP was 25% of the total GDP of the world when the British began their rule. When they departed in 1947, this came down to only 1%. William Durant, an American historian wrote, "I was filled with astonishment and indignation at the apparently conscious and deliberate bleeding of India by England throughout a hundred and fifty years. I began to feel that I had come upon the greatest crime in all history." There were two unforgivable barbaric atrocities committed by the British during their rule over India. The first was Jallianwala Bagh massacre in 1919 and the second deliberately failing to alleviate the suffering of the people during the 1943 Bengal famine in which 3 million people perished. Prime Minister Winston Churchill refused to divert troop ships to transport food to save the starving millions in Bengal. This was a crime against humanity. As a young student and later as a young officer in the British Indian Army, my cherished ambition was to see the end of British rule over my country. I am not an Anglophile. Yet I am conscious of many advantages that accrued to India through her British connection.

British scholars and administrators through research and study made us aware of our past heritage. An Imperialist like Curzon took special measures to preserve our ancient monuments including the Taj Mahal. Through English education, Indians were exposed to modern thinking and scientific knowledge. It is interesting that most of our great stalwarts of the Independence Movement had the benefit of being educated in England. Mahatma Gandhi, Muhammad Ali Jinnah, Jawaharlal Nehru, Sardar Vallabhbhai Patel, Subhas Chandra Bose and many others had been to England for higher education. Even those who had not been to England had all received English education. Today, English is an international language and India has the largest English speaking population in the world. In this respect, we have an edge over our potential adversary on our Northern border.

Although India had the first Republic at Vaishali, in the history of mankind, Parliamentary democracy adopted by India is based on the British pattern. Independent Judiciary based on Anglo-Saxon jurisprudence, a neutral and efficient bureaucracy which was the steel frame of the administration and a highly professional and apolitical modern Army. The British connection also helped India to emerge from a feudal to a modern society.

However, after Independence most of the institutions of governance set up by the British have got undermined. After the first couple of decades of Independence when the generation of our great political leaders of the era of freedom struggle passed away, the quality of our political leadership has been disastrous. Dynastic rule, corruption, servility and arrogance of power have been eating into the vitals of our polity and society. The malady has been so great that it would need more than a generation to improve the political and administrative scenario in our country.

Time and Space

From the dawn of Creation, mankind has been trying to conquer Time and Space. The wheel was invented, the horse tamed, the stirrup introduced, the boat with sail brought into use, steam and internal combustion engines invented, and aviation introduced. These have drastically reduced, travelling time. Flying by air is now the most popular mode of travel for those who can afford it.

Pilgrims from South India visiting holy places in the Himalaya once trekked for months and even a year or more. Horse riders took few weeks to cover the distance. Now that distance is covered in hours. Similarly it took six months to travel from England to India by sea until the nineteenth century. My first trip by sea to England soon after Independence took me nearly a month. This distance is now being covered by air in less than half a day.

Another aspect of mankind overcoming limitations of time and space has been the information and knowledge explosions of recent times. Internet, Mobile Phones and Social Media have changed the style and tenor of life. We now live in an age of instant communication. News of the historic victory in the battle of Waterloo took a few days to reach London and news of the death of Napoleon took about two months to do so. It is said that when the news of the death of Napoleon reached London, King George IV was at a Ball in Buckingham Palace. The Prime Minister and Duke of Wellington were present at the Ball. The Prime Minister asked the Duke to convey the news to the King. The Duke went up to him and announced, "Your Majesty's, worst enemy is dead." The King inquired, "Is the Queen dead?"

In my young days one was lucky if one got a trunk call through on a telephone from one place to another within the country and it would take a few hours for it to materialise. Telegrams were faster and more reliable. Today one can communicate with any part of the world instantly. Telegraph service which served us well for 163 years was wound up in 2013. Government Postal Services may also be wound up. Internet and Net banking are making them redundant. Private Couriers are more reliable and faster.

Video-conferencing within the country and across countries and continents is catching up increasingly. Drones have started delivering food from restaurants to private homes. Self driven cars are being developed. There is also talk of cars with vertical air lift capacity like helicopters being invented to reduce traffic rush on roads in metropolitan cities.

Very recently a Solar power aircraft has done a non-stop 14,000 miles round trip of the world. In the future aircraft may all be solar driven and requirement of petrol for them may be dispensed with. A stage may come when petrol may not be required for cars and other industrial use. This will greatly reduce pollution. The Sheikhs who travel in Cadillac instead of Camels may have to go back to doing so on Camels once petrol becomes redundant.

§

Then and Now

India's great philosopher President, Dr Radhakrishnan, in a Convocation Address to University students, had said that Life is a game of Chance. I have found that Life has been full of surprises. In my young days, I had never thought of joining the Army till a chance incident a few months earlier made me decide to do so. Similarly, when I resigned from the Army I thought that I had reached the end of my active career. Very unexpectedly, I was repeatedly given important assignments in the service of the Nation. Before I conclude this book, I want to record changes that I have seen, both big and small, in the course of my long life.

In the old days almost all families, rich, middle or poor class, were village-centric. Even those working in cities with an establishment there, when asked about their home would invariably refer to their village and not to the city where they may be working and living. Mahatma Gandhi had rightly said that India lives in villages. Nowadays the home for the middle-class people has increasingly become cities, particularly after land ceiling laws came into force. Fragmentation of land holding also accelerated the process. Gradually the village connection has been eroding and urban population has been increasing. In the cities, the upper and middle class lived in houses with compounds. This was largely so even in metropolitan cities. There was enough vacant land space in cities. There were no multi-storied flats except a few in metropolitan cities like Kolkata and Mumbai. In Patna, where I grew up, buildings in the city had mostly tiled roof. There were no high-rise buildings. Land was cheap and constructing a house was more expensive than the plot of land on which it was constructed. With population explosion, land has become more expensive than buildings. In summer one slept out on the lawn with mosquito nets and one felt quite secure. There were then no air conditioners. Today people sleep in air conditioned rooms and travel in air conditioned cars. The society has become violent and it is unsafe to sleep in the open. Air pollution level is high in big cities and air purifiers have begun to be used. As in the case of land and buildings, the equation between cloth and tailoring has changed. Tailoring was cheaper than the cloth used for stitching. Now cloth has become cheaper than tailoring. Readymade clothes are increasingly replacing stitched clothes.

When the society was village-centric the joint Indian families thrived. With urbanisation, the concept of the joint Indian families has been changing rapidly. Most families are now nuclear families. No doubt joint family system had certain weaknesses but all in all, it provided social insurance for the members of the joint family particularly for people in old age.

My ancestors from both my father's and my mother's side were from the middle class. I grew up living in big houses with a bevy of servants. Most of the middle-class families whether Hindu or Muslim knew each other and participated in each other's functions like family members and addressed each other as Brother or Uncle. After Partition, most of the middle class Muslim families migrated to Pakistan. Patna had a population of a little over 1 lakh. It was the only city in Bihar with a population of more than 1 lakh. Today the population of Patna is 14 million and almost all the old private bungalows have been replaced by multi-storey flats. The tempo of life is high and in many cases one does not know others living in the same building.

While I was growing up in Patna, horse driven carriages were in use in large numbers. The total number of cars in the city was a few hundred. Traffic jams were unheard of. Today the roads in Patna as in all cities, big and small, get choked with traffic particularly during office and school rush hours.

During my forty years Army career, I hardly ever lived in a flat. Even as a junior Army officer, I had small independent homes with compounds for my residence. As I became senior in rank, I lived in elegant Flag Staff Houses which became bigger as I rose up the promotion ladder. As a General officer in the Army, I lived during my assignments in Delhi in nice single-storey bungalows with compounds, most of them having peacocks in the compound. In my last assignment in the Army when I was Vice-Army Chief, I lived in a bungalow on Race Course Road which is now the residence of the Prime Minister.

In my post-Army career as Ambassador and Governor, I lived in palatial buildings with extensive grounds. On my final retirement, I have settled down in Delhi, in a ground floor flat in an open area adjacent to a park away from busy road or traffic noise. I am happy at the change that has come about in my style of living conforming to changing times. However, I still have a few private servants from Bihar. My wife and I would find it difficult to manage without servants. The young generation now is learning to live without servants.

§

Women used to live mostly in *pardah* (veil) in my young days. They would seldom go out of the house. Hence every house of a middle-class family used to have courtyards for the womenfolk. The men wore either *Dhoti* or *Pajama* and the women wore *Saris*. When I was a student at school I wore shorts and at college I wore trousers. Very few students would be dressed like that in these days. I wore *Dhoti* or *Pajama* only for religious or other functions at home. Today trousers for men have become wide-spread among students and others in cities. Even in villages, the wearing of trousers has become very common. Women wore *sarees* or *salwar* and had their head covered. Today the young generation wears trousers, jeans and other Western dress. In fact in big cities like Delhi or Mumbai hardly any student in schools and colleges wear *Dhoti, Pajama,* or *Saris*. The latest trend is of American informal dress replacing British formal dress.

§

Women empowerment in politics began in the latter half of twentieth century with women becoming Heads of State and government. This was unthinkable in my early days. In the early days, women did not have the right to vote. It is interesting that women started getting top political appointments in Asian countries before this happened in the West. Sirimavo Bandaranaike in Sri Lanka, Indira Gandhi in India and Golda Meir in Israel became Prime Ministers of their countries before Margaret Thatcher in UK and Angela Merkel in Germany. Even in a conservative Islamic State, like Pakistan, Benazir Bhutto became the Prime Minister. The USA has not yet had a woman head of government. Hillary Clinton may become the first woman Head of State in the USA in 2016. Three of the major powers in the West would then have women Heads of Government, Hillary Clinton in the USA, Angela Merkel in Germany and Theresa May in UK.

Two women Prime Ministers were in their time known to be very powerful Heads of Government. It used to be said that Indira Gandhi and Margaret Thatcher were the only 'Men in the Cabinet' of their countries.

In India we have also had a woman President and many women Chief Ministers of States. Three of them in their own ways have been strong Chief Ministers. Jayalalithaa in Tamil Nadu, Mayawati in UP and Mamata Banerjee in West Bengal. Jayalalithaa was worshipped like a goddess by her followers.

§

Our food habits have also changed radically. Earlier generations of Indians till eighteenth century did not eat potatoes. Now there is hardly a home where potatoes are not eaten. Today potato is the staple food in Indian families. In my young days, I had not heard of South Indian food like Idli, Dosa nor of any Chinese food like Chow-mein, noodles, momos and so on. These have now become popular all over the country, even in small towns and villages. In big cities, different foreign cuisines like Italian, Mexican, Japanese etc, have also become common.

In the old days travelling within the country was restricted largely to one's district or State. I remember that till I joined the Army I had hardly gone out of Bihar. Nowadays most middle-class families have relations working or studying abroad. This is part of the globalization process. International marriages have become very common and in well to do families weddings are attended by foreign guests from abroad. Destination weddings to exotic locations in the country and abroad have become popular in many rich families.

Students mostly went to schools and colleges near their homes or within their Province. The very few who could go abroad would go to Britain for higher education. Nowadays the US has become the Mecca of higher education for Indian students. New subjects like Management, Information Technology, Computer Science etc, are very popular. As a student, I had not heard of these disciplines. The emphasis nowadays is on job-oriented education rather than education in humanities or science. In the UK, knowledge of Greek and Latin was a hall mark for the elite. This has now become virtually defunct just as Sanskrit or Persian in India.

Social values have also changed. The trading class did not have a high place in society in spite of being wealthy. All over the world, Trade followed the Flag. Trade flourished in well-governed countries or Empires. An exception took place in India when Flag followed Trade. East India Company was perhaps the biggest business organisation in the world. It established an Empire demonstrating how Flag could follow Trade. Some historians have said that the British acquired an Empire in India in a fit of absent-mindedness. When I joined the Army it was fashionable for Army Officers to look down upon businessmen, calling them *Boxwalas*. That attitude has now changed. Leaders of the corporate sector now enjoy much prestige in society and influence in government.

§

English language, English dress and English style of living are now in use much more than during British rule over India. Even among the lower and uneducated class, children use terms like Daddy, Papa, Mummy or Mama. English is used for conversation much more than during the British era. There are now more English-speaking people in India than in Britain. English. It has replaced French as a language of diplomacy. At the time of Independence there was a move in States like Bihar and UP to completely do away with English both in educational institutions and in government offices. Its use was considered a badge of slavery. The States that took such an extreme position suffered and became BIMARU (backward) States. A Chief Minister of UP maintained that use of computer is something foreign and should be banned. A Chief Minister of Bihar maintained that tarmac or modern roads were used by the rich people who owned cars. They were not very necessary as the poor constitute the bulk of the population and do not have cars.

In certain areas local dialects are fast disappearing. Born at Gaya and brought up in Patna, I come from the heart land of Magadh. Maghi was the common dialect in the towns and villages of this region and as it was in our family. Today that dialect has almost disappeared in middle class families and in the cities. However, it still survives in the villages. The Bihari indentured labour that settled in places like Mauritius, Fiji and West Indies continue to use their dialect which they took with them from Bihar and Eastern UP. Some of their descendants have now become Heads of Government in those countries.

§

The middle-class population of India has been increasing exponentially. It was a mere 2% of the population in 1947. It has now become 23% of India's population. With a population of 1.25 billion, the Indian middle class being 300 million is now more than the total population of Europe. India has thus become a very attractive market for investment propelling her economic development.

The standard of living of the middle class in India has gone up considerably. There is hardly a family which does not have some of its members in Europe or US. This was very rare in my young days. The cost of children studying at good private schools has shot up to astronomical figures like 25,000 per month for a small child and more for older children. The standard of education in government schools has become deplorable. My generation got good quality education at government schools. I was educated in a government school for ₹3 per month and in college for ₹8 a month.

In my early days many well to do landlords would open schools in their villages as an act of philanthropy and not for making money. Nowadays many political leaders open schools and colleges primarily to earn money.

Middle-class families nowadays frequently go on holidays abroad to exotic places. In my own family many are going on cruises on the Mediterranean, Malacca Straits and even Black Sea. Within India, one often sees Indian tourists at different tourist spots more than foreign tourists. When I was young, on my small Army salary, I hardly ever took holiday tours. My holidays invariably were going home to my parents or for a while to my wife's parents. This shows the level of prosperity that has now come about among our middle class.

When I saw a mall in Delhi for the first time in the late twentieth century, I thought that the American style of high living and shopping in mall will not work in India. The malls would have very few customers. I later found that I was completely off the mark. Due to the prosperity among the middle class, malls have become very popular all over India. There is hardly any big city in the country which does not have malls and metropolitan cities have numerous malls doing good business with a large clientele.

The quality and style of social life have also changed radically. Western style sitting rooms, chairs and tables have replaced the old Indian style of furniture. Eating food sitting on the ground has become uncommon. Even in the villages one now comes across chairs and tables. In our own family till early twentieth century, we did not have Sofa Sets or Chairs and Tables.

After Independence, the upper caste that had provided leadership for the Freedom Movement held political power in government. This started gradually changing and with universal suffrage and reservations, the hitherto depressed lot started calling the shots in politics. Increasingly they influenced electoral results and were often used as vote banks by political leaders and parties. This created some very strange situations. In Bihar, a Chief Minister with no formal education came to power who could barely put a signature to the document and could not read its contents. In the same State, sons who are school drop-outs are in the State Cabinet, one as Deputy Chief Minister and the other one is a Cabinet Minister with an important portfolio.

Political leaders of Nehruvian era had made great personal sacrifice in service of the Nation. They were shining examples of simple living and high thinking. Today, politics has become a profession of profit and our leaders have become the byword of High Living and Low Thinking. The level of debate in the Parliament compared to the old age of even the Central Legislative Assembly has become very low, and ugly incidents of shouting and even violence have become common. Often the dignity of our temples of democracy at the Centre and in the States witness unbecoming rowdy and violent acts. In Lok Sabha members rushing to the well, raising slogans and even tearing Resolutions is quite common. Once a member in Lok Sabha even used chilli spray inside the house. We had adopted the British Parliamentary system of Democracy. In hundreds of years of its history, the House of Commons has never witnessed such ugly scenes, nor did the Central Legislative Assembly in Delhi or the Lok Sabha during the first two decades of Independence.

The dignity of language has been the hall mark in British Parliament and also in our Parliament. Winston Churchill spoke about Clement Attlee in dignified language saying, "Mr Attlee is a modest man and has much to be modest about." One may also recall Krishna Menon's response to Kriplani when he complained that he could not get what the former was saying. Kriplani interrupted by saying, "Sir, I can provide information to the Opposition but I cannot provide understanding." This was in 1962 when the Lok Sabha was debating the threat from China. One feels sad when our political leaders indulge in name calling against their opponents and use the language of the street. Chief Minister Arvind Kejriwal recently attacked Prime Minister Narendra Modi calling him a coward and psychopath. The Prime Minister has kept his dignity ignoring all his diatribe. On his birthday, Narendra Modi sent him birthday greetings wishing him happiness and a long life. Similarly, the Lt Governor Najeeb Jung's response to unbecoming language used by Kejriwal against him has always been very dignified.

§

With universal suffrage the educated middle class, mostly from upper castes, who were small numbers, lost their dominance in electoral politics. They showed little interest in voting during elections and did not bother to queue at polling booths to cast their vote. This has now been changing. With increase in their numbers, the middle class also are becoming important and have started going to polling booths in increasing numbers and influencing poll results. However, the caste factor affects both the middle class and others. During my Army career, I never voted in any election because the postal ballot system for the military personnel was so complicated that one used to receive postal ballots after the election was over. After my retirement, I have been voting in all elections. The old postal ballot system for the military personnel has now been modified making it easier for exercising their franchise but there are still some lacunae which need to be looked into.

§

In my childhood and early youth, marriages were organised in a totally different manner. A barber from the girl side would bring information about suitable boys within the sub-caste from neighbouring areas. Horoscope of the boy would be obtained and the family astrologer would select a suitable match for wedding. The astrologer's verdict was considered sacrosanct and had to be adhered to. The marrying couple had no say in the matter. Their wedding was decided by the parents. Brides and bridegrooms met each other only after the wedding had taken place. It may sound strange that even when I had served in the Army for five years, I had no say in my marriage nor did my wife have any say. Our parents on both sides took the decision and we met for the first time after we got married. Nowadays young couples decide on their weddings themselves and their parents have to accept their decision. Often couples court each other for some time before they decide to tie the knot. I have also heard of several cases, even in the US, when marriages have got arranged through advertisements in the Press. In a few cases in the US, I have known even international marriages being arranged through the Internet or social media. The society has changed so fast all over the world. With all its drawbacks, the old arrangement used to work and one seldom heard of divorce. Today divorce in India is becoming very much more common than in the olden days.

In the first half of the previous century, I saw weddings in my family and also in the society with functions spread over a number of days. Extended families would gather for weeks for weddings in the family and elaborate rituals were performed. Life moved at a leisurely pace. The bridegroom's party would go to the bride's place and remain as guests of the bride's family for three or four days. The latter would, of course, have to foot the bill in addition to providing a dowry. I remember some weddings in our family and friends being elaborate affairs. Elephants, horses and horse carriages would be in the procession. For the entertainment of the bridegroom's party, there would be dancing girls for *mehfils* in the evening. The pace of modern life does not allow such long drawn out functions for weddings nowadays. Often weddings are one- or two-day affairs with *Mehandi/Sangeet* and a reception on different days. Amongst the rich, life style has become so different. At wedding receptions in Delhi, I have seen half a dozen or more stalls serving different National cuisines like Mughlai, Western, Chinese, Mexican, Japanese and so on.

Another feature in the old days was that having two or more wives was something fairly common. It was only a couple of years after Independence that a legal embargo was imposed to prevent plural marriages. I remember that in Bihar there was a Chief Secretary, Director Public Instruction, and a Commissioner who all had two wives each at the time of Independence. The IG Police was a Muslim and he had three wives. Even in the Army when I joined I came across two interesting cases. In 1944, at the Jat Regimental Training Centre, Bareilly, there was a Muslim Lieutenant who had risen from the ranks and had four wives with sixteen children, four from each wife. In those days Army Officers were allowed family allowance of ₹100 per month per wife and ₹75 per month for children. This Lieutenant's salary and allowance were more than that of the British full Colonel commanding the Centre. Another such example of 1948 was that of a non-Muslim Major-General, commanding a Division who died in a road accident. It was said that up to the rank of Brigadier he used to acquire a new wife whenever he was promoted. However, he could not marry on promotion to Major-General in 1947 because he was in a field area and died soon after his promotion.

§

Cinema started becoming a popular mode of entertainment after the First World War. In early 30s, around 1932, I saw a silent movie for the first time in Patna. After a few years, we started having Talkies in which the voice of actors and actresses could be heard. In my student days cinema had become quite a craze. Most of the songs would be classical or neo classical. When I joined the Army in the Jat Regiment we had written orders in the Officers' Mess that Indian music would not be played. For the British officers, classical Indian music appeared strange and some of them called it Kettle and Drum music. Today Bollywood music has become popular all over the world. On the television, I have seen and heard Hollywood actors and actresses singing and dancing in Bollywood style. Bollywood music, with Western musical instruments along with dancing and singing style, has no doubt itself been influenced by the West. However, it has also developed its own culture and identity. Recently I saw the complete Hanuman Chalisa sung by American actors to the accompaniment of Western orchestra sung in a strong American accent. I also saw a concert in Vienna where a Hindi tune was being sung by Austrian artists.

§

Due to better health care longevity has been steadily increasing in India. In the old days when the retirement age in government service was 55 years, one did not see many pensioners. By the time they reached the age of 60, most of them used to pass away. Today, even when the retirement age is higher, pegged at 60, the number of retired personnel has become much higher. Large numbers of pensioners even above 80 years of age and more are living. People now joke that soon we would have more retired people than serving personnel.

Another interesting feature is that pension rates have increased considerably. In the old days, it was difficult for an individual to live on his pension and he had to supplement living with additional resources generated from continuing to work. The pension age has increased considerably and now a pensioner can afford to live on his pension. A new feature has been added to the pension scheme by providing higher percentage of pension for people as they reach beyond 80 after five yearly intervals. A person scoring a century receives double his pension as old age benefit. This is a good social welfare measure.

§

Today, one of our big problems is rampant corruption in the society. Even in the old days, corruption was wide spread in the country but it was confined primarily to lower levels of administration. Instances of corruption in officers rank were very rare. For example, in the Police corruption was rampant up to the level of the Police Station and almost nonexistent above that level. Unfortunately, our political leadership has been providing a bad example and corruption is to be found at all levels of the administration. It is often said that democracy and elections have become a major reason for this. Even in developed countries corruption at the higher political level can be seen because of the need of funds for political parties to participate in elections. All out efforts need to be taken to eradicate corruption in our administration and in our society.

No doubt there has been no scam at the Centre during the past two years of Modi government in power. Corruption at the lower level is so deep rooted that it will take a long time to eradicate. There are two limitations in achieving a corruption-free society. The first is our electoral system and the second is that India is a Union of autonomous States. The latter cannot be fully under the control of the Centre.

§

Mahatma Gandhi advised the ministers who had assumed power saying, "Today you have worn on your head a crown of thorns. The seat of power is a nasty thing. You have to remain ever wakeful on that seat. You have to be more non-violent, more humble and more forbearing.... You are there to serve the villagers and the poor." Jawaharlal Nehru in an anonymous article wrote about himself, "Nehru has all the makings of a dictator in him, vast popularity, a strong will directed to a well-defined purpose, energy, pride, organisational capacity, ability and hardness with all the love of the crowd, intolerance of others and a certain contempt for the weak and the inefficient. From the far North to Cape Comorin, he goes like some triumphant Caesar blazing a trail of glory and legend behind him. It is his will to power that is driving him from crowd to crowd. His conceit is formidable. He must be checked. We want no Caesar." Apart from Nehru's warning to the Nation not to allow anyone to become a dictator, Dr BR Ambedkar addressing the Constituent Assembly on 23 March 1949 had also warned against bhakti in politics.

Through Hero-worship of the political leader in power, our present society in India has promoted abject sycophancy and feudal arrogance among people in authority. This has resulted in promoting family rule and a tendency in the country that is promoting the arrogance of power. Like a dangerous disease this has been eating into our National self respect and undermining democratic values. The result has been that dynastic rule has become a wide-spread disease in our democracy. This is destroying our democratic culture and instruments of governance. Family rule pioneered by the Congress has become common among political parties barring the Left parties and the BJP. Thus we have family rule of Abdullahs in Kashmir, Yadavs in Bihar and UP, Badals in Punjab, Lals in Haryana and the Karunanidhi clan in Tamil Nadu. Even in Bengal, Mamata Banerjee's nephew has begun to wield political power. The bureaucracy and the administration seems to have lost its spine. The craze for Red Beacons on cars by parliamentarians and legislators promote a culture repugnant to democratic values. Chief Ministers in their States with trappings of power have become tin-pot dictators. Ministers whether in the Centre or in the States have acquired unbearable arrogance of power. Sometime I feel that the colonial administration before 1947 was more responsive to the needs of the common man as they generally functioned as benevolent rulers except when imperial interests were involved.

§

Let me now reflect on our instruments of governance developed by the British during their imperial rule. British tradition of the functioning of judiciary was based on the fundamental concept of the Independence of the judiciary. Way back in 1857 some interesting incidents took place which show how the judiciary during British rule functioned. A banker of Patna city named Luft Ali was accused of providing funds for Indian soldiers who had rebelled against the British. After normalcy was restored in 1858, he was tried by the District Judge, Mr RN Farquharson, for treason. Mr William Tayler, Commissioner of Patna, then a sort of mini-Governor of Bihar, which was part of Bengal Presidency, wrote a letter to the District Judge asking him to convict the banker and give him maximum punishment. The judge took umbrage at this and sent a copy of the letter to the Governor of Bengal saying that the Commissioner was encroaching on the independence of the judiciary. The Governor was unhappy with the Commissioner for other administrative reasons and, taking advantage of this complaint, dismissed him. This was perhaps the first and only time that such a high-ranking official was dismissed for misconduct. There is another interesting incident when in 1922 Mahatma Gandhi appeared as an accused during the Non-Cooperation Movement before the British District Judge at Ahmedabad. On the Mahatma entering his Court, the Judge stood up in his honour. All present in the Court also did so. The Mahatma pleaded guilty of the charge against him. While delivering his judgment, the Judge observed that he never had an occasion to try such a great person who was worshipped by his Nation and respected the world over, nor was he likely to do so in the future. On the basis of the evidence before the Court, he convicted the Mahatma giving him the sentence of imprisonment for six years. While delivering his judgment, he said that no one would be happier than him if higher authorities acquitted the Mahatma or reduced his duration of imprisonment. Whereas the bureaucracy, the Army and the Police were often accused of committing excesses during the Independence Movement, the judiciary was never criticised on this score. No doubt the Anglo-Saxon jurisprudence of equality before the law and a person not being guilty unless he has been proved to be so, is a superior legal system than our indigenous system of Manu Code and Islamic Shariyat Code which differentiate between caste in the case of the former and between believers and non-believers in the latter. After Independence, we have rightly chosen to continue with Anglo-Saxon jurisprudence. However, it is distressing that nowadays legal cases take years to conclude and have become so expensive that the common man does not get justice in short time. Justice delayed is justice denied.

§

Our bureaucracy which was the steel frame of administration during the British period, is no longer so. The efficiency of Indian bureaucracy was widely recognised and considered better than the bureaucracy even in Britain at that time. Both were recruited on the basis of a common competitive examination and the better ones normally opted for Indian Civil Service in preference to Home Civil Service. Civil servants in India exercised much authority in the Sub-Divisions, Districts and Divisions while their British equivalent had to serve in Borough or Councils as Town Clerks under the elected political executives. They did not have an opportunity to exercise initiative and acquire experience in governance like their counterparts in Indian Civil Service.

Political interference and sycophancy as well as unchecked ambition have totally destroyed the old high standards of bureaucracy during British rule. In the old days, bureaucrats showed much strength, character and determination to look after the interest of the common man. The Indian bureaucracy was rated as the best in the world. Deputy Commissioners of districts in Punjab were asked to work from the 'saddle of their horse'. This meant that they had to tour their districts extensively and be accessible to the villagers to solve their problems. Today, district officers like to spend more time in their air-conditioned offices and are more involved in pleasing their political masters and working to advance their career rather than looking after the common man. It is a pity that the Indian bureaucracy today is rated below the civil bureaucracy of many South-East Asian countries. In the British days, if an ordinary person wrote any letter to a civilian authority whether a high executive or a junior bureaucrat, he would get an acknowledgement. Even if his request could not be agreed to he would be informed about it. Today, no matter how senior a person may be, his letters to ministers or bureaucrats are hardly ever replied to.

As mentioned earlier, the Police was corrupt up to the Police Station level and was also very oppressive. This continues to be so even now. However, the Police Station which is the cutting edge of Police administration is today much neglected. Corruption in Police has spread to the highest level and the functioning of the Police Station is much neglected. The Police has become more militarised and lost its culture and ethos of functioning, leading to lamentable deterioration in the quality of its functioning.

The Army continues to be apolitical and highly professional. It has always risen to the occasion in the service of the nation in war and peace. During natural disasters it has provided excellent relief for the affected people. Despite all its service to the nation, it has been greatly marginalised in the process of decision-making on military matters at the highest level. Further its status is being constantly lowered compared to civilians and its emoluments constantly made less than civilians. This can have an adverse impact on the nation's last weapon.

§

Population explosion has not only led to congested living and travelling but has also degraded the environment. I had not heard in my early days of distilled water for drinking. One drank water from wells and rivers. Railway travel was comfortable with no crowding at Railway Stations or on railway trains. Air travel was unknown. Nowadays there is over crowding not only on trains but also in air travel, both National and International.

I recall that in Patna during my childhood there were never any traffic jams. There were less than 500 cars in the city. When I first came to Delhi in 1946, it was the same at the National Capital. There were, of course, many more cars in New Delhi but traffic jams were unheard of. When I first came to live in New Delhi, it was confined to Connaught Place in the North, Safdarjung/Lodhi Gardens in the South, Viceroy's House (present Rashtrapati Bhavan) in the West and Purana Quila/Irwin Stadium (now National Stadium) in the East. There were no restrictions of driving clockwise in Connaught Place and there were plenty of parking spaces lying vacant in front of shops at this elite shopping area. Old Delhi was miles away from New Delhi with hardly any built up area connecting the two. All that has changed in New Delhi, which, with adjoining areas, has become what is called National Capital Region with population of several millions. Air Pollution and traffic snarls have become a menace. Neighbouring Gurgaon was a small Mofussil town with dusty roads and plenty of camel carts in 1947. Gurgaon has been the fastest growing modern city of the world. Numerous high rise modern buildings, many with glass exterior, have come up. The city has all the accompaniments of a modern society in the most advanced cities in the West. Camel carts and women with veil-covered heads are now not to be seen as in the old days. Modern cars, including luxury ones often driven by women, are now a common scene. The name of the city may have been changed to ancient Guru Gram but most of the modern buildings have English names.

§

In the feudal society in which I grew up, the higher class and middle class enjoyed many privileges and the deprived classes were denied good living. Yet the latter remained quite content and resigned to their fate. Much has now been done to improve their lot as it should be. They also nurture legitimate aspiration. It is interesting that when I joined the Army the salary of the Indian Sepoy was ₹16 a month while that of a British soldier was ₹80 per month. Apart from difference in salary, the British soldiers had better entitlements in terms of rations, accommodation and travel. This was not resented by the Indian soldiers who had a complex because the British were the ruling race. Moreover, most of them being illiterate accepted this invidious distinction. In those days, people from rural areas were resigned to their lot and did not have aspirations. Today, such unfair distinctions would not be acceptable to the present generation of our soldiers. The Indian Army sending contingents to serve with United Nations Peace Keeping Forces get the same lavish salaries and other benefits as soldiers of any other Army. Field Martial Slim who commanded the Army in Burma during Second World War had seven Indian Divisions and two British Divisions under his command. He was honest enough to record in his memoir that his Indian Formations which cost the government much less than his British Formations produced better results in war during the Burma Campaign.

So far as officers of the Army were concerned, Indian and British officers were treated at par in terms of emoluments and privileges when I joined the Army. The Regimental mystique developed by the British in the Indian Army was unique. Officers subordinated their own personal identity to the identity of their soldiers. Field Marshal Auchinleck was an Indian Army Officer and was said to be partial to Indian troops in North Africa during the Second World War. Field Marshal Montgomery was a British Army Officer and he was partial to British rather than Indian troops. I am glad that the Regimental mystique developed by the British in the Indian Army continues to this date in which Indian officers identify themselves with their soldiers in terms of language and Regimental spirit.

§

I have been reflecting at random on the changes that I have seen in my life. Somehow despite progress and better facilities of today, when I close my eyes I have nostalgia for old times. Life used to be so peaceful and leisurely. Today, the pace of life has become so fast that the British poet WH Davies has conveyed this feeling in his poem, "What is this life if, full of care, We have no time to stand and stare." Alas! the old age cannot now come back in today's world. Let me conclude my reflections by quoting from the Rubaiyat of Omar Khayyam:

"The moving finger writes and having writ,
Moves on; not all thy piety and wit
Shall lure it back to cancel half a line
Nor all thy tears wash a word of it.
Lift not thy hand to the inverted Bowl
We call the sky
For it rolls on as helplessly
As you and I."

§

Crystal Gazing

Population explosion has been having a tremendous impact on our planet. World population in 1800 was one billion, three billion in 1960 and it is seven billion now. It is estimated that by 2050 the world population may go up to ten billion. At this rate of growth of population, our planet would not be able to sustain human population. Human beings will have to consider migrating to other planets. Space travel has been steadily picking up since 1969 when Neil Armstrong was the first man to take a step on the Moon. At that time he said, "One small step for man, one giant leap for mankind." Centuries of poetic imagery in different languages became a scientific realty in that year. Since then space missions have been establishing new records. Mars is the furthest planet from Earth and is at a distance of 225 million kms. In 2014, both the NASA and ISRO, sent successful missions to this planet and it has been established that oxygen is there to support human life. Booking for a one-way trip to Mars at a cost of 7,000 US Dollars has commenced and so far 1,65,000 people from 40 countries have done their booking for this trip. Of these 8,107 are Indians. At this rate in a century or more mankind may have established themselves on different planets. Already the military in advanced countries are planning to develop capability for Space Warfare. Perhaps there would be a requirement for United Planetary Nations as a counterpart of United Nations on Earth.

§

Scientific discoveries have helped to increase the longevity of human beings. Various incurable diseases have now become curable. Scientists are working on finding a cure for Cancer and providing spare organs to replace diseased organs in the human body. An artificial heart is also being worked upon. At this rate the world may have many Centenarians. There are quite a few in this category now and the oldest living individual is 125 years old. At this rate, we may even start having double Centenarians. All this, at present a fantasy, may well become a reality in the future Centuries.

A lot of work has been done by scientists on the Big Bang theory. The secret of Creation may get unravelled but possibly unravelling the secret of Death may not be found. All this is mind boggling speculation. It is however certain that, like in the recent past, in the coming future we may have developments that at present the human mind cannot even imagine. Shakespeare wrote in Hamlet, "There are more things in Heaven and Earth, Than your philosophy dreams of."

§

Appendix 1

ENGLISH TRANSLATION OF ABOVE LETTER

BHAI NANDKEOLYAR,

The account of the yarn spun by the Kerala spinners during the Khadi Jayanti made me very happy. I have also received the draft for Rs.236 sent by you for that yarn. Please convey my congratulations to all the spinners. I hope this enthusiasm will endure and the Khadi atmosphere will spread.

Blessings from
BAPU

From a copy of the Hindi: Pyarelal Papers
Letter No. 453: *Collected Works of Mahatma Gandhi*, Volume 81

MAHABALESHWAR,
May 13, 1945

BHAI NANDKEOLYAR,

I know you refrained from coming so as to save me trouble. I will lovingly use the tumblers when they arrive. You and Priyamvada have asked for my blessings for Mohandas and his bride. My fear is, theirs may not be an inter-caste marriage. Has the bride given up *purdah*? Will both of them give themselves up to service? Will Privamvada keep the bride engaged in household work or give her time to do work of service? I hope the bride's parents do not keep her like a slave. If you can give satisfactory replies to all these questions, then here are heaps of blessings for the bride and bridegroom.

Blessings from
BAPU

Barrister Nandkeolyar
Nand Vilas
Gaya (Bihar)

April 1, 1946

BHAI DEVDOOT*,

There was considerable discussion in the Working Committee about you. Now Priyamvadabehn** is in charge of the whole work. It is, therefore, your duty to co-operate with her loyally and sincerely. It is possible that you are more capable than her. But if we think along this line, women will never rise. Whatever it is, while under a single management it is not right for anyone to hold such an opinion about oneself.

Blessings from
BAPU

Shri Devdoot Vidyarthi
Kasturba [Gandhi National] Memorial Trust Camp
Madhubani (Darbhanga), Bihar

From a copy of the Hindi: Pyarelal Papers
Letter No. 288: Letter to Devdoot Vidyarthi, *Collected Works of Mahatma Gandhi*, Volume 90

*Devdoot Vidyarthi, worker of Kastruba Gandhi National Memorial Trust, Madhubani

Appendix 2

Correspondence between Sardar Patel and Chief Minister of Bihar pertaining to Shri MK Sinha, IP. (Extract from Volume 5, page 95 of *Sardar Patel's Correspondence* edited by Shri Durga Das.)

New Delhi
13 February 1947

My dear Sri Babu,

I understand that there is some difficulty in your sparing Mr. M.K. Sinha who is our Intelligence Officer in Bihar for service with the Central Intelligence Bureau. You know how anxious we are to Indianise the Bureau as soon as possible, and amongst the intelligence officers Mr. Sinha was the only Indian who could be considered for the post of Deputy Director. I do hope that you will be able to spare him for the purpose and inform our office accordingly. We require him to join the Bureau as soon as possible and I shall be glad if very early arrangements could be made for his relief. My letters to you remain unanswered. Please attend to them without delay.

Your sincerely,
Vallabhbhai Patel

The Hon'ble Mr. Sri Krishna Sinha

Patna

* * *

Patna
18 February 1947

Dear Sardar Sahib,

I am in receipt of your letter of the 13th inst. I have passed order yesterday before receipt of your letter that Mr. M.K. Sinha was to be spared for service in the Central Intelligence Bureau. I am asking the Chief Secretary to see that he is relieved at once.

I am sorry to find that some of your letters have remained unanswered. I will see that a reply to them are sent soon.

Your sincerely,
S.K. Sinha

The Hon'ble Sardar Vallabhbhai Patel
New Delhi

FOOTNOTE: Shri M.K. Sinha, IP came to Delhi in February 1947 and took over as Number 2 to Sir Norman Smith who was the then Director Intelligence Bureau. Shri Sinha was the first Indian Officer posted to the Directorate of Intelligence Bureau. Sardar Patel wanted only an Indian Officer to work for him on sensitive issues on the eve of Partition, particularly on matters dealing with Princely States. He did not trust a British Officer for this. Shri Sinha was the only Indian Officer in the country who had worked both in the CID and as a Field Officer of Intelligence Bureau. After one year, at the insistence of the Chief Minister of Bihar, he returned to his home State to become Police Chief of Bihar.

Index